JIMMY CARTER AND CHINA

A NANCY BERNKOPF TUCKER AND WARREN I. COHEN BOOK ON
AMERICAN-EAST ASIAN RELATIONS

NANCY BERNKOPF TUCKER and WARREN I. COHEN
Books on American–East Asian Relations

EDITED BY

Thomas J. Christensen
Mark Philip Bradley
Rosemary Foot

Founded in 2014, this series advances the legacy of the scholars Nancy Bernkopf Tucker and Warren I. Cohen. It publishes groundbreaking interdisciplinary and discipline-based studies across history and social sciences that explore the past, present, and future of U.S. relations with the Asia-Pacific. These books aim to bring analytical clarity to the complex ties linking the United States with one of the most consequential regions in world politics.

Deborah Davis and Terry Lautz, eds., *Chinese Encounters with America: Journeys That Shaped the Future of China*

Hongshan Li, *Fighting on the Cultural Front: U.S.-China Relations in the Cold War*

Thomas Larkin, *The China Firm: American Elites and the Making of British Colonial Society*

John T. Downey, Thomas J. Christensen, and Jack Lee Downey, *Lost in the Cold War: The Story of Jack Downey, America's Longest-Held POW*

Anne F. Thurston, ed., *Engaging China: Fifty Years of Sino-American Relations*

Andrew B. Kennedy, *The Conflicted Superpower: America's Collaboration with China and India in Global Innovation*

Jeanne Guillemin, *Hidden Atrocities: Japanese Germ Warfare and American Obstruction of Justice at the Tokyo Trial*

Michael J. Green, *By More Than Providence: Grand Strategy and American Power in the Asia Pacific Since 1783*

Nancy Bernkopf Tucker was a historian of American diplomacy whose work focused on American–East Asian relations. She published seven books, including the prize-winning *Uncertain Friendships: Taiwan, Hong Kong, and the United States, 1945–1992*. Her articles and essays appeared in countless journals and anthologies, including the *American Historical Review*, *Diplomatic History*, *Foreign Affairs*, and the *Journal of American History*. In addition to teaching at Colgate and Georgetown (where she was the first woman to be awarded tenure in the School of Foreign Service), she served on the China desk of the Department of State and in the American embassy in Beijing. When the Office of the Director of National Intelligence was created, she was chosen to serve as the first Assistant Deputy Director of National Intelligence for Analytic Integrity and Standards and Ombudsman, and she was awarded the National Intelligence Medal of Achievement in 2007. To honor her, in 2012 the Woodrow Wilson International Center for Scholars established an annual Nancy Bernkopf Tucker Memorial Lecture on U.S.–East Asian Relations.

Warren I. Cohen was University Distinguished Professor Emeritus at Michigan State University and the University of Maryland, Baltimore County, and a senior scholar in the Asia Program of the Woodrow Wilson Center. He wrote thirteen books and edited eight others. He served as a line officer in the U.S. Pacific Fleet, editor of *Diplomatic History*, president of the Society for Historians of American Foreign Relations, and chairman of the Department of State Advisory Committee on Historical Diplomatic Documentation. In addition to scholarly publications, he wrote for *The Atlantic*, the *Baltimore Sun*, the *Christian Science Monitor*, *Dissent*, *Foreign Affairs*, the *International Herald Tribune*, the *Los Angeles Times*, *The Nation*, the *New York Times*, the *Times Literary Supplement*, and the *Washington Post*. He was also a consultant on Chinese affairs to various government organizations.

JIMMY CARTER AND CHINA

MULTILATERAL COMPETITION IN THE GLOBAL COLD WAR

SHENG PENG

Columbia University Press
New York

Columbia University Press
Publishers Since 1893
New York   Chichester, West Sussex
cup.columbia.edu

Copyright © 2026 Columbia University Press
All rights reserved

Cataloging-in-Publication data is available from the Library of Congress.

ISBN 9780231211949 (hardback)
ISBN 9780231211956 (trade paperback)
ISBN 9780231559133 (epub)
ISBN 9780231565288 (PDF)

Cover design: Noah Arlow

Cover image: Deng Xiaoping and Jimmy Carter during the Sino-American signing ceremony in Washington, DC, on January 20, 1979. (Photo: Jimmy Carter Library)

GPSR Authorized Representative: Easy Access System Europe, Mustamäe tee 50, 10621 Tallinn, Estonia, gpsr.requests@easproject.com

CONTENTS

Acknowledgments ix

INTRODUCTION 1

I. STRATEGIC COMPETITION

1. THE DECLINE OF DÉTENTE AND THE NORMALIZATION OF US-CHINA DIPLOMATIC RELATIONS 19

2. THE CHINA-FRANCE NUCLEAR ALLIANCE AND THE FAILED COMPREHENSIVE TEST BAN NEGOTIATION 61

II. TECHNOLOGICAL COMPETITION

3. WESTERN EUROPEAN MILITARY AND DUAL-USE TECHNOLOGY TRANSFERS TO CHINA 93

4. CHIANG CHING-KUO AND TAIWAN'S SEARCH FOR SECURITY 133

III. IDEOLOGY

5. FROM CLASSMATES TO ENEMIES: DENG XIAOPING AND CHIANG CHING-KUO   159

6. THE GLOBAL RESPONSE TO CARTER'S CHINA POLICY: UNHEEDED WARNINGS FROM MOSCOW TO WASHINGTON   188

CONCLUSION: MULTILATERAL COMPETITION BEYOND THE COLD WAR   221

Notes   243
Bibliography   287
Index   313

ACKNOWLEDGMENTS

The writing of this book, with its focus on the Cold War, has been quite a journey, crossing multiple countries and cultures and combining both traditional historical archival research and some inevitable detective work, which involved a great deal of improvisation and luck. This book also could not have been written without the help of many other scholars, colleagues, and friends worldwide, whose knowledge and connections—what the Chinese would call *Guanxi*—have opened many doors.

I would especially wish to thank my DPhil mentor, Professor Rana Mitter at the University of Oxford, for his continuous support and expert guidance during my research. There is a rumor among the History Faculty that no other historians would play Pub Quiz with Professor Mitter because he would always win with his immense knowledge on any given topic. When he received the OBE from Queen Elizabeth in 2019 for his contribution to China studies, all of his students rejoiced, and none were really surprised. I would also like to thank another Oxford historian, Professor Margaret MacMillan, the first historian who encouraged me to come to St. Antony's College for my DPhil and taught me to "not only look into what policymakers knew, but also what they didn't know when they make decisions," a reality that applied to most scenarios during the Cold War.

I would also wish to thank other mentors who have guided me professionally through the years before I arrived in Oxford. Professor James

Hershberg, my master's thesis adviser at George Washington University, was the first person who, in his own words, "dragged me away from the dark side of International Relations to Cold War History." At GWU, my intellectual growth also benefited from studying with an unlikely pair of policymakers-turned-academics: Professor Henry R. Nau and Professor Paul Stronski. Professor Nau is a conservative and a former economic adviser under President Reagan, while Professor Stronski is a liberal who served as the Russian expert on President Obama's National Security Council. I was always mystified that they could have such opposite worldviews and yet both could sound absolutely reasonable in their arguments. This unusual learning experience turned out to have prepared me for the study of ideologies in the making of foreign policy. I would also like to thank another GWU professor, Robert Sutter, who taught me to examine the intricacies of modern U.S.-China relations and kindly invited me to audit his class on Taiwanese history and politics, which helped me to formulate the Taiwanese section of this book.

I had my first research position after my DPhil training at the University of Vienna, which provided crucial financial and logistical support as I was revising this manuscript. In particular, I was able to conduct additional fieldwork and present my findings in neighboring Germany. In addition, my colleagues in Vienna also provided valuable insights on the European and Russian chapters of this book, and I especially wish to thank Professor Philipp Ther, Professor Claudia Kraft, Professor Jannis Panagiotidis, Dr. Magdalena Baran-Szołtys, Irena Remestwenski, Professor János Mátyás Kovács, Dr. Rosamund Johnston, Dr. Thuc Linh Nguyen Vu, Dr. Mischa Gabowitsch, and Dr. Katarzyna Nowak.

In the summer of 2024, I was very fortunate to be offered an Ernest May Fellowship in History and Policy at the John F. Kennedy School of Government at Harvard University by Professor Fredrik Logevall. This fellowship allowed me to access the school's vast collections of rare manuscripts, particularly those on Taiwanese history, and to catch up with the current debate on US foreign policy. I am incredibly grateful for the applied history seminars organized by Professor Graham T. Allison and the work-in-progress workshops organized by Professor Logevall, Professor Mary Elise Sarotte, and Professor Rana Mitter. The unique policy-oriented environment at the Harvard Kennedy School enabled me to give my work a more significant and relevant perspective. Lastly, I am tremendously grateful to our host, the International Security Program at the Belfer Center for Science and International Affairs—and particularly our manager, Susan Lynch, and the ISP program director, Professor Steve E. Miller, who spent every "Bagels and Babble Tuesday" with the fellows to share their wealth of knowledge in security studies and history. Finally, this manuscript went through one last round of rigorous reviews by my current cohort of Ernest May applied history fellows: Lyudmila Austin, Kate Birkbeck, Mary Bridges, Anne Boniface, Kevin Keller, Chloë Mayoux, Joseph Passman, and Madelyn Lugli.

There are also many other scholars and colleagues who have helped me with my research professionally along the way.

University of Oxford: Aimee Burlakova (St. Antony's), Professor Roger Goodman (St. Antony's), Professor Pekka Hämäläinen (St. Catherine's), Professor Dan Healey (St. Antony's), Professor Halbert Jones (St. Antony's), Professor Matteo Legrenzi (St. Antony's), Dr. Helena Lopes (Merton), Dr. Toby Matthiesen (St. Antony's), Caroline Heilig (St. Antony's), Dr. Hongping Annie Nie (China Centre), Mr. Richard Ramage (St. Antony's), Dr. Elizabeth Sandis (Merton), Professor Robert Service (St. Antony's), Dr. Cristina Blanco Sio-Lopez (St. Antony's), Professor Steven Smith (All Souls), Dr. Jodie Zhou (Keble College and now Fudan University).

Other universities and institutions: Dr. Dmitry Asinovskiy (European University of St. Petersburg), Nicole Bodishteanu (National Research University Higher School of Economics, Moscow), Camille Boullenois (Australian National University), Dr. Giovanni Cadioli (Sciences Po), Dr. Hao Chen (University of Cambridge), Professor Fumitaka Cho (Rikkyo University), Dr. Khue Dieu Do (Seoul National University), Professor Koji Hirata (Monash University), Professor Benjamin D. Hopkins (GWU), Clay Kastky (University of Texas at Austin), Dr. Yulia Klimova (University College London), Professor Alexander Lukin (Moscow Higher School of Economics), Hanna Matt (The University of Manchester), Professor Mary McCarthy (Drake University), Professor Edward McCord (GWU), Hannah Munday (St. Anne's College, whose grandpa used to spoon-feed Stephen Hawking at the University of Cambridge), Professor Dmitry Novikov (Moscow Higher School of Economics), Professor Timothy Nunan (Free University of Berlin), Professor Deepa Ollapally (GWU), Brittany Paris (Carter Library), Dr. Douglas Paul (Carnegie Endowment for International Peace), Professor Sergey Radchenko (Johns Hopkins University, School of Advanced International Studies [SAIS]), Professor Eric Saylor (Drake University), Professor David Skidmore (Drake University), Professor Darcie Vandegrift (Drake University), Professor Xia Yafeng (University of Maryland), Dr. Jingdong Yuan (University of Technology Sydney, who wrote a very insightful and constructive review of the article version of my third chapter).

I would also like to thank all my friends who helped me in many other ways during my years of fieldwork. Many of them live in different parts of the world and have hosted me through my long research trips abroad. Some of them are also excellent academics in their respective fields, including the classics, philosophy, and theoretical physics, and their different perspectives of the natural world and human society have not only enriched me as a historian but also made me a better-informed individual. For your convenience, I will arrange their names based on where I met those wonderful people.

China: There are many scholars in China who provided me with priceless insights into Chinese politics and history. Some of them, not without risk, even shared with me books and rare manuscripts that are banned or no longer available in the public realm. However, for reasons obvious to Chinese intellectuals, though they might be difficult for Westerners to understand, I shall not name those individuals, but I hope you know who you are, and I give you my sincere thanks.

United Kingdom and the European Union: Ville Aula, Emily Barton, Julia Blaski, River Cambrell, Joe Cap, Alex Chen and Valerian Hall-Chen, Dr. Nicole Chen, Maciek Chrzanowski, Federico Cortigiani, Dr. Michael Jonathan Dangerfield, Dr. Leonardo Davoudi, Sergii Drobysh, Nicolas Du Buis, Dr. Luis Vargas Faulbaum, Dr. Ira Federenko, Dr. Cosima Clara Gillhammer, Dr. Deirdre Ruscitti Harshman, Dr. Saher Hasnain, Sebastian Hoffmann, Irim Idiz, Kara Juul, Dr. Marten Krijgsman, Dr. Nina Kuglinova, Dr. Ivan Lidarev, Tommy Lo, Philip Longley, Lavi Melman, Soumya Mishra, Dr. Jean Christopher Mittelstaedt, Mike Monaghan, Dr. Laiza Poletii, Mayesha Quesem, Patrick Quinton-Brown, Felipe Roa-Clavijo, Dr. Ira Roldugina, Michelle Rorich, Anna Sands, Dr. Abhijit Sarkar, Dr. Carl-Maria Scandolo, Endri Shabani, Alen Shadunts, Elena Shumskaya, Marie-Louise Sieber, Arkady Silverman, Elizabeth Rosser

Smith, Vita Spivak, Kelly Tse, Julia Vassileva (who soon will be joining me at the ISP program at the Harvard Kennedy School), Sarah Walsh, Woody Wu, Xiaochu Wu, Rocky Yuen, Yunyun Zhou.

Russia: Dr. Anna Antonova, Lia Fakhrutdinova, the Galina family and their gigantic Siberian cat Basia (without her fluffiness, I would not have survived the Russian winter), Tonya Gromyko, Dr. Liang Jingyu, Dr. Fedor Part and his family, George Pashinski, Ambassador Yve Rossier.

United States: Jessica Bachmann, Greg Boal, Stephanie Borria and her family, Mike Bouffard, Laurisha Cotton, Lauren Fabijanski, Zhoujun Fu, Jon Gabriel, Michele Gilbert, Dr. Deirdre Ruscitti Harshman, Mary Howard, Chris and Colleen Adele Johnson, Bob and Susan Judkins Josten (as well as their cats Zip and Mia), Emily Katherine, Vineeth Mma, Tom Padrick, Andrew Parker, Dennell Reynolds, Jeremy Shao, Daniel Van-Sant, Haoying Wang, Courtney Weatherby.

Because of the multilingual nature of the sources used in the book, I owe a significant debt of gratitude to the excellent staff and highly competent language instructors at the following institutions where I received my language training: Department of Romance, Germanic, and Slavic Languages and Literatures at the George Washington University, Oxford University Language Centre, Belarusian State University, Preparatory Department for Foreign Citizens, Moscow State Institute of International Relations (MGIMO University), Liden-Denz Moscow, Goethe-Institut Mannheim, and Goethe-Institut Freiburg. I also am grateful to the fantastic staff and German teachers at the University of Vienna Sprachenzentrum, with whom I shared an office building from 2020 to 2024. Learning new languages, meeting new friends, discovering new feline species, and trying out new food, in reflection, have always been the most enjoyable experiences for me as a historian.

JIMMY CARTER AND CHINA

INTRODUCTION

In this book, I examine how the two competing Chinese regimes, the People's Republic of China (PRC) on the Chinese mainland and the Republic of China (ROC) in Taiwan, aggressively pursued their own global objectives and how their independent Cold War ambitions complicated the United States' overall China policy and its position in the late 1970s global Cold War. I cover the period from 1977 to 1981, the entirety of Jimmy Carter's presidency, with parts of the story extending further into the 1980s. I argue that both the PRC's and the ROC's independent Cold War aspirations—often at odds with the interests of the United States—made it impossible for the Carter administration to conduct a balanced policy toward both sides: The PRC's hostile attitude toward US-Soviet arms control contributed to the collapse of détente, Deng Xiaoping's and Chiang Ching-kuo's competing efforts to obtain advanced military technologies from Western countries caused serious strains between the United States and its allies, and, finally, the PRC's and the ROC's hostile attitudes toward one another, as well as their lobbying and counterlobbying efforts, polarized the US domestic debate on China and left the sovereignty and security of Taiwan an unsolved question even today, long after the end of the Cold War.

I decided to study President Carter's relations with the two competing Chinese regimes because this period is central to our understanding of both the end of the Cold War and the United States' relations with

China and Taiwan today. In 1979, the Carter administration severed official ties with the ROC, controlled by the Chinese Nationalist Party (the Kuomintang, or KMT), and recognized the PRC. The ROC, then led by Chiang Ching-kuo, the son of China's World War II leader Chiang Kai-shek, had been a traditional ally of the United States, while the PRC, controlled by the Chinese Communist Party (CCP), had just emerged from the Cultural Revolution and had not been recognized diplomatically by the United States. You can certainly imagine—and if you are old enough, remember—the excitement, confusion, hope, and expectations that the United States' sudden change of sides unleashed in the public imagination. "We Americans landed on the moon in 1969," an older American English teacher in China once reminded me, "but for a long time, Mao's China was further and more mysterious than the moon; then suddenly, in 1979, you could travel to China again."

RETHINKING CARTER'S LEGACY

President Carter, who made such travel possible by playing the most decisive role in establishing US-PRC diplomatic relations, passed away peacefully on December 29, 2024, at 100. His presidency (1977–1981) is often remembered for its ambitious yet complex foreign policy legacy during that period's turmoil, uncertainty, and rapidly changing international political landscapes. Unfortunately, for Carter, this happened in the context of his gradual, irreversible decline in public trust and popularity domestically, leading to his failed reelection bid in November 1980 against the popular and charismatic Republican candidate, Ronald Reagan. Nevertheless, he had several major achievements. The most notable highlights include the Camp David Accords in 1978, which brought long-lasting peace to Egypt and Israel for the first time since the 1973 Arab-Israeli war. Also, in Latin America, Carter peacefully transferred control of the Panama Canal back to Panama by signing the 1977 Torrijos-Carter Treaties. This decision rectified Panama's historical grievances regarding US control of the canal. It improved the United States' relations with Latin American countries until this issue became controversial again recently.

Carter's foreign policy was also severely tested by the Iranian Revolution of 1979 and the subsequent hostage crisis; the image of blindfolded American hostages taken from the US Embassy in Tehran left a dark scar on the American public psyche and exposed the limitations of US power and influence in the Middle East. After years of difficult negotiations, Carter and the Soviet Union's General Secretary Leonid Brezhnev signed the second Strategic Arms Limitation Talks (SALT II) Treaty in June 1979, designed to limit nuclear weapon arsenals on both sides and reduce Cold War tensions. Yet the Soviet invasion of Afghanistan in December 1979 led to the severe deterioration of US-Soviet relations, and later to the return of violent great power interventions in the last decade of the Cold War, causing Carter to boycott the 1980 Moscow Olympics and cease US grain exports to the USSR.[1]

With the former president's recent passing and the 2024 US election, Carter's foreign policy legacy returned to the center of the US political debate. After learning about Carter's death, President-Elect Donald Trump commented admirably on Carter's patriotism and character: "The challenges Jimmy faced as President came at a pivotal time for our country, and he did everything in his power to improve the lives of all Americans. For that, we all owe him a debt of gratitude."[2] Yet he also said, "Nobody wants to talk about the Panama Canal now. . . . It's a bad part of the Carter legacy." Carter was "a good man," Trump insisted, and "a very fine person," but "giving the Panama Canal to Panama was a very big mistake."[3] Richard Haass, on the other hand, served under President Carter and justified this decision as "the only way to keep the canal open." Carter was a president who "was able to live with contradictions." In the late 1970s, Hass reminded us, the United States faced "a rough world at times, and other countries don't play fair."[4]

However, I argue that the part of Carter's foreign policy legacy that had the most impact in the long run was not in the Middle East or Latin America but in East Asia. The one decision that fundamentally reshaped the end of the Cold War and the current-day international order was, in retrospect, Carter's decision to pivot away from the United States' traditional ally, the ROC, and embrace the PRC in the Cold War struggle against the Soviet Union. This act changed the nature of the Cold War from a global anti-Communist struggle to an anti-Soviet struggle, where the PRC, as the most important anti-Soviet Communist country, was brought onto the United States' side. Carter's policy toward the two competing Chinese regimes was thus a tremendous political gamble for him and the United States, as US economic and technological assistance, continued open and covert military cooperation, and political support to a certain extent helped the CCP avoid the demise that befell other socialist regimes in the Eastern bloc and in the Soviet Union itself.[5] Carter's decision, one could argue, in the long run helped Communism in China to survive the Cold War.

Carter's decision to embrace the PRC also raised important questions: Would the new relations with Deng Xiaoping, one of Mao's most ruthless and deceitful comrades, really help the United States recover from any real or perceived disadvantages against the Soviet Union in the Cold War? Would the two Chinese regimes sort out their differences peacefully, as US officials had expected? Would the Taiwanese leader Chiang Ching-kuo—now abandoned and angry but not defeated—continue to fight for the ROC's survival? Would the Soviet Union under Brezhnev, still mired in a long and bitter struggle with China within the socialist bloc, stay quiet and ignore the fact that the United States' new relationship with the PRC was built upon their shared anti-Soviet basis? Would US conservatives, still seeing the Cold War through an anti-Communist lens, be able to tolerate Carter's decision to abandon "our good free China" in Taiwan in favor of the "red bad Communist China" on the mainland? Most importantly, how would the United States' unclear and sometimes self-contradictory policy toward the two Chinas shape the emerging multilateral world order in the last decade of the Cold War?

With those questions in mind, I did not write this book to repeat the diplomatic side of the story of how Carter made friends with Deng and, in the words of a Taiwanese diplomat whom I met at George Washington University, "throw Taiwan under the bus." This story of establishing US-PRC diplomatic relations has already been popularized in the memoirs of Zbigniew Brzezinski, Cyrus Vance, and Jimmy Carter.[6] Those contemporary accounts generally had an optimistic tone about the conduct of US-PRC relations, ignoring the ROC side of the story or leaving that perspective unclear. President Carter, for example, was quite satisfied after he decided to switch sides and praised Deng and his comrades as "the most civilized people in the world."[7] This optimism, I will prove, had arrived too early.

Later generations of scholars have questioned the wisdom of Carter's diplomacy toward mainland China and have contemplated whether it was possible to have reached a different outcome that was more accommodating toward the ROC's interests, or they have looked inside Taiwan's political and economic transformation to understand the ROC's troubled relations with the outside world.[8] Nancy Tucker, for example, wrote a highly valuable study on the intricacy of Washington, D.C.'s decision-making process and the failure of each subsequent administration to resolve the tension in cross-strait relations.[9] Carter's China policy also attracted the attention of political scientists: Robert C. Ross, for example, applied international relations theories to security dilemmas in the study of cross-strait tensions during this period.[10] In Chinese-speaking academia, Carter's China policy caused much heated and emotional debate among both professional historians and less professional pundits. Official CCP historians, such as Gong Li, tend to praise Deng's "wisdom and far-sightedness" in his "decisive dealing" with Chiang Ching-kuo,

FIGURE 0.1 Jimmy Carter signs a document in the Oval Office. (Jimmy Carter Presidential Library and Museum)

who, in their opinion, was an illegitimate leader of a rebellious regime. Taiwanese scholars with more nuanced views, such as Hsiao-ting Lin, looked at the United States' policy priorities and the Taiwanese Nationalist leaders' own mistakes. Chinese dissident writer Yu Jie, a maverick independent thinker, blamed all three sides: both Deng and Chiang were ruthless dictators and pathological liars, and Carter was a naïve policymaker. Yu's argument was a bit extreme, but not without some wisdom.[11]

MAINLAND CHINA AND TAIWAN DURING THE 1970S GLOBAL COLD WAR

I move beyond those bilateral or trilateral arguments and look at what the most crucial issues were in the global Cold War at the time and how they interacted with Carter's China policy in a multilateral and global manner. Thus, my story has a far more extensive scope: It is about how both the ROC's and the PRC's multifaceted Cold War agendas complicated the ways US officials debated, perceived, and fought the global Cold War in the late 1970s. At the time, the US-Soviet arms race, superpower proxy wars, conflicting political ideologies, and the increased worldwide proliferation and transfer of military and dual-use technology all made it much more difficult for the Carter administration to manage the old and emerging issues around the world, which were still mainly, and inadequately, perceived from the perspective of the bipolar US-Soviet superpower rivalry.

As the historian Nancy Mitchell pointed out, the 1970s were a strange era for US officials when the president had to confront the country's past failures after the Vietnam War and restrict the direct use of—or the threat to use—force in the competition with the Soviet Union.[12] The United States' reluctance to be directly and militarily involved in global conflicts—such as Angola, the Horn of Africa, and later Afghanistan—and US officials' insistence on viewing those conflicts as black-and-white, zero-sum competitions against the Soviet Union made it tempting to redelegate the responsibility to fight the global Cold War to allies and partners, including post-Mao Communist China. As none of those partners were entirely reliable and not all their interests were perfectly aligned with those of the

United States, this proxy-based strategy left plenty of potential for independent actions, intrigues, and betrayals.

This study is one of the first serious academic efforts to document how both the PRC and the ROC considered themselves partners of the United States in the late 1970s, while also actively engaging in the global Cold War and pursuing objectives that often contradicted or even undermined US policies. Lorenz M. Lüthi, for example, pointed out that when the United States withdrew from Indochina, it left the Cold War in Asia in the late 1970s in a fluid state, which offered emerging players, such as mainland China, the opportunity to both pursue their regional interests and bargain for better bilateral relations with the United States.[13] I argue further that one of the deadly disadvantages Taiwanese leader Chiang Ching-kuo faced was that he and his Nationalist regime were incapable of filling either such a regional role or a much more significant global role as a US partner in the fight against the Soviet Union. Taiwan, as it turned out, was just too small in the arena of giants. I will demonstrate with archival evidence that Chiang desperately *tried* to play a much bigger role in the Cold War. However, his and the Nationalists' efforts—secretly pursuing nuclear weapons, seeking rapprochement with the Soviet Union, purchasing advanced weapons from US allies, and lobbying for Taiwan's anti-Communist cause— were constantly stalled and sabotaged by Carter's hardcore anti-Soviet advisers, who perceived mainland China under Deng Xiaoping and the Chinese Communists as a more valuable and realistic partner in winning the global Cold War. That mainland China's superior position—in terms of its territorial size, population, growing nuclear arsenal, and vast industrial potential—could be translated into tremendous military power as a counterweight to the Soviet Union was especially valuable in the eyes of Secretary of Defense Harold Brown, who believed that "the stronger the [mainland] Chinese military establishment, the more military resources the Soviet Union would have to divert to counter it and the better off NATO and the United States would be."[14] Taiwan could not distract and fend off a million Soviet troops at its border like mainland China did throughout the Sino-Soviet split, and it could not invade a Soviet ally, Vietnam, like Deng did in 1979, despite how unjustifiable, unethical, and costly the war was.

Therefore, US-China relations then, just like today, were not about a *bilateral* relationship between the United States and either of the two

Chinese regimes. Instead, they were about a *multilateral* network of people, ideas, and events that dynamically interacted with all three parties in a rapidly changing global context that decisively favored the larger PRC over the smaller ROC. But by choosing the CCP in mainland China over the KMT in Taiwan as the primary partner, Carter had to pay other prices. In this book, I discuss a series of global Cold War issues that negatively impacted the United States in one way or another due to its cooperation with the PRC. These issues include the US-Soviet arms race, nuclear nonproliferation, and the United States' relations with its allies. In domestic politics, the Carter administration also paid the price as the PRC and ROC lobbying and counterlobbying efforts became deeply embedded in the increasingly polarized domestic debates regarding what China—and which regime of China—really meant for the US effort to win the Cold War.

The best way to approach this wide range of issues, I believe, is through a book that provides an international history of the Cold War. To write such a book, I used a variety of primary sources: diplomatic records, policy papers, diaries, letters and memoirs, newspapers, and contemporary academic writings from not just mainland China, Taiwan, and the United States but also many other countries. Aside from documents collected in the United States, the additional international material I used for this book comes from the United Kingdom, Germany, France, and Russia. Many of those sources, such as former West German foreign ministry records on West German–PRC nuclear cooperation, Russian Academy of Sciences papers on Soviet policy toward the PRC, and British Ministry of Defence papers on UK-China anti-Soviet cooperation, have rarely been used or are used here for the first time in the study of US-China relations. A significant portion of my time and effort in writing this book involved learning foreign languages—including German and Russian—and conducting archival fieldwork. In total, I spent one year in the United States visiting a dozen presidential and university archives, two years in total learning Russian and working in Moscow's archives and libraries, and another year learning German and working with West German documents in Berlin and the nuclear bunker-like archive in Koblenz, where the West German government hid its national archive in fear of a potential Soviet strike. In the case of French sources dealing with Sino-French nuclear cooperation, I spent quite a lot of time making coffee and Chinese food to motivate my first-year PhD French housemate Camille Boullenois, now an excellent China scholar based in Berlin, to find them in Paris for me and have them translated.

Those efforts, some more academic and others more detective-like, eventually paid off. Going through historical records in multiple languages, as well as speaking to witnesses who personally shaped those historical events, allowed me to paint a very different picture of the United States' engagement with mainland China and Taiwan during those fateful years of the late 1970s, a time of uncertainty, radical changes, and emerging new crises. Many of the people to whom I spoke are still influencing policy debates in Moscow, Beijing, Taipei, and Washington—or they have children currently in high positions, which added a sense of relevance and urgency to my research. Based on all the information so far, I conclude that Jimmy Carter, the American president, was not just making policy toward China. He was, in fact, fighting the Cold War in different geographic regions and various policy areas, with China as an increasingly important piece of the puzzle, while at the same time getting sidetracked by the two Chinese regimes' bitter engagement in the Cold War. It is a much messier yet far more dynamic, multilayered, and fascinating story than the bilateral or trilateral view of US-PRC-ROC relations that most existing scholarship tends to confirm.

WHAT HAS BEEN WRITTEN SO FAR

I am by no means the first historian to try to research the history of the United States' relations with the PRC or the ROC during the Carter administration. Since the 1980s, a steady flow of scholarly work has offered different approaches to and perspectives on this topic, though far more literature has focused on the actions of President Richard Nixon and National Security Adviser/Secretary of State Henry Kissinger. Despite its vintage, much of the earlier literature still offers valuable insights, such as those of Michel Oksenberg, President Carter's top China adviser, who looked at ideology, political structure, and strategic thinking in the making of PRC policy toward the United States. In addition, John Fairbank traced the problem of US relations with the two Chinese regimes to two profound but conflicting historical trends: each US administration's natural attempt to treat both sides as equal through the old "open door policy" tradition versus the Chinese "echoes of the dynastic circle" to pursue unity under a single regime.[15] After the end of the Cold War and with more access to Chinese materials, recent scholars have taken a bottom-up approach and looked at elements inside the United States and China that shaped their relations. This school of thought includes Harry Harding, who investigated policy debates in both Beijing and Washington; Robert S. Ross, who paid specific attention to Chinese leaders' perceptions of US politics; Richard Solomon, who studied Chinese diplomats' negotiation strategies; David Shambaugh, who conducted a multiagency analysis of policymaking in both countries; and Rosemary Foot, who looked at border structure problems in the United States' attempt to integrate China into the US-led liberal international global order.[16]

However, mainland China's role in the much broader global Cold War is less studied due to linguistic difficulties and the lack of access to PRC diplomatic records. Recently, John W. Garver's survey of PRC diplomatic history started to carefully examine how Deng Xiaoping's attempt to build an anti-Soviet alliance in Europe played a central role in China's late Cold War strategy, a collected volume edited by William Kirby looked at the international impact of the opening of US-China relations, and a special issue, *Cold War History*, dealt with the European dimension of China's Cold War in the late 1970s.[17] European historians, such as Martin Alber and Frank Bösch, have also started to investigate how Carter's diplomatic opening impacted Europe's arms sales to and military cooperation with the PRC, a new theme that I will delve into in more detail.[18]

In writing this book, I also benefited from the emerging literature on Taiwan and the late 1970s Cold War, a theme that had been largely ignored by historians until the 2000s. This literature includes Jay Taylor's biographies of Chiang Kai-shek and Chiang Ching-kuo, which detailed the Chiang family's complex love-hate relations with the United States from World War II until the democratic movement in the late 1980s; Nancy Tucker's study of Taiwan's important role in overall US security policy; and a new biography of Chiang Ching-kuo by the Taiwanese historian Hsiao-ting Lin, in which he shows the ROC's Cold War diplomacy had a much more active role—pursuing its secret nuclear program, initiating back-channel negotiations with the Soviet Union, and conducting lobbying efforts in the United States.[19] In addition, a large body of legal studies literature has examined the 1979 Taiwan Relations Act and its deliberate ambiguity regarding the United States' security commitment to Taiwan.[20]

The works mentioned here are, of course, not comprehensive. Because of the wide range of issues covered in this book, I also consulted hundreds of studies in highly specialized areas. For the convenience of my nonacademic audience, I will leave most of the literature in detailed footnotes in each chapter and mention only a few of the most important ones here for those curious about my book's larger historical background. Sources on the broader Cold War include Odd Arne Westad's new comprehensive survey, Raymond Garthoff's account of the collapse of US-Soviet détente, Nancy Mitchell's study of US-Soviet intervention in Africa, and Elizabeth Wishnick's work on Brezhnev's policy toward China.[21] Examples of more specialized studies include Hugo Meijer, Frank Cain, and Jing-dong Yuan's works on US export control policy toward China, Brian J. Auten's study on US rearmament programs under Carter, Xiaoming Zhang's account of the 1979 Sino-Vietnam war, and Shen Zhihua and Li Danhui's studies on Sino-Soviet relations (although, unfortunately, some of them are available only in Chinese).[22]

STRUCTURE OF THE BOOK: STRATEGY, TECHNOLOGY, AND IDEOLOGY

I have organized this book into three parts. Each deals with a critical aspect of how the United States' China policy complicated its other Cold War objectives. The first part is about the US-Soviet strategic competition in the nuclear arms race and in arms control, the second is about military and dual-use technology transfer, and the last is about ideology and competing world visions in the Cold War.

In the first part, I focus on the United States' relations with the PRC. Chapter 1 discusses how Deng Xiaoping skillfully played the US domestic Cold War political debate and allied himself with anti-Soviet officials both inside and outside the White House. This political alliance allowed Deng to pressure the Carter administration to sacrifice the United States' traditional security guarantee toward Taiwan amid increased US-Soviet tension during the collapse of détente, symbolized by the difficult new negotiations around SALT II and the two superpowers' indirect support of the Ethiopia-Somalia conflict in the Horn of Africa.

Chapter 2 analyzes how the PRC's Cold War policy contributed to the collapse of a major pillar of US-Soviet détente, the proposed Comprehensive Test Ban Treaty (CTBT). It shows that the PRC-French alliance against the US-Soviet-British efforts to negotiate the first CTBT was the most important contributor to the disintegration of this joint trilateral effort to ban the testing of nuclear weapons. The chapter also includes a parallel study of mainland China's intercontinental ballistic missile (ICBM) project to demonstrate that Deng had placed his faith in mainland China's technological progress, not in a US-led multilateral treaty, to ensure China's future security.

In the book's second part, I introduce the theme of military and dual-use technology transfer. The two chapters provide two case studies comparing mainland China's and Taiwan's separate and competitive efforts to acquire advanced US and Western military technology and the way those efforts strained the Carter administration's relations with its allies and created a regional arms race across the Taiwan Strait.

Chapter 3 studies the PRC's effort to undermine the US-led Coordinating Committee for Multilateral Export Controls (COCOM) system by importing advanced military and dual-use technology from Western Europe, which affected East-West détente and transatlantic relations between the United States and its NATO allies. A significant part of the story also focuses on the development of Chinese strategic and technical thinking behind the PRC's technology acquisition policy, so that importing expensive weapons became less of a priority than acquiring military and dual-use technologies that could be integrated into existing military and civilian platforms.

Chapter 4 focuses on the ROC and Chiang Ching-kuo's effort to enhance Taiwan's own security through its secret nuclear weapons buildup and its failed effort to acquire advanced fighter jets from Israel, both of which were sabotaged by the Carter administration, which put nonproliferation, US-PRC anti-Soviet cooperation, and US domestic business interests ahead of Chiang Ching-kuo's need to gain a technological edge against the Communist regime on the Chinese mainland.

Suppose the Cold War was an ideological battle. What did President Carter's engagement with Communist mainland China and his abandonment of anti-Communist Taiwan mean for the ideological dimension of United States' Cold War? With this question in mind, in the last part of the book I examine both sides of China's engagement in the multilateral ideological battles of the Cold War. Chapter 5 studies the competing lobbying efforts of both the PRC and the ROC in US domestic politics surrounding the passage of the Taiwan Relations Act, as well as the effort of each Chinese regime to force its own vision of "one China" on the other. Deng's failed effort to lure Chiang Ching-kuo to the negotiating table and Chiang's resolute, though very nuanced, anti-Communist attitudes, this chapter suggests, shaped cross-strait relations long after the end of the Cold War.

Chapter 6 focuses on the Sino-Soviet dimension and studies the Brezhnev regime's response to and criticism of Carter's handling of mainland China. This often came at the cost of US-Soviet détente and Brezhnev's attempt to repair relations with the mainland Chinese comrades in the brief window between early 1977 and early 1978, an idea that was born after Mao's death and the end of the Cultural Revolution. Furthermore, taking advantage of materials collected in the Archive of the Russian Academy of Sciences, which is now no longer available to Western researchers, I examine two very similar voices in Moscow and Washington that were critical of Carter's China policy: Even the Soviet Union's top Chinese studies experts discussed privately how unsustainable the United States' China policy was when it was solely based upon anti-Soviet military cooperation with the mainland, although Taiwan still played—and for a very long time would still play—an indispensable strategic role in United States' overall Asia-Pacific security policy.

Finally, in the conclusion, I summarize the historical legacy of Carter's policy toward both Chinese regimes at the end of the Cold War and beyond. I further argue that the main themes I discuss in this book—strategic competition, technological transfer, and the battle for ideology—are still relevant in the post–Cold War context. There are, however, significant variations and new developments. During the Cold War, the competition between the PRC and the ROC, no matter how fierce it looked, was limited and contained mainly by their mutual pro-American policies. Today, however, mainland China, ever more oppressive and autocratic, leans toward Putin's Russia, while Taiwan, now a thriving democracy, has become firmly integrated into US-led liberal political and economic systems. During the late 1970s, the PRC and the ROC were competing on the American side of the Cold War; today they are in a much more deadly struggle against one another, representing two opposing international orders.

A NOTE ON NAMING CHINA

This book is titled *Jimmy Carter and China* partially because President Carter never visited China during his presidency and partially because the concept of China in this book is a contested geographic space rather than a political entity, as the division and independent nature of the two competing Chinese regimes were, and still are, an obvious political reality that politicians in the West do not wish to officially acknowledge and often deliberately choose to ignore. During the Cold War, both Deng Xiaoping and Chiang Ching-kuo identified themselves as Chinese nationalists. They both insisted there was only "one China," except they disagreed with which one it was. At the same time, US officials did not want to get involved in this hopeless debate or to offend any of their Chinese partners. Thus, from Kissinger's "Shanghai Communiqué" to the first year of Carter's presidency, the United States dutifully played along—until Carter made the hard choice, selecting the PRC as the United States' main partner in the Cold War. Since then, for the politically savvy leaders in the United States and in both Chinese regimes, "one China" has been a commonly accepted fictional concept, a euphemism to avoid complexity, or, depending on which side of the Taiwan Strait one is situated, a symbol of stubbornness born out of either unfinished ambition for the future or unforgettable defeat from the past. However, the divided "two Chinas" was the unavoidable reality each side faced in the Cold War.

Also, during the late 1970s, the Indigenous Taiwanese cultural and political identity associated with the various democratic movements had not yet become a mainstream political force, and the debate about whether Taiwan should not be a part of the PRC or whether the ROC should just be called simply Taiwan wouldn't surface until after the Democratic Progress Party candidate Chen Shui-bian defeated the KMT candidate James Soong in the 2000 presidential election.[23] This was not the case during the Cold War, when Chiang Ching-kuo and his KMT comrades often proudly and nostalgically referred to their regime as the Dang Guo, meaning the "Party State." For the convenience of the readers, the PRC, the Communist regime, China, and mainland China are used interchangeably, as are the ROC, the KMT regime, and Taiwan, depending on the historical or linguistic context. However, I do not wish to engage here in an argument over which term is correct, as scholars on cross-strait relations have shown that, in this part of the world, the name is a political metaphor, a discursive site of struggle.[24]

I

STRATEGIC COMPETITION

1

THE DECLINE OF DÉTENTE AND THE NORMALIZATION OF US-CHINA DIPLOMATIC RELATIONS

Taking advantage of stalled US-Soviet negotiations at SALT II and Soviet intervention in the Horn of Africa, Deng Xiaoping, the new PRC leader who had just won a power struggle with Mao's designated successor, Hua Guofeng, allied himself with anti-Soviet US officials both inside and outside the Carter administration and skillfully pushed his terms for normalizing US-PRC diplomatic relations: The United States must abandon its diplomatic ties with and security commitment to Taiwan in exchange for the PRC's cooperation in the global Cold War.

KISSINGER'S LEGACY: DÉTENTE AND ITS CRITICS

From 1969 until President Jimmy Carter took office, Presidents Richard Nixon and Gerald Ford had carefully balanced two major foreign policy priorities: to establish and maintain détente with the Soviet Union and rapprochement with the PRC. During the Nixon years, the initiation of dialogue with Mao Zedong's China was an important step in getting US troops out of Vietnam. The Vietnam War was, as the historian Henry William Brands observed, not just a US war but also a Soviet and a Chinese war. The Soviet Union and Mao's China were North Vietnam's primary supporters; thus, for Nixon and Kissinger, détente with the Soviet Union and a simultaneous rapprochement with China were two necessary steps to be considered.[1] Until 1968, mainland China, guided by Mao's anti-imperialist beliefs, was the main supporter of North Vietnam's continued fight against the United States. Historians believe Mao wanted to fight the Americans so much that he even actively blocked other socialist countries' attempts to mediate peace between North Vietnam and the United States.[2] However, Nixon and Kissinger took advantage of the Sino-Soviet split, especially the Sino-Soviet border conflicts of 1969, to negotiate with Mao and work out a gradual Chinese disengagement from the Vietnam War, paving the way for the final US withdrawal.[3]

At the same time, US-Soviet relations were carefully maintained in what Nixon frequently called "a structure of peace"—the détente. At the center of this policy was the Strategic Arms Limitation Talks Treaty (SALT), negotiated by both superpowers between 1969 and its final signing on May 26, 1972, by President Nixon and General Secretary Leonid Brezhnev at a summit meeting in Moscow. The treaty maintained the nuclear arms race between the United States and the Soviet Union in a way that subjected each side to the other's nuclear deterrent. Political scientists called this "Mutual Assured Destruction (MAD)," a situation in which peace between the superpowers was maintained because, regardless of who started the war, both sides would be completely destroyed in mutual nuclear exchanges, thus making the option of war illogical and suicidal.[4] The SALT allowed the two countries to achieve such an exactly calculated balance that each country would have the capability to destroy the other in the event of nuclear war; thus, in theory, the two nuclear superpowers would stay at peace.

In reality, each country always wanted more from this treaty than the other would tolerate. From the US perspective, Nixon and Kissinger wanted to use the SALT Treaty to limit the Soviet Union's nuclear ambitions, thus saving the American people from a potentially far more expensive nuclear arms race. They simultaneously wanted the SALT to serve as a "code of conduct" for peaceful coexistence between the two superpowers. A better US-Soviet relationship based on the treaty would further restrain the Soviet Union's global adventurism, which was also checked and restrained, on a second front and particularly in Asia, by the improvement of US relations with mainland China. Thus, in the eyes of Nixon and Kissinger, the SALT Treaty would be the cornerstone of détente with the

Soviet Union: There would be no risk of nuclear war, each superpower would take care of business in its own sphere of influence, and the world would be at peace.[5]

This additional benefit to be derived from the SALT Treaty—that of restraining Soviet ambitions—was far from becoming a reality; rather, it was more of a one-sided US aspiration. The Soviet Union did the opposite of dismantling détente precisely because the treaty guaranteed peace at the superpower level. Brezhnev and his comrades saw the SALT Treaty as an American acceptance of the Soviet Union as an equal superpower, thus making it a basis on which the Soviet Union could further solidify its self-imposed, unpopular grasp of Eastern Europe. Even further, the Soviet leadership saw the treaty as a safeguard, a guarantee that the Soviet Union could safely disrupt and replace the United States' global influence in the Third World without the risk that those actions would escalate into a nuclear war. In the words of the Russian historian Vladislav Zubok, "Both sides viewed détente as managed competition, as a continuation of the Cold War by less dangerous means."[6]

The United States was also seeking advantages outside of détente to regain its lost prestige after Vietnam. For example, it was selling weapons to the shah of Iran and backed up Israel at the most critical moments of the 1973 Yom Kippur War. According to Raymond L. Garthoff, an American SALT negotiator, "Détente was a more sophisticated and less belligerent way of waging the Cold War, rather than an alternative to it."[7]

The détente also did not prevent the two superpowers from conducting their separate policies toward the PRC. While the Brezhnev regime desperately tried to contain mainland China's competing influence in the socialist world, Nixon and Kissinger conducted a rapprochement with mainland China to constrain the Soviet Union on the global stage (figure 1.1). Thus, the détente, in the words of Robert Gates, offered a false sense of hope to both superpowers, with mainland China being a key disruptive external factor: The Soviet leader had hoped that détente would encourage the United States to use its improved relations with Mao's China to restrain and regulate Mao's anti-Soviet behaviors. At the same time, US officials wished that the détente could stop the Soviet Union's military buildup. Both sides, as it turned out, were greatly disappointed.[8]

In summary, the US-Soviet détente had always been characterized by a careful balance between strategic cooperation and competition, with

FIGURE 1.1 Détente at its peak: US President Richard M. Nixon and a stylish Soviet General Secretary Leonid Brezhnev, the two leading architects of détente, aboard the presidential yacht USS *Sequoia*, June 19, 1973. (National Archives and Records Administration White House Photo Office Collection)

mainland China being an increasingly important factor. Starting in the autumn of 1977, however, the cooperative aspect of US-Soviet relations, as demonstrated by the negotiations for a new SALT treaty (SALT II), became increasingly strained, and the competitive aspect, characterized by the proxy wars in the Horn of Africa and later in Afghanistan, was moving beyond the superpowers' control.[9] President Carter was still committed to SALT II but needed another option to pressure the Soviet Union without directly breaking down US-Soviet relations. Thus, reaching out to mainland China's post-Mao generation of leaders seemed to be an increasingly tempting choice in an effort to recreate Nixon and Kissinger's 1972 scenario in which the United States was the leader in the "strategic triangle." US-Soviet relations could be maintained through arms reduction talks, and mainland China could be used to balance the perceived US loss in the Third World—a term coined by Mao to describe the developing nations beyond the US, the USSR, and industrialized Europe.[10] This time, however, the US role in the tripolar political situation came with a cost. Unlike Mao Zedong, Deng Xiaoping actively and skillfully exploited the division in US domestic politics to press for his position on how the normalization of US-China relations should proceed. Deng stipulated that the United States had to abandon the ROC in Taiwan and grant the PRC access to advanced Western military technologies. In addition, he sabotaged US-Soviet arms control negotiations whenever he had the chance. This posed two separate but closely linked challenges to the Carter administration: namely, trying to maintain the US commitment to Taiwan, while not allowing the Soviet leadership to think that the US linked negotiations on SALT II to China.

In the view of Taiwanese leaders Chiang Kai-shek and later Chiang Ching-kuo, the Nixon and Kissinger years, as well as the brief Ford administration, were a pure nightmare, as the US shifted its focus from building a traditional, anti-Communist alliance with the ROC to what they saw as a counterproductive policy of flirting with their Communist rival on the Chinese mainland. Chiang Ching-kuo was glad to see that Ford lost the 1976 election because this meant Kissinger, the person Chiang saw as un-American, traitorous, and most responsible for the US shift in focus from the ROC to the PRC, would no longer be part of the political scene.

Chiang Ching-kuo, however, remained cautious about Carter, the rather unknown and untested president-elect, and wrote the following in his diary on November 8, 1976, the US election day: "For us, whoever becomes the US president does not really matter; the most important thing is to 'get rid of the knots tied by Henry Kissinger,' as Ford was an American, so was Carter, both of whom have American blood, but Kissinger is not an American. Observing clearly his actions, all are harmful to America; his sin is not just playing power politics but selling out American national interests and selling out America's friends." He observed that the election of the relatively unknown Carter reflected the American people's "dissatisfaction with bureaucratism, corruption, the current state of American politics, and an urgent need for renewal and change."[11] Chiang would soon be disappointed, as Carter went even further than his predecessors and officially severed US diplomatic ties with Taiwan.

CARTER'S FIRST YEAR IN THE WHITE HOUSE

When Jimmy Carter arrived at the White House on January 20, 1977, he inherited détente together with its promises and failures. As a former nuclear submarine officer, he understood the danger of nuclear war all too well. He was determined to complete a SALT II treaty, as negotiations under both President Nixon and President Ford had not achieved concrete results, and to bring the US-Soviet nuclear arms race under greater control. Carter's campaign notes were filled with thoughts and proposals such as the following: "The ultimate goal of this nation should be a reduction of nuclear weapons in all nations of the world to zero. This should be done by carefully controlled public proposals to Russia and other nuclear powers for step-by-step, carefully monitored mutual reductions." He wanted to reduce nuclear weapons carriers—meaning missiles and bombers—on all sides to approximately 1,320—a drastic reduction from 2,360 for the Soviets and 1,710 for the Americans, which Nixon and Brezhnev had agreed to in the 1972 SALT Treaty.[12] A faithful Christian, Carter also quoted the prophet Isaiah during his campaign for this noble cause: "They shall beat their swords into plowshares and their spears into pruning hooks, and nation shall not lift up sword against nation, neither shall they learn war anymore."[13]

This drastic departure was too much for Carter's domestic critics, who believed that a new SALT treaty with deeper arms reductions would give unfair advantages to the Soviet Union and further encourage Brezhnev's global ambitions, which were detrimental to US national interests. Those opponents of a new treaty were drawn to an intelligence project commissioned by the Ford administration, the Project Team B. The report resulting from this study, led by then director of the CIA George H. W. Bush and the legendary Cold War hawk Paul Nitze, argued that Soviet strategic forces were catching up to the United States in terms of nuclear weapons. It also stated that the Soviet nuclear strategy was not entirely defensive, as the CIA had previously concluded: a euphemistic way to say that the Soviet leaders were willing to launch a surprise nuclear attack against the United States in the future because they could potentially wipe out the US ability to retaliate—contrary to what the theory of mutually assured destruction had predicted.[14]

This new analysis, while not entirely honest about the United States' own overwhelming and much more technologically advanced nuclear capability, was nevertheless leaked to the *New York Times* during Carter's election campaign, causing severe criticism from the conservative wing of Washington's foreign policy establishment.[15] Carter, who was never involved in this study and certainly not a fan of either Bush or Nitze, found it increasingly difficult to deal with the polarized opinions regarding his policy toward the Soviet Union.[16]

The Soviet leadership, too, was totally unprepared for this proposed deep reduction and immediately started to view the new president's proposal and personal character with suspicion. During his first week in the White House, Carter learned his lesson when he enthusiastically laid out his goal to "see the total number of nuclear missiles [on both sides] reduced to several hundred" to Soviet Ambassador Anatoly Dobrynin.[17] From the Soviets' perspective, the cut that Carter asked for was too big to be realistic, and they thought he was threatening the Soviet Union by asking them to disarm their nuclear forces. In addition, the Soviet negotiators fundamentally disagreed with the US proposal to consider their Tupolev Tu-22M Backfire bombers as strategic weapons. As the Soviets argued, these intermediate-range bombers could not reach the United States. They also regarded as unfair the Americans' insistence that their own cruise missiles were not strategic weapons when, in fact, their functions were similar to those of ballistic missiles.[18]

Linguistic differences caused further confusion: Cruise missiles are called "winged missiles" in Russian. Brezhnev wrote a frustrated letter on this issue to Carter in February 1977, complaining about the seemingly absurd American position: "What is the difference indeed for people, regarding what kind of missile will kill them—a winged missile or a missile without wings?"[19] In addition, the Soviet military had needed many years to build up its nuclear force to catch up with the United States. The Soviet leaders were thus unwilling to sacrifice their newly gained strategic parity. They thought that Carter was using the "radical cuts" approach as "a political demagogue and putting propaganda pressure on us."[20]

Carter, however, was undeterred. In March, he sent Secretary of State Cyrus Vance to Moscow with his "deep cut" proposal that would limit both sides to 1,800–2,000 nuclear delivery vehicles, with additional limitations on the number of nuclear warheads each such vehicle could carry; limit multiple independently targetable reentry vehicles (MIRVs) to 1,100–1,200 on each side; freeze the deployment of a variety of new missiles; and limit cruise missiles to a range of 2,500 kilometers (just over 1,500 miles). The aging Brezhnev saw this plan as not only too advantageous to the United States but also too far away from what the Ford administration had once agreed to with the Soviet Union. The Soviet leadership outright rejected this proposal as well as Carter's fallback proposal, which would have deferred some of the most challenging questions, such as cruise missiles and Soviet Backfire bombers, to future negotiations.[21] The first stage of the negotiation thus failed to achieve any concrete result.

THE LINKAGE WITH CHINA

The Taiwanese Nationalist leader Chiang Ching-kuo proved himself a surprisingly keen observer of the US-Soviet negotiations at SALT II. Earlier than anyone else we know of in the historical record, he sensed the fundamental impact of the stalled negotiations on future US policy toward China: "The US-Russia SALT II negotiation has been derailed due to Russia's tough attitude. This is an expected event, but also something severely disadvantaged/disadvantageous to us [the ROC]; American left-wing politicians will use it as an excuse to push for a policy of 'uniting with the [Chinese Communist] bandits to balance the Russians.' We will be walking on a tightrope from now and must remain cautious!"[22]

Chiang had good reason to understand that a closer and more disruptive linkage between US-PRC policy and US-Soviet policy was not far away. After all, he had clearly observed that on the world stage, it was his Chinese Communist rivals, from Mao Zedong and Hua Guofeng to Deng Xiaoping, who were the most vociferous critics of US-Soviet arms reduction negotiations. Deng had fiercely criticized every US-Soviet treaty from the Limited Test Ban Treaty of 1963 and the Non-Proliferation Treaty of 1968 to the Vladivostok Accord of 1974. Deng expressed his full contempt for this accord: "The so-called disarmament, called by both the United States and the Soviet Union, has in fact concealed the danger of a new world war and masked the breakneck military expansion on both sides."[23] He maintained this position during the Carter years. For example, on April 14, 1977, Deng's trusted messenger PRC Foreign Minister Huang Hua warned Thomas S. Gates, director of the US Liaison Office, of the danger of believing that arms talks could improve the US position vis-à-vis the USSR:

> The Soviet Union is trying to squeeze the US out of various areas. Disarmament, detente, and SALT are various forms taken to continue this

rivalry. In negotiation, each side tries to improve its position. Neither will accept a concession or submit to a position of defeat. Disarmament has never succeeded in history. This was the case before the First World War and the Second World War. It still holds true today. Take the SALT talks, for example: since Vladivostok up until now, the strategic weapons of the Soviet Union and the US have increased, and weapons have become more accurate instead of being reduced and weakened. This is a fact no one can deny. Whether or not the SALT talks between the US and the Soviet Union succeed will not alter the basic situation of rivalry between the two countries, even if you can reach some agreements. An agreement amounts to just an empty piece of paper.[24]

Complex and sometimes self-serving calculations lay behind the CCP leaders' warnings against détente, and not all were honestly communicated to the Americans. First, even though Mao had died, the current leaders had inherited the deceased chairman's anti-imperial and antihegemonic worldview; thus, they saw both the United States and the Soviet Union as imperial powers and did not want to see them make peace through détente, which would give either of them a chance to focus their pressure on mainland China. Second, among the post-Mao leaders, Deng Xiaoping, in particular, needed to present mainland China as an indispensable partner in the global anti-Soviet struggle led by the United States and to use mainland China's cooperation in fighting the Cold War to force the Americans to give up their security guarantee for Taiwan. In other words, if the United States and the Soviet Union made real peace, all the massive concessions on Taiwan that the United States had given to the PRC could have been lost or reversed. There is enough evidence to suggest that the last thing Deng wanted at this moment was for the Soviet Union and the United States to end their confrontation.

The PRC's post-Mao leaders held a complex view of détente, the arms race, and Taiwan, which was first openly laid out by Hua Guofeng, Mao's immediate successor, during the Eleventh Chinese Communist Party Congress in August 1977: "They praise 'détente,' yet the more they praise, the more tension there is. They scream 'arms reduction,' yet the more 'reduction,' the more arms they have. They talk about 'peace' every day. Still, every day they prepare for war." Comparing the two superpowers, Hua believed that "the Soviet Socialist Imperialists present a bigger danger" because "in the current US-Soviet rivalry, the Soviet Imperialists are on the advance, and the American Imperialists in retreat." To counter this threat, Soviet expansion had to be resisted throughout the world from Europe to Africa, to Latin America and Japan. China was willing to work with the United States because "the difficulty China had with the United States [seemed] to be rather small." However, "China and the United States have different social systems and different ideologies, and they have some fundamental differences," especially demanding that "America must withdraw forces from Taiwan, cut off diplomatic relations with the Chiang [Ching-kuo] bandits, and abrogate the so-called Sino-American Mutual Defense Treaty. We will absolutely liberate Taiwan," Hua emphasized. "When and how [we deal with Taiwan], this is our domestic policy, no other countries should meddle with it."[25] Even though Deng eventually replaced Hua after the post-Mao power struggle, I will demonstrate that Deng's antihegemonic worldview, hostile attitude toward the US-Soviet détente, and resolute determination to take control of Taiwan were very similar to those of his rival and predecessor.

THE CONVERGING WORLDVIEWS OF BEIJING'S LEADERS AND WASHINGTON'S HARD-LINERS

In 1977, one group of policymakers at the US Department of Defense was increasingly worried about Carter's lack of progress in improving cooperation with the PRC. If Deng Xiaoping and his comrades were so hostile toward the Soviet Union, why not exploit their worldview to put more pressure on the Soviets? Harold Brown, a former nuclear scientist and secretary of defense at the time, was especially concerned about the expanding Soviet nuclear capability, given the lack of progress in the negotiations at SALT II. He also believed it was mainland China, with its massive population and industrial potential—not Japan and certainly not Taiwan—that could help the United States counter the Soviet Union. Secretary Brown wrote to President Carter and Zbigniew Brzezinski on February 9, 1977: "In the past six years, building a new Sino-American relationship has been a central element in Washington's efforts to construct counterweights to and constraints on the Soviets." He noted: "I am concerned that the new Administration, in its first weeks, may be giving the impression that the weight of its national security diplomacy will be cast in the familiar framework of the Western alliance (and Japan) versus the Soviet Union and ignoring China." Brown urged exploration of a range of options from arms sales to military contracts to improve US-PRC relations and issued a slightly cynical review of the "feasibility of US-PRC relations as a means of sustaining the Sino-Soviet split."[26] Based on post–Cold War interviews, Brown was, in fact, the first person to suggest to Carter that the United States use mainland China to pressure the Soviet Union to gain the upper hand in SALT II.[27]

Outside of the White House, the Cold War hawks associated with the Committee on the Present Danger (CPD) had already started their moves on mainland China. The CPD was formed by conservative anti-Soviet politicians in the 1950s to lobby for Paul Nitze and Dean Acheson's policy of remilitarizing the United States against the Soviet Union and actively intervening to "roll back" Soviet victories symbolized by the Communist victory in mainland China and later by Soviet-PRC intervention in the Korean War. It opposed the more moderate containment policy proposed by George F. Kennan, the author of the famous "long telegram" about Russia's aggressiveness and then director of policy planning at the State Department.[28] After two decades of inaction, it was re-formed during the 1976 presidential election to lobby against détente and then, after the election, against Carter's perceived appeasement policy toward the Soviet Union. Its members were not friends of Carter and promoted precisely the kind of confrontational policy toward the Soviet Union that the Carter administration wanted to avoid.[29]

Given Carter's new drastic reduction proposal, SALT II naturally became the CPD's primary target. While supporters of SALT II, such as Secretary of State Vance and the president himself, believed that US-Soviet relations could be regulated with arms control, those associated with the CPD were convinced that SALT II offered the Soviet Union too much advantage and would only encourage Brezhnev's aggression in other areas where the superpowers were competing. Nitze initially tried to get a cabinet position in the Carter administration but failed to do so because his views were fundamentally different from the current State Department's policy on US-Soviet relations. Greatly disappointed but not defeated, Nitze spent 1977 working for the CPD to publicize the Soviet threat across the United States—speaking at universities, community meetings, and policy conferences. Nitze's grandson remembered with great amusement his grandfather's strange behavior during the Carter years: "Nitze liked to use models to demonstrate Soviet military supremacy. He would carry around re-creations of Soviet ICBMs, ten inches long and black. The American models were five inches long and white. Sometimes, in speeches or meetings, he would arrange the black missiles to point upward while laying the white ones horizontal."[30]

It has previously gone unnoticed among historians that Nitze soon attracted willing listeners in Beijing (figure 1.2). From November 24 to December 13, 1977, Nitze and his wife, Phyllis Pratt Nitze, as well as a few other members of the CPD, went on a three-week grand tour in China, thanks to "tourist visas" offered by the PRC's Ministry of Foreign Affairs. Nitze, a retired official according to his title and a military intelligence officer in disguise, closely coordinated the tour with the Defense Intelligence Agency at the Pentagon. He toured major cities and industrial

FIGURE 1.2 The pair of unlikely anti-Soviet hard-liners: Paul Nitze (*front row, fourth from the left*) and PRC Vice Premier Li Xiannian (*front row, fifth from the left*). (Library of Congress, Paul Nitze Papers)

centers and, as part of the Chinese male bonding ritual, drank *baijiu* with Chinese officials at every stop.[31] Nitze even inspected Chinese military bases, offered advice to Chinese generals, and sent back more reports to his American generals before finally having a three-hour meeting with the PRC Foreign Minister Huang Hua on December 1, 1977.[32] The two immediately formed a friendship over their shared worldview that Soviet expansionism was the biggest threat to the world. "The Committee feels the Soviet Union is seeking hegemony over the entire world, including the Asian landmass and the United States," Nitze told the Chinese and asked: "What measures should the PRC and the United States take together against the 'Polar Bear'?" Huang Hua answered: "The most important question is to fight against [Carter's] appeasement policy, and we must have no illusions about that." Huang then laid out his conditions both to inform and to influence the American visitor: "SALT II and all these negotiations are transitory and false. . . . We are prepared to struggle against the Soviet Union ideologically and militarily as well for one thousand years." However, the ROC on Taiwan was the only obstacle between the United States and China. Huang then laid his cards on the table: China could not promise to reunify Taiwan only through peaceful means. "The right road is the use of force because there is such a bunch of counter-revolutionaries in Taiwan."[33]

Nitze's trip was only part of mainland China's effort to court American anti-Soviet hard-liners and thereby use Carter's domestic opposition to pressure the president into yielding to their demand on Taiwan. Henry "Scoop" Jackson, the leading Democratic senator from the state of Washington, was known for his strong anti-Soviet views and was also unhappy with Carter's SALT II proposals. He repeatedly wrote to Carter, stating that the concessions he had made were unfair and that the "Soviets desire a SALT agreement on terms that they regard as advantageous."[34] This position was very much shared by the Joint Chiefs of Staff, who resisted Carter's proposal and openly supported the anti-Soviet position advocated by the CPD.[35] Carter, known for his politeness and stubbornness, would always write back, "Scoop, your SALT memorandum is excellent and of great help to me," and then stay on his own course.[36]

Jackson then made his point by opposing Carter's appointment of Paul Warnke, a supporter of the drastic reduction proposal, as the director of arms control negotiations in March 1977. This which forced Carter to adjust his first SALT II proposal to be much more restrictive on Soviet land-based heavy missiles, which, in turn, caused further anger and mistrust on the Soviet side.[37] For example, when Vance met with Brezhnev in Moscow in the same month and asked the Soviets to eliminate half of their land-based heavy ICBMs, Brezhnev was quite shocked at how much Carter had deviated from what President Ford had promised during the Vladivostok Summit. Land-based heavy ICBMs, after all, were the only advantage the Soviet military had against US strategic forces, which, in turn, had the overwhelming technological edge in air- and submarine-launched nuclear missiles. Minister of Foreign Affairs Andrei Gromyko even privately told Vance that Carter's position on Soviet ICBMs was "not just unacceptable but also absurd."[38] Brezhnev's concern fell on deaf ears in both Washington and Beijing. However, now the mainland Chinese had learned about Jackson's harsh stance toward Carter's SALT II policy, and later, in 1978, they invited Jackson to Beijing. The mainland Chinese leaders believed he could play a helpful role in bringing mainland China into the global anti-Soviet alliance.[39]

Deng Xiaoping's attitude toward SALT II had several effects on the later development of the US-PRC normalization process. First, when Carter switched to a stricter policy toward the Soviet Union in his second year in the White House, "playing the China card" became an easier choice, as Deng's anti-Soviet messages had already been echoed loudly inside the United States for a while by people like Nitze and Jackson. Second, since the Chinese were always very clear about the link between their position on Taiwan and US-China normalization, it was very difficult for Carter administration officials to separate these two issues and not abandon Chiang Ching-kuo and his Nationalist regime in Taiwan if they hoped to receive anti-Soviet military support from Deng.

BRZEZINSKI, THE ANTI-SOVIET SCHOLAR IN THE WHITE HOUSE

All the critics of SALT II inside and outside the White House were overshadowed by Carter's national security adviser, Zbigniew Brzezinski, who was the most instrumental in moving the US-PRC diplomatic reopening forward at full speed. Brzezinski was born into a Polish diplomat family that witnessed the rise of fascism before World War II. He was educated at McGill University in Canada and in 1953 obtained his PhD at Harvard as a political scientist specializing in the political system of the Soviet Union.[40] Already in his earlier writings, Brzezinski had shown fundamental disdain toward the Soviet system—with its lack of freedom, cruelty, and perpetual violence. In his 1956 book, *The Permanent Purge: Politics in Soviet Totalitarianism*, he argued that political purges served as an institutionalized process that kept the highly centralized power structure alive.[41] Fear, oppression, and violence were not just the result of Stalin's paranoia; they were also used as systemic tools to maintain ideological purity and loyalty. In this book, Brzezinski provided a fresh new explanation of the violent nature of the Soviet system for Western readers and made him a rising star in the academic field of Sovietology. In his next book, *The Soviet Bloc: Unity and Conflict*, published in 1961, he dealt with Soviet ethnic relations and foreign policy and argued that under the apparent unity, significant tensions between Moscow and its satellite states existed and that nationalism still played a silent yet important role in other Eastern European nations' struggle to assert their political and ethnic independence from the Russian-dominated Soviet Union.[42]

In 1970, Brzezinski discussed the question of modern technology in the superpower competition in his third book, *Between Two Ages: America's Role in the Technetronic Era*. Computer and communication technologies, he argued, would transform the power structures of the future, and the United States would have a clear competitive edge against the Soviet Union, which was losing the free market–driven race in computer technology and its applications, including in modern military equipment.[43] However, to achieve success, there had to be closer economic, technological, and geopolitical cooperation among the world's three main blocs of capitalist democracies: the United States, Western Europe, and Japan.

Armed with those sharp ideas and a star teaching profile, including positions at Harvard, Columbia, and Johns Hopkins University School of Advanced International Studies, Brzezinski waltzed into the policy world with the financial sponsorship of banker and philanthropist David Rockefeller and established the Trilateral Commission in 1973.

The commission advocated, as Brzezinski had earlier, closer cooperation among the United States, Western Europe, and Japan to address the challenges posed by increasing interdependence among these regions. In addition, commission members were interested in discussing emerging problems in the context of an increasingly interconnected world, a result of the phenomenon of globalization, as later generations would call it. In the commission's 1974 mission statement, for example, they listed as a major topic of interest the "confrontation between the advanced and the developing countries"; they argued that this situation "must be avoided and progress must be made towards an equitable world order, which takes full account of the problems of those nations lacking in material wealth" and that "the vitality of the industrialized nations," including the Soviet Union, "is an indispensable condition for the solution of the problems of all countries."[44] The Trilateral Commission, initially made up of "180 private citizens" from around the world, eventually became the intellectual cradle for Jimmy Carter's 1976 presidential election campaign.[45] Carter himself became a member in 1973, while many other members served in his administration, including Vice President Walter Mondale, Secretary of State Cyrus Vance, Secretary of Defense Harold Brown, Secretary of the Treasury W. Michael Blumenthal, and the chief US delegate to the first SALT, Gerald C. Smith, whom Carter later appointed as his special representative on nuclear nonproliferation matters.

A closer examination of the Trilateral Commission files left by Brzezinski and Carter suggests that even during the initial stage of Carter's political campaign in July 1975, both men shared similar doubts about the US-Soviet détente initiated by Nixon and Kissinger and now inherited by Ford. For example, Brzezinski wrote to Carter on July 31, 1975, "It occurred to me that you may soon have to speak on the question on U.S.-Soviet relations. . . . I am generally troubled by the way the [Ford] Administration is handling the US-Soviet détente, though, on the whole, I do feel that it is in the American interest to promote an American-Soviet détente. However, that détente ought to be more reciprocal, and it ought to be shaped with clearer American political objectives in mind."[46]

It was also interesting that their internal communications showed Brzezinski was not happy with the Trilateral Commission's policy impact in Japan. "Japanese participation in our last two executive Committee sessions was not quite as strong as it should have been." Brzezinski complained to his benefactor David Rockefeller on January 9, 1975, "Japanese activity in our task force is perfunctory. In our North-South task force, it has been minimal." In addition, "I am disturbed by [Japanese Trilateral Commission member] Yamamoto's assertion that nobody reads our report in Japan."[47] In retrospect, it is easier to understand that Japan—with its binding postwar peace constitution, its conservative culture, its lack of nuclear weapons and only a small self-defense force, and its leaders who were terrified of offending the Soviet Union—would focus more on internal development and trade rather than play the risky game of geopolitics in the late 1970s Cold War. Thus, when the CCP leader Deng Xiaoping offered Brzezinski his version of a "multilateral" anti-Soviet alliance spanning Western Europe, the Middle East, the United States, and the PRC, Brzezinski and like-minded Trilateral Commission members would quickly ditch their Japanese colleagues and make the PRC their next partner in boosting the United States' global alliance against the Soviet Union and in reshaping the modern world.

INTENSIFIED GLOBAL COMPETITION

Skeptics of détente, such as Brown, Jackson, Nitze, Brzezinski, and eventually Carter soon had more reasons to question the effectiveness of using arms control negotiations such as SALT II to limit Soviet global ambitions, even though the administration's consensus that SALT II was an absolute necessity never changed. At the beginning of Carter's term in the White House, US officials had already noticed a concerning pattern in Africa and the Middle East, as the Soviet Union and its Cuban allies were expanding their influence in these regions.

In the Middle East, for example, the Soviet Union had taken advantage of the rising Arab nationalism and anti-American feelings in the wake of the 1973 Egypt-Israeli War to expand its influence in the region. It also took advantage of Egyptian President Anwar Sadat's decision to seek a separate peace process with Israel after 1977 to demonstrate to Arab nationalists in the Middle East that only the Soviet Union could be trusted with respect to their national aspirations. As a result, the Soviet Union gained support from Hafez al-Assad's Syria and Aḥmad Ḥassan al-Bakr's Iraq, both of which became the primary recipients of Soviet aid in the Middle East.[48]

Near the Gulf of Aden, a strategic deep-water region linking the Red Sea to the Indian Ocean, the Brezhnev regime took advantage of anti-colonialism in the region and exerted its influence. It became an ally of the nationalist elite in the former British colony of South Yemen, which formed a Marxist, pro-Soviet government, the People's Democratic Republic of Yemen (PDRY), in 1969. Calling itself "the only socialist regime in the Arab world," the PDRY pursued the Soviet model of domestic reforms, received massive Soviet and Cuban military aid, and entered into military conflict with North Yemen in 1972.[49] The PDRY's pro-Soviet and interventionist policy—especially its support of Communist rebels in the region—seriously threatened US access to Middle Eastern oil and became a thorn in the side of the Saudis, who were a vital US ally in the region. "South Yemen has more arms than the Sheiks of the Gulf," Saudi Crown Prince Fahd bin Abdulaziz Al Saud complained to Secretary of State Vance on December 14, 1977. "Suppose that South Yemen attacks one of the Gulf states and that Iraq comes to the support of South Yemen. . . . If such a thing were to happen at a time when the US was incapable of helping Saudi Arabia, the outcome would be terrible."[50] The situation would only get worse in 1978 when the Soviet Union firmly established a naval stronghold in the South Yemen port of Aden and started to deploy cruise-missile attack submarines, amphibious landing ships, and guided missile frigates at the mouth of the Red Sea.[51]

Another major conflict in North Africa would finally bury détente and give Deng Xiaoping momentum to push his Cold War agenda forward. Before Carter, in the period from 1973 to 1974, America's traditional ally Ethiopia was suffering from escalating rebellion and a devastating famine. In September 1974, Haile Selassie, the Ethiopian emperor and friend of the United States, was overthrown by a group of military officers who called themselves the Provisional Military Government of Socialist Ethiopia, or the Derg. The Derg was initially supported by students, urban residents, and police officers and collaborated with the other leading revolutionary group, the Ethiopian People's Revolutionary Party (EPRP). However, during the internal rivalry among revolutionary groups that began in 1975, political struggles became increasingly ideological and violent. On February 3, 1977, the Marxist-Leninist-inspired Mengistu Haile Mariam murdered forty political officers who opposed him in a mafia-style shoot-out and emerged as Ethiopia's new dictator. The following year Mengistu turned his guns on his former political allies, including the EPRP, and initiated a wave of violent purges known as the Ethiopian Red Terror, which caused somewhere between 55,000 and 150,000 deaths, according to differing accounts.[52]

As Mengistu's faction embarked on a program of self-proclaimed Soviet-style socialism, Americans, Ethiopia's traditional allies, were no longer welcome, and the country gradually gained the attention of the Soviet Union and Cuba.[53] The Cuban Communist leader Fidel Castro was so impressed by Mengistu and the Ethiopian revolution that he sent a two-hundred-man military mission to help Mengistu build up his army.[54] The Cuban military setting foot in Ethiopia immediately alarmed the US intelligence service: It proved that "Mengistu sees clear-cut advantages in closer relations with the Soviet Union and other Communist countries," as the CIA reported on March 28, 1977.[55] The US military was also very disturbed by the presence of Cuban military personnel in Ethiopia. It started to extract its secret communication centers and personnel from the Kagnew intelligence station in Asmara, which was still a part of Ethiopia, both as a precaution and as "a political message to the Ethiopian military regime that we are disengaging from them."[56]

These precautions could not be taken soon enough. On April 19, 1977, Carter told Brzezinski that the United States would withdraw all military advisers and suspend all military aid to Ethiopia and would, along with its allies, start using military assistance to "turn" Ethiopia's neighbor Somalia into a new US proxy in the region. They believed Somalia's military dictator Mohamed Siad Barre would be a replacement for Mengistu, who had gone astray to the Soviet and Cuban side.[57] The Carter administration's decision to switch support from Ethiopia to Somalia was now supported by the UK, France, West Germany, and Egypt and bankrolled by Saudi Arabia; each promised military aid to Somalia as a way to "keep Siad on the Western Hook" and to create a possible break between Somalia and the Soviet Union.[58]

However, Siad Barre was not easy to work with, as he, too, had regional ambitions that were beyond the West's control. The situation in the Horn was further complicated on July 23, 1977, when Somalia launched a sudden attack on Ethiopian military outposts in the Ogaden region, just as US intelligence had feared.[59] For Moscow and Havana, Siad Barre's attack on a fellow socialist country was both inconvenient and intolerable, especially considering that both Cuba and the Soviet Union traditionally had enjoyed good relations with both warring parties. The Soviet Union's relations with Somalia further fell apart after Moscow's mediation effort had little impact during the first half of 1977. Cuban leader Fidel Castro confirmed during his visit to Ethiopia that the Ethiopians were true Communists. In contrast, East German leader Erich Honecker, who made a mediation trip to Somalia, suggested the Somali regime was being increasingly driven by right-wing politicians who were getting "closer to Saudi Arabia and the imperialist countries."[60] In a last attempt to restrain Siad Barre, the Soviet Union airlifted around twelve hundred Soviet military advisers out of Somalia and sent them instead to Ethiopia, along with advanced weapon systems such as SS-N-2 Styx antiship missiles and MiG fighters.

On July 23, 1977, the Soviet Union also suspended the delivery of spare parts for military equipment to Somalia.[61] In August, the Soviet Union gave Siad Barre an ultimatum to withdraw his troops and denied his plea for arms assistance during his final, fruitless meeting in Moscow with Brezhnev. Siad Barre ignored this: Ogaden was too important to his national ambitions, the Somali troops were winning the war, and he considered Ogaden valuable enough to risk losing Soviet support.[62]

Robert G. Patman, a scholar who closely studied the conflict, noted that in mid-August 1977, Somalia embarked on a collision course with the Soviet Union. Meanwhile, the Soviet Union's top priority was strengthening its ties and military position in Ethiopia. Patman noted that "in late September, [Ethiopian capital] Addis Ababa for the first time received substantial quantities of MiG-21 jet fighters, Stalin Organs (batteries of 40 122mm rockets mounted on lorries) and new T-55 Tanks," together with South Yemeni troops and growing numbers of Soviet and Cuban military advisers, who "were rushed to the front line." These supplies, additional troops, and military advisers would soon turn the tide of the war in favor of Ethiopia.[63]

LINKING CHINA WITH SALT II AND THE HORN OF AFRICA

The distant war in the Horn of Africa happened while the Carter administration was significantly changing its overall national defense policy. Throughout 1977, Carter's critics claimed that the alternative review of the US-Soviet strategic balance—the Team B study undertaken during the Ford administration, which painted a threatening picture of the Soviet Union—was correct; thus, the new president could not afford to base his entire Soviet policy solely on a SALT II treaty.[64] The United States, they argued, had to show its strength. For instance, the Joint Chiefs of Staff at the Pentagon were eager to join a new space-age arms race and tried to convince Carter to initiate the development of antisatellite weapons instead of using an agreement with the Soviet Union to ban them altogether. The Soviet Union had already developed an antisatellite weapon, they argued; thus, it was intolerable that the United States had not.[65] Carter also faced pressure from the older generation of Cold War veterans. On August 4, 1977, Secretary of Defense Harold Brown invited six members of the CPD to the White House to explain their view on the Soviet Union to the president. Paul Nitze and his fellow hawks told Carter that the administration was on the wrong track in its handling of the Soviet Union: First, the Soviet Union would use its nuclear superiority to coerce the United States and its allies; second, Moscow would bargain in SALT II only to the extent that it faced growing US military capabilities; and third, the current military balance did not favor the United States—a fact that would hurt the United States if the negotiations dragged on for too long.[66]

New troubles in the ongoing negotiations at SALT II compounded the United States' differences with the Soviet Union over the Horn of Africa. In 1978, the Soviet leaders, pushed by their military, argued for harsher terms and unleashed their own anti-American propaganda campaign. In addition to the disagreement on Soviet ICBMs, the United States' inclusion of the Soviet Tu-22M Backfire bombers as strategic weapons, while excluding US cruise missiles from the same category, and its strict limitation on Russian heavy strategic missiles were seen as a trick to preserve American advantages at the cost of Soviet deterrence capabilities.[67] As a part of the Soviet public opinion campaign, The official newspaper of the Central Committee of the Communist Party of the Soviet Union, *Pravda*, published a flaming editorial in February 1978 blaming all the problems in SALT II on its opponents inside the United States, who were composed of "retired high-ranking military personnel, 'theoretical specialists' on the issues of strategy, the organization of the so-called 'Committee on the existing [Present] danger,' [and] some organs of the press, who are direct agents of the Pentagon and the military-industrial complex." These people, *Pravda* argued, were pushing for new proposals that were meant to give the United States "significant nuclear advantages over the Soviet Union," while the true goal was to "pervert, and defame the Soviet Union." After listing all the new weapon systems that the United States had developed unilaterally, deployed in "forward bases" along the Soviet border, and "aimed at targets inside of Soviet territory," it criticized American cynicism and warned that "there should be no illusions about the fact that the Soviet Union would resort to such restrictions that would give unilateral advantages to the United States."[68] Senior US diplomat Raymond L. Garthoff observed that the Soviets were trying to use this article to warn US officials that if they refused to reduce the number of American cruise missiles during the negotiations, the Soviet Union would be compelled to develop its own, which would further escalate the arms race.[69]

Meanwhile, US diplomats were pointing out to the White House that the Soviets were playing the same game: Soviet negotiators at SALT II were pushing to further restrict submarine-launched ballistic missiles (SLBMs), in which the United States had an overwhelming advantage, while the Soviet military was hiding the antisatellite weapons tests that Americans felt were highly threatening.[70] To the Soviet military engineers' credit, they invented some truly genius ways to cheat, some of which were discovered only long after the signing of the SALT II Treaty itself. As US defense experts assumed that one missile silo typically holds just one nuclear missile, the Soviet military developed a "rapid reload" system that allowed used SS-18 silos to be quickly recycled in order to launch additional missiles like a giant revolver, so those additional missiles would not be counted in the agreement by the less-imaginary, silo-fixated Americans.[71] Neither side, it turned out, was entirely sincere during the negotiations.

It was within this tense atmosphere in the summer of 1977 that SALT II, the Horn of Africa, and the PRC became interconnected. From the mainland Chinese perspective, the conflict in the Horn of Africa presented Deng Xiaoping with the perfect opportunity to convince the United States that his warnings about the Soviet Union had always been correct and that the PRC was willing to play a role on the United States' side of the Cold War—if the Americans are willing to sacrifice the ROC in Taiwan. The timing was also convenient: Since Mao's death, the new mainland Chinese leaders had lost interest in competing with the United States in the developing world. Instead, China started using its existing intelligence and diplomatic assets abroad to help the Americans.[72]

As early as February 26, 1977, mainland Chinese diplomats had already started to feed intelligence to their American counterparts regarding Cuba's involvement in the African conflict, which confirmed the worst fears of some anti-Soviet hardliners in the United States. "A PRC official in an African embassy revealed Somalia and Cuba have signed a defense agreement," Brzezinski reported to Carter. "PRC officials believed that there are about 700 Cubans in Somalia, and the number of military instructors will increase, and that the training of guerrillas will be more open and on a larger scale."[73] In early 1977, US and mainland Chinese diplomats had also been exchanging information about Cuba's involvement in Ethiopia, while the PRC, according to information shared by Somali diplomats, had replaced the Soviet Union as Somalia's supplier of spare parts for its Soviet-made weapon systems.[74] Fostered by intelligence sharing, the United States and mainland China seemed to be gradually taking the same side in the Horn of Africa.

On August 23, 1977, Secretary of State Vance flew to Beijing to seriously probe the possibilities of normalizing diplomatic relations with mainland China. He did not arrive with a specific timeline or terms of normalization, but both sides did reach conclusions on Soviet expansion in the Horn of Africa. Vance said: "We have made basic changes in our approach to our African policy. In Africa, we have opposed interference by outside powers through efforts to encourage African solutions to African problems. Turning specifically to the Horn of Africa, this area is of obvious strategic importance because of its location on the route through the Canal and leading to the Persian Gulf." In terms of Somalia, Vance told the PRC foreign minister that the United States had already initiated economic aid to and military ties with Siad Barre and that it was working with other allies to provide weapons to Somalia. Vance also predicted that "Mengistu made a very major and, I think, dangerous decision when he concluded that he was going to put all of his reliance on the Soviets as a military supplier, and I think he is bearing the consequences of that now."[75]

The next day, August 24, PRC officials steered the discussion to Taiwan. During the conversation, Chinese Foreign Minister Huang Hua expressed his utter contempt for Chiang Ching-kuo and the Nationalist regime, the KMT. In the morning's meeting, for example, Huang warned Vance that the United States should not support Chiang any further:

> You Americans were reluctant to give up your privileges in China in the past, and you were reluctant to give up your design to control China in the past. You regarded Chiang Kai-shek as your pet and you boasted about the Chiang Kai-shek clique and gave it support. When Chiang Kai-shek was driven out of the mainland and fled to the island of Taiwan, you were reluctant to lose Taiwan. First, you regarded Chiang Kai-shek as your pet, and then Chiang Ching-kuo as your pet. You would go to any lengths to protect them. If you continue to act in this way, sooner or later, you will meet the same fate as you have met on the mainland in the past.[76]

Taiwan also dominated Vance's next meeting with Deng Xiaoping. On this topic, Deng used his parallel negotiations with the Japanese to pressure the United States, as he had demanded similar terms from Prime Minister Takeo Fukuda: Taiwan's current separation from the mainland should be considered a Chinese domestic issue, and the PRC would not renounce the use of force.[77] To make this "Japanese formula" more convincing, Deng skillfully tied the issue of Taiwan to the threat the United States faced from the Soviet Union: "The Polar Bear you are confronting is one with wild ambitions—wild ambition to conquer the world and to establish its hegemony over the world." However, what was preventing the United States and the PRC from working together was, Deng emphasized, America's current diplomatic and military relations with the ROC, led by Chiang Ching-kuo: "It is the United States which is occupying Taiwan, and it will not do if you try to put equal blame on both sides. . . . The issue we are confronting now is the United States, which wishes to control Taiwan and obstruct China [the PRC] from reunifying its own motherland. Only the United States owes a debt to China. China owes nothing to the United States." The measures that the United States needed to take to earn mainland China's cooperation were "severance of so-called diplomatic relations with the Chiang clique on Taiwan, withdrawal of US forces in Taiwan and the Taiwan Straits area, and [abrogation of the defense] treaty. Those are the short words for the Japanese formula, and, to be honest, agreeing to use the Japanese formula was a concession for the mainland Chinese to the United States side." Citing Chairman Mao, Deng asked: "With such a bunch of renegades and counter-revolutionaries in Taiwan, do you think it would be able to be peacefully liberated?"[78]

Because Vance made no breakthrough in normalization, the US public did not receive the trip well, and some of Vance's opponents inside the Carter administration called it a "disaster" because of the lack of clear progress toward a formal normalization of diplomatic relations.[79] Yet it was on this trip that mainland Chinese officials confirmed their position on the Horn of Africa. According to Nancy Mitchell, a prominent scholar on Carter's policy in Africa, mainland China's strong interest in the Horn was also confirmed by US intelligence. What Huang and Deng did not directly tell the Americans was that mainland China was funneling large quantities of arms through Pakistan to Somalia to support their fighters in the Ogaden; the CIA later confirmed that "in the second half of 1977, the PRC had sent small arms, ammunition, and anti-tank and anti-aircraft weapons to Somalia."[80] The United States and the PRC, it now seemed, were being pulled together by the most bizarre, brutal, and now largely forgotten conflict in the least habitable part of the world.

It should be noted that even though Vance's negotiations on the trip had been inconclusive, the mainland Chinese leaders spared no expense to entertain, impress, and influence the US secretary of state. The official dinner Vance enjoyed in Beijing on August 24, 1977, was particularly extravagant and included seven lavish main courses, aside from the numerous appetizers and desserts:

Jasmine-flavoured stinkhorn mushroom soup
Braised shark fins with three types of fine-shredded meats
Peachwood smoked duck breast
Squirrel-shaped fried fish

"Luohan" style king prawns
Bamboo sprouts and chicken in oyster sauce
Stir-fried Japanese mustard spinach[81]

These menu items actually shed light on the intricate web of actions behind what is known as food diplomacy. We know that to get these items, the PRC Ministry of Foreign Affairs needed to issue emergency political orders to provincial governments all across mainland China to collect these exotic ingredients and fly them fresh to Beijing on chartered flights for such state dinners. For foreign items such as caviar, foie gras, and cheese, PRC embassy staff abroad purchased them with precious foreign currency and delivered them specially. According to one CCP historian, the particular type of stinkhorn mushroom used to treat "distinguished foreign guests," like Vance, had to be picked fresh in the mountain forests in Sichuan, thousands of kilometers away. Likewise, harvesting exotic seafood items in the frozen depths of the East China Sea placed divers at great personal risk.[82] Moreover, the exorbitant relative costs the PRC willingly spent on its food diplomacy for Vance's August 1977 visit become all the more striking when we remember that the common people had hardly begun recovering from the economic deprivations of the Cultural Revolution. In short, though Vance's visit did not result in concrete diplomatic agreements, the tenor of his reception by the PRC had been quite favorable (figure 1.3).

In Taiwan, Chinese Nationalist leader Chiang Ching-kuo followed Vance's trip to Beijing anxiously and with anger and frustration. His personal file from that month was filled with newspaper clips of the visits from various domestic and international news outlets. "The Communist bandits have three main objectives in their collusion with the United States," Chiang wrote in his diary on August 25, 1977. "One is to crush our Republic of China, their biggest and most serious rival; the second is to attack United States' credibility and reputation in the world, and last, to increase the weight of their bargaining chips towards the Soviet Union."[83] "I have clearly warned our ambassador to the US that we will not enter any kind of contact with the Communist Bandits," he wrote the next day, "and any exchanges will harm the mutual interests between [the Republic of] China and the United States."[84]

FIGURE 1.3 Secretary of State Cyrus Vance kept many lavish banquet menus from his 1977 trip to China. (Yale Law School)

"THE SOVIETS COULD NOT HAVE A FREE RIDE"

Despite Chiang Ching-kuo's concerns and warnings, the momentum of the global Cold War was not on Taiwan's side. As officials in Beijing entertained their American guests, the war in the Horn of Africa took a dramatic turn, which made a potential US-PRC partnership much more attractive to Washington's anti-Soviet Cold War warriors. On October 18, 1977, the Soviet Union stopped supplying arms to Somalia and was now fully behind Ethiopia. It also severed Soviet-Somalian diplomatic relations on October 21. On the battleground, meanwhile, the Somalian offensive had halted by the end of the year due to overextended supply lines and heavy casualties. Having the lessons of the Vietnam War in mind and unwilling to send US troops on another adventure, the Carter administration found itself with limited options to avoid an Ethiopian victory. UN Ambassador Andrew Young and Secretary of State Vance both believed that US military intervention in Somalia was out of the question, as it would run contrary to African nationalism and to the US noninterventionist policy in Africa as a whole.[85] In addition, the Organization of African Unity, during an October meeting, had adopted the view that Somalia's invasion of the Ogaden was illegitimate and violated Ethiopia's state sovereignty, and it called on Somalia to withdraw, a position that the Soviet Union supported.[86] In Vance's words, these unfavorable conditions for Somalia and the United States' lack of influence in the region put the Soviet Union in "a position to mediate the dispute and to gain substantial additional influence in the Horn."[87] Even the technocrats in the Pentagon, such as Secretary of Defense Brown, admitted that "the Horn is a poor part of the world in which to operate" and that the United States would have great difficulty maintaining a flow of military supplies to Somalia.[88] Additionally, US allies were incapable of turning the tide of the war for Somalia. Even the French, who had long been interested in the region, admitted that Somalia was the aggressor and refrained from sending weapons.[89]

The moral probation given to the Somalis, in turn, only emboldened the Soviets and Cuba, and they increased their military support of Ethiopia. In January 1978, the Ethiopians revived their fighting against Somalia with the addition of newly arrived Cuban troops led by General Arnaldo Ochoa Sánchez, a veteran of the 1975–1976 Angola campaign.

The initial Cuban force of three thousand men grew rapidly to thirteen thousand within a month. They were equipped with Soviet T-62 tanks, heavy artillery, armored personnel carriers, and modern radar and anti-air units. Large numbers of Soviet military advisers also took over command positions in the Ethiopian forces, many of them switched directly from their former posts in Somalia. In addition, the Cuban and Ethiopian joint forces enjoyed overwhelming air superiority due to previously supplied US F-5 fighters equipped with AIM-9 Sidewinder missiles, as well as newly arrived Soviet MiGs and Sukhoi fighters operated by Cuban pilots.[90] The mix of these weapons' origins demonstrates not only how quickly the alliances had shifted but also how military technology transfer could shift the regional military balance during crucial moments in the Cold War.[91]

Carter's personal relations with Brezhnev also started to deteriorate. Between December 1977 and March 1978, the two exchanged a series of letters in an effort to do some damage control. However, they mostly ended up blaming one another for being unfair and insincere, while Soviet weapons continued to flow into Ethiopia and, to a less impactful degree, mainland Chinese weapons continued to reach Somalia. In April 1978, Vance flew to Moscow to advance the negotiations at SALT II and found a frustrated Brezhnev complaining that the United States was backstabbing the Soviets by reaching out to the mainland Chinese. "Soviet-American relations must develop without prejudice to the interests of third countries," Brezhnev said. "It was not in our mutual interest to tolerate attempts by third world countries to undermine the relations between us or to play on the differences that inevitably arise between us." However, he did not mention that forces from Cuba—also considered one of the "third world countries" from an American perspective—were fighting for Ethiopia[92]

It was during what Brzezinski called "those troublesome months" that his imaginative mind roamed to mainland China and "started reviewing more systematically the advisability of developing strategic consultations with the Chinese to balance the Soviets."[93] During a Special Coordination Committee meeting on the Horn of Africa on February 22, 1978, Vance insisted that "he would not put any US troops in Africa." Brzezinski recommended an alternative: "We should get the regional powers to act and make the Soviets and Cubans bleed." If they could not do it, then "with respect to other actions against the USSR and Cuba," the United States should "consider further steps with respect to space cooperation and technology transfers to the Chinese." Vance again rejected this option.[94]

But Brzezinski and his analysts had already decided to make a move. "The Soviets have chosen Africa as their principal focus of competition for the foreseeable future, and we find it difficult to develop appropriate local responses," wrote Michel Oksenberg and Michael Armacost, the two leading experts on Asia on the National Security Council, in a paper sent to Brzezinski on February 22, 1978. "Our response should not be confined to Africa. Nor should we rely heavily on a linkage with arms negotiations since a SALT II agreement can serve our own interests." They wanted to make a daring move to open relations with the PRC as a countermove to the Soviet Union's victory in the Horn of Africa and as leverage to pressure Soviet concessions at the SALT II. They predicted that moving closer to mainland China and establishing diplomatic relations with Beijing would "increase Soviet incentives to cooperate with us in other areas, including SALT II. It would strengthen mainland China's commitment to a moderate policy in Asia, thereby limiting further opportunities for the Soviets to translate their growing military power in the Pacific into any significant political influence."[95]

Brzezinski immediately liked the idea: "The Soviets could not have a free ride in some parts of the world while pursuing détente where it suited them." He continued: "The Chinese and American relationship bears very directly on the American-Soviet relationship."[96] On March 10, he pointed out to President Carter that mainland Chinese diplomats were sending signals by offering the US Liaison Office a new building in Beijing and allowing Chinese military attachés abroad to interact with Americans. Mainland Chinese propaganda organs also "featured [journalist] Edgar Snow on the front page of *People's Daily* as an American who had contributed to Sino-American friendship." "I do not mean to suggest that the Chinese have altered their position on Taiwan," Brzezinski reported to Carter. "Rather, I simply draw your attention to indications that the Chinese may be receptive to overtures from us to restore some momentum to the relationship."[97] This was the moment that Carter decided to follow Brzezinski's advice to fast-track US-PRC normalization, knowing full well that it would be an unpopular decision at the State Department. On March 16, 1978, with only short notice to Vice President Mondale and Secretary of State Vance, Carter wrote: "I've decided it would be best for Zbig to go to China—perhaps as early as next month if it is mutually satisfactory with the Chinese. We need to expedite the arrangements and plans." At the bottom of the page, Carter wrote: "bcc: Dr. Brzezinski."[98] Thus, Carter authorized Brzezinski to actively explore options he knew were at odds with the advice coming from Vance and the Department of State.

On the Sino-Soviet front, US intelligence suggested that the Soviet Union had increased military pressure on mainland China. Soviet troops deployed on the Sino-Soviet border increased from 130,000 men in fifteen combat divisions in 1965 to 415,000 men in forty active divisions in 1977. Most alarmingly, nuclear-capable short-range rocket systems—NATO-designated FROG launchers—were detected, in addition to nuclear-capable self-propelled 230mm and 240mm heavy artillery deployed along the Soviet-Chinese border.[99] The CIA also predicted that Sino-Soviet relations would get no better. A 1977 report on Soviet foreign policy intentions stated: "Moscow sees no prospect of a complete restoration of the relationship of the 1950s. . . . The roots of the dispute are deep, and the USSR, in its conciliatory approach, is not prepared to give up the option of military pressure."[100] In February 1978, another comprehensive study by the CIA suggested that "we see no change for better or worse in Sino-Soviet relations forthcoming."[101]

The CIA also kept abundant records on Deng Xiaoping that showed him to be the most militant anti-Soviet PRC politician around. The CIA noted, for example, that as early as 1963, when Mao sent Deng, one of his chief lieutenants, to Moscow at the beginning of the Sino-Soviet split, Deng planned and executed strategy in the anti-Soviet contest.[102] After Zhou Enlai's death, the CIA correctly reported that if Deng emerged as premier, he would "try to operate under the guidelines set down by Mao and Chou, to wit continued hostility with the Soviet Union, emphasis on China's role in the Third World, and restrained manipulation of the US connection."[103] The presidential intelligence briefing on April 10 1978, right before Brzezinski's breakthrough trip, suggested that Soviet intentions would be of "paramount importance" to the Chinese. Meanwhile, maintaining China's links with the United States remained "a major foreign policy theme" because it was the "only country capable of countering the USSR."[104] Another report stated that "Peiking has rejected a number of Soviet overtures for improved relations and polemics between the two sides remain at high level." Meanwhile, Deng was calling for a "united front of Western Europe, Japan, and the US and the Third World to contain the USSR"[105]—a strategy like the one Brzezinski had been advocating since his Trilateral Commission days.

This combined intelligence from the Soviet Union and the PRC provided a geopolitical background and rationale for Carter's final decision to push for a fast-track normalization option with mainland China. Deng, whom the CIA had credited as the most anti-Soviet CCP leader since Mao, seemed a natural ally. On the other hand, Deng had laid the international groundwork to pressure the United States to accept normalization based on his conditions. Exploiting Japan's fear of the Soviet Union, Deng and Japanese Prime Minister Takeo Fukuda had agreed to restart diplomatic negotiations disrupted by the Cultural Revolution. As a result, they were able to move PRC-Japan relations one step forward from the 1972 Japan-China Joint Communiqué issued by Zhou Enlai and Kakuei Tanaka, which normalized PRC-Japan diplomatic relations, to the much more concrete and mutually beneficial 1978 Treaty of Peace and Friendship Between Japan and China.

The new treaty brought more than additional economic benefit for China: Deng specifically insisted that a new antihegemonic clause be included in the 1978 treaty, thus adding Japan to his global anti-Soviet network and sending a strong signal to the anti-Soviet officials in the Carter administration.[106] In addition, the new treaty reiterated an agreement from the 1972 Japan-China Joint Communiqué that Japan would acknowledge Taiwan as a part of the PRC. This diplomatic breakthrough with Japan allowed Deng to achieve several additional goals: He made peace with mainland China's historical enemy, secured precious Japanese investment for his domestic reform, and gained access to Japanese politicians who could influence US policy toward Asia in his favor.[107] Most crucially for this study, Japan's reaffirmation of the "one China" position encouraged Deng to make similar demands regarding Taiwan to President Carter.

DENG'S THREE DEMANDS AND CARTER'S COMPROMISE

In January 1978, Senator Henry Jackson had a "nonofficial" meeting with Deng Xiaoping. Deng played up the Soviet threat and mentioned to the senator that there were pro-Soviet elements in Chinese politics, a vague threat that the PRC could turn back to the Soviet Union if US-PRC normalization made no progress. Jackson and Oksenberg indeed got the message and explained to Carter that Deng was expressing dissatisfaction with the lack of progress in the US-China normalization talks. As Deng clarified, "The quality of our strategic dialogue as well as our level of commercial and scientific exchange would be severely constrained without formal diplomatic relations." Curiously, Jackson also met a People's Liberation Army (PLA) general, Deputy Chief of Staff Wu Xiuquan, who in 1976 was the head of the special military court that sentenced Mao's wife, Jiang Qing, and the rest of the Gang of Four to prison, a key event in Chinese politics that paved the way for Deng's rehabilitation and political rise. Jackson asked Wu if the PRC "would be turning to the West for military capability." Wu said: "The principle of the four modernizations is to rely on our efforts mainly, but we do not rule out introducing advanced technology from advanced countries. We wish for them, but we will not beg for them." Jackson was the first member of the US Congress to meet a mainland Chinese military leader, and the general's interest in Western technology intrigued him. This news was reported to Carter and Brzezinski.[108]

Mainland Chinese diplomats meanwhile paid close attention to the stalled negotiations at SALT II and Soviet interventions in the Horn. They made several moves to show the Americans they were ready to proceed with normalization talks. Through a meeting with Prime Minister Kriangsak Chamanan of Thailand, Deng passed a note to the US Liaison Office, which ended up in Carter's April 11, 1978, daily report. Deng wrote to the American president using the same tactics of overemphasizing the Soviet threat by ridiculing détente and of blaming the Americans for meddling in Taiwan:

> In the past, we were enemies and did not have much contact.... In 1972, a new situation developed.... We signed the *Shanghai Communiqué* and established semi-diplomatic relations. We share a common point: how to deal with the Polar Bear to frustrate its war designs.... We are concerned that some people in the US still have false hopes about detente. Some people in Europe doubt that the US will come to their rescue.... Our only difference is Taiwan.... The US has accepted that Taiwan is part of

China and is willing to withdraw militarily, provided Peking will not use force, but we tell them this is our problem. When and how we liberate Taiwan is our own question.[109]

Other anti-Soviet US officials also pushed Carter toward a fast-track normalization with China. Secretary of Defense Brown had already stated in October 1977 that the PRC's view on an anti-Soviet global alliance aligned with the US military's interests. He suggested that the United States invite mainland Chinese officials to receive a high-level NATO briefing and observe NATO military exercises—a position that Secretary of State Vance would reject.[110] Brown was the first to propose that the United States "activate the Chinese to agitate among the members of the non-aligned movement against the Cubans" in the Horn of Africa.[111] Aware of the immense pressure from within and outside the Carter administration to "do something to the Soviets with the Chinese," mainland Chinese diplomats pushed their cause in all diplomatic and private channels, asking the administration to cede to the PRC's three demands on Taiwan. Between March and May 1978, Carter's Nation Security Council reached a consensus that the United States had to make a compromise as Carter himself faced increasing public pressure to respond to the Cuban-Soviet victory in the Horn. For example, on May 5, the *New York Times Magazine* published a full-page, triumphant portrait Brezhnev in military dress decorated with medals, titled "Can Carter Handle Him?"[112]

On May 10, under pressure both at home and abroad, President Carter finally approved a secret memo laying out the fast-track option to normalize relations with the PRC based on Deng's three demands: Close down official US representation in Taiwan, terminate the US-ROC Mutual Defense Treaty, and withdraw remaining US military personnel and installations. The memo further instructed that this move should happen before 1980 and that the timing should be closely coordinated with US-Soviet negotiations at SALT II and the US midterm congressional election. This would "demonstrate domestically and abroad that in seeking a SALT agreement with the USSR, we were also taking steps to enhance our strategic position in other ways."[113]

Thus, in a Nixon-and-Kissinger-like secret manner, the compromise was made by President Carter even before Brzezinski went to China and without consulting the rest of the administration or the US Congress.

Meanwhile, to warm up the following negotiations, Brzezinski and Frank Press, the White House science adviser, called in Han Xu, the first deputy chief of the Chinese Liaison Office in Washington, on May 15, 1978, and promised to send a sizable scientific delegation to China and to start cooperating with the Chinese in science and technology.[114] Deng's strategy seemed to be working: He was getting not only the US compromise on Taiwan but also the US science and technology urgently need to implement the domestic reforms set out in the Four Modernizations.

BRZEZINSKI GOES TO CHINA

On May 20, 1978, Brzezinski landed in Beijing to make the final deal. "I have come to the People's Republic of China because President Carter and I believe that the US and China share certain common, fundamental interests and have similar long-term strategic concerns," he informed PRC Foreign Minister Huang Hua. "The most important of these is our position on global and regional hegemony. Thus, our interest in relations with the PRC is not tactical in nature but is based on certain long-term and strategic objectives." Mixing up the vastly different roles the Nationalists and the Communists played during WWII, Brzezinski reminded his guests that China and the United States had been allies and that both shared a vision for a pluralistic world. He said that, furthermore, the two countries today "should cooperate again in the face of the common threat, for one of the central features of our era is the emergence of the Soviet Union as a global power."[115] He listed new military inventions on both the US and the Soviet sides, and he reviewed trouble spots worldwide where the Soviet Union was making dangerous moves: Rhodesia, Angola, and the Horn of Africa. He then assured Huang that President Carter was committed to both normalizing diplomatic relations with the PRC and confronting the Soviet Union strategically and conventionally—in other words, the United States was fully committed to gaining a technological advantage in the nuclear and conventional arms race with the Soviet Union.

To speak in terms that the CCP's generals and technocrats would understand, Brzezinski even showed them a list of five types of still-in-development, top-secret US weapons. Curiously, except for the cruise missiles, these are still too secret to be shown in the declassified transcripts four decades later. When it came to nuclear weapons, he assured the CCP comrades that the United States had a lead in MIRVs and the total number of warheads (twelve hundred were to be allowed according to SALT II), most of which were "capable of liquidating a city." "We continue to enjoy significant technological advantages in the strategic area," Brzezinski bragged. "The Soviet ICBMs are large, but their accuracy is not as good as ours."[116]

The CCP officials liked Brzezinski's bravado. The next day Huang complimented him: "I have already read several volumes of your works. It is true that our exchange of views can only succeed." Huang then warned that "the Soviet Union is the most dangerous source of war" and that "the Soviet Union is seeking strategic superiority over the US." At the same time, SALT II or any agreement reached between the two superpowers "cannot deter the speed of the arms race." When it came to Third World intervention, Huang said: "In Africa, the Soviet Union is making infiltration and expansion and making an open challenge to the US." The solution was for the United States to "follow the Japanese formula"—to abide by the principles of the Shanghai Joint Communiqué to work with the PRC. "Chairman Mao said to Dr. Kissinger," Huang related, "as long as we do not try to harm you, nor you try to harm us, we therefore can work together to cope with the [Soviet] SOB."[117]

With the groundwork finished by the deputies, Brzezinski laid out his cards before Deng Xiaoping on May 21, 1978. After they complimented one another on their "straightforwardness," Brzezinski told Deng frankly that he wanted to move normalization forward as fast as possible: "I was instructed to confirm to you the US acceptance of the three basic Chinese points and to reaffirm once again the five points that were made to you by the previous US Administration." "The President," he said, "is prepared to undertake the political responsibility at home of resolving the outstanding issues between us. In our relationships, we will remain guided by the *Shanghai Communiqué*, by the principle that there is only one China and that the resolution of the issue of Taiwan is your problem." The deal was made, and the two men proceeded to the timely topic of the Soviet threat around the world: SALT II was unfair, détente was an illusion, Europe was in danger, and Cubans, with Soviet help, "are acting aggressively in Ethiopia and Zaire." Finally, Brzezinski and Deng shared the most recent update on Soviet infiltration in Afghanistan, with Deng predicting that "Afghanistan may become Cuba in the East."[118] Both men reached an understanding, Taiwan was abandoned without even being informed about the negotiations, and Brzezinski personally secured the biggest deal of his career.

Brzezinski's trip to Beijing marked both the end of the eight-year-long US-PRC normalization process started by Kissinger's secret trip to Beijing in July 1971 and the beginning of a de facto PRC-US anti-Soviet alliance. This would change the global strategic balance of the Cold War in the United States' favor. Mainland China, too, received a benefit: Close diplomatic and military cooperation with the United States opened doors for the mass transfer of Western military and dual-use technologies to its own military-industry complex. I will develop this new theme in the next chapter and provide more details in part II of this book. Returning to Washington, Brzezinski ordered a "special" COCOM exemption to export to mainland China Daedalus airborne reconnaissance radar equipment that could be used for both resource mapping and military reconnaissance, despite loud protests from the Department of Energy and the Arms Control and Disarmament Agency. Those deals, Brzezinski hoped, would help smooth out their new relations with Deng.[119]

Deng and his comrades had an appetite for advanced US technology that seemed insatiable; however, there were more sensitive technologies that the United States, at the time, was still unwilling to sell. Furthermore, Deng and other PRC diplomats were still deeply worried about and sometimes completely perplexed by the different and self-contradicting aspects of US Cold War policy. Why, they asked, would the Americans build up such vast nuclear arsenals while at the same time telling other countries, such as the PRC, to stop building similar weapons? They also had trouble understanding the role of the US Congress in making foreign policy. Why, they often asked, after Carter promised to cut ties with the ROC, would the United States, especially the US Congress, continue unofficial relations with Chiang Ching-kuo's Nationalist regime? Who was really making China policy in the United States?

THE 1979 VISIT THAT CHANGED THE WORLD

In the biting cold of late January 1979, Deng Xiaoping stepped onto American soil from a Boeing 707 aircraft at Andrews Air Force Base in

Maryland. This was the first time a PRC leader had ever officially visited the United States. At 74, having survived Mao's purges and the chaos of the Cultural Revolution, Deng now represented the CCP's new vision of China's future. This future included embracing the very nation that his party once deemed its greatest enemy. During the eight-day visit, Deng had nearly eighty talks and meetings, attended about twenty banquets or receptions, gave twenty-two formal speeches, and met with the press on eight occasions.

Washington, D.C., stopped traffic and rolled out the red carpet for Deng's arrival. He was welcomed by a grand military ceremony at the White House, with President Carter standing beside him (figure 1.4). This moment symbolized the completion of a dramatic shift of Cold War alliances that started with Kissinger's secret trip to Beijing in 1971 and Nixon's

FIGURE 1.4 Madame Zhuo Lin, First Lady Rosalynn Carter, Vice Premier Deng Xiaoping, and President Jimmy Carter at the arrival ceremony for the vice premier at the White House on January 29, 1979. (Jimmy Carter Presidential Library and Museum)

visit to China in 1972. In fact, former President Richard Nixon was at this ceremony in the presence of the very leaders who had helped finally realize and transform his legacy. The image of Deng, Carter, and Nixon smiling at each other at the White House reception with champagne glasses in their hands would symbolize the "good old days" of US-PRC relations in later, more troubled years. Brzezinski, too, had the most glorious moment of his career when Deng arrived at his private home to have dinner with Brzezinski's family and was offered "an American menu, reinforced by some very nice Soviet Vodka," gifted earlier by Soviet Ambassador Anatoly Dobrynin (figure 1.5). "Deng," Brzezinski bragged, "was greatly amused when I told him that he was being toasted with Brezhnev's favorite drink."[120]

Deng was not in the United States just to gain publicity and catch up with old friends; he was there to sell a vision. He knew that mainland China, still reeling from the devastating Maoist years, needed economic and technological aid from the West. With the careful precision

FIGURE 1.5 Deng Xiaoping and Zbigniew Brzezinski enjoy a bottle of Leonid Brezhnev's favorite vodka at the US national security adviser's home. (Jimmy Carter Presidential Library and Museum)

of a master manipulator, he navigated discussions on trade, science, and military concerns, even hinting at China's intentions to attack Vietnam. Behind closed doors, Deng made no secret of his distrust of the Soviet Union. He warned Carter that Vietnam, backed by Moscow, was becoming the "Cuba of the East" and strongly hinted at China's readiness to strike.[121] Days later China would indeed invade Vietnam, proving Deng was not merely making idle threats.

In Atlanta, Deng visited the tomb of Dr. Martin Luther King Jr., where he met with Coretta Scott King, Dr. King's widow. The moment was deeply symbolic and somewhat ironic.[122] Here was a Chinese Communist leader, ruling over a country with a history of internal repression, honoring a man who fought for civil rights and liberty in the United States. In comparison, the forty demonstrators protesting Deng's visit outside his hotel in Atlanta, mostly made up of evangelical Christians and members of pro-Taiwan groups, "seemed a tiny minority" compared to the audiences that welcomed him.[123] Deng and his companions also showed tremendous interest in US industrial power and technology. He toured a Ford Motor Company assembly plant in Hapeville, Georgia, in a golf cart with Henry Ford II and met with American workers, while Fang Yi, the deputy prime minister for science and technology, visited the Georgia Institute of Technology, examining displays on solar energy and computers.[124]

But it was in Texas where Deng truly captured the American public's imagination and where American technological wonders inspired the Chinese leader. In Houston on February 2, he attended a rodeo and did something no one expected—he put on a cowboy hat presented to him by two cowgirls. The crowd erupted in cheers, and the image of this small, elderly Chinese Communist leader grinning beneath a cowboy hat became an instant sensation.[125] On the same day, Deng visited NASA's Johnson Space Center in Houston and was given a full review of NASA's manned space program by the center's director, Dr. Christopher C. Kraft, using exhibit-scale models. Deng also climbed into the NASA space shuttle flight simulator and experienced a full launch-return simulation. According to a Chinese state-sponsored documentary, Deng was so awestruck by this experience that it influenced his later decision to launch the 863 Program, which led to China's manned space flight program.[126]

Deng's industrial tour continued on February 3 in Seattle at Boeing, the world's leading aerospace manufacturer, where he viewed assembly lines and was offered an in-depth look at modern aviation technologies. His meeting with Boeing executives led to China's first major commercial aircraft purchases from the United States and initiated an unspoken tradition: Every CCP leader would visit Boeing headquarters during their official visit to the United States, and the size of China's aircraft orders would serve as a barometer for US-PRC relations for decades to come.[127] Perhaps more profoundly in the long run, Deng also secured a new US-China Agreement on Cooperation in Science and Technology with the Carter administration, which allowed Chinese scientists to be trained in US universities and opened the door for collaborations—as well as for sabotage—between the two countries' scientific institutions.[128]

Deng's visit to NASA, with its strong focus on science and technology, was not just a diplomatic stop; it also marked something more profound: the moment the PRC turned away from radical internal political struggles and toward economic modernization, driven less by communist ideology as in the Mao period and more by science, technology, and business models acquired from the West. Reportedly, on the flight back to China, Deng told his assistants: "If we look back, we find that all of those [Third World countries] that were on the side of the United States have been successful [in their modernization drive], whereas all of those that were against the United States have not been successful. We shall be on the side of the United States."[129] This dramatic shift would eventually make China a major technological competitor of the United States after the Cold War.

In his personal diary, President Carter reflected that Deng's 1979 visit to the United States was "one of the delightful experiences of my Presidency." He characterized Deng as "smart, tough, intelligent, frank, courageous, personable, self-assured, friendly" and found it "a pleasure to negotiate with him."[130] But despite the mutual good wishes, lavish state banquets, and Deng's cowboy hat–waving stunt, something unsettling and cynical lay under the glamourous surface of the celebrated new PRC-US relationship that is so well documented in films, photographs, and personal memoirs: How to exploit the United States' internal division over Cold War policy in the context of the gradual collapse of the US-Soviet détente would become the underlying, unspoken, and crucial goal of mainland China's policy toward the Carter administration.

Very soon Deng and his comrades would launch several major assaults on détente, seriously testing their new relationship with the United States.

On February 17, 1979, two weeks after returning to Beijing, Deng ordered the PLA to invade Vietnam, then a close Soviet ally. This sudden attack caused severe alarm in Moscow and immediately the United States' new relations with the PRC became a major flashpoint in the US-Soviet détente.[131] There was also a less well-known but equally damaging challenge the PRC posed to détente in the area of US-Soviet arms reduction efforts: When Carter tried to enlist the Soviet Union and the United Kingdom to establish a new ban on the testing of nuclear weapons, Deng was determined to spoil it.

Most importantly, Carter's secret deal with Deng behind Taiwan's back shocked and awakened the equally capable and strong-willed Taiwanese leader Chiang Ching-kuo, who would undermine domestic support for Carter's China policy. "The United States and the [CCP] Bandits all have their internal and external problems under the larger global context," Chiang wrote the day after he learned that Brzezinski was heading to Beijing. "They kept running into walls and yet without any better ideas, Americans, however, felt ashamed of themselves, while the arrogant [mainland] Communists tend to use intimidation [to achieve their goals]. There are no real politicians in the United States anymore; they are like blind people riding on blind horses; no one knows where they will end up."[132]

CONCLUSION

Chiang's comments, though sarcastic, rang partially true. As Deng Xiaoping and Jimmy Carter celebrated their new friendship in Washington, D.C., in January 1979, few US officials could have foreseen how complicated the United States' future relations with the two competing Chinese regimes would be. Gliding on the momentum created by the collapse of the US-Soviet détente, the PRC, led by Deng and the CCP, had successfully pushed its way onto Washington's political stage at the expense of the ROC. At the same time, Chiang Ching-kuo, the ROC's Nationalist leader, refused to leave the scene without a fight. Both Chinas, from that moment on, became forever entangled in the US politics of the Cold War.

2

THE CHINA-FRANCE NUCLEAR ALLIANCE AND THE FAILED COMPREHENSIVE TEST BAN NEGOTIATIONS

The PRC's rejection of the US-USSR-UK trilateral proposal for a comprehensive nuclear test ban treaty dealt a severe blow to President Carter's efforts to integrate China into the US-led global nonproliferation regime. Furthermore, China's alliance with France in nuclear affairs led to the collapse of the proposed treaty and significantly complicated the nuclear dimension of the US-Soviet détente, adding another layer of tension and complexity to the Carter administration's attempts to manage the global Cold War.

CARTER'S DILEMMA: CHINA AND THE QUESTION OF NUCLEAR TESTING

Deng Xiaoping and his comrades' attack on the US-Soviet détente was not limited to rhetoric in US domestic politics. In this chapter, I further examine the PRC's role in the collapse of the détente, looking specifically at the Carter administration's failed effort to convince the PRC to support the Comprehensive Test Ban Treaty (CTBT) negotiations. The proposed trilateral treaty, which had been negotiated among the United States, the Soviet Union, and the UK, was designed to slow the spread of nuclear weapons and to curb the escalating superpower nuclear arms race. Even though the United States and the PRC had established official diplomatic relations on January 1, 1979, based on mutual anti-Soviet grounds, Deng was far more interested in having the PRC develop its own nuclear weapons than in participating in any US-led nonproliferation efforts. Furthermore, Deng was able to convince the anti-Soviet hard-liners in the Carter administration to secretly transfer US underground nuclear testing technology to the PRC to help the PLA's ICBM program, a move that not only violated the United States' own nonproliferation policy but also caused serious consequences long after the end of the Cold War.

In this chapter, I fill a major gap in the literature on mainland China's historical role in US-led nonproliferation efforts. Thus far, scholars have debated why US-China nuclear nonproliferation cooperation started only in President Ronald Reagan's second term and not during the "honeymoon" Carter years. The predominant view is that it took a long time for the Americans to engage and educate Chinese leaders to the point they understood the importance of nonproliferation.[1] Others have argued that China preferred a more representative nuclear order, in which second-tier nuclear powers such as China, the UK, and France would have a stronger voice in international nuclear affairs, and this led to China's slower adoption of US-dominated nonproliferation efforts.[2] In this study, I examined a serious yet understudied attempt by the Carter administration to bring China into the US global nonproliferation order through the CTBT negotiations. These negotiations failed, however, because the US- and Soviet-dominated nonproliferation order was fundamentally at odds with the worldviews and nuclear weapon ambitions of Deng and his comrades.

As observed by senior diplomat Raymond L. Garthoff, a veteran of the negotiations at SALT I, disarmament and arms control were Carter's priorities, and they required "continuing and even expanded American-Soviet collaboration." As a gesture, four days into his presidency, Carter called for a halt to nuclear weapons testing and arranged a series of new arms control talks that would consider a new CTBT.[3] From the US perspective, the proposed CTBT was one of the two pillars of Carter's nuclear policy. It was designed to slow down the nuclear arms race between the United States and the USSR, what Dr. Herbert York, Carter's representative at the CTBT talks, would refer to as *vertical proliferation*. The second pillar of Carter's nuclear policy was the prevention of the further spread of nuclear weapons in the Third World, what arms control experts would conceptualize as *horizontal proliferation*.[4]

Carter's two-part policy was based on two crucial treaties. First, the new Strategic Arms Limitation Talks that began in 1972 (SALT II) were intended to result in a treaty that would limit the number of nuclear weapon delivery vehicles owned by, and exclusively within, the two superpowers—the United States and the Soviet Union.[5] However, because SALT II would not limit the quality and explosive power of the individual nuclear warheads carried on those vehicles, the second treaty, the CTBT, would play a complementary role in both halting vertical proliferation by slowing the testing of new and more powerful nuclear weapons by countries already having such weapons and by stopping horizontal proliferation by preventing ambitious countries without nuclear weapons from going nuclear. Regarding its scope and target countries, the SALT II treaty was to be a superpower agreement between the United States and the Soviet Union. At the same time, the CTBT was to cover the whole world, including second-tier nuclear powers such as China, France, and India. In addition, many of the issues in the two treaties—verification, qualitative restraint on nuclear weapons development, and confidence building between the United States and the USSR—were linked. Supporters associated with the Arms Control Association argued that because there was enough popular demand among the US public for a halt to nuclear testing, finalizing the CTBT would help the Carter administration further convince the US Congress to approve the eventual SALT II treaty.[6]

The critics of Carter's nuclear policy, most of whom were associated with the military establishment, argued that the CTBT would inflict too high an opportunity cost, as it would reduce the reliability of US nuclear weapons; increase US reliance on conventional forces, in which the Soviet Union had a perceived advantage; degrade the capability of US weapons laboratories; and eliminate the United States' capability to modernize its nuclear weapons.[7] Further, in March 1978, at the early stage of the negotiations, US arms control officials had no guarantee that they could convince second-tier nuclear powers, especially France and China, to stop testing.[8]

From China's perspective, accepting the CTBT would put it in an unequal position because the United States could afford to stop testing nuclear weapons—in the late 1970s, its nuclear warhead technology was already decades ahead of that of China, while China and, to a lesser degree, France still needed to do more testing to catch up. The PLA had not yet tested a functioning nuclear warhead for its ICBM program when Carter approached Deng Xiaoping on this issue. The Soviet experts understood this rationale well and during the negotiations did not shy away from pointing out their own hypocrisy. Roland Timerbaev, the chief Soviet delegate to the CTBT negotiations, bluntly pointed out that the superpowers themselves were ready to talk about the CTBT in 1977 only because both sides had already exploded so many nuclear weapons in the previous years: "By 1974–1976, after the Threshold Test Ban Treaty was signed . . . the USA, and USSR., had already developed too many overpowered nuclear warheads for Intercontinental Ballistic Missiles, Submarine-launched Ballistic Missiles, and Multiple Independently Targetable Reentry Vehicles, thus the necessity for [the two superpowers] to test such overpowered nuclear warheads further had already disappeared."[9]

At this point, China had no comparable weapons. Nicola Horsburgh, an expert on Chinese nuclear policy, compared the strategic forces Deng inherited in 1978 to those of the superpowers:

> China started the post-Mao period with no second-strike force capabilities in place. This meant that China's declared policy of NFU [No First Use] rendered the country extremely vulnerable to a nuclear first strike. At that time, China's nuclear arsenal consisted of around 80 TU-16 bombers that could not penetrate US or USSR air defenses; between thirty and forty intermediate-range ballistic missiles (IRBMs) that could not reach the US, and only a few Soviet cities; no ICBMs; and no SLBMs. In fact, China's ICBM and SLBM systems were several years behind schedule. Throughout the late 1970s and most of the 1980s, relative to other nuclear states, China was arguably the weakest nuclear actor in the nuclear order.[10]

Given all this, Carter faced an unsolvable dilemma: His nonproliferation policy toward China depended on getting Deng to support a treaty that would damage China's already weak nuclear deterrence capability versus that of the superpowers. China's relative weakness was also reflected in its number of nuclear tests. According to the Arms Control Association, in China's entire history with nuclear weapons, from 1962 to 1996, it conducted a total of 45 nuclear tests, while the Soviet Union conducted an astonishing 713 nuclear tests before its dissolution, at which point Russia ceased all testing. Ironically, the United States tested the most: 1,030 from 1945 to 1992.[11]

President Carter sincerely intended to conclude a test ban treaty with the UK and the Soviet Union. However, it was difficult for his administration to exclude China from the calculation because the US debate regarding the banning of nuclear tests had always been connected to China. As an aspiring second-tier atomic power, China's attitudes and actions greatly influenced the rest of the world. Furthermore, its nuclear weapons development was too deeply entangled in the US-Soviet Cold War to be ignored by either US or Soviet nonproliferation officials. For example, during the first year of the President John F. Kennedy's administration, both the Joint Chiefs of Staff and the CIA warned that China would acquire a nuclear weapon as early as 1964 and achieve short-range missile capability by the end of the 1970s.[12]

Unwilling to conduct a military strike on China's nuclear facilities,[13] President Kennedy, during the 1961 Vienna summit, probed the willingness of Soviet Premier Nikita Khrushchev to accept a test ban treaty that would prevent China from getting the bomb.[14] However, Khrushchev did not wish to damage Soviet-China relations and deemed a test ban aimed at China unnecessary.[15] As Sino-Soviet relations deteriorated in the following years, Khrushchev finally agreed to the Kennedy administration's proposal to use a test ban to stop China from getting the bomb and made a significant compromise: permitting on-site inspections.[16] On June 10, 1963, Kennedy formally announced his endorsement of a limited ban on nuclear testing that would prohibit all nuclear testing in the atmosphere, in outer space, and underwater. Kennedy hoped that the technical challenge of underground nuclear testing would slow China's nuclear weapons development, and he turned to Khrushchev for help, hoping the Soviet Union would have better leverage to force China to accept the proposed treaty.[17]

The United States, UK, and Soviet Union formally signed the Limited Test Ban Treaty (LTBT) on July 25, 1963, at a time when both the United States and the Soviet Union were themselves pursuing vertical proliferation, trying to outmatch one another in nuclear weapons development. Earlier, in 1961, the Soviet Union had tested the Tsar Bomba, which had three thousand times the destructive power of the Hiroshima bomb.[18] On the other hand, US engineers had developed some of the most bizarre and unconventional "portable nuclear devices," such as the infamous M29 W54 Davy Crockett nuclear bazooka developed in 1961. The bazooka, which was known as a "suicidal weapon," weighed only twenty-three kilograms (about fifty pounds) and could be fired by five or even just one infantry soldier. With a firing range of no more than four kilometers (about two and a half miles), it was designed as an ambush weapon to "surprise" advancing Soviet armor divisions on the front line of Central Europe, and depending on which direction the wind was blowing on that day, it could give the unfortunate users a heavy dose of radiation poisoning as well.[19]

The rationale behind these developments was a bizarre military strategy based on US military thinkers' further development of the 1960s deterrence doctrine and on what political scientists called the escalation ladder or nuclear brinkmanship. When tactical nuclear weapons were deployed at the front lines and backed up with even bigger strategic weapons at home, even a small armed conflict between the two superpowers could quickly escalate out of control and turn into an apocalyptic nuclear mutual destruction. Thus, based on a somewhat convoluted logic, the very fear of such escalation would prevent a minor conflict from starting in the first place—at least on paper.[20] The Soviet Union, in response, developed a series of unguided nuclear artillery shells in 1965, some with a caliber as small as 152 mm, that could be fired from self-propelled artillery. Only after the Cold War, cooler heads on both sides admitted that this nuclear brinkmanship based on portable nuclear devices was not an intelligent idea and bilaterally halted their deployment in 1993.[21]

Keenly aware of the vertical proliferation of nuclear weapons by the two superpowers, Mao Zedong, upon the signing of the LTBT in 1963, became increasingly suspicious that the United States and the Soviet Union were utilizing double standards to smother China's nuclear projects while pursuing an arms race to maintain their hegemony in the nuclear field. On the diplomatic front, Mao issued a three-part response to the LTBT. First, he claimed the moral high ground by calling out the hypocrisy of both superpowers by requiring "all nations, nuclear and non-nuclear," to "ban and destroy all nuclear weapons" and to "outlaw the production, transfer, testing, and storage of nuclear weapons." Then Mao, portraying himself as a "leader of the Third World," pointed out that the LTBT would not prevent the superpowers from testing bombs underground. At the same time, it would hinder other independent, "peace-loving nations from obtaining the weapons to protect themselves."[22]

Later that year China issued a series of public statements known as the Nine Articles of Polemics, which blamed the two superpowers for using the arms reduction talks to hide the fact that both were pursuing an arms race and endangering world peace. In addition, those statements had the strong anti-Soviet flavor typical of Chinese propaganda produced during this period of the Sino-Soviet split. The LTBT was described in those polemics as "a worthless piece of paper that was never intended to be fulfilled" and a result of both Khrushchev's "false belief" that "nuclear weapons could erase the law of class conflict" and his "false hope to maintain world peace" simply by "US-Soviet nuclear cooperation," the cost of which was the "betrayal of socialism and communism."[23]

Chinese historians generally agree that the main intention of the polemics was to discredit Khrushchev, whom Mao had blamed for causing the Sino-Soviet split.[24] Curiously, the person whom Mao had put in charge of drafting that anti-Soviet propaganda was the future Chinese leader Deng Xiaoping.[25] A decade and a half later, when President Carter excitedly told Deng about a possible brand-new US-Soviet-British joint comprehensive test ban treaty, it immediately triggered the new Chinese leader's unhappy memories.

After President Kennedy's death, China's complex relations with US nonproliferation efforts continued into President Lyndon Johnson's administration. From a global perspective, China's stance against nonproliferation enjoyed increasing popularity with other rising, second-tier nuclear powers because of its antihegemonic overtone. Early in July 1963, French President Charles de Gaulle suddenly announced that France would formally recognize the PRC on January 27, 1964, becoming the first Western European nation to do so. France's diplomatic recognition, which came after a series of secret minister-level Sino-French negotiations, was mainly based on their shared dislike of the LTBT, which both China and France viewed as a superpower conspiracy to prevent second-tier nations like themselves from developing their own nuclear weapons.[26] Then came the Chinese nuclear test on October 16, 1964, just a day after the CIA had wrongly assured President Johnson that "a Chinese nuclear test probably would not occur before the end of 1964."[27]

As the Johnson administration was distracted from test ban issues by the escalating Vietnam War, China began an all-out race to catch up with the superpowers in nuclear weapons design and delivery capabilities. On June 30, 1966, China launched its first nuclear-capable ballistic missile, code-named DF-2 A.[28] The, on October 27, 1966, a sister missile carrying a live atomic warhead delivered a fission explosion to the target area, propelling China into the nuclear missile age.[29] Less than a year later, on June 17, 1967, China exploded its first hydrogen bomb and then, together with France (which was developing its own thermonuclear device through Opération Canopus), refused to sign the Nuclear Nonproliferation Treaty when it opened for signature in 1968. By then, the United States' test-ban-centered nuclear policy toward China had entirely collapsed.[30]

THE FIRST STRATEGIC ARMS LIMITATION TALKS TREATY AND CHINA'S REACTION

From the Chinese perspective, the Cultural Revolution, which coincided with the Nixon years, had a devastating effect on China's nuclear weapons development and cost the lives of a large number of China's best scientists; many of them had been educated in the West, making them the natural targets of the Red Guards, who viewed anything Western as suspicious. An independent study by a Hong Kong–based human rights nongovernmental organization showed that in the Chinese Academy of Sciences system alone, twenty-three of the seventy academy fellows were persecuted to the point of death by the Red Guards, and another ten committed suicide. Even those who survived suffered severe trauma and humiliation.[31] Many of those who died were military scientists or scientists involved in military-related fundamental research. Dr. Ye Qisun, a physicist who was educated at the University of Chicago and Harvard and who contributed to China's atomic bomb program, for example, was accused of being an "imperialist walking dog" because of his American study experiences. He was tortured by the Red Guards and died "mysteriously" in Beijing in 1977. Zhou Ren, China's leading metallurgist and special materials expert trained at Cornell University, was persecuted as a "traitor to the nation" because his wife was from an old Manchu noble family. He was beaten to death at seventy-five years of age in 1973. Dr. Rao Yutai, who trained at Harvard, Yale, and Princeton, was known as the "father of modern Chinese physics." After his arrest, he was paraded in the streets from 1966 to 1968 and killed himself inside his apartment at Beijing University. Even Dr. Deng Jiaxian, the much-revered founder of China's atomic weapons program, nearly died from injuries after he was beaten and tortured under the scorching sun at a nuclear research base.[32]

Some of the deaths were excruciatingly brutal. According to an oral history essay written by Hua Xinming, a student at University of Science and Technology of China's Mechanic Engineering Department, where Qian Xuesen was the director, on June 8, 1968, China's top UK-educated rocket and aviation materials scientist Yao Tongbin was beaten to death with steel pipes in an internal military struggle within the Seventh Machine Building Department, the predecessor of today's Ministry of Space and Aviation; in October 1968, Zhao Jiuzhong, Berlin University–educated director of the Chinese Academy of Sciences' Earth Science Department, committed suicide at his home after persecution; and then on December 11, 1968, Xiao Guangyan, the University of Chicago–educated chemist and rocket-fuel researcher, committed suicide after being tortured by local mobs, his action followed three days later by the suicide of his wife and young daughter.[33]

Those senseless persecutions and murders slowed down China's nuclear development and its overall scientific progress significantly and terrified other scientists who had studied abroad. The situation was so bad that eventually Premier Zhou Enlai and several high-ranking generals, such as Liu Bocheng and Nie Rongzhen, directly intervened in 1969 to prevent the Red Guards from harming the three most crucial strategic projects: the nuclear weapons, ballistic missile, and nuclear submarine programs. A few key personnel, such as the missile scientist Qian Xuesen, were saved through these efforts, but the damage was already done and irreversible.[34]

The external environment was more nuanced: China's internal weakness and the unfolding Sino-Soviet split led to a reevaluation of the Chinese nuclear threat toward the United States on January 27, 1969, led by the CIA, Department of Defense, Atomic Energy Commission, and NASA. The joint study determined that many previous fears were unfounded and estimations regarding China's nuclear program were inaccurate. Most importantly, it suggested to Nixon that China's nuclear arsenal would moderate China's behavior rather than make it more aggressive, as the previous administration had assumed. According to the study, "So long as the Chinese strategic force remains relatively small and vulnerable, a condition which is likely to persist beyond the period of this estimate . . . the Chinese will almost certainly recognize that the actual use of their nuclear weapons against neighbors or the superpowers would involve substantial risks of a devastating counterblow to China."[35]

The Sino-Soviet split also led Nixon and Kissinger to consider China, however severe its internal problems were, as a strategic asset in the Cold War against the Soviet Union rather than as a problem for US nonproliferation efforts. As Kissinger wrote to Nixon, the United States should "work towards putting US-Chinese relations on a more rational and less ideological basis than has been true for the past two decades."[36] In regard to nuclear weapons, the US intelligence community again confirmed the previous opinion that China's nuclear weapons program was too small and immature to pose any threat to the United States and that, in fact, acquiring nuclear weapons would "not necessarily make China more willing to risk a direct clash with the US; indeed, it is more likely to have a sobering effect."[37] Those reevaluations of China's strategic posture contributed to Kissinger's famous 1971 secret trip and provided a relatively secure environment in which China could pursue its strategic capabilities.[38]

The US-China rapprochement did not, however, change Chinese leaders' hostile attitude toward US- and Soviet-led nuclear nonproliferation efforts. In fact, in 1969 Mao had linked US-Soviet arms reduction talks with the ongoing Sino-Soviet border conflicts and believed the talks were a conspiracy to force China to give up its nuclear weapons. According to a recent study, China's top leaders firmly believed that it was not a coincidence that the 1969 Helsinki US-Soviet SALT I happened at the worst time in the Sino-Soviet split. The same study, based on Zhou Enlai's letters and meetings with foreign dignitaries, also suggested that the Chinese leaders firmly believed the Soviet Union was trying to use arms reduction to maintain its nuclear hegemony, as well as to collaborate with the United States to put even more pressure on China.[39]

Even after Nixon's historic trip to China, Mao and his comrades remained suspicious of US-Soviet arms reduction efforts. In fact, Nixon faced severe criticism from China when he signed the SALT I Treaty with Brezhnev in 1972. Zhou complained afterward to the US liaison officer that "the Soviet leader's visit to the US enhanced our suspicion that two big powers intend to dominate the world." And Mao, even more doubtful, seriously contemplated the possibility that the United States had betrayed China through its détente with the Soviet Union.[40]

DENG'S DECISION TO PURSUE INTERCONTINENTAL BALLISTIC MISSILE CAPABILITY

The Carter administration chose the wrong time to bring up the CTBT to Deng Xiaoping. As the Cultural Revolution came to an end in China, the technocrats in the PLA had already set the modernization of the Chinese military as their long-term objective. One of the key promoters of such modernization was General Zhang Aiping, the director of the National Defense Science Committee (NDSC) and a close ally of Deng. Zhang and Deng were both purged briefly from 1976 to 1977 during the last political movement of the Cultural Revolution. After returning to his post at the NDSC, Zhang gave a speech on April 24, 1977, in which he stated that bringing China's best scientists who had managed to survive the purges back to the strategic rocket force should be the army's priority. Meanwhile, the state should "cherish and pay special care to the intellectuals working on the frontline of national defense research and development," whose work was so valuable that they should not be forced into "endless political studies" and "manual labor," "which wasted valuable time for scientific research." With the realities of starvation during the Cultural Revolution still vivid in his memory, Zhang commented: "Planting vegetables, raising pigs, and cooking food in communal canteens should occupy no more than one-fifth of our scientists' daily schedule" (figure 2.1). "Hard manual labor," according to the general, "[is] only meant to help their brains get some relaxation!"[41]

In July 1977, Deng was also rehabilitated and returned to Beijing. Two months later, with both Deng and General Zhang present, China launched its ICBM program, code-named Project 718. The records show the scale of the project: Eight central-level government ministries and representatives from twenty-seven provinces, four universities, thirty-nine factories, and thirty-four research institutes were called in to receive military orders to

FIGURE 2.1 Li Yue Fei, *Gathering in the Crops*, July 1975. The Chinese propaganda poster depicts PLA soldiers harvesting pumpkins after a shooting range exercise. (chineseposters.net, Landsberger collection)

design, produce, and test China's first ICBM.[42] Also invited to the launch was the MIT-trained American Chinese missile scientist Qian Xuesen, who delivered a nationalistic speech filled with an antihegemonic message (figure 2.2). Qian, once a top rocket scientist at NASA, was famous for having been deported back to China by the Eisenhower administration in 1955 for his anti-American views and alleged Communist associations.

FIGURE 2.2 After MIT-trained NASA missile scientist Qian Xuesen was deported back to China by the Eisenhower administration during the Red Scare, he became Mao's chief rocket designer and later the chief scientist for China's ICBM program under Deng Xiaoping. (NASA Riverside Archive)

"The Intercontinental Missiles," Qian said, "in the hands of the imperialists, are just tools to help them to perpetuate their hegemony. But in the hands of the Chinese people, they will become a guarantee for world peace and stability!"[43]

A more detailed strategy was laid out by General Zhang at a meeting with NDSC members on May 5, 1978. China, the general advised, needed to "catch up with the United States and the Soviet Union by 1985" in both "conventional and strategic weapon development." "According to acquired intelligence," he said, "the Americans are developing 3rd generation nuclear weapons. We must catch up and surpass them, which does not mean step by step following the Americans, the Soviets, and what the other capitalists have already done, but to acquire the advanced things from them, combine with the [technological] basis we already have to leap forward." "It can absolutely be achieved by 1985," Zhang assured his fellow comrades, "and I do not just mean in terms of quantity!"[44]

Those developments paralleled Deng's consolidation of power from late 1977 to December 1978. For the Carter administration, this meant that they had to face Deng's personal and almost pathological animosity toward US-Soviet disarmament collaboration when they tried to bring China on board for any sort of multilateral nuclear test ban effort. On March 12, 1975, during the Cultural Revolution, for example, Deng had stated that US-Soviet disarmament talks were a disguise for their military expansionism. Commenting on the 1974 US-Soviet Vladivostok Summit Meeting on Arms Control, he said: "Ford and Brezhnev's agreement was essentially a military expansion pact, not a disarmament pact. They avoided the issue of the quality of the nuclear weapons. Thus, the number of nuclear warheads agreed upon in the treaty had increased. Even though the increase in number was small, without the control of their quality, it was essentially a strategic military expansion." Mindful of the LTBT, which he had already attacked during the Mao period, Deng said: "Since 1963, they [the United States and the USSR] signed three nuclear arms agreements, 1963, 1972, 1974. After each agreement, the nuclear arms race intensified even further, with one specific characteristic: Every time, the Soviet Union raced faster. If the Soviet Union still lagged far behind the USA in 1963, then we can say that now the nuclear weapons on both sides are almost equal."[45] This hostile attitude toward arms control did not diminish with the end of the Cultural Revolution. After Deng became the supreme leader of the PRC in December 1978, the CTBT became his main point of conflict with President Carter.

CARTER'S FIRST ENGAGEMENT WITH CHINA ON NONPROLIFERATION

President Carter issued the Sixteenth Presidential Review Memorandum on January 25, 1977, requesting the National Security Council to conduct a comprehensive study of the prospects of a new nuclear test ban. In the response, officials warned him that China's attitudes would be a major obstacle:

> Even after a bilateral/multilateral CTBT has been achieved, it is likely that China, France, and perhaps other nations would continue to test. China has accorded high visibility to weapons testing, which it has indicated that it would continue and could be expected to severely criticize a CTBT as a superpower collusion. . . .
>
> The fact that some nations, particularly China, will continue to develop nuclear explosives would undoubtedly be viewed with concern by the Soviet Union. However, since current Chinese weapons technology is believed to be significantly inferior to that of the USA and USSR, the Soviets would probably be less concerned about a short-term continuation of Chinese testing. In the long term, this situation would be viewed as a serious problem by the Soviets and could even pose a problem for the USA from the national security standpoint. The result is that an indefinite duration CTBT without periodic reviews is unlikely to be acceptable to Soviets.[46]

Brzezinski, too, warned Carter on February 7, 1977, that Carter should choose carefully between a test ban with all five nuclear powers and a bilateral ban with the Soviet Union because the former would be deeply resented not only by the Chinese but also by the French. So as to not damage US-China relations, Brzezinski proposed that the president pursue the issue bilaterally with the Soviet Union.[47]

Despite these warnings, Carter was not discouraged from presenting his proposal. The next day, February 8, 1977, Carter met with the director of the Chinese Liaison Office, Huang Zhen, who also happened to be the Chinese ambassador to France from 1964 to 1971, the period when China and France sided together against the United States on the LTBT. Huang had also played a critical role in convincing France to break the United States' technological embargo against China after the Korean War. For a while, their meeting was cordial and polite, and they talked about the "traditional friendship between our two peoples," the importance of "the Nixon-Mao Shanghai Communiqué," and the timely topic of how much both Americans and Chinese distrusted the Russians. The chemistry was good until Carter suddenly brought up nonproliferation: "We have offered the Soviet Union a Comprehensive Test Ban treaty. This would be a bilateral agreement with the Soviets. If it can be worked out, then perhaps others such as China or France can consider joining in some form."[48]

Those words—*France*, *China*, and *Test Ban* must have touched a nerve with Huang, and he suddenly turned the conversation into a monologue on how the Soviet Union can't be trusted, how disarmament talks with the Russians are an illusion, and how

> in recent years the Soviet Union under the camouflage of détente has been stepping up military preparations for expansion. Not only have the Soviets caught up with the US in conventional forces, but they are seeking overall military superiority.... They bully the ones who are soft but are afraid of the ones who can act tough. Quite often, they do not mean what they say. They talk about disarmament but do the opposite. While they discuss disarmament, they build more weapons.... I would also say a few words about our northern neighbor—a neighbor that is not too far from your country either. We are vigilant and prepared.[49]

Huang's rejection of nonproliferation and his hostile attitude toward any US-Soviet arms reduction talks deeply concerned Secretary of State Vance, who oversaw the negotiations for the SALT II Treaty and the CTBT—both of which had become targets of China's criticism. The following month Secretary Vance went to see Director Huang and politely and indirectly probed his interest in "the possibility of negotiating for a ban on all tests of nuclear weapons for a limited period, as the President had indicated." This tactic did not work. No longer dealing with the American president, Huang went into another monologue: "The PRC has never been interested in the so-called disarmament agreements reached by the Soviet Union and the US." China's consistent policy is to "oppose the nuclear blackmail proposed by the Soviet Union and the US, and China will not take part in any of these activities." Directly pointing out the United States' hypocrisy, he said: "The PRC feels that the Soviet Union and the United States have now conducted enough tests and don't want to allow others to do so." He then used a Chinese idiom to describe the irrationality of a CTBT targeted at China: "There is no reason for this under Heaven!"[50]

FRENCH-CHINESE OPPOSITION CREATES TROUBLE FOR THE COMPREHENSIVE TEST BAN TREATY

While President Carter failed to bring China on board with the CTBT, the British-American-Soviet multilateral negotiations, which ran from 1977 to the end of 1978, turned into a love triangle involving cheaters trying to catch the others cheating. For example, the British priority at the time was not to ban nuclear testing but to develop a new type of submarine-launched warhead code-named Chevaline for the Polaris missiles launched by its Resolution class nuclear submarines. The British Ministry of Defense feared that a newly installed Soviet antiballistic missile defense system around Moscow would render the UK's already-thin atomic deterrence against the USSR useless.[51] Due to the high velocity and high temperature the experimental Chevaline warheads had to endure before hitting their targets, they could not be guaranteed to work without live nuclear tests.[52] In early 1978, Brzezinski reported that the British secretly asked the Americans "to conduct one additional test in late autumn of 1978 for their Polaris improvement program."[53] Only after conducting three tests in 1979 and 1980 would Britain fully commit to the CTBT negotiations.

The Soviets, on the other hand, resolutely refused to have monitoring stations on Soviet territory, saying that "trust" would be enough to replace verification, a term never clearly defined.[54] Meanwhile, the Americans had clear evidence that the Soviet Union was violating the LTBT by testing warheads above 150 kilotons throughout the CTBT negotiations, which made the Soviet refusal to accept on-site verification measures even more troubling and suspicious.[55] In addition, Russian scholars have recently revealed that the Soviet military in the late 1970s was very fearful of the United States' burgeoning computer industry, which would allow it to use computers to conduct as many simulated nuclear tests as it deemed necessary and without violating any test ban agreement. The Soviet Union, on the other hand, did not have any comparable technology to do simulated tests and thus had to rely on the old-school method of lighting up real nuclear warheads. This became another reason for the Soviet nuclear weapons industry to oppose the test ban.[56]

While all three parties cheated, the single issue on which they all had the most similar opinion for was the Soviet proposal that the CTBT be enforced for only three years. However, the Soviet delegation also insisted that the treaty *automatically* self-terminate if the Chinese or the French continued to test their weapons. The rationale for the Soviet proposal was that if the treaty failed, the French and the Chinese, who were most likely to continue to conduct more tests, would be to blame. The US delegation agreed with a three-year moratorium but wanted to reserve the right to withdraw *voluntarily* rather than automatically. The Americans calculated that if the treaty failed after three years, the Russians would be blamed—because the Soviets were lagging in MIRV technology and would be the party most likely to pull out. In addition, they believed the Soviet leadership would be much more sensitive to continued Chinese testing than would the Americans. The Soviet representative Timerbaev saw right through the American trick: "The [American] formula seemed politically motivated. The United States must recognize that the Soviet Union was the party most likely to be put in that difficult position, given the threat posed by continued Chinese testing. Although the Americans would withdraw as a result of the Soviet Union's decision to withdraw, it would be the Soviet Union that would shoulder the responsibility for destroying the treaty."[57]

Observing the negotiations closely, France and China did not wish to be the scapegoats for the failure of the treaty when they deemed it unfair and did not even take part in the negotiations. Although French President Valéry Giscard d'Estaing was considered to be more cooperative with the United States in nonproliferation matters compared to Charles de

Gaulle, Giscard d'Estaing and his advisers were also nationalists and had no intention of letting the superpowers dictate whether France could test nuclear weapons.[58] Thus, Giscard d'Estaing engaged in a double-dealing game with the Americans and the Chinese. On the one hand, he promised the Americans that France would do more to promote international nonproliferation regimes—and indeed achieved certain success in stopping reactor sales to Pakistan—while, separately, the French Ministry of Foreign Affairs worked with the Chinese against the US monopoly over the CTBT.[59] As early as 1977, fearing Carter would start a new round of test ban negotiations, the French ambassador to China met with Chinese Foreign Minister Huang Hua and found out that they were on the same page:

> [Huang asked,] "If the new president of the United States goes on with his plan to offer all nuclear powers a comprehensive test ban treaty, what will be your reaction?" I confidently answered: "The same as yours, which we will act together for the joint interests of France and China." During this conversation, the [Chinese] minister asked me another question, "What measures are you taking to face the recrudescence of the military threat from the USSR?" I then reported our defense effort, which is even more intense than a few years ago, as evidenced by the budgetary data. Secondly, I exposed our concept of deterrence, which, given the inferiority of our conventional forces, required that we keep the possibility of using tactical or strategic nuclear arms open. Suffice it to say that we cannot take the same position as China, consisting of formally renouncing the first use of atomic weapons, which my interlocutor seemed to understand very well.[60]

Instead of cooperating with the United States on the CTBT, France and China stepped up their bilateral cooperation in nuclear affairs the next year and reached an understanding that a superpower monopoly should not hinder both countries' nuclear weapons development. For example, on October 11, 1978, France submitted an Intervener Agreement on the Supply of Nuclear Reactors to the Chinese Embassy in Paris. Meanwhile, French officials began to work on a deal to sell China two nuclear reactors. The following week the director of the Chinese Academy of Sciences and Vice Premier Fang Yi visited Paris and toured France's top scientific institutions; during that time, both sides reached the agreement that

"France is a military nuclear power. She refuses to sign the non-proliferation treaty for reasons that are fully understood in China, because she intends to continue to develop its nuclear armament in all independence."[61] Quite comically, French diplomats even served as mentors to the Chinese in 1979, showing them how to get around US-led nuclear technology export-control restrictions. The French advised that instead of "buying raw uranium," which was under the control of the US- and USSR-led Nuclear Suppliers Group, they should get the reactor, which is "already supplied with fuel rods by France." Also, they told the Chinese to provide "peaceful use assurances" to get around the US State Department's legal restrictions when an American patent was involved.[62]

It was no wonder that François de la Gorce, the French representative at the Geneva Disarmament Conference, reported back to the French Ministry of Foreign Affairs on January 21, 1980, that the Chinese representative, An Yang, shared France's concerns about the CTBT negotiations:

> The words of Mr. An and his colleagues confirmed the position that we know on the convergence of French and Chinese interests [in the nuclear matter in particular] and on the advisability of close cooperation. . . . My interlocutor stressed the importance of the role [of decision], which belongs to the disarmament committee as a negotiation body. China can, of course, only reject the idea of the privileged responsibility of those two superpowers, from which the committee itself would derive a subordinate role, reduced to the recording of their decisions. The Chinese delegation also attaches great importance to the negotiations on chemical weapons, and they wonder if the next session regarding [chemical weapons] would open at all, particularly given the current state of the American-Soviet relations. . . . Mr. An asserted that the disarmament issues could not be resolved after Afghanistan [was invaded], as China has thus concluded that [disarmament] has not taken place.[63]

France's sympathy toward the Chinese position was further laid out in a memorandum prepared by its Ministry of Foreign Affairs: "The Chinese, as well as we, think that disarmament is a matter that concerns all." They opposed a bipolar conception in which the superpowers would negotiate deals that other countries would have to follow. The "fundamental issue" the French and Chinese agreed on was that "given the enormous [nuclear] superiority both superpowers have, *they should be the ones* substantially reducing their arsenal first. It's only when the disproportion between American and Soviet arsenals and those of the three other powers [China, France, and India] will have changed that the latter will consider reducing theirs."[64]

France and China disliked the exceptionalism and hypocrisy displayed by the Americans and Soviets, but this did not prevent them from feeling exceptional and displaying hypocrisy themselves. French sources show diplomats from both countries agreed that because the United States and the Soviet Union were already nuclear-armed states, any nonproliferation restrictions should apply only to nonnuclear weapon states and not to France and China; they were already members of the nuclear weapons club and therefore believed they could do whatever they wanted. Further, because both France and China were peace-loving nations, their nuclear weapons program could only contribute to world peace. "All non-proliferation agreements, international or bilateral," both countries agreed, should "reflect the fact that French-Chinese nuclear cooperation is entirely peaceful."[65] One such "peaceful" cooperation happened in December 1980: In the heat of the CTBT talks, France agreed to sell China two nuclear plants capable of producing both electricity for the grid and weapons-grade plutonium out of the back door. However, during the sale, the only "safety guarantee" French officials sought from the Chinese was a verbal guarantee that China would use those plants for peaceful purposes and "electricity generation only." This no-strings-attached position greatly irritated Secretary Vance, who personally complained to the French ambassador that France could have asked for firmer, written, legally binding safety guarantees.[66]

The French-Chinese resistance would create problems for the three parties involved in the CTBT negotiations. First, as long as France and China refused to follow the treaty and continued developing nuclear weapons technologies, the treaty signatories would be tempted to quit complying as well, not to mention the related issue of how to enforce the test ban on other nonnuclear states that would point to France and China as convenient excuses for their own tests. Second, since the Soviet Union was attempting to withdraw on the grounds of continued French and Chinese testing, a US official complained that the Soviets "will not move on the crucial details of the verification system until they are assured that we are serious about wanting a treaty that could be continued—as opposed to a mere three-year pause in testing."⁶⁷ The Soviet position was clearly aimed at France and China and turned out to be detrimental to the fate of the CTBT negotiations.

KEEP THE BOMB UNDERGROUND: CARTER MAN-TO-MAN WITH DENG

By the beginning of 1979, President Carter had already given up hope of convincing China to be a part of the CTBT. However, at least he still had the hope of pressuring China to support SALT II—the last silver lining before the complete collapse of US-Soviet relations. Unfortunately, Carter used the wrong language with Deng Xiaoping. During their first face-to-face meeting when Deng finally visited Washington after the normalization of US-China diplomatic relations, Carter asked Deng if China could support SALT II and "several agreements with the Soviet Union," noting, "contrary to your own belief, that the Soviets have complied with the previous agreement, including the Limited Test Ban, the Anti-Ballistic Missile Treaty, SALT I and the agreement reached at Vladivostok." The words *Limited Test Ban* immediately triggered a knee-jerk reaction from Deng:

> We are not opposed to negotiations. And we are not opposed to your reaching this or that agreement. At the same time, we believe that such an agreement cannot really restrain the Soviet Union. . . .
> And after each agreement, the Soviet Union stepped up its efforts to catch up. . . .
> Even if you are able to carry out effective supervision on the question of nuclear weapons, they will still look for loopholes in another direction. For instance, Afghanistan, Iran, South Yemen, Angola, Vietnam, Ethiopia, and so on constantly engage in such actions. So, we repeatedly said that what we really need to do is real, solid, down-to-earth work.⁶⁸

After this exchange, Carter gave up. Instead, he took a step back and at a later meeting urged Deng to start complying with the unwritten norm already adhered to by the two superpowers: namely, to stop testing nuclear weapons in the open air and instead do it more quietly underground. It was a not-so-honorable practice that former US presidents secretly recommended to close allies to help them avoid Soviet attention and pursue their nuclear weapons ambitions in a more low-profile manner.[69] Carter told Deng: "One other sensitive matter . . . is the nuclear testing that you conduct in the atmosphere. Each time you conduct a test, the nuclear fallout comes on my people. If it is possible for you to conduct such tests underground as we ourselves do, this will be a very fine announcement that could be made." Deng brushed the request away and, as a seasoned poker player, used this perfect chance to ask for nuclear testing technologies: "At the present time we are not able to commit ourselves not to conduct atmospheric tests. If we were to talk reason on this matter, we could say that the Soviet Union and the United States have conducted many atmospheric tests whereas the number of tests we have conducted is very small. . . . If you are able to supply us with some technical help in this respect, maybe it could be solved easily."[70]

The very next week Brzezinski wrote to Carter, urging him to offer technical assistance to help the Chinese test nuclear weapons underground, just as "we have provided such assistance but only to our closest allies, the UK and France."[71] The technical assistance must not have worked as smoothly as Brzezinski once hoped. China conducted a one-megaton atmospheric test the following year on October 16, 1980, allegedly for a new type of ballistic missile warhead.[72]

THE COLLAPSE OF THE COMPREHENSIVE TEST BAN TREATY NEGOTIATIONS

As negotiations dragged into the closing months of 1978, Paul Warnke, the director of the Arms Control and Disarmament Agency and chief negotiator for CTBT, became so exasperated with attacks from anti-Soviet critics who thought he was making too many concessions to the Soviet Union that he resigned from the Carter administration.[73] Carter resolved this internal crisis on February 2, 1979, by appointing Dr. Herbert York, the former nuclear weapons designer, to be the new chief CTBT negotiator (figure 2.3). There was an sense of urgency to the CTBT negotiations that

FIGURE 2.3 Dr. Herbert York began his career as a Manhattan Project nuclear physicist and later became a champion of arms control. He served as the Carter administration's ambassador to the CTBT talks. (University of California San Diego Library)

year, as newly emerging intelligence suggested that Pakistan was on its way to developing nuclear weapons; one such piece of intelligence even indicated that "China has almost certainly been involved in some mutually beneficial cooperation with Pakistan, particularly in connection with nuclear power, but the precise nature and extent of this cooperation is uncertain."[74] The fear of what they called an Islam Bomb pushed the US and British CTBT teams to speed up their negotiations. In the words of British chief negotiator Sir Clive Rose, "If we can get Indian support for a CTBT, this will help to alleviate the Pakistani problem."[75]

The negotiation was also blocked by the Soviets' insistence on the automatic withdrawal amendment because "few would believe it likely that France and China will stop testing in three years."[76] The paranoid Soviet military representatives also opposed having any national seismic station (NSS), designed to monitor nuclear test–triggered earthquakes, on Soviet soil, fearing the US-made equipment was essentially a spy tool that would "not only register earthquakes but also listen to other events and activities."[77] The British also refused to have more than one NSS on British home territory and wanted absolutely no NSS on British overseas islands, a position York believed was "in effect stalling the negotiation."[78]

The Soviet negotiator Timebaev, on the other hand, sarcastically commented that he was "less concerned about [British] Ambassador Edmonds's testing his own bomb in some remote places than about Edmonds's allowing [US] Ambassador York to test one of his on British territories." Despite being allies, there was also a significant misunderstanding between the British and the Americans. The British cabinet did not believe the NSS was an essential obstacle to the CTBT, contrary to what York had thought, and blamed the slow negotiation progress on the overall deterioration of US-Soviet relations.[79] As late as July 1980, British Foreign Secretary Peter Carrington insisted on having only one NSS in Scotland and none in independent territories.[80] Strangely, the British colonial legacy blocked the path of nonproliferation efforts during the Cold War. On May 3, 1979, Margaret Thatcher's Conservative government won the election and replaced James Callaghan's Labour cabinet members. Thatcher was not a fan of the CTBT and believed that "if one [NSS] was good enough for Callaghan, one is certainly good enough for me."[81] By the end of the year, the entire negotiation was stalled.[82]

On May 22, 1979, at the most difficult stage of the negotiations, York received an ominous "Top Secret" instruction from James A. Geocaris, a top lawyer in the Office of General Counsel at the Department of Defense: "Nations are bound under international law to obligations and interpretations of treaties to which they explicitly agree," the lawyer explained; therefore, "the CTBT could contain a provision allowing nuclear weapons states to experiment up to some specified limit while prohibiting no-nuclear weapons states from experimenting at all," and the department should make "a US unilateral statement [that] would provide the United States with good but not indisputable evidence for an interpretation allowing it to conduct experiments." This is justified because "no authoritative international tribunal exists to halt US experiments while the international legal dispute occurs." Meanwhile, another special statement should be made to prevent others from following the United States' example: "We could avoid the legal effect of our unilateral statement stopping us from disputing the right of non-nuclear weapons states to experiment up to the level specified in our unilateral statement by making a statement that allows nuclear weapons states to experiment but prohibits non-nuclear weapons states from doing so."[83] In other words, the Pentagon would test nuclear weapons as it wished, and the CTBT should prevent every other nation but the United States from testing nuclear weapons. This instruction represents the American military-industrial complex's unilateralism in the most cynical form. York's dilemma, as aptly put by his Soviet counterpart, was "being a person who makes nuclear materials for the bomb but at the same time tries to protect the world from the same bombs."[84]

Lying behind this Pentagon memo was the US military's increased sense of urgency for nuclear tests. As US-Soviet relations deteriorated, domestic support for a CTBT was also lost to those who argued for preparation for a nuclear war.[85] For example, the US Navy pressed Carter on a series of new nuclear tests, some of which not only violated current arms control treaties but also were downright absurd. For example, the admirals first wanted to test a nuclear warhead used for the SM-2 air defense missiles that would cause a nuclear explosion in orbit to destroy incoming enemy nuclear missiles—a clear violation of the 1972 Anti-Ballistic Missile Treaty, which specifically banned the use of nuclear explosives in outer space. Thankfully, Carter rejected this proposal.

Then the admirals asked to test a new type of "ammunition" codenamed Knighthead, which consisted of "insertable nuclear components for naval weapons" that would "permit conventional use of firing positions and magazine storage currently reserved for nuclear weapons use." An educated guess based on the US Navy's own ordnance records suggested that the four decommissioned Iowa-class fast battleships built during World War II—the USS *Iowa*, USS *New Jersey*, USS *Missouri*, and USS *Wisconsin*—equipped with sixteen-inch main guns, were the only Navy ships capable of firing both conventional and nuclear warheads.[86] Carter, a Navy man himself, could not resist the temptation to give those legacy battleships a new lease of life and checked the "Approve" box and signed with a "J."[87] Thus, with a stroke of his pen, Carter, the nonproliferation president, created a whole new level of nuclear warfare on the high seas. Those four ships would soon be recommissioned into service during the Reagan administration as a quantitative answer to the swelling Soviet fleet, having been upgraded with cruise missiles and modern antiaircraft systems and able to fire this type of unguided nuclear artillery shell.

The negotiations with China also took a strange turn. Pro-China officials at the State Department—especially Assistant Secretary of State Leslie Gelb, Director of Policy Planning Antony Lake, and NSA East Asia specialist Roger Sullivan—started to push Secretary of State Vance and President Carter to seriously consider Deng Xiaoping's request for US underground nuclear testing technology. On March 15, 1979, they suggested that instead of seeking China's support for the CTBT negotiations, Carter should encourage China to hide its nuclear tests underground and offer technical assistance if possible. They even formulated a backup plan if the story got leaked to the public: The Carter administration would "declare China's nuclear weapons program in our security interests" to avoid export control legal problems and congressional oversight.[88] It seemed that Carter's pro-China officials had started to stab Carter's nonproliferation officials in the back.

The CTBT negotiations went nowhere throughout the latter half of 1979 and were essentially stalled in late 1980. On November 11, 1980, Carter lost his ill-fated presidential reelection bid. A week after Reagan's victory, the Soviet negotiators understood there was no point in negotiating with the Carter administration anymore. They told York's lame-duck US delegation that they would have no new proposal until the next US administration was in office.[89] The newly elected President Reagan wanted to build up the United States' nuclear arsenal before engaging in negotiations with the Soviets. Following this "negotiation from strength" strategy, Reagan formally ended the CTBT talks on July 19, 1982, declaring that the United States would no longer continue negotiations "because of the need to keep testing new nuclear weapons."[90] As the CTBT negotiations came to an end, the superpowers rushed into a new round of nuclear arms tests.

In retrospect, the CTBT negotiations had no impact on the nuclear testing activities of the superpowers. The United States tested fifteen nuclear weapons in 1979 and fourteen in 1981, and the Soviet Union had thirty-one tests in 1979 and twenty-four in 1980. The British tested one in 1979 and three in 1980, and France, an opponent of the CTBT, tested ten in 1979 and twelve in 1980, while China, the most antagonistic of all toward CTBT negotiations, tested much fewer: one in 1979, three in 1980, and one in 1981. All the nuclear powers continued to test nuclear weapons in large quantities well after the end of the Cold War, although the United States and the Soviet Union did far more testing than the others.[91]

On May 8, 1980, a PLA Navy fleet of eighteen ships sailed out of the South China Sea and across the equator to guide and monitor China's first ICBM test. When the missile was successfully launched and landed in the water near Australia, Deng Xiaoping was jubilant, and even CCP General Secretary Hu Yaobang, remembered as a pro-American liberal reformer, jumped up and shouted, "We won! We won!"[92] Deng's wartime comrade Vice Premier Wang Zhen called this test "a blow to the imperialists' nuclear blackmail and expansionist ambition" and reminded the world that "our ICBM can reach any place in an imperialist country, and if they dare to use nuclear missiles against us, they will have to consider the consequences."[93] Ignoring the CTBT negotiations, in October 1980, China tested a new one-megaton warhead that would make its ICBM fully functional. Because France and the UK focused exclusively on submarine-based nuclear deterrence and thus never developed comparable long-range missiles, China finally made its leap into the exclusive ICBM club, side by side with the superpowers.

China's pursuit of ICBMs and related nuclear tests could be read as the need for an extra layer of security for Deng Xiaoping's rather risky global realignment with the West at the fall of détente. Those rapidly acquired ICBM capabilities with tested, proven nuclear warheads also explained why China was much more comfortable joining a series of nonproliferation talks with the United States in the late 1980s. It was not because international liberal institutions ensured China's sense of security, as American liberal academics and policymakers had hoped.[94] Nor was it because Ronald Reagan was a better dealmaker in handling China.[95] This episode of forgotten history also demonstrated the extent to which Deng Xiaoping would go to attack US-led nonproliferation efforts and US-Soviet détente in the name of Chinese national security—with the help of an important US ally, France—when President Carter had just started to rebuild the United States' relationship with the PRC. The failed CTBT can thus be seen as the first major casualty of China's independent engagement in the global Cold War, but it certainly would not be the last.

Ironically, in 2021, when the major nuclear powers celebrated the twenty-fifth anniversary of the 1996 CTBT, Zhang Jun, Chinese ambassador to

THE CHINA-FRANCE NUCLEAR ALLIANCE 89

FIGURE 2.4 This Soviet propaganda cartoons depicts radioactive clouds from Chinese nuclear testing floating across the Pacific to the United States. It appeared in Russia's satirical magazine *Krokodil* in 1980 (issue 33). (East View Information Services)

the UN, lectured nonnuclear nations on the importance of not testing nuclear weapons, just like the superpowers lectured China during the Cold War, pointing out that the new test bans were all about "maintaining world peace and safety" through "disarmament," with the aim of "eventually banning all nuclear weapons in the world." He further noted that China signed the treaty purely for altruistic reasons such as "fulfilling its international responsibility" and "abandoning double-standard and discriminatory methods."[96] Here, too, is a sense of hypocrisy as Ambassador Zhang did not mention how the treaty was never officially ratified by the CCP-controlled People's Congress.[97] To demonstrate how much China loved "disarmament" and "world peace," weeks later the PLA announced it had secretly conducted a successful nuclear-capable hypersonic missile test that circled the globe. That this missile was capable of evading modern missile defense systems triggered anxiety in Washington, D.C., especially considering that a month earlier the United States had conducted a similar test that failed. At the same time, China enjoyed its success. "They look like a first-use weapon," a rather jealous US general commented. "That's what those weapons look like to me."[98]

CONCLUSION

Jimmy Carter's invitation to Deng Xiaoping to support US-led arms control efforts was met with a cold shoulder in the case of SALT II and the proposed CTBT. The joint refusal of the PRC and France to support the US-, UK-, and Soviet-led CTBT was one of the main obstacles that led to the collapse of the treaty negotiations. Instead of relying on international arms control regimes to ensure the PRC's security, Deng and his military technocrats decided to pursue ICBM capabilities and work with France in both civilian and military nuclear weapon research. The PRC's attitude toward arms control changed only when the PLA felt confident about its nuclear deterrence capabilities. It turned out that both Chinese regimes had little trust in the superpowers and wished to take security into their own hands. As I demonstrate in the next part of the book, the ROC in Taiwan also tried to acquire independent nuclear weapons capability under the leadership of Chiang Ching-kuo but had much less success.

II

TECHNOLOGICAL COMPETITION

3

WESTERN EUROPEAN MILITARY AND DUAL-USE TECHNOLOGY TRANSFERS TO CHINA

Deng Xiaoping's China aggressively pursued advanced military and dual-use technology from US allies in Western Europe as a way to circumvent US export controls. This action undermined the US-led COCOM export control system, caused friction between the Carter administration and its European allies, and created another point of contention in the deteriorating relationship between the United States and the Soviet Union.

In this chapter, I examine another understudied aspect of US-China relations under the Carter administration: the transfer of military technologies from American allies in Western Europe to the PRC during and after the US-PRC opening of relations and the central role those transfers played in Deng Xiaoping's overall Cold War strategy. I show that the Carter administration's decision to relax military technology export control toward China based on mutual anti-Soviet grounds resulted in unexpected consequences. Western Europeans ended up competing with one another in business deals, which made it impossible for the Carter administration to regulate their technology transfers to China. Meanwhile, the anti-Soviet officials in the Carter administration were far more interested in arming the Chinese to counter the Soviet Union than in fulfilling the COCOM system's original intention of limiting the transfer of Western military technology to the Communist bloc. As a result, the quality and quantity of the weapon systems and technologies that Western Europeans and China were willing to trade eventually became a matter for Western Europeans themselves to decide—a situation that was capitalized on by Deng and his comrades, whose long-term military ambitions reached far beyond the Cold War.

These Western European–Chinese military exchanges did not go unnoticed by US officials who had concerns about the proliferation of Western military technologies in Communist countries—China included; these transfers to China were also closely tracked by the Soviets around Brezhnev, who were even more suspicious of—if not paranoid about—China's long-term strategic goals. As a result, European arms sales to China became a potential point of contention in US-European relations. Further, they complicated the already deteriorating East-West relations within the context of the collapse of détente.

European-Chinese relations during and after the US-China diplomatic opening, as well as China's opening and reform, is an emerging but still relatively understudied topic of Cold War history;[1] however, very little has been written on security cooperation, especially the transfer of Western European arms and dual-use technology to China as a result of US officials' relaxation of restrictions (if not direct encouragement to disregard them).[2] The political scientist David Shambaugh, for example, briefly mentioned those arms sales as China's "window shopping" trips in the West: a metaphor to illustrate the lack of fruitful results due to China's limited financial capability to purchase large items and its much stronger desire to acquire the means of production that the Europeans were hesitant to hand out.[3] This emerging strategy of focusing on technology transfer instead of purchasing military hardware also foreshadowed China's dominant technology-importing strategy after the Cold War, when the diffusion and commercialization of military technology, together with the collapse of multilateral export control regimes like COCOM, made it much harder for the United States to control what type of technology China could access and from whom, especially when the transactions were disguised as civilian business deals or academic scientific exchanges.[4] Utilizing new materials from British, French, German, and Russian archives, I provide a unique opportunity for readers to understand China's strategy in this early phase of technology acquisition and the Western European countries' inescapable role in the collapse of global export regimes.

TRADING WITH THE ENEMY THROUGH THE EUROPEAN BACK DOOR

The United States' trade embargo against China, enacted during the Chinese Civil War and expanded during the Korean War, caused unease among its Western European allies, who had far less of a security commitment in Asia but plenty of business interests at stake. The British, in particular, felt it was unfair that British Hong Kong had to follow the COCOM, established in 1949, and the China Committee, also known as CHINCOM, established in 1952, which regulated the port city's trade with the Chinese mainland. In fact, CHINCOM was specifically created by the Truman administration after the Korean War to target Mao's China because, as it turned out, the less industrialized PRC had very different import needs compared to the much more industrialized Soviet Union.[5] By restricting even essential commodities such as food, rubber, and fuel, the embargo severely damaged the economies of Hong Kong and, by extension, the British Empire. "Hong Kong must trade with the mainland to live," British Foreign Secretary Herbert Morrison complained to US officials in September 1951. The United States, however, was less sympathetic, as the Defense Department under George Marshall believed that Hong Kong "was not strategically important in the defense of the West" in their undeclared war against Communism. The US Congress, now dominated by anti-Communist Republicans, called the trade between mainland China and the West, such as that which occurred through Hong Kong, "trading with the enemy behind the back of the US."[6]

The Chinese leaders, especially Zhou Enlai, knew that the British had a weak spot in Hong Kong and strove to drive a wedge between the UK and the United States in the embargo against China. Zhou employed the strategy of *gege jipo*, which was understood as "striking at the weakest link, then the next weakest link, one at a time, to break the embargo." Indeed, British-Chinese trade talks continued behind the backs of the Americans in Geneva throughout the 1950s, turning Hong Kong into a black market for the two countries' bilateral trade. By 1954, China was already the third-largest Communist trading partner of the UK from the Sino-Soviet bloc, ranked only behind the USSR and Poland.[7]

During the Sino-American rapprochement, British-Chinese trade reached the area of strategic weapons, and the UK remained a "weak link" within the COCOM system. In 1974, British Cabinet Secretary John Hunt even convinced Kissinger to allow Rolls-Royce to sell China Spey 202 turbofan military jet engines and its production line in a semisecret manner outside of the COCOM system. Because of Kissinger's interest in improving relations with China, this sale went through despite opposition from the US Commerce, State, and Defense Departments, which argued that it would severely damage the COCOM system and boost Chinese military capability far beyond what they deemed necessary.[8] Those concerns were rightly raised as in the long term this sale severely reduced the prestige of COCOM. Further, it inspired other nations to follow Britain's "business model" and bypass COCOM to sell restricted weapons to China.[9] Britain's action not only started the demise of the COCOM system but also created unintended consequences for US security long after the Cold War. In the 2020s, Chinese JH-7 tactical bombers equipped with those British engines and armed with reverse-engineered French antiship cruise missiles patrolled the Taiwan Strait and the South China Sea, posing a real challenge to the US Seventh Fleet.[10]

France posed another challenge to the COCOM structure, and this has something to do with the unpredictable personalities and anti-American sentiments of French leaders, particularly Charles de Gaulle and Valéry Giscard d'Estaing. Already during Mao's time, China and France did plenty of business deals through unofficial diplomatic channels established in 1955 in Geneva.[11] Also, in 1964, France became the first of the major European powers to establish full diplomatic relations with the PRC, far ahead of West Germany, which opened relations in October 1972, and the UK, which attained formal mutual recognition in 1950 but posted no ambassador until March 1972. France's friendly foreign relations with China further facilitated the growth of France-China trade during the earlier stages of the Cold War. One scholar described President de Gaulle as being most interested in using this connection with China to revive France's great power status in Southeast Asia and as "playing cat-and-mouse with allies" when it came to dodging pressures caused by the Kennedy administration's anti-PRC stance.[12] The United States knew that France remained another weak link in its embargo on China, as the CIA had warned in 1963 that France could easily evade the COCOM by rerouting direct trade between France and China on a proxy route through French African colonies to British Hong Kong.[13] Colonial legacies, strangely, played handily into the economic games of the Cold War.

France played the most prominent role in the transfer of nuclear technology to China, creating a painful headache for US nonproliferation officials. During the earlier stages of the Cold War, France and China often worked together to oppose US-led nonproliferation efforts, such as the LTBT of 1963 and the proposed CTBT during the Carter administration.[14] The US-China rapprochement under Carter encouraged France to upgrade its nuclear cooperation with China from secret deals to full open collaboration. In 1977, France was already prepared to sell nuclear reactors with integrated US technologies to China, which soon became a dilemma for nonproliferation officials and trade embargo experts in the Carter administration.

The only Western European country complying with the US embargo against China, it seemed, was West Germany, although this was the result of the complicated relations between West Germany and China. In 1969, at the height of the Sino-Soviet split, Mao had already placed both German states in the "intermediate zone" in his geopolitical view of the Cold War, which, in his mind, should not be controlled by either superpower.[15] Based on this philosophy, China under Mao tried to drive a wedge between the Democratic Republic of Germany (GDR, or East Germany) and the Soviet Union and between the Federal Republic of Germany (FRG, or West Germany) and the United States. This policy, however, was not well received in West Germany, where the *Ostpolitik* conducted by Chancellor Willy Brandt was more focused on keeping the peace with the Soviet Union while maintaining good relations with the United States—and thus incompatible with Mao's radical antisuperpower position.[16] This comparatively more complex political situation, scholars of Sino-German relations argued, contributed to the low level of Sino-FGR relations overall during most of the Mao years. It was not until 1975 that China reached out to conservative politicians in Western Europe in hope of building a new anti-Soviet front, that Helmut Kohl and Franz-Josef Strauss, both representing the conservative anti-Soviet wing of German politics, visited China. Chancellor Helmut Schmidt, the same year, also visited China in a pragmatic manner and thus opened up the Chinese market for western German companies.[17] However, the West Germans were very self-conscious about their militaristic past during the fascist period and did not wish any arms sales to a potential conflict zone to be seen as a repeat of that history. For example, during the West German–British debate on Rolls-Royce's Spey engine sales to China in 1973, The State Secretary of the Foreign Ministry (likely Hans-Georg Sachs) told British Ambassador Nicholas Henderson on July 13 that Bonn refused to give an opinion on the British sale because it affected *Ostpolitik* with Eastern Europe and the USSR and also that the FRG's hesitation to sell arms to China, "given the principle of unanimity applied by COCOM" and the current Sino-Soviet split, was an act of "restraint from engagement in an international conflict that we see as a direct consequence of the Second World War."[18]

However, West Germany's stated intent to keep sales within the COCOM limit and allow no weapons into conflict zones did not mean that it did not offer China crucial, dual-use technologies outside of the COCOM rules under the guise of civilian technological exchanges. I suggest that the West Germans were, in fact, in secret competition with the French in a nuclear reactor sale to China. Meanwhile, the Chinese under Deng Xiaoping used all necessary means—including gifting a pair of adorable giant pandas named Bao Ba and Tjen Tjen to the Berlin Zoo—to smooth their relations with the FRG and facilitate the purchase of technologies, as well as the training of Chinese scientists in the FRG.[19] Because those civilian scientific exchanges were not sensitive enough to require the United States to intervene directly, they tended to work much more smoothly than the provocative nuclear deals between France and China. This was also due to the larger number of Chinese scientists being trained in West Germany compared with other countries and the much broader scope of the technological exchange between the FRG and China. By the 1980s, West German scholars discovered that the FRG and Japan were second only to the United States in the number of Chinese scientists and technical experts each hosted. West Germans, even within the broadly defined COCOM limit, played arguably the most prominent role in the general modernization process in post-Mao China.[20]

FROM CIVILIAN SCIENCE AND TECHNOLOGY EXCHANGES TO ARMS SALES

Using the US-China rapprochement to pursue advanced technology was a common objective among the top Chinese leaders. Even the CCP's conservative wing agreed China had a once-in-a-lifetime opportunity to catch up with the West. For example, already in early 1976, when Deng Xiaoping was still enduring his second purge, Premier Hua Guofeng explained how the international circumstances favored China:

> The development of international politics demands that we seize this opportunity. The Second World [Europe] strongly urges establishing better relations with us to do business. . . . Even the Americans wanted to do business with us. The capitalists in Europe, Japan, and North America have seen the improving situation in our country and are competing with each other to propose big business deals. Such a great situation is unprecedented since the founding of the People's Republic of China. This situation, however, has raised a question for us: [we] must be good at using this momentum based on independent development to absorb foreign technology and capital, to speed up our development, to catch up with the world standard . . . if we are not good at exploiting this great international situation, then that would be a mistake. [Because] we must understand that the Americans and Soviets are competing furiously for global hegemony, one day there will be war, not to mention the Soviet Revisionists still want us dead. We must plan well and prepare for the worst; we might live peacefully now, but we must not forget the dangers. [We need] to hurry up our development before the war arrives, to prepare for everything, and to have no disillusionment.[21]

Chinese military leaders fully supported this perspective (figure 3.1). General Zhang Aiping, a technocrat in the PLA whom Deng appointed director of the National Defense R&D Council, also believed that China now had one, and probably the only, chance to catch up with the West by getting military technologies directly from Westerners. During the council's opening conference, General Zhang said:

> Science and technology have been developing extremely fast in recent decades. But, the Gang of Four disrupted us . . . and now we are stuck on the path and not moving forward. The gap between the developing countries and the US is now even bigger. Thus, we must double our efforts and catch up with [the West]. Now, we have the plan till the year 1985. Whether in strategic or conventional weapons, we must catch up—or be close to the level where Americans and Soviets are now. We ask all our

FIGURE 3.1 Li, *Striving to Modernize National Defense*, September 1978. The Chinese propaganda poster bears the slogan "Struggle for the modernization of national defense" (为国防现代化而奋斗). (chineseposters.net, Landsberger collection)

comrades to increase our research in basic [scientific] knowledge and bring advanced foreign expertise. We don't have to walk the paths that the Americans, Soviets, British, and French had once walked. Choosing a "shortcut" is entirely possible. From what we know, the Americans are already working on the third generation of nuclear weapons. We must catch up and surpass them, but it does not mean we must always follow them. It is possible to take their advanced technologies over, build our own based upon them, and even surpass them.[22]

PRC politicians had already shown a strong interest in pursuing scientific and technological exchanges with the United States shortly after Brzezinski's deal-making trip to China in May 1978. They started aggressively lobbying for new American technologies, but for the moment, they did not propose to acquire US weapons and military technologies. Instead, they focused on less sensitive civilian technologies and institution-level scientific exchanges. On June 19, 1978, Han Xu, the first deputy chief of the Chinese Liaison Office in Washington, D.C., invited Frank Press, the head of Carter's Science and Technology Policy Office, to bring a delegation of scientists and science policymakers to China. Han specifically asked that the delegation include Secretary of Energy James Schlesinger, a Harvard-trained nuclear physicist and vocal anti-Soviet hawk.[23] President Carter, too, showed his interest in such a visit and generally hoped scientific exchanges would allow China to "play a central role in the maintenance of the global equilibrium." In addition, Carter and his advisers agreed that technology transfers to China would enable it to be "self-sufficient in agriculture and not become a major claimant on world food supplies," to "contribute to natural resource supplies," to "remain confident it can deter a Sino-Soviet conflict," and, most importantly, to "be a part of the global community and contribute to solving global problems."[24]

When Press visited China from July 6 to July 10, 1978, the members of his delegation included many high-profile scientists and policymakers, such as Robert A. Frosch from NASA, Richard C. Atkinson from the National Science Foundation, Rupert Cutler from the Department of Agriculture, Jordan A. Baruch from the Department of Commerce, John M. Deutch from the Department of Energy, and Donald S. Fredrickson from Department of Health, Education, and Welfare, as well as Benjamin Huberman and Anne Keatley, experts from the Office of Science and Technology

Policy. This impressive delegation—accompanied by Michel Oksenberg and Scott Halford, experts on Asia from the State Department—met with Vice Premier Fang Yi, who was also the director of the State Scientific and Technological Commission and the key architect of the development of China's strategic sectors: material science, energy, computer science, space science, lasers, and genetics.[25] Deng also met with Press's delegation and told them, "The United States and China's scientific exchanges have special importance. America is more advanced in science and technology compared to the other countries, we are willing to absorb some of your technologies . . . we need to learn from developed countries, including you." He also asked to send more Chinese students to the United States: "You have agreed to take 500 students, but we want to send more and to invite more scientists, engineers, and scholars to help us, to reform some of our enterprises." In addition, he expressed concerns about China's financial capabilities and export control restrictions and said he wished the United States would relax some of the restrictions and allow China to "import equipment [first] and then pay back with our products."[26]

The opportunity for scientific and technological cooperation arrived with the normalization of US-PRC diplomatic relations on New Year's Day, 1979. Deng traveled to the United States on January 29, 1979, and on January 31, he and President Carter signed the U.S.-China Agreement on Cooperation in Science and Technology. The treaty was to be renewed every five years and set "equal and mutually beneficial" conditions for the two countries' scientific and technological cooperation at both the governmental and the institutional levels. The treaty was accompanied by fifty subagreements, covering energy, environment, agriculture, fundamental research, informatics, earth sciences, natural resources, traffic, water resources, medical science, public health, quantitative research methods, civilian nuclear technology, safety, statistics, biotechnology, earthquake prediction, atmosphere studies, and many other areas.[27]

Even though US-PRC scientific and technological exchanges were institutionalized with this treaty, many anti-Soviet hard-liners in the Carter administration believed that the United States could do more and move beyond civilian science and technology exchanges. The United States, they argued, should start to deliver weapons directly to the PRC to incentivize Deng Xiaoping to continue his anti-Soviet policy. Brzezinski, in particular, believed US permission for Western arms sales to the PRC should be a pillar in building a long-lasting relationship with China, a position he expressed in a January 1979 memo to President Carter before Deng's visit: "Our common concern with the Soviet Union, however, is an insufficient basis for building a long-term relationship with China. More positively, we want to build a durable relationship based on (1) extensive commercial, scientific, and cultural relations; (2) shared views on world affairs, exploiting parallel interests on specific issues like Indochina, the Middle East, and Korea, and (3) weapon deployments that are aimed at our common adversary rather than at each other." Brzezinski further argued that selling arms to the Chinese was in the interest of the United States and world peace because "our effort to attain security in a world of diversity parallels the current Chinese desire for a stable, non-hegemonical world order." Thus, "we have no interest in a Sino-Soviet accommodation secured through Chinese submission to Soviet pressure. We are interested in a strong, secure, and peaceful China and are willing to acquiesce to limited Western European arms sales."[28]

President Carter, however, was unsure whether giving US weapons and military technologies directly to the PRC was a wise idea, especially in early 1979 when SALT II was still hanging in the balance and direct US military assistance to the PRC might antagonize the Soviet Union in a way that would be detrimental to the already difficult efforts to maintain détente. Nevertheless, he mused that there should be other ways to arm the PRC without the United States' direct involvement. On February 6, 1979, under the White House's direction, the US State Department decided to allow US allies to be the first to sell weapons and dual-use technologies to China and to no longer require the cumbersome COCOM reviews: "We have told the Allies that if they want our views on particular sales, they should come to us bilaterally at the highest political level, rather than through COCOM." Meanwhile, to evade responsibilities and possible Soviet accusations, the policy instructed, "Allies should not necessarily expect an opinion from us before their plans on a particular case have taken shape."[29] The United States, the founding member of COCOM, would soon face the unintended consequences of this new policy, as US allies and eventually, the US arms industry competed with one another to deliver military technologies to China, which significantly undermined the COCOM system.

CASE STUDY 1: BRITISH HARRIER JET SALE TO CHINA

Ever since the Sino-Soviet split, the CCP's armed forces, the PLA, had wanted better fighter jets than those in their Stalin-era Soviet-made MiG fighter fleet and their domestic made copies, so when they could not purchase such planes from the United States, they tried to get them from US allies in Europe. As we have seen in previous chapters, Deng Xiaoping attempted to purchase F-16s from the United States without apparent success. However, UK intelligence reports in 1978 stated that China was trying to use licensing agreements and other means to evade COCOM restrictions in its attempts to purchase Harrier jets from Britain, Mirage fighters from France, and Saab 37 Viggen fighter-bombers from Sweden—all of which were comparable alternatives to the F-16s the United States refused to sell.[30]

The Chinese military was particularly interested in the Harrier jump jets manufactured by UK-based British Aerospace because of their short and vertical takeoff capabilities. Chinese diplomats had already raised the issue with the British in 1972, testing the goodwill of the West from the earliest years of the US-China rapprochement. Negotiations had slowed down due to the internal chaos in China during the Cultural Revolution and the British fear of disrupting détente with the Soviets.[31] However, in 1977, the Chinese raised the question to the British again when Chinese Foreign Trade Minister Li Qiang, a Yan'an-era old-time revolutionary, a military engineer, and a crucial figure in the PRC's military aid to North Vietnam during the Vietnam War, visited the UK and specifically asked to purchase seventy or more Harrier jump jets. This new request caused heated internal debates among top British officials. On the supporting side, for example, Sir Percy Cradock, British ambassador to China, believed that the deal made sense, since China could use a credible defense against the Soviets and "we have so much of what the Chinese want. . . . It was a good business opportunity, and the UK should take advantage of the 'warming of Sino-British relations' to approve the sale." In addition, "it would have a very damaging effect if we were now to refuse to consider further orders."[32] The Department of Industry also supported the sale, believing the sizable Chinese order would give significant financial relief to "the most depressed industries, notably steel plants and power plants." Eric Varley, secretary of trade and industry, believed a deal with China would open the door to China's raw materials and give the UK an edge in the ongoing trade competition with France and West Germany.[33]

However, other officials, such as Foreign Secretary David Owen and Prime Minister James Callaghan, were quite concerned about violating the COCOM procedure and facing the rage of the Soviets. Hence, they decided to consult the Americans. After all, they had created COCOM, and their opinion should be the deciding factor in NATO-China military cooperation. However, when British Defense Secretary Fred Mulley—following NATO COCOM procedure—consulted his American counterparts led by Secretary Brown, the Americans only pushed the decision back to the British. Brown, another anti-Soviet hard-liner in the Carter administration who had been pushing for the normalization of US-China diplomatic relations based on mutual anti-Soviet grounds, was glad to use the British to arm the Chinese. However, he surmised that the Americans should not be the ones to face the Soviet Union's blame, as they still required Soviet cooperation on a series of issues related to détente and disarmament. In addition, he did not want Americans to be responsible for the unpleasant consequences such a deal would cause in US-Taiwan relations, since the Harriers, according to the British, "had just enough range" to reach Taiwan. "For political reasons, primarily connected with US/Soviet relations, the US would not sell weapons, even defensive ones, to China," Brown told Mulley, "but they did not propose to lead an arms blockade against China, which could only benefit the Soviet Union." The Americans "therefore put no pressure on their friends not to sell arms to the Chinese, but considered that we [the British] should be careful about what items we were willing to sell."[34]

Getting no clear answers from the Americans, the Callaghan government turned to fellow NATO allies, hoping, first, to gain their support on the Harrier deal and, second, to accept responsibility together in the face of a possible hostile Soviet response. Comically, state officials from all COCOM members were called to London for a special meeting on November 17, 1978, to discuss the British Harrier exports to China, and it turned out that every member state was planning military sales to the Chinese, with some deals more visibly military-related than others. Each member state sought innovative methods to evade COCOM restrictions and dodge Soviet retaliation. The report of the meeting said the Italians and Dutch were trying to sell China missiles, drones, and naval ships. In contrast, the West Germans and Japanese "would not sell to the Chinese weapons suitable for making war."[35] Still, the Chinese were interested in "acquiring modern technology of all types, including items covered by the industrial list of embargoed items"—items that the Japanese and West Germans were happy to see exempted from COCOM restrictions. The French did not even bother to attend the meeting because they were in the process of selling the Chinese nuclear reactors and a large number of other grey-area items that the French themselves had defined as non-COCOM-related.

Facing a delicate situation in which no one wished to take any more responsibility than the others, the COCOM members unanimously agreed to the British proposal of a "no comment policy" at the end of the meeting. This meant that each government should make its own decisions regarding what to sell to the Chinese, and when an issue had to be brought to the COCOM meeting to be examined—a step that would not always be entirely necessary—other member states had the right to "not make any comment" of objection and allow the questionable sale to pass quietly.[36] According to the British Foreign Office, this "no comment policy" was a "gentleman's understanding."[37]

The late 1970s were a difficult time for the British aerospace industry, as its strategy to enter the lucrative US market based on niche products such as the Harrier had not succeeded. This was mainly because the Americans were determined to build a whole generation of aircraft based on the hard lessons they learned from the violent encounters US-produced aircraft had with Soviet MiG fighters during the Vietnam War. In the American market, the US Air Force was already focused on purchasing the next generation of F-15 air-superiority fighters developed by McDonnell Douglas and the lighter and cheaper F-16 multirole fighters developed by General Dynamics. The US Navy focused exclusively on two carrier-based jets: the F/A-18 multirole fighters jointly developed by McDonnell Douglas and Northrop and the Grumman F-14 interceptors designed to counter Soviet MiGs.[38] Only the US Marine Corps wanted to import the Harrier as a vertical-takeoff, short-distance air-support aircraft useful in war zones without airfields. Thus, the Harrier filled only a very specific and limited need in the US market.

The British trade unions, afraid that the US Marine Corps would not buy enough Harriers to sustain the production line, argued that the UK should sell them to the Chinese instead, as this would maintain "over 10,000 jobs" in Britain.[39] Others, however, had doubts. Lord President of the Council Michael Foot was especially concerned about the repercussions for British-Soviet relations, as well as the much bigger question of China and its future relations with the UK. "Are we really convinced that China has become the progressive, peaceful power that is now represented to us?" he asked the prime minister. "If it is, why should the sale of military equipment be so important to them as a test of our intentions? It would appear from this that China will be seeking to dictate to us the terms on which they are prepared to trade with us generally—and if that is the case, I certainly do not believe that we should accept it."[40]

DEDICATED RELATIONS WITH THE UNITED STATES

For those who wished for the UK-China deal on the Harriers to go through, everything seemed to look brighter at the end of 1978, when the United States and China announced they would normalize their diplomatic relations in 1979. First, the Callaghan government received notice from all the COCOM members except Portugal, whose representative skipped the COCOM meeting, that they would pose no objection to the sale.[41] To pacify the American doves who were concerned about the détente with the Soviets and the safety of the Taiwanese, the British officials in Washington, D.C., assured Secretary of State Vance that the Harriers the UK was contemplating selling to the Chinese were the eighteen-year-old version designed by Hawker Siddeley, British Aerospace's predecessor, that were in service with the Royal Air Force and not the "advanced version we were working on with the Americans," which British Aerospace had redesigned.[42] However, the British never mentioned in front of the Chinese that the Harrier version they proposed to sell was outdated, at least according to available records. Instead, the British officials and arms dealers used every opportunity to convince Chinese officials that they "have an advanced aerospace industry" and that when it comes to airplanes, military or civilian, it is best to buy those made in Britain.[43] To prove their point, they even allowed PLA Air Force pilots to make a few test flights in the UK. However, no visible record of this was found because British officials were anxious to prevent any photos from being leaked to the media and instructed British Aerospace to keep the test flights absolutely secret.[44] Everyone, it seemed, had a little game to play.

With the change in US-China relations, British officials such as Andrew Duguid, private secretary to the prime minister, no longer saw the United States as an obstacle preventing the British from doing business with the Chinese, which it had been earlier, but rather as a potential long-term competitor. Thus, the UK determined that it should sell the Harriers to the Chinese, as "we have something special to offer to the Chinese, and the Harrier is unique."[45] Likewise, Ewen Fergusson of the Eastern European and Soviet Department in the Foreign Office assured the prime minister's office that "the opportunities for effective short-term Soviet reprisals are correspondingly meager" as "at worst[,] cost in trade lost with the USSR is unlikely to approach the potential value of the Harrier sale and other business under consideration with China." The deal, Fergusson suggested, should go ahead.[46] China, too, started to play the Westerners against one another and dropped hints on multiple occasions that the British fighters, in fact, were not that unique. "China cannot wait," said an official through a secret channel in Hong Kong. "There are always the US and others who could move in if Britain was not prepared to supply."[47]

To convince the British to make the offer, the Chinese, through multiple channels, played up the Soviet threat rhetoric. One of the key Chinese officials who engaged in this rhetoric was Vice Premier Li Xiannian, one of the earliest economic reformers advising Deng Xiaoping, who had a keen interest in bringing in foreign expertise to modernize China. Li was involved in foreign trade even before the Cultural Revolution and had already noted in 1959 the necessity of bringing in foreign experience from both socialist and capitalist countries to modernize Chinese industry, a surprisingly open-minded position during that closed-minded period.[48] During the Great Leap Forward, he was one of the few top Chinese leaders who dared to tell Mao that his agriculture policy was wrong and was causing starvation.[49] Li then served as finance minister and played a key role in stabilizing the country's finances at the end of the Cultural Revolution. Now Li was overseeing financial reforms and foreign trade issues under Deng. As a plain-spoken person, Li was unsatisfied with using the old Soviet model with the Chinese economy, where, in his own words, "old heavy industries' fat asses are sitting in others' [modern industries'] seats." He tried to redirect financial resources to importing foreign technologies to create those modern industries.[50] He once half-joked about his experiences dealing with foreign trade delegations: "The advanced sciences and technologies we can master now are not just not enough, but seriously not enough. . . . But foreign businessmen are clever; negotiating with them is hard work."[51]

In July 1978, a delegation of British members of Parliament from the Labour Party led by Lord Goronwy-Roberts arrived in Beijing, and Li offered them a Maoist-style monologue on the Soviet threat to Europe as a reason Britain should sell the Harrier jets to China: "In the Russian vocabulary, peace means war, disarmament means the build-up of arms and detente means tension," and "the European Security Conference was a sham" that was "immediately followed by the Cuban action in Angola, and the Horn of Africa." China would not retreat in front of Soviet pressure, and it would not surrender in times of war, Li assured his British guests. "China was an ardent lover of peace. But what could she do if the Russians wanted war? China would fight back, even at the expense of 200 million, 300 million, or half her population; there would still be 400 million left." After those exaggerations, Li switched to the actual topic: whether the British would agree to sell some Harrier fighters to China. He pointed out it would be even better if they would also sell China the entire production line. "The difficulty was that if China should buy 200 planes and they were destroyed in the war, she would need to manufacture replacements. China might initially wish to buy Harriers," Li said, "and then acquire the right to manufacture them herself." However, Li did not receive a definite answer, and the person who read those records at the British Foreign Office drew several exclamation marks beside Li's mention of the millions of people he was willing to sacrifice to win the war.[52]

COMPLICATIONS AND DELAY

The Harrier sale negotiations were complicated by several factors in 1979. British Aerospace, it turned out, was also selling Harriers to India, and

China still had unresolved border disputes with India as the result of a war fifteen years earlier. The Chinese also had to tolerate the inconvenient fact that the Indian navy was buying the Sea Harrier that had been redesigned by British Aerospace, so it was at least ten years more advanced than the Hawker Siddeley stock version offered to China. As India was a nonaligned country and outside of the COCOM restriction, the Harrier deal also had far fewer strings attached regarding how India could use the Harriers and what additional weapons could come with them.[53] It was not that simple for China because each attached weapons system needed special clearance from the other COCOM members as a group and from the United States specifically. Moreover, when the Chinese requested a type of cluster antiarmor bomb—the BL755—which it would use to attack concentrated Soviet tank columns, numerous British Ministry of Defense and Foreign Office officials raised humanitarian concerns. They argued that even though the bomb was mainly designed to split into multiple small explosive units in a large area, each of which would penetrate the relatively weak armor on the top of a Soviet tank turret, it still had a secondary function as an infantry killer. When dropped into a crowd of people, those explosive units could spread shrapnel horizontally and kill human targets in a very large radius. Those concerned officials warned that, however unlikely the circumstances, such weapons could still be used by the Communist government to kill protestors crowded in a public square.[54] Because antiarmor warfare against large Soviet tanks and armored infantry fighting vehicles was the key reason the Chinese needed to deploy Harriers along the Sino-Soviet border in the first place, the British refusal to sell the BL755 bombs greatly disappointed the Chinese negotiating team.[55]

Those humanitarian concerns only became more serious when Chinese forces invaded Vietnam in February 1979. This sudden attack turned the Harrier sale into a public relations crisis for those in the Callaghan government after they had spent the previous year trying to convince fellow NATO partners—and themselves—that after Mao, China was turning into a peace-loving country. Prime Minister Callaghan and his cabinet members had to try their best to dodge awkward questions from the media and their opposition, who used the UK-China military connection in the wake of the Sino-Vietnamese war to question the government's moral standing in the upcoming 1979 parliamentary election.

For example, British Foreign Secretary David Owen was grilled by BBC Radio 4:

> BBC: If the Labour Government is returning in the next election, will it consider its position, please, regarding the selling of arms to China in view of the Viet Nam campaign and some disquiet in the minds of some British people?
>
> DAVID OWEN: It is not always a decision whether you are to sell arms; it is also a question of whether you refuse to sell arms to people who ask you to. Now, I do not believe that we should sell offensive weapons to China. I think there is a case for selling defensive weapons to a country that has requested it and has made some very dramatic changes in its policy over the last year or two.
>
> BBC: You know, at the same time we are selling jump jets, China has become an aggressor.
>
> DAVID OWEN: Yes, and I think it is a very bad way of solving border disputes . . . [but] we must take account of the border disputes which have long been part of the history of that region.[56]

The Labour Party's own international affairs committee was also concerned. Considering China had just attacked Vietnam, Member of Parliament Tony Benn told his peers in an emergency meeting on the Harrier sale, "No one could say that there would not be another Cultural Revolution in a few years and the Harrier jets would not be used against Hong Kong."[57] According to a contemporary account, the Chinese attack on Vietnam was such an embarrassment to Callaghan that he had to withdraw permission to sign the Harrier deal from the British delegation that was in China at the same time to finish up the final negotiations.[58]

"MONEY CANNOT BUY US FOUR MODERNIZATIONS" AND THE CHINA DIFFERENTIAL

Although the Harrier jet deal was indefinitely postponed, real change was coming from the Chinese side. Throughout late 1978 and 1979, the Chinese had been reevaluating their military modernization priorities.

Acquiring technologies became a much more urgent need than purchasing large items of military hardware that would be expensive to develop and even more expensive to maintain. In 1978 alone, PRC officials, often without clear communication and coordination with one another, signed US$7.8 billion in technology import deals, a cost higher than the PRC's 1977 export revenue, which was US$7.6 billion. Furthermore, 1978's technology transfers focused mainly on heavy industry, which accounted for two-thirds of the costs. According to the economic historian Xiao Donglian, few projects were "moderate in investment, fast to see the result, and able to earn back foreign currencies."[59] Provincial officials who hosted those technology import projects also grossly overestimated their local governments' abilities to make the necessary domestic investment in infrastructure, labor, materials, and domestically produced parts, if they could be produced at all. In 1978, technology imports alone required RMB 130 billion in local investment, which far exceeded the entire government's total revenue of RMB 87.4 billion.[60]

During a Politburo meeting held from March 21 to March 23, 1979, Li Xiannian admitted that 1978's hastily made technology import policy was a mistake. The forecasts were too optimistic, Li concluded, and the sudden US$80 billion budget increase was too much for a country with limited means to earn foreign currencies. He summarized three mistakes: "All projects were bought with precious foreign currency reserves; we imported things even we can domestically produce; we signed US$7.8 billion worth of contracts but acquired no or very few patents."[61] In another meeting, he laid out the nine new strategies:

1. If we can make them ourselves, even if the quality is not as good as foreign-made, we will make them ourselves and gradually improve them.
2. If we can import the technology and make the equipment, then we won't buy the equipment.
3. If we can buy key components and make up the rest ourselves, then we won't buy the entire set of equipment.
4. If we have to buy the entire set, we will try to make some parts that fit the standard.
5. We will systematically import equipment and technology . . . and gradually produce our indigenous versions.

6. If the project is too big or complicated, we can hire foreign experts to help us design and build [it] and help us manage and build it in the future.
7. We will utilize foreign consulting agencies and let them offer us technical information and advice to make better decisions.
8. Any technology transfer and equipment import projects must be registered with the government to avoid monopoly and repetition.
9. We will simultaneously organize scientific and technical forces to research imported technology, digest it domestically, and innovate further.[62]

The end goals, Li suggested, were to save money, to acquire the foreigners' technical know-how, and eventually to produce those high-tech goods locally and cheaply in China. In addition, he urged them to find more imaginative ways to pay for those projects—through leases, foreign loans, joint ventures with foreign investors, and modern financial instruments.[63] Li recited Premier Zhou Enlai's slogan on modernizing China's agriculture, industry, national defense, and science and technology many times that year as a warning to his fellow comrades: "Money cannot buy us Four Modernizations."[64]

China did make a significant change in the finance models it used for technology acquisition: instead of making down payments using hard-earned foreign currency reserves, which caused a deficit by the end of 1978, PRC officials increasingly turned to foreign investment, loans, and modern financial instruments such as leverage leases to reduce the costs of technology acquisition. Deng and his comrades realized that technology transfer, financial innovation, and China's domestic economic reform had to be linked. In May 1979, the PRC State Council, with Deng's permission and Li Xiannian's detailed involvement, established the China International Trust Investment Corporation (CITIC). Its main aim was, as it still is today, to attract foreign investment—particularly at that time from the global Chinese diaspora communities—to help finance much-needed foreign technology transfer deals and the creation of jointly owned companies.[65] Led by Rong Yiren, a former businessman turned Communist politician who had been educated at Christian-run St John's University in Shanghai, the CITIC grew grow into the largest state-owned enterprise in China by the late 2010s and became the most critical and controversial financial institution in China's global quest for advanced foreign technologies.[66]

This new, more intelligent approach was reflected in the 1979 round of PRC-UK negotiations, as bringing down the price and acquiring a local Harrier production line were the Chinese negotiating team's two new demands. British negotiators noted that Chinese tactics had significantly changed and that the Chinese negotiating team complained that they were paying too much for too little.[67] During a British Aerospace delegation's visit to China, the Chinese frankly told British officials that they could not accept the fact that the US Marine Corps was paying less for a more advanced version of the Harrier than the Chinese had to pay for a watered-down version that was ten years behind the Marine Corps model.[68] The Americans also reported a change in the Chinese attitude toward arms acquisition in 1979: "Despite a flurry of speculation last fall that China would become a major arms buyer, China appears still to be studying what it should do given its domestic priorities and limitations. We expect that the Chinese will continue to examine the foreign arms market closely, but it will take some time before concluding significant agreements, if any. China will probably opt to acquire only technology and samples to evolve Chinese-modified weaponry, which can be produced in quantity."[69]

The negotiations slowed down significantly in the 1980s, while another vital factor made the Chinese change their mind. The Soviet invasion of Afghanistan in December 1979 completely transformed the way the Carter administration's military export policy operated toward China. Now, seeing China as a potential ally in the Cold War, US officials quickly realized that allowing US companies to sell weapons directly to the Chinese was far more convenient—and lucrative. Why let the Europeans make all the money when Americans could do the business themselves and put pressure on the Russians at the same time? In January 1980, Secretary Brown flew to Beijing with a newly sanctioned list of defense-related items—a new "Made-in-America shopping menu" for the Chinese military that ranged from aviation equipment, targeting electronics, and trainer simulators for pilots to military satellites and radars. Thus, Brown kick-started the unprecedented and rather strange episode of US-China military cooperation that characterized this period in the Cold War.[70]

To make doing business easier, the rules had to change. On March 13, 1980, a US State Department official announced to fellow COCOM members that the United States would apply a new set of regulations to China; this China differential proposal would allow it to sell "to China all types of COCOM listed arms and equipment, whether for military or civilian use," while restrictions on the Soviet Union and other Eastern bloc countries would remain the same. To make other COCOM members feel better and allow them to get a share of the profit, the State Department promised to publish a new guideline in case "other COCOM members should propose export to China too."[71]

For British Aerospace, serious competition had started. "China may have had second thoughts about making an agreement with the UK for the Harrier ground-attack aircraft for operational and economic reasons," observed the Americans, but "the Chinese continued to emphasize the acquisition of electronics, components, manufacturing processes, and test equipment that will improve their ability to develop and produce sophisticated military hardware." For example, "they recently signed an agreement with Pratt and Whitney of Canada to obtain the technology to manufacture the PT-6 Turboshaft engine that they have installed on Chinese-made MI-4 Helicopter[s] and possibly on a new helicopter."[72] Thus, in 1980, there was a bizarre period when the US and UK governments were competing with one another not just in weapons sales to China but also in their diplomatic efforts to dismantle COCOM regulations, very much to the bewilderment of more rule-abiding members such as West Germany and Japan. German records showed that on September 26, 1980, the British government proposed to COCOM members that a special exception be applied to China on three sets of items: "industry list, international munitions list, and atomic energy list." Further, it proposed that "in the absence of agreed procedure in COCOM" on the sale of "equipment or even weapons," the British government could just assume that it had permission, and the deal could go ahead.[73] When all the member states finally sat down to discuss this proposal in November, most countries had no opinion on what to do with the British proposal. The United States, Japan, and Norway agreed with minor amendments, and West Germany was the only member that opposed the change.[74]

CASE STUDY 2: FRENCH–WEST GERMAN COMPETITION IN A NUCLEAR REACTOR SALE TO CHINA

Even though the British Harrier sale came to an unsatisfying end, more doors in the West opened to China. On October 15, 1979, CCP Chairman Hua Guofeng started his twenty-two-day European tour in Paris and made headlines worldwide (figure 3.2). It was, according to the *New York Times*, "the first time in its 4,000-year history [that] China's leader has ventured out to Western Europe." Hua, as reported, was on a mission to seek help from the Europeans in modernizing China's industry and military.[75]

Hua's choice of Paris as his first stop had great symbolic significance. After all, France was the first Western European country to publicly recognize the PRC in 1964.[76] This was an act humorously described by the witty and sarcastic American diplomat-historian Warren Zimmermann, who was a foreign officer in Paris at the time, as de Gaulle's attempt "to

FIGURE 3.2 Hua Guofeng with Paris Mayor Jacques Chirac during his 1979 visit to the French capital. Image by Raymond Mesnildrey. (Bibliothèque de l'Hôtel de Ville)

demonstrate an independent foreign policy (vis-a-vis the US)" and had more to do with "French pride and France's image of itself as a world power." Zimmermann thus concluded that "France, as the maverick and independent member of the West, was the logical target of China's preliminary and instant step into the world stage." On a more practical note, he reported that China would like to give the French "preferential trade treatment in return for arms sales and weapons technology."[77] Besides China's unique role in French national pride, there was a deeper historical reason for Hua's warm reception in Paris at this particular moment. In the late 1970s, Europe was hit by the full weight of the energy crisis, compounded by decades of deindustrialization, as well as competition from emerging markets because of globalization. The working class, traditional unions, and people who earned their living in conventional heavy industries suffered the most in those crises.[78] The benefits of the service and information technology boom of the 1990s were still a decade and a half away. At that moment, the beginning of this continent-wide economic "sector shift" caused only high unemployment and deepening political crises in traditionally industrialized countries like France and West Germany.[79] A Chinese market that was suddenly open for technology and industrial products seemed too good for Europeans to pass up.

Hua specifically wished to purchase two Framatome nuclear reactors capable of generating 900 MW of electricity from the French. It was an important business opportunity for the French, and the deal would be worth F 5.2 billion in cash or F 5.3 billion if the Chinese needed to take out loans. According to French sources, the Chinese Ministry of Commerce had forwarded the formal request a year earlier, in December 1978.[80] In addition, Chinese sources suggest that Li Xiannian specifically gave a written reminder to Vice Premier Gu Mu, who was in charge of external economic relations and oversight of the reactor project, that they should find a way to access French technologies through the deal. "Even if technology transfer is not allowed [in the initial agreement], you must find a way to get those technologies."[81]

The French-Chinese reactor negotiations alarmed US officials on two different but related grounds. First, those reactors were not entirely French, as they incorporated patented US technologies and were thus subject to the US Commerce Department's export control measures. Second, because those reactors could produce plutonium as a by-product, they could be used in making atomic weapons in addition to generating electricity. Therefore, they were considered American-made strategic goods, fell under COCOM regulations, and were not supposed to be sold to Communist countries. Overall, the deal ran against the Carter administration's arms control and nonproliferation principle that no Western country should facilitate the spread of nuclear technology in the developing world, especially when it had potential military uses. Thus, this sale was highly problematic for US nonproliferation officials.

Rumors about the French-Chinese deal first surfaced as early as 1977. Secretary Vance wrote to Brzezinski that those French reactors would allow China to access fuel-processing technologies they did not yet possess and that it was likely they could pass it to the Pakistanis, whose request for similar technology from the French had been refused. He noted, "We have, of course, a strong interest in encouraging Chinese cooperation on non-proliferation in general, including safeguards as a condition of any supply the PRC might undertake."[82] Throughout late 1977 and 1978, the Americans repeatedly expressed their concern to the French and asked them to obtain assurances from the Chinese that they would use those reactors only for generating electricity and would not pass secret information about them to others; specifically, the Americans sought the inclusion of this clause in the sale contract: "The materials produced [from the reactors] shall not be used by the PRC for explosive and military purposes."[83]

"EXCLUSIVELY CIVILIAN AND PEACEFUL... TOTALLY FREE FROM ANY SUSPICION"

Records suggest that the French diplomats knew very clearly from the beginning of their negotiations with the Chinese that any reactor the French sold to China would be used to make atomic bombs, but they chose to ignore it. As early as November 1975, a delegation from the French nuclear industry led by Jean Teillac, a well-known nuclear physicist and later the French representative to the European Organization for Nuclear Research, conducted a two-week inspection tour in China as an ice-breaking trip to foster future French-Chinese nuclear cooperation.

Teillac and his team inspected most major Chinese nuclear facilities, from uranium mines to nuclear power plants and research institutes. The tour was so detailed that the Chinese insisted the French not publicly disclose any portion of it. In the final report to the French Ministry of Energy and the Ministry of Foreign Affairs, Teillac warned that he had reached a "quasi-conviction" that China's nuclear activities were meant for military purposes because "the existence of plutonium production for military purposes . . . had followed a similar path to that of France" in both "the production of fissile materials" and "the plutonium extraction" processes. The overall picture also tipped off the French scientists because there were far more activities "linked to the nuclear fuel cycle, on a scale compared to other big countries," in contrast to a "lack of dynamism for other activities such as reactors and laboratories." Teillac concluded, "This contrast can be explained only by a high strategic [military] priority given to the former [plutonium production] over the latter [research and electricity generation]."[84]

However, the French expedition's purpose was not to judge whether China's nuclear activities were designed to make bombs. Instead, Teillac's team was highly interested in China's extensive uranium resources and the possibility of exchanging them for French nuclear reactors. Their Chinese counterparts, too, were interested in such mutually beneficial exchanges, as "they don't exclude the possibility of selling raw material in exchange, oil for example, but no uranium for now." At the end of their tour, the French delegation even met with Premier Hua, who lectured them about the monopoly of the imperialists (Americans) and imperialist socialists (Soviets) on nuclear affairs and, quoting from Mao's little red book, about the need for China and France "to rely on their own strength in the face of the hegemony of the two superpowers."[85] Upon receiving the delegation's report, Jean Simon, the secretary general of defense and national security, completely ignored the fact that French-Chinese nuclear cooperation might not be peaceful and pushed for another meeting with a focus on "exports of sensitive materials" and "the confidential openings of the Chinese authorities on [French] reactors."[86]

The French interest in Chinese uranium sources continued in 1976 and 1977, prior to the formal Chinese request for the two Framatome reactors. In fact, French scientists eagerly worked all over China and helped the Chinese survey uranium deposits. For example, the French geologists' delegation wrote back an enthusiastic report after their visit in November 1976, saying "China has great potential in uranium resources (perhaps a million tons)." They are "investing heavily into them [extractions]" and, quoting their Chinese counterpart, "could be able to sell soon." This was a signal that "the Chinese are starting to be more open to French-Chinese cooperation and says the French should seize the opportunity."[87] Thus, the French had a far more substantial interest in getting Chinese uranium and selling reactors to the Chinese than in telling the Americans all the inconvenient secrets about China's nuclear program. It was no wonder the French officials, especially those at the French Ministry of Foreign Affairs, decided to play a cat-and-mouse game with the Americans—one the Chinese were happy to play. On October 9, 1978, President Giscard d'Estaing's confidante Secretary General Jean François-Poncet, soon to be appointed as the next foreign minister, reached a gentleman's agreement with the Chinese ambassador that France did not care what China would do with French reactors, and that as long as both France and China pretended their cooperation was peaceful, he would give the Framatome deal the green light. François-Ponce, in a humorous way, said:

> The nuclear cooperation between France and China is moving in a satisfactory direction. . . . We certainly know that everything nuclear has a political aspect to it because the atom has both civil and military applications. France, however, does not intend to do anything in its foreign policy which may appear to contribute to the development of nuclear weapons. As both of our countries are both nuclear weapons states, it is of the utmost importance that our nuclear collaboration, which is exclusively civilian and peaceful, be totally free from any suspicion. This is why we believe that an intergovernmental agreement should accompany the eventual contract between the industrialists, an agreement designed to demonstrate the peaceful character of the French-Chinese nuclear cooperation . . . in doing so, we have no intention of preventing the development of China's activities in the military nuclear field. We do not intend to ask China for the type of guarantees that we ask other Framatome customers. But we want to show that our nuclear cooperation is in no way related to the military programs which are being developed independently in each of our countries.[88]

It is no wonder that French officials in the United States were acting suspiciously a week before testimony to the US Congress on the request for American permission for the French sale. "De Laboulaye [the French ambassador] came in today," noted an American nonproliferation official. "He said that he had authority from Paris to say that it was all right to pass the substance of the Framatome proposed deal to the [US] Congress . . . [for a final review]." However, the French government did not want any original text of the Chinese-French contract to go to Congress, as there was no need for US congressmen to read the contract. "It [the contract] was pretty much the same as I [the American official] had seen before," promised the slick French ambassador. "It talked about pacifist uses, physical security."[89]

WEST GERMAN CONDITIONALITIES

The Americans and, to a lesser degree, the French also faced another complication: The Chinese engaged in parallel negotiations with the FRG for possible reactor purchases. German records suggest that the Chinese had already informed FRG officials in December 1977 of their interest in purchasing a nuclear reactor. Both sides began to consult one another every month, and in a high-level visit, Gu Mu, Deng's top economic aide, met with Otto Graf Lambsdorff, the West German federal minister for economic affairs. However, those negotiations were likewise delayed—but now because the more cautious West Germans had a much stricter interpretation of COCOM regulations, which meant they had to consult with the Americans separately at each step.[90]

Comparing British, French, and German records shows that West Germany was the only rule-following member of COCOM in that that refrained from selling obviously military-use goods to China. The German company Siemens, for example, in 1977, dutifully applied for a COCOM license for the export of a second-generation electronic data processing system for a shipyard in Hangzhou.[91] However, the FRG was the buzzkill for other, more "business-oriented" countries when it came to dual-use or military goods. In May 1977, the West German delegation blocked Japan's proposal to export computers to China, citing the case as "a special treatment . . . [and] thus would lead to discrimination against the other countries subject to the COCOM embargo." Concurrently, the British and Americans asked for "more flexible interpretations."[92] Throughout 1978, West German diplomats tried to convince their French counterparts that unilaterally selling French–West German coproduced long-range HOT antitank missiles to China—even if already approved by the Carter administration—was a violation of COCOM and, according to Peter Hermes, a state secretary at the Ministry of Foreign Affairs, an act that "would hardly be understood by the [West German] public."[93] Even as late as May 1979, when the British notified COCOM members that they would send China a list of armaments—radar, imaging tubes, artillery computers, motor targeting devices, and tank night vision equipment—and would do so under the "no comment policy" regardless of others' opinions, the West German government sent an official demarche to the UK Foreign Office, stating that this action would "constitute a violation of COCOM policy" and that "we do not agree with the British 'no-comment' policy."[94]

Bonn's literal interpretation of COCOM regulations concerned those who advocated better West Germany–China relations. The most radical proposal came from Erwin Wickert, the West German ambassador to China. Ambassador Wickert wrote to Chancellor Helmut Schmidt on August 15, 1978, that West Germany should do more to improve relations with China and that there was no such thing as basing its China policy on Soviet policy. "Since Brzezinski's Beijing visit on May 4, the relationship between Beijing and Washington has changed and greatly improved. . . . Chinese high-ranking figures are touring the USA, some even incognito! It would be a shame if China prioritized the USA and became less interested in us." He concluded, "Germany's opportunity in world politics would grow when we are more closely linked economically and politically with China." However, "our economic connections were severely hindered by COCOM restrictions and we hear from German merchants all the time that Japanese, British, and the French are defying the rules." What the government in Bonn can do to help, then, "is for you, Chancellor, to publicly declare that China should be excluded from the circle of countries subject to COCOM restrictions."[95] The other politicians in Bonn were not ready to go this far. During September's cabinet meeting,

Volker Hauff, the federal minister for technology and research, called the ambassador's proposal "problematic in multiple sections" and instructed the ambassador "to leave no impression" on his Chinese contact Fang Yi, the vice premier and Deng's close ally, that improving relations between the two countries could mean that "we will change the COCOM regulation to specifically benefit China."[96]

The rest of the cabinet also moved cautiously, especially on the nuclear reactor deal. As the FRG did not have nuclear weapons and did not wish to anger the Soviets, how to make a responsible deal became a central theme in Bonn's internal discussions. Even the energy sector's workers' union, which had a financial interest in the sale, wrote a carefully phrased letter to State Secretary Hans Hilger Haunschild in the Federal Ministry of Research and Technology that the reactor sales should go ahead only when considered alongside "the political consequences of China's role as a nuclear-weapon state" and "after [the FRG has] fully explored the opinion and received acceptance from friendly countries within the COCOM structure."[97]

Chinese officials thus became concerned about West German conditionalities—COCOM approval, safeguards, and a clear definition of what is and in not a weapon—and tried to use their current negotiations with the French to bargain for "equal treatment." A memorandum dated July 15, 1978, from Minister of Economy of the Federal State of Hesse Heinz-Herbert Karry to Foreign Minister Hans-Dietrich Genscher laid out this complex picture. Karry reported that Xie Peiyi, the Chinese commissioner on foreign investment and import-export, had told him and other West German officials that the Chinese had to "give it a second thought," considering that "West Germany was in the complete opposite position to France who had no attached [nonproliferation] conditions." He was also concerned that "the delivery of reactors from West Germany to China could only be possible if China subjected itself to supervision by the International Atomic Energy Organization's control in Vienna, while the delivery of French reactors had no such attached conditions." Karry nevertheless judged the Chinese proposal for the West Germans to "do it like the French—export the reactors without any different or additional restrictions" was incomprehensible and challenging to accept. The conversation with Xie caused West German officials to realize that the French were outsmarting them—and perhaps with American help.

"French sales, in principle, should also be like the case in Germany—to be subject to COCOM reviews. It is thus in our opinion that the French must have gotten some leeway from their direct negotiations with the Americans. West Germany so far hasn't done anything similar to it [meaning to talk to the Americans] but should do it soon and do it craftily."[98]

A comparison of documents in Paris, Bonn, and Washington shows a strange dynamic surrounding China's reactor purchase in the last few months of 1978. The Chinese were bargaining over price with the French, saying that they could go to the West Germans at any moment. Meanwhile, the West Germans, especially the energy workers' union representatives, watched the more advanced French-Chinese negotiations with both jealousy and anxiety and then used the fact that China was indeed talking to their French competitors as an excuse to press their own officials to approve the sale.[99] In Washington, meanwhile, Carter administration officials tried their best to keep the French–West German competition under control. On December 6, 1978, French embassy staff finally reported to the US State Department that they had obtained a written, albeit vague, assurance from the Chinese that those reactors would be used for "peaceful purposes" and that Framatome would "minimize any transfer of technology beyond that needed to ensure the safe operation of the reactor." In addition, "the manufacturing technology will not be transferred, and there will be contractual provisions against replication or subsequent retransfer of technology."[100]

Also, because the French reactors contained US technology while the West German reactors did not, the Carter administration determined that it still had some legal control over what China could do with the French reactors. Finally, the State Department decided that it would prefer the French to make the first sale rather than the West Germans.[101] On December 18, 1978, Gerard Smith, Carter's special representative on arms control, and Assistant Secretary of State Thomas Pickering dumped the White House's decision on the poorly informed US Congress in a passive-aggressive manner during a hearing: "The significance is that the French had obtained from the PRC at our behest . . . a government-to-government peaceful uses assurance . . . and minimum subsequent transfer from the PRC [to third countries], and the fact [is] that the West Germans would likely make the sale, without any US involvement, if we were to deny it to the French."[102] Without much choice, the members of Congress "gave no sign they would object" but "said they wished they had been consulted earlier." On December 25, 1978, Pickering formally gave the green light to Framatome Vice President Yves Girard, who was in Washington, D.C., eagerly waiting for the Americans' final decision. The French, it seemed, had finally secured an excellent business deal with China.[103]

In 1979, the French reactor sale suffered a fate similar to that of the British Harrier deal—not only were the talks stuck on pricing issues, but also China wanted the transfer of technologies related to the reactors that the French were unwilling to give.[104] Li Xiannian, who in 1978 had been enthusiastic about this project's potential to access French nuclear technology, became more reserved in 1979 and instructed the negotiating team on April 1 to "reevaluate the project, carefully study the pros and cons." He also asked the team to eliminate any political consideration from negotiations; "this deal," Li assured, "does not have to accommodate the friendly relations between China and France."[105] The West Germans also adjusted their policy but far too late. For all of 1979, they had refused to conduct the sale bilaterally with China and waited patiently for US instructions, which never came. Only on September 10, 1980, after the United States had announced the China differential in March of that year and after six months of intense debate did Chancellor Schmidt, supported by the ministers of defense and commerce, finally agree to match the French position: i.e., to trade the reactor bilaterally with China instead of multilaterally through COCOM and to ask only for an oral instead of a written safeguard. But the chancellor still insisted that West Germany would not deliver weapons to China, even though, admittedly, "we were in no position to stop our European partners from doing so."[106]

By that time, China's priority also had changed. Instead of purchasing two commercial reactors from either France or West Germany, the Chinese in 1980 started a different negotiation. China asked for just one experimental reactor from France, as well as the transfer of an extensive list of associated technologies and training for Chinese operators and technicians. This strategy, it turned out, worked for both sides and was far more economical and beneficial in the long term for China.[107] Sixteen years later, in 1996, this new project finally bore fruit as China fired up the new jointly built French-Chinese reactors in Daya Bay after the French had trained a new generation of Chinese nuclear experts.[108] This cooperation continued far beyond the Cold War, as demonstrated by the

Taishan Nuclear Power Plant, which opened in 2018, powered by two new French-designed reactors. The opening ceremony was lavish and symbolically praised in the Chinese press as a sign of China's ability to win friends in the West despite the escalating US-China trade war and a new round of US technological embargos on Chinese firms.[109]

EUROPEAN ARMS SALES TO CHINA AND THE EAST-WEST DÉTENTE

From a Cold War perspective, the European technology transfer negotiations with China just described also coincided with the Soviet Union's reevaluation of its Asia strategy in the face of rapidly advancing US-China military cooperation. It seems that the Soviet Union's own containment policy against China was also failing on the European front in addition to the American and Japanese fronts. For example, after two Chinese military delegations visited London in May 1978 to discuss arms purchases, Soviet diplomats told their GDR colleagues that the British effort to arm China, as well as "Owen's statement that [the] USSR is the common enemy of China and Britain," contributed to the worsening Soviet-British relations, which were already strained by the two countries' competing interventions in Africa.[110]

What China was doing in Europe only confirmed the fear of Brezhnev and his foreign policy analysts that the United States was arming the Chinese so as to encircle the Soviet Union. Mikhail Sladkovskii, the director of the Far East Institute, painted a grim picture in his February 1978 report titled "The political situation in Asia and the problems of collective security:" "The opposition force against the Soviet Union in East Asia now included the USA, Japan, South Korea, and the extremely anti-Soviet China. . . . Carter was playing the China card when he said America had parallel strategic interests in Asia, which was intended to incorporate China's anti-Soviet principles under the disguise of collective security."[111] According to Sladkovskii, in his opening address to the Soviet Communist Party Central Committee's special meeting on China, China's relations with Europe were intended to "allow Beijing to coordinate with the imperialists, to use anti-Soviet propaganda to attack socialist countries . . . and to get close to NATO. China's new relationship with Western Europe, under the guise of 'mutual security,' is now an emerging threat to the Warsaw Pact."[112]

Furthermore, Brezhnev's advisers were especially disturbed by China's purchases of weapons from NATO countries, which they saw as a more extensive and deeper Chinese conspiracy to ally itself with the military-industrial complex in Western countries. In a joint report by the American and Canadian Studies Institute and the Far East Institute, the Soviet experts on both Chinese and American politics agreed that the current trade and economic cooperation between China and the West "cannot just be seen as China's way to get technologies, weapons, or means of production, but also as China's attempt to mobilize anti-Soviet resources in capitalist states, in the form of [China's] support of NATO." Americans, of course, were the masterminds behind the conspiracy. "Brzezinski had nothing new; he was trying to arm the Chinese to pressure the Soviet Union."[113]

On November 20, 1978, Vyacheslav Ivanovich Dolgov, the Soviet ambassador's political counselor, delivered to the British Foreign Office a personal letter from Brezhnev. While the letter was intended for the prime minister, it is unclear whether Callaghan read the letter, since George G. Walden, secretary at the Foreign Office, shoved Dolgov out, saying the "United Kingdom's relations with China were not directed at any third country." That letter, preserved in the British Foreign Office files, showed Brezhnev's frustration:

Dear Mr. Prime Minister,

I am addressing you on a major issue that is not only important for a due mutual understanding in our bilateral relations but also transcends them and has a direct bearing on the problems of detente and maintaining peace. This issue is military sales to China. I would share the view that the question of supplying arms to this or that state cannot be considered alienation from the policy of this state. This is yet more so with regard to China, whose leadership is advocating war and is doing so openly, in front of the very eyes of everybody. . . . Recently, one can, however, hear statements about the possibility of postponing the war . . . but in fact,

Peking leaders applaud any aggravation of international tensions, and where they can provoke and cause them, and on the contrary, anything that benefits detente is anathema to them. How can one turn a blind eye to that?

Then Brezhnev talked about the lack of a clear distinction between "defensive" and "offensive weapons"; further, "China, having as it is one of the biggest armies in the world, takes a stand against disarmament, has not signed a single treaty concerning disarmament and makes a stake on further growth of arms of its own." Therefore, "military deliveries to China... must be stopped, and stopped in time, without delay."[114] It seemed, from Brezhnev's perspective, that two of the Soviet Union's most evil enemies, the Maoist-Revisionist Chinese and the Imperialist-Militarists in NATO, were forging an anti-Soviet alliance in a nightmarish scenario.

However, Deng Xiaoping and his comrades argued precisely the opposite: that the Soviet Union, not China, was the evil empire that needed to be contained. Or as Hua Guofeng told Vice President Walter Mondale on August 28, 1979, "We have told many visiting American friends that we must work together to cope with the Polar Bear. Our late Chairman told visiting American friends that we should form a line stretching from the United States, Western Europe, China, and Japan. This is because we recognize that the main danger of war at present comes from the Soviet Union.... The Soviet Union is still trying to take advantage of openings everywhere to expand."[115] In Europe, Chinese top officials and diplomats engaged in a similar polemic against the Soviet Union in order to get the weapons that Brezhnev warned Europeans not to sell. Chinese Foreign Minister Huang Hua, for example, told Prime Minister Callaghan during the Harrier sale negotiations that "the Soviet Union talked about detente, disarmament and economic cooperation in Europe but at the same time was extending her influence ... in the countries peripheral to Europe. If a crisis came about or if an emergency arose, China feared that the West would find itself in a situation in which it wanted to resist the Soviet Union but could not do so." The British prime minister, in return, "expressed he had similar concerns."[116]

France, too, became a battleground of opinions between the Chinese and the Soviets. This was despite the fact that the French were driven by their desire to become an independent nuclear power alongside both of the superpowers, a view that was very much shared by their Chinese partners. For example, the French complained among themselves about the United States and its COCOMs and its "excessive insistence on the question of controls [that] could lead to China preferring the German partners."[117] Meanwhile, they fondly recalled France and China's shared special status as nuclear weapons states and cited this as a reason for China to stick with the French on nuclear matters.[118] In a bid to both inform and influence, Chinese diplomats told the West Germans that they should not expect the Chinese-French negotiations to be slowed down by COCOM restrictions. "Why [should we care] about the COCOM?" asked the Chinese. "China and France will not let their nuclear cooperation be influenced by the superpowers."[119]

It was the Carter administration, however, that faced the strongest pressure from the Soviet Union on European arms sales to China, as Brezhnev and his advisers saw the United States' dirty hands behind every European arms delivery to China—small and large, real or imagined. NATO arms sales to China turned out to be a major point of contention in US-Soviet relations. As early as 1977, anxious Soviet diplomats had visited the US Liaison Office in Beijing multiple times trying to confirm rumors, mostly picked up from Hong Kong street tabloids, that NATO members were selling weapons or military-related technologies to the Chinese. In 1977, the Americans could still pretend those rumors were unsubstantiated and send the curious Soviet visitors away: "The US has no plans to sell weapons to the PRC, while, in any case, [the] PRC probably would not wish to buy weapons from the US" was the standard response.[120] However, a year later, as additional evidence confirmed those tabloid rumors to be true, the Soviets decided to bring the issue to the highest level of US-Soviet relations.

By late 1978, Western arms sales had become a significant cause of tension between the United States and the Soviet Union. On September 30, 1978, Soviet Foreign Minister Andrei Gromyko protested to President Carter that he had noted reports "appearing from time to time in the press to the effect that China intended or had already begun to purchase large quantities of arms from various countries, perhaps from some of the US allies and perhaps from the United States as well. . . . If something like this were indeed taking place, it would be a very major problem that could seriously impact the relations between our two countries."[121] Brezhnev himself was even more direct in a message intended to pressure the

United States to prevent its allies from selling weapons to China. He wrote to Carter that "a number of US allies are preparing—and this is an open secret—deals for deliveries of arms and transfer of technology to Peking," where "it is well known that the US has not the least role to play." It was a dangerous move on the part of the United States that could only lead to actions by the Soviet Union to further arm itself, Brezhnev argued, and as a result, "there can hardly remain any doubts that contributing to the armament of China does not strengthen but, on the contrary, erodes trust in our relations which is being built with such difficulty."[122]

However, arming the Chinese was precisely what US hard-liners wanted, and the warning of the Soviet officials was brushed aside. On January 6, 1980, a week after the invasion of Afghanistan, a delegation of US Defense Department officials, led by Ambassador George Seignious, the director of the Arms Control and Disarmament Agency, arrived in China and met with Admiral Liu Huaqing, another of Deng's supporter in the PLA, who was also remembered in China as the father of China's modernized navy. Seignious told Liu that times had changed "since the days when COCOM was formed" and that "we have been considering on a case-by-case basis the transfer of technology to China, which we would not provide the Soviet Union."[123] At the same time in Washington, Secretary of Defense Brown told visiting Chinese Vice Premier Gen Biao, another of Deng's trusted generals who was now a politician, that the Soviet invasion of Afghanistan required a new level of strategic cooperation between the United States and China, such that the "tightening up of technology transfers to the Soviet Union and high-technology sales" would "also take place at the same time [as] technology transfers to the PRC are moving in the reverse direction."[124] Carter's change of policy, which started to show results in 1981, was continued by the Reagan administration. From 1982 to 1986, the United States sold US$88.8 million in arms to China and transferred another US$520.5 million in military and dual-use technologies.[125]

CONCLUSION

The West European "weak link" in China's global technology acquisition strategy was a critical yet understudied point of contention in the

US-Soviet détente during this period of the Cold War. In 1978, Western European countries offered the PRC their military and dual-use technology with a clear green light from the White House. US defense industries entered the competition with Western Europeans to see technology and arms to China after the Soviet invasion of Afghanistan in December 1979, and the 1980s marked the decline of the COCOM system and a turning point in China's industrial and military development. As shown in table 3.1, China enjoyed unprecedented access to Western arms and technology. Its access to European military and dual-use technology even survived the Tiananmen Square massacre in 1989 under the disguise of civilian trade deals.[126] Western Europe—mainly the UK and France—remained a weak link in the US-led effort to maintain global export controls toward China long after the end of the Cold War.

TABLE 3.1 Major Western Arms Sales to China, 1979–1993

Supplier	Number ordered	Weapon designation	Weapon description	Year(s) of order/license	Year(s) of delivery/ production	Comments
Canada	3	Challenger 601	Transport	1985	1986	For VIP transport
Canada	2	Challenger 601	Transport	1988	1988–1989	Deal worth $35 million; for VIP transport
France	50	AS-365N Dauphin II	Helicopter	1980	1982–1992	Chinese designation Z-9 Haitun; includes production for civil use
France	6	AS-332 Super Puma	Helicopter	1985	1985–1986	
France	3	SA-321H Super Frelon	Helicopter	1985	1985–1989	For PLANavy; Chinese designation Z-8
France	5	Rasit E	Radar	1986	1986	
France	—	AIFV turret upgrade	Armored vehicle turret	1986	1986	

(continued)

TABLE 3.1 (continued)

Supplier	Number ordered	Weapon designation	Weapon description	Year(s) of order/license	Year(s) of delivery/ production	Comments
France	—	A-5K avionics upgrade	Avionics system	1987	1987–1989	
France	8	SA-342L Gazelle	Helicopter	1988	1988–1989	
France	96	HOT-2 ATM	Antitank missile	1988	1988–1989	
France	—	Crotale SAM	Surface-to-air missile	1989	1989–1993	For 1 Luhu Class and refit on 1 Luda Class destroyer; deal worth $91.5 million including Crotale naval modular launchers and radar
Israel	—	Python III SAM	Air-to-air missile	1990	1990–1993	Chinese designation PL-9
Italy	—	Aspide SAM	Surface-to-air missile	1989	1990–1991	For planned J-8 II (F-8 II) fighters; status of last 30 uncertain after J-8 II development stopped in 1990
UK	200+	F-7M avionics upgrade	Avionics system	1979–1989	1979–1989	
UK	—	AIFV turret upgrade	Armored vehicle turret	1984–1986	1984–1986	
UK	—	T-59 MBT turret upgrade	Turret	1985	1985	
UK	4	105 mm main gun	Tank gun	1987	1987	
UK	1	Watchman	Radar	1987	1987	
FRG (West Germany)	8	Bo-105C	Helicopter	1979–1980	1979–1981	
FRG (West Germany)	—	Diesel engine	Engine	1984–1989	1984–1989	Licensed production

Source: Based on table 2.2 and appendix 1 of Stockholm International Peace Research Institute's *China's Arms Acquisitions from Abroad: A Quest for "Superb and Secret" Weapons* (Stockholm International Peace Research Institute, 1994).

4

CHIANG CHING-KUO AND TAIWAN'S SEARCH FOR SECURITY

The ROC's efforts to enhance its security in the late 1970s were often constrained by its limited capabilities, diminishing US support, and constant threats from the CCP regime on the mainland. From the secret attempt to acquire nuclear weapons to the failed fighter jet deal with Israel, Taiwanese leader Chiang Ching-kuo, despite his ambitions, had to make significant compromises in the ROC's pursuit of security.

In the late 1970s, Deng Xiaoping was not the only Chinese leader who lived under the shadow of the US-Soviet arms race and felt threatened by the technological gap between the military under his command and those of the two Cold War superpowers. Chiang Ching-kuo, the Nationalist leader in Taiwan, also feared the consequences of an inadequate military. The Republic of China Army (ROCA) was too far behind the others to protect the country, especially after 1979, when the United States not only abandoned its formal security commitment to the ROC but also started selling weapons and technologies to its Communist rivals in the PRC. How to ensure Taiwan's security with diminished US support became a priority for Chiang and for the ROC's multilateral Cold War diplomacy (figure 4.1).

Before we delve into Taiwan's secret nuclear weapons program and its attempted fighter jet purchase from Israel, it is essential to point out

FIGURE 4.1 KMT leader Chiang Ching-kuo and his Belarusian wife, Chiang Fang-liang. When his father, Chiang Kai-shek, was alive, Chiang Ching-kuo was already in charge of Taiwan's secret nuclear program. (Academia Historica)

that both Chiang Kai-shek and his son Chiang Ching-kuo had ambitious plans for the ROC. However, their Cold War competition with the CCP on the mainland led to many unfortunate episodes in their already complicated relations with the United States long before Jimmy Carter became the US president in 1977. Formally, the ROC was placed under US protection by the 1954 Mutual Defense Treaty Between the United States and the Republic of China, negotiated between Chiang Kai-shek and the Eisenhower administration in response to the PRC's entry into the Korean War and the first Taiwan Strait Crisis, during which the PLA shelled and partially took over one of the Nationalist-controlled offshore islands.[1] Chiang Kai-shek, however, was not entirely satisfied with the 1954 treaty because it guaranteed US protection only over the territories that the ROC controlled—Taiwan and the Pescadores. Furthermore, the treaty would protect the ROC only when it was under external attack and stated nothing about lending US support to the ROC if Chiang launched an invasion against the mainland.² Those restrictions, as the excellent research by the Taiwanese historian Lin Hsiao-ting has shown, "limited the Nationalists' rule within the confines of Taiwan and the offshore islands," which "fundamentally crushed the Nationalists' future attempt to reclaim the Chinese mainland militarily."³

The Chiangs' deep dissatisfaction with the US security guarantee to the ROC led them to take a series of independent actions that severely strained the ROC's already fragile relations with the United States, particularly with the Jimmy Carter administration. I argue that these efforts, from their secret plans to reinvade the Chinese mainland to their backdoor diplomacy with the Soviet Union, from their global nuclear weapons technology shopping spree to their proposed advanced fighter jet purchase from US allies, show that the ROC's leaders always harbored strong Cold War ambitions. Still, they suffered from a combination of lack of resources and immediate threats from the mainland and, worst of all, from the Carter administration's decision to sacrifice Taiwanese security for the sake of seemingly more critical US-PRC cooperation in the larger global Cold War.

TAIWAN'S SECRET NUCLEAR PROGRAM

During the second Taiwan Strait Crisis, when in 1958 the PLA under Mao's command again started to shell the ROCA-controlled offshore islands of Quemoy and Matsu, US Secretary of State John Foster Dulles and PRC leader Chiang Kai-shek conducted three days of intense negotiations, trying to find a way to prevent the conflict from escalating further and possibly dragging the United States into another major war in Asia. On October 23, 1958, Chiang and Dulles issued a joint communiqué in which the United States expressed its solidarity with Chiang's Nationalist regime and its will to defend Taiwan, as well as the two offshore islands under PLA artillery fire. However, as insurance to prevent Chiang from using this crisis to start a full-scale war with the PRC, which would complicate US positions in Asia, Dulles forced Chiang, albeit grudgingly, to issue a guarantee within the communiqué that the ROC would not try to unify the country through military invasion.⁴

Dulles believed this would prevent Chiang from dragging the United States into a conflict with mainland China, while leaving the prospect of reunifying China under the Nationalists open, once the Communist regime on the mainland collapsed.[5] Behind the scenes, both sides were disappointed. Dulles could not ignore that Mao's CCP controlled most of China, and the United States could not possibly pretend that Chiang's KMT could take the mainland back—or even encourage such a military adventure. Chiang, however, felt even greater dissatisfaction, as he saw the United States' desire to make peace with the Communists and to maintain the status quo in the Taiwan Strait as a dangerous step toward creating a "political reality of two Chinas" in the international community, following the divisions of Germany and Korea. For Chiang, this was unacceptable because acceding to a two-China reality meant surrendering his claim to the Chinese mainland, a reality that would severely damage his domestic rule's legitimacy and national aspirations. In addition, Chiang was greatly disappointed that the United States refused to launch an attack to destroy the PLA's coastal artillery bases, which, for him, was the only sure way to stop the PLA from shelling those islands again.[6]

Chiang's disappointment at the United States' handling of the second Taiwan Strait Crisis gave birth to more secret and wild initiatives. Recently declassified Taiwanese documents demonstrate that in the early 1960s, Chiang, over the clear objections of US military advisers and the new Kennedy administration, was seriously reconsidering the possibility of invading the Chinese mainland by force—this time *without* US prior knowledge or military support. His unilateral crusade against the PRC led to a diplomatic disaster just weeks into the new administration: On February 15, 1962, as a part of a larger plan to invade the Chinese mainland through the jungles of South Asia, a ROC Air Force PB47 cargo plan was secretly dispatched to Burma to support local KMT commandos' guerrilla warfare against CCP forces along the Yunnan Province border. En route the plane was shot down by the Burmese Air Force, and the American-made weapons and supplies it carried were captured by the Burmese government, leading to nationwide anti-American protests in the small South Asian country.[7]

The Kennedy administration, already preoccupied with the escalating French-Indochina War, did not want another proxy war in another South Asian country involving both the ROC and the PRC. President Kennedy responded with harsh words and pressured Chiang to withdraw the KMT guerrilla forces from Burma. However, this disaster did not stop Chiang's ambition to reclaim the Chinese mainland.[8]

To avoid US suspicion, in 1961, Chiang secretly established the Guo-Guang Jihua [Nation's Light Plan], a bureau that he tasked with developing a new strategic plan to take over the Chinese mainland through a frontal assault across the Taiwan Strait. Between 1961 and 1965, the Guo-Guang planners drafted twenty-six different proposals on how to invade the PLA-controlled mainland and presented eighty-one secret studies to Chiang personally. All of these were developed under the specific condition that military operations would be carried out without US naval or air support. As a result, these reports were filled with topics such as "compact equipment transport," "speed offload," "using merchant ships to carry equipment," "sea-crossing capabilities," and "airborne attacks," all of which were essential to launching a surprise attack before the PLA—and, to a lesser degree, the United States—could react. The most detailed invasion plan was proposed to Chiang in December 1962, in which a "first wave of 39,000 troops, 1,174 vehicles, and 13,000 tons of equipment" would depart from Quemoy to attack the mainland city of Xiamen, opening up a landing zone for the successive waves of attacks. However, the plan noted several conditions that were essential for the rest of the invasion to succeed:

(1) The first phase of the "Guo-Guang Plan" must have achieved the expected results.
(2) Our naval and air forces must have gained and maintained naval and air superiority in the Taiwan Strait and target areas.
(3) Transport ships must be able to supply the needs of this operation.
(4) In this operation, neither the Communists nor our military forces can have the ability to use atomic weapons.[9]

THE COMMUNISTS AND THE BOMB

The Guo-Guang's secret invasion plan showed how determined the Chiang family was to commit Taiwan's limited resources to independent actions in the Cold War, especially considering it was planned with clear instructions that the United States would not be expected to support the invasion. The planning, detailed as it was on paper, never worked out in reality. The nightmarish scenario of atomic weapons being involved in such an invasion—and, worse, being used by the Communist PLA—came ever closer to reality in the early 1960s. In August 1963, both the US and the Taiwanese intelligence services suggested that Mao's nuclear program had entered its final stage.[10] In public, Chiang Ching-kuo—then in charge of "political warfare," a euphemism for internal propaganda and indoctrination, within the KMT Army—gave an anxious and self-contradictory speech to fellow political commissars in the army to boost their morale: If "Communist bandits exploded a nuclear weapon," it "would be totally political, and only good at scaring people" because "the Communist bandits don't have any scientific base." Even if an explosion happened, "it would be like the nuclear explosion conducted by the French—a nuclear explosion but not a nuclear warhead, and without any capacity to kill people."[11]

In secret, however, both father and son were deeply disturbed by the development on the mainland. Chiang Kai-shek sent Chiang Ching-kuo to Washington, D.C., to lobby the Kennedy administration to launch a joint attack on the mainland, during which the US Air Force would airlift platoons of brave ROCA commandos deep inside mainland China to launch a suicide attack on PRC nuclear facilities. This proposal, wild and unrealistic as it sounded, indeed raised some interest in the US intelligence community but came to nothing as the United States soon faced its own crisis with the assassination of President Kennedy.[12] After the ROC had been waiting anxiously for almost a year and had received no help from the new Johnson administration, the PRC exploded its first functioning nuclear weapon on October 16, 1964—and it was not just a simple experimental explosive device as Taiwanese and US intelligence officials had expected. Despite the Chiangs' public rhetoric, US records suggest that the family was in full panic behind closed doors. "The Republic of China and [Chiang] himself were the principal targets of the CHINCOMs," Chiang Kai-shek told US officials, and Taiwan "could be wiped out in one attack." Then he asked the Americans again to provide equipment and support to "destroy CHINCOM Nuclear Installations."[13] Chiang's unrealistic suggestions were rejected, as President Lyndon Johnson had no interest in involving the country in a war with China when US troops were already becoming entangled in the fighting in the jungles of Vietnam. Chiang Kai-shek responded most logically: The ROC needed its own nuclear bomb.

SHOPPING AROUND THE WORLD

In 1965, Chiang Kai-shek appointed Chiang Ching-kuo to be the ROC's new minister of defense in charge of its secret nuclear program, operating under the vague facade of "participating in the research and development of the nuclear industry."[14] Meanwhile, US diplomats started to pick up signals that the KMT was sending scientists worldwide to purchase nuclear technologies that could be used to produce a fusion bomb. On December 8, 1965, the US Embassy in Tel Aviv noticed that the director and the assistant directors of the Nationalist Chinese Atomic Energy Institute had made a suspicious trip to Israel, where they "met with Israeli scientists engaged in atomic research" and inspected one of Israel's nuclear reactors.[15] The Americans raised their eyebrows further when the US ambassador to West Germany noticed that the Taiwanese were negotiating with the West German government to buy "multi-purpose research nuclear reactors" from Siemens.[16] Meanwhile, Taiwanese officials awkwardly avoided questions when the International Atomic Energy Agency (IAEA) sent a team to visit their proposed reactor site, which the agency suspected was for military use.[17] In June, the US Embassy in Taipei concluded that the KMT was developing a nuclear weapons program despite the so-called peaceful research and development disguise.[18]

Over the next decade, the ROC Atomic Energy Council and the subordinate Institute for Nuclear Energy Research (INER), the cover agency for its nuclear weapons program, went on a global shopping spree. A truly multilateral project involving a dozen Western nations, the ROC's secret nuclear weapon program included a small heavy-water reactor purchased from Canada in 1969 and additional equipment from France, West Germany, and even the United States. INER also hired a Norwegian scientist to operate the reactor using uranium smuggled from South Africa. In 1973, the ROC imported more nuclear technologies from France. By 1975–1976, it had set up another plutonium reprocessing lab, which produced military-grade metallic plutonium based on American liquid-form plutonium it had initially imported for "civilian research" purposes. According to Professor Wu Ta-you, former president of Academia Sinica and an internal opponent of Taiwan's nuclear weapons program, "Chiang Ching-Kuo, the President's son, then at the Defense Ministry, secretly decided to pursue the separation of plutonium without his father's knowledge." This claim, however, cannot be verified from other Taiwanese sources.[19]

For the time being, the Nixon and Ford administrations made no substantial effort to stop Taiwan from achieving nuclear weapons capability. A nonproliferation scholar described the two administrations as playing a Whac-a-Mole game with Taiwan's nuclear program: US nonproliferation officials would cut off transfers and fuel supplies once in a while and occasionally threaten to cut off military aid, but they were never able to eliminate the program.[20] This game continued until the Ford administration, when Kissinger finally determined that Chiang Kai-shek's nuclear ambitions would damage the much more critical Nixon-Mao rapprochement. However, even then the administration made no serious efforts to stop Chiang; instead, US officials asked him only for an empty assurance that Taiwan would "cease [weapons-grade plutonium] reprocessing processes." Chiang Kai-shek, of course, gladly assured this, and yet his nuclear weapons program went ahead and even speeded up after his death in 1975 as his son, Chiang Ching-kuo, eventually replaced him as the leader of the KMT.[21]

JIMMY CARTER, THE NONPROLIFERATION PRESIDENT

Taiwan's nuclear weapons development attracted far more attention from US nonproliferation officials when Jimmy Carter arrived at the White House, as he was determined to prioritize nuclear nonproliferation in his foreign policy agenda and would not take empty assurances as a response. Carter encouraged the Nuclear Supplier Group and the IAEA to implement much stricter controls over the flow of nuclear materials and the reprocessing of nuclear fuels—in other words, to cut off the supply of nuclear materials to aspiring nuclear weapons states such as the ROC, which received uranium from South Africa and plutonium from the United States.²² To ensure that Carter's policy on Taiwan would succeed, on March 5, 1977, Leonard S. Unger, the US ambassador to the ROC, pressured former foreign minister Chou Shu-k'ai, Chiang Ching-kuo's close friend, to obtain another guarantee that Chiang would not acquire nuclear weapons capability. Hard-pressed, Chou assured the American ambassador that Chiang had made such a promise: "It had been made clear, and could be in the future also, that the ROC does not intend to produce weapons."²³ Still, IAEA inspectors discovered that the Taiwanese research reactor had a unique backdoor port from which plutonium, the nuclear fission material used to make atomic bombs, was spirited away—a clear violation of IAEA regulations—indicating that a weapons program was secretly running. The alarmed IAEA officials contacted the Canadian contractors who built the reactor and were told that this unique back door was made "at the request of the Taiwanese."²⁴

When news of the IAEA discovery reached Washington, it caused quite a sensation in the American nonproliferation community, and this time Carter cracked down hard on the Taiwanese. On March 26, 1977, Secretary of State Vance cabled Ambassador Unger that far stricter measures had to be taken: "All present and future ROC nuclear facilities and materials" would be monitored "under the US/ROC bilateral Agreement for Cooperation," "spent fuels" would be "disposed [of] under mutually acceptable conditions," "all fuel cycle activities and reorientation facilities involving or leading to weapons-usable materials" would be terminated, the research reactor program would be suspended, and, last but not least, "all plutonium should be transferred to the United States." In addition, American nuclear experts and inspectors would be on their way to Taiwan. In other words, US nonproliferation officials would take over all of Taiwan's nuclear activities and make sure it did not get the bomb.²⁵ A study by former IAEA inspector David Albright and nonproliferation expert Andrea Stricker suggests that the ROC and the Carter administration reached an agreement between March and May 1977, under which the United States would be "afforded unlimited access to all ROC nuclear facilities" and all nuclear materials, equipment, and facilities would be subject to the trilateral US-ROC-IAEA safeguards agreement. As a reward, the administration agreed to provide technology and technical assistance to redirect INER from weapons production to nuclear power generation, thus altogether transforming Taiwan's nuclear program from a rogue secret military program to a civilian power generation program under close US supervision.²⁶

Chiang Ching-kuo never admitted that he was secretly developing nuclear weapons in his diary. Still, some entries were filled with complaints about the Carter administration and the regrets that Taiwan had to cease its "nuclear energy development":

> Everything I think about Americans' vile appearances, their evil intentions, and their despicable methods, how they are terrified of enemies yet they bully their friends, which will only hurt them regardless of enemies or friends—I am filled with pain and hate.
>
> —March 31, 1977²⁷

> I respect all the hard work and efforts made by researchers who participated in the nuclear energy research. However, [the research] has to be terminated today, and I feel deeply guilty and worried. In comparison [with the United States], our country's strength is weak; it is the most painful feeling to have to face such bullying, and there is a countless amount of bitterness in my mind!
>
> —April 1, 1977²⁸

The crackdown was likely a joint operation between the nonproliferation liberals in the State Department and the Cold War realists who did not want Taiwan to become a flashpoint in the much more critical US-PRC relations. After all, a nuclear Taiwan Strait crisis was not something they could afford when the global Cold War required mainland China's cooperation. This conclusion could be traced to a particular presidential briefing prepared by Brzezinski, Carter's pro-PRC national security adviser who typically deemed Taiwan useless in his grand strategy to counter the Soviet Union. "It is now quite clear that the Taiwanese Institute of Nuclear Energy Research has been ordered to terminate its heavy water reactor project and close the hot laboratory," Brzezinski wrote to President Carter with a sense of satisfaction. "The American effort to crack down on this project yielded its desired results."²⁹

The Carter administration's shutdown of Chiang's nuclear weapons program had several impacts on future US-Taiwan relations. First, it destroyed Chiang's last hope of having an independent security guarantee against a possible mainland attack, further increasing Taiwan's dependence on conventional arms purchases from advanced Western nations. Senator James A. McClure (R–Idaho), a longtime sympathizer with the Taiwanese cause, addressed precisely this point. When US-PRC normalization was on the agenda, McClure, with a sense of regret, told Taiwanese Ambassador Shen Hongjian on September 7, 1978: "There could have been another way [for Taiwan to protect itself]—if Taiwan followed the original path to speed up the development of nuclear power, it could have saved itself." But it was already too late, as the heavy water reactor suspected of weapons production had been dismantled under pressure from the Carter administration. Taiwan, McClure admitted, was now in such a peculiar situation that its leaders "cannot be allowed to approach the Russians, cannot be allowed to develop nuclear weapons, and do not have enough support from the American public."[30] Secondly, on a personal level, this episode might have increased Chiang's distrust of Jimmy Carter, as suggested by Taiwan's later engagement with his domestic rivals and the discovery in the late 1980s of further secret nuclear weapons activity when an INER scientist, Chang Hsien-yi, defected to the United States.[31] Strangely, the biggest beneficiary of this episode was CCP leader Deng Xiaoping. With a stroke of his pen, Carter removed a significant roadblock in Deng's goal of taking back Taiwan by force.

NEW SECURITY CONCERNS AND THE TAIWAN-ISRAEL FIGHTER JET DEAL

The increasingly close Cold War cooperation between the Carter Administration and the PRC disrupted Taiwan's nuclear ambitions and severely limited Chiang Ching-kuo's options for obtaining advanced military technologies from US allies. The Taiwanese could no longer independently determine their access to military technologies abroad; rather, they faced a game of political compromise, diplomatic betrayal, and gangster-style business blackmail played among the Carter administration, American arms makers, and, strangely, the mainland Chinese Communist regime.

Chiang Ching-kuo was determined to reverse this trend, but where could the ROC purchase advanced modern fighters aside from the United

States and its NATO allies, who were all subject to the Carter administration's strict export control measures? Where could the ROC find a sympathetic seller that could offer modern fighters without strings attached and teach them how to maintain, modify, or even build these fighters domestically?

By late 1977, the Taiwanese military urgently needed to upgrade the ROC Air Force's aging fighter jet fleet, composed mainly of Lockheed F-104 Starfighters, small, agile, short-range interceptors the Eisenhower administration had sold to Taiwan after the 1958 crisis. Those single-engine fighters, built in the 1960s, were known for their fast takeoff and Mach 2.2 top speed, but they were also notorious for their poor gliding distance because they had tiny, narrow wings. Whenever the engine suffered a dysfunction, the F-104 would quickly fall out of the sky and crash into a ball of flame, leaving little time for the pilot to escape. Taiwanese Defense Ministry records show that there were 144 crashes caused by mechanical failure during the F-104's service history between 1960 and 1996, killing an astonishing number of Taiwanese pilots—sixty-two—without having even engaged in actual combat. Taiwanese military experts, however, did blame themselves for part of the unusually high casualty rate: The lack of a modern aerospace industry and technical know-how in the ROC prevented its air force from modifying and improving those fighters to make them safer, which was what US allies did as a common practice. A study jointly conducted by three former and current high-ranking ROC Air Force officials admitted it was a lesson learned in blood.[32]

For Chiang Ching-kuo, the options to upgrade the ROC Air Force were the American McDonnell Douglas F-4, a twin-engine, all-weather, long-range supersonic jet interceptor, and its slightly smaller counterpart the Israeli Kfir, a single-engine, multirole fighter. Both were very advanced fighter jets at the time, which could help Taiwan defend against an invasion from the mainland by protecting the sky and attacking incoming sea and ground units. Chiang's initial plan was to purchase the American F-4, the most advanced fighter in service in the US Air Force.[33] The choice, however, was not up to Taiwan, as Carter asked his two top Asia experts, Mike Armacost and Mike Oksenberg, to decide the matter.

According to the official military technology transfer policy in Presidential Directive 13, US aerospace companies could not sell their most advanced weapons system to a customer unless it was urgently needed to "serve America's security interests." Commonly, US companies sold only watered-down, older-generation equipment to foreigners to prevent leaking US technology to distrusted customers and to reduce the chance of causing a regional arms race, while still making enough profit.[34] When interpreting the transfer policy, Armacost and Oksenberg, instead of being more sensitive to Taiwan's urgent need to defend itself, were far more worried about antagonizing their new Communist allies in the PRC. Furthermore, however unlikely the situation, no arms sales should encourage Taiwan to launch an attack on the mainland and drag the United States into another unnecessary war in Asia. In their report to President Carter, the two experts concluded that US arms sales should be straight to the point: not too little, not too much, not too old, and not too advanced. They stated that US weaponry should help the ROC deter "an invasion of the island," "a blockade of the island," or an "over-assertive PRC patrolling of the Strait." However, sales of such weaponry should be limited so as to "to deprive the ROC of an offensive capability against the mainland" and "a capacity to patrol the strait in an overly assertive fashion." The report thus offered four choices:

1. The F-4E, which could significantly boost the Taiwanese Air Force but, with an operating range of one thousand miles, might be flown to the mainland. Therefore, the United States would insist that "the planes are not to be flown within 50 miles of the PRC coast except in the event of PRC-initiated hostilities."
2. The F-5E, a cheaper, trimmed, and less capable export aircraft based on F-4 technology, which the ROC Air Force already operated (mostly in older models) and had a license to produce locally. The F-5Es would arrive without the modern black box that would have enabled them to use precision-guided munitions and Maverick antiship missiles. This would be a quantitative but not a qualitative boost to Taiwan's defenses.
3. The new F-5E with the black box, precision-guided munitions, and Maverick air-to-ground missiles, bundled with another sale of land-based AGM-84 Harpoon antiship missiles.
4. The Israeli Kfir, which the report described as perfect, as it "stands in between the F-4 and the F-5E."[35]

The Kfir was the premier Israeli fighter developed by Israeli Aerospace Industries (IAI) in the 1970s—and a classic example of industry espionage, sanction evasion, and the way much military technology traveled multilaterally back and forth between both friends and enemies. The Kfir fighter contained crucial American technology, including its General Electric J79 turbojet engine. It shared many parts with and played a similar role to the General Dynamics F-16 multirole jet. The Kfir also contained French technologies that Israeli spies had stolen from the Mirage fighter jet made by the French company Dassault through a compromised Swiss engineer who traded "$200,000 from Israel for about 200,000 jet engine blueprints smuggled in crates."[36] In fact, Israel stole those technologies in the first place because France had decided to cancel Mirage 5 sales to Israel as a part of a multilateral embargo against the belligerents after the 1967 Six-Day War.[37] Those bought or stolen technologies traveled farther as the Israeli Air Force equipped the first batches of Kfirs themselves, and then later models were exported to countries with dubious human rights records, such as Ecuador (1981), Sri Lanka (1995), and Colombia (1989)—countries that were on US sanctions lists and could not purchase American-made fighters. By the end of the Cold War, a small number of Kfir fighters were finally repurchased by a private company in Texas to be used as "enemy aircraft" for studies and in tactical training with the US Air Force.[38]

But why was the ROC military interested in this niche type of Israeli fighter jet instead of battle-tested American and Western European products? Chiang Ching-kuo had a long-standing interest in the Israeli defense industry as a part of the ROC's strategy to diversify its foreign sources of advanced military support, going back to the days of his father's presidency. ROC Foreign Ministry records suggest that at some point in the 1950s, ROC Air Force General Hu Xu-guang secretly carried a personal letter from Chiang Kai-shek to the Israeli Air Force, proposing nuclear and military cooperation.[39] A study by Hong Kong Chinese University cited Israeli scientists' letters in confirming that the ROC and Israel had already started a secret nuclear collaboration in the 1960s.[40] A similar US Department of State source also suggests that Israel was the first country that Taiwanese scientists approached to acquire nuclear technology.[41]

In the summer of 1977, there was already enough intelligence for Chiang Ching-kuo and his KMT comrades to foresee an immediate break in

US-ROC relations. Even US Ambassador Unger told Taiwanese officials he might be the last US ambassador to Taiwan.[42] "The American policy towards us is increasingly clear that they will abandon us and go to the Communist bandits," Chiang wrote in his diary on May 29. "They have used multiple channels to try to convince me to accept their terms, and they tried to use arms sales as a guarantee, toying with us like children. America is willingly falling into a trap, how pathetic."[43] Thus, no longer willing to put Taiwanese security in the hands of unreliable and "pathetic" Americans, Chiang needed to find a non-US partner with advanced military technologies.

According to a study by the historian Thomas A. Marks, Israel and South Africa were the two key sources of the ROC's advanced military technology in the late 1970s, when US technology became increasingly challenging to acquire due to the US-PRC rapprochement.[44] In 1976, for example, the ROC's National Chung-Shan Institute of Science and Technology (NCSIST), a state-owned national defense enterprise, with Israeli help, redeveloped and repurposed the Israeli Gabriel II antiship missile into the Hsiung Feng I (Brave Wind I) land-attack cruise missile, capable of crossing the Taiwan Strait and striking PLA airbases and ports in Fujian Province. Encouraged by this achievement, the NCSIST also proposed coproducing with Israel a more powerful medium-range missile capable of attacking farther targets on the mainland.[45] In comparison, Taiwan failed to acquire missile technology from the United States.

The NCSIST, in association with the ROC Ministry of National Defense, also launched a joint program with MIT to train missile scientists for its medium- to long-range missile development program, including a proposed Sky Horse missile with a range of 890 kilometers (over 550 miles), enabling it to strike major mainland Chinese cities. The Ford administration severely disrupted those efforts, and in July 1976, fifteen Taiwanese missile science students at MIT were deported by the U.S. Department of State's Office of Munitions Control.[46]

The ROC's strategic missile program, according to Chiang's diary, started up once more on the eve of US-PRC normalization, almost as an irrational emotional response to what Chiang saw as the United States' betrayal of Taiwan.[47] But again, during the Reagan administration, Chiang had to halt missile development under renewed US pressure.[48] Nevertheless, the ROC's missile ambitions resurfaced for a third time after the Cold War when, despite US opposition, it successfully tested a land-attack cruise missile with a range of 500–1,000 kilometers (about 300–620 miles) in 2005.[49]

Compared to dealing with American companies restricted by export control measures, doing business with Israel was relatively more straightforward. By the early 1970s, the ROC Air Force and IAI were already closely linked, exchanging information and preparing for the mutual transfer of military technologies. For example, IAI's founder and first CEO Adolph William Schwimmer visited Chiang Ching-kuo in Taiwan and gave him a list of naval and aerospace technical data. Then, on November 11, 1970, after his return to Israel, Schwimmer wrote Chiang a letter, saying he hoped to secure a market and close cooperation "between your Air Force and our Air Force and IAI."[50]

This potential deal was equally crucial for the Israelis. According to a CIA report from the late 1970s, Israel was determined to become militarily more independent from the United States, as past American unwillingness to provide the best weapons to Israel had limited its regional ambitions. Israel sought to "reduce the country's dependence on foreign suppliers and maintain its qualitative edge in weaponry over the Arabs." Being able to export Kfir fighter jets played an indispensable role in financing Israel's regional military ambitions; the Israeli defense force was too small to provide a large enough market to fund critical indigenous weapons programs. This was especially true for IAI, where development of the Kfir project alone cost US$1.1 billion and its production accounted for one-fourth of its workload. Kfir exports generated US$200 million annually and provide sustained employment for 5,000 technicians. Without exports, the CIA estimated that 3,000 IAI employees would face immediate unemployment.[51]

Throughout 1978, both Israel and the ROC exchanged visits and letters, and Chiang Ching-kuo's files were filled with news about IAI's recent developments.[52] On June 2, 1978, Chiang made his first move. Like a scene taken straight from a Cold War spy movie, at Tiberio, a small Italian restaurant located at 1915 K Street N.W., in Washington, D.C., Wen Haxiong, the procurement officer of the ROC Army, had a secret lunch meeting with Marvin Klemow, IAI's US representative. Klemow told Wen, "I shall soon return to Israel for business and will report the issue regarding the sale of Kfir to your country. From what we heard during the past few weeks, there is still a high chance for you to get the [American] F-4E, but there is no hope for the F-16. Even then, the number of F-4E you will receive could be minimal, or [Americans] will remove their air attack abilities."[53]

The Israelis were nevertheless concerned about offending the US military-industrial complex. They were also worried about the possibility US officials or industry insiders might spoil the sale with leaks and fake news. "If America allows Israel to sell you Kfir, this will offend the American aerospace industry, especially the company that makes F-4E, McDonnell Douglas. The American officials announced to the public and Israel that the Republic of China was not sincere about purchasing the Kfir. This was a trick: their goal was to speed up US aircraft sales to the ROC." But there was still a chance: Since the US Congress had pushed through the sale of different types of aircraft to Israel, the Saudis, and Egypt over Israel's protest, the Carter administration felt it owed Israel a favor:

> Vice President Mondale and his subordinates asked Israel many times if there were ways they could increase American assistance towards Israel. In response, we proposed that Americans approve Israeli sales of Kfir to the ROC. On the eve of American-Communist [China] normalization, the last [US] sale to Taiwan might just be a parting console. After US-PRC normalization, the likelihood of a US sale to the ROC will seriously decrease. Also, around the world, few countries except Israel are willing to offer the ROC fighter planes. Consider all the political elements. The ROC should buy the F4-E if the Americans are willing to offer, but also consider buying the Israeli Kfir—that is a wise choice.

Wen thanked his IAI contact and promised to pass these words on to Taipei. In a report he wrote to the ROC Foreign Ministry, Wen stated that he had complete confidence in Klemow and trusted his analysis.[54]

However, even before the deal with Taiwan, the United States had blocked Israel's Kfir sale to Ecuador by withholding licenses for the American-made components, which, in Secretary of State Vance's own words, cost Israel "a loss of about $300 million in foreign exchange."[55] The reason the United States intervened was relatively straightforward—and easily understood by anyone involved in organized crime. By the 1970s, the two superpowers had divided the world's arms sales market using an unspoken, drug cartel–style rule of partition. The Carter administration considered Latin America the exclusive turf of American defense companies, just as Eastern Europe, in the USSR's backyard, belonged to Soviet defense companies. "The Kfir is an Israeli plane with a US engine, and it cannot be produced without some exports," Israeli Defense Minister Shimon Peres complained in front of US officials after that hard lesson. "There is a limited potential market for sales because Israel is closed out of any market where the US or USSR sells planes."[56]

Still, Israeli officials tried their best to lobby for their Taiwanese friends. On August 2, 1977, Josef Ciechanover, the Israeli Embassy's military attaché in charge of Israeli military procurement in the United States, probed Assistant Secretary of State Leslie H. Gelb about possibly acquiring a US license for Kfir sales to Taiwan. It was terrible timing, as Secretary Vance would soon fly to Beijing to meet Deng Xiaoping, and Gelb was unsure how the mainland Chinese officials would react. "It would be premature to request US approval for Kfir sales to Taiwan, even informally," Vance advised. He wanted to talk first to the mainland Chinese: "We would know better after that what our position would be."[57] The following month the Taiwanese Ministry of Defense secretly visited Israel and formally signed the contract. Ciechanover again called the State Department to request American permission for the sale. "[Israel] recognized the sensitivity of this request for permission to transfer American components," he said, "but asked that we [the United States] give a response to his approach as quickly as possible." "The ROC is ready to sign a contract immediately," the Israeli director said, "and that delivery would start 12 to 14 months after the signing of a contract." Again, the Americans did not answer.[58]

The United States' inaction agitated even the very top members of the Israeli government. The following month Israeli Minister of Defense and future president Ezer Weizman flew to Washington, D.C., himself and pushed the issue with Secretary of Defense Brown. He said that if Israel could not sell the Kfir, the United States should provide enough parts for Israel to produce more by itself, at least to save the production line. "If we [the United States] were to provide financial support to expand Kfir production from 18 to 24 per year, Israel would regard this as an alternative to our permission to sell Kfirs to Taiwan." Again, Brown did not answer, and Weizman left idisappointed.[59]

Carter never wanted to pass this lucrative deal to IAI; he was determined to let an American company win the $300 million contract. The only question was which plane was appropriate, considering possible bad reactions from his new best friend, Deng Xiaoping. During a discussion on April 11, 1978, the pro-ROC officials, including Secretary of State Cyrus Vance and Deputy Assistant Secretary of Defense Morton Abramowitz, favored the McDonnell Douglas F-4. This all-weather, long-range fighter-bomber first entered service with the US Air Force as its primary air-superiority fighter during the Vietnam War. They argued that "this is possibly the last sale of new equipment to the ROC before [US-PRC] normalization" and that the F-4 was advanced enough to "keep them going ten to fifteen years." The pro-PRC officials, however, pushed back. Leading this camp, Brzezinski favored the less capable Northrop F-5, a low-cost aircraft explicitly developed for export to allies, as its sales would be less provocative to Deng Xiaoping. In addition, the ROC Air Force already operated several older F-5 models—the A, B, and E—so it would be very familiar with maintaining and operating the new planes. Secretary of Defense Brown, also a pro-PRC realist, again suggested the less advanced F-5, citing a secret agreement made years back during the Nixon administration, in which Kissinger had promised PRC Premier Zhou Enlai that the United States would not sell any F-4s to Taiwan.[60]

The indecision dragged on, as the United States gave priority to US-PRC normalization talks. Increasingly disillusioned, Chiang Ching-kuo decided during June and July of 1978 not to pursue the Israeli airplane further.[61] Israeli officials, unable to get a green light from President Carter, were equally disillusioned and started to blame the Americans, whom they believed had deliberately put legal restrictions on Israeli fighter exports to weaken IAI and prevent Israel's independence from the United States.[62] The decision was finally made on October 26, 1978, by Brzezinski. Having just secured his grand deal with Deng Xiaoping on US-PRC normalization negotiations, he could not care less about Taiwan's security and decided that the "F-5 would do the job." He was much more worried about the security of mainland China from a surprise Taiwanese attack using American fighter jets. Brzezinski told Carter that the F-5 could be paired with "500 laser-guided bombs" because, "given the limited range of the F-5, these munitions would not pose a threat to targets in the PRC but would improve Taiwan's defense, particularly against the numerically superior PLA navy." Furthermore, he said the United States should not give the ROC too much hope by giving it the advanced F-4 or even the future generation of long-range multirole fighters such as F-16 or F-18, and it should not authorize Taiwan's "creation of a follow-on aircraft to the F-5."[63]

Carter, unwilling to offend Israel and yet equally unwilling to offend Deng Xiaoping, made a well-timed passive-aggressive offer to Chiang Ching-kuo in November 1978, right before the official US-PRC diplomatic opening. Through the State Department, Carter offered Chiang the choice of either the Kfir from Israel or an upgraded version of the F-5—the F-5E—from the United States, possibly with further upgrading.[64] The belated and unexpected approval of the Kfir sale, tied to another package of US arms transfers, threw Chiang off. With the Americans getting even closer to his enemy on the mainland, he had no choice: Instead of taking the better Israeli deal, he had to stick with the American offer so he could stay politically close with the US defense industry. Chiang's disappointment could not have been better expressed during his call to US Ambassador Unger, who himself would be downgraded to "representative" as official diplomatic ties between the United States and Taiwan were about to expire:

> The common objective of the USG [United States Government] and GROC [Government of the Republic of China] is to maintain peace and security in this part of the world. However, a fundamental prerequisite is that between the two contending parties, the Communists and the ROC, there must be maintained "Parity or Equilibrium" in military power. If the other side should gain a substantial advantage over the ROC, peace would be sabotaged. The most important factor is air power, on which ROC defense mainly depends.... The Communists already have a great quantitative advantage over the ROC, for whom quality is important. The main elements of ROC air power, the F-100s, F-104s, and F-5Es, are already in a category that should be replaced with follow-on aircraft. The ROC is now far behind others in this respect. For instance, South Korea has the F-4, and Japan has the F-16. Obviously, if the ROC's weakness in this regard increases, it will lead to the strategic weakening of the whole free world. Therefore, the ROC feels it needs the F-5G now. It has waited a long time, and it is a great disappointment to receive this answer....

Although the Kfir is a better aircraft than the F-104, the ROC does not want to go to Israel or any country other than the US for new types of equipment, which would lead to maintenance and supply problems. We want US planes and equipment; please convey this to the USG and ask President Carter to give personally favorable consideration to the F-5G and thus help us solve our present problems.[65]

Carter's belated decision to announce the Kfir approval, coming on the eve of the US-PRC opening, wounded both allies. The ROC was forever stuck with US airplanes for both maintenance and political reasons. Israel tried to sell an upgraded Kfir to Taiwan again in 1992, and the George H. W. Bush administration waited to announce its approval until Taiwan had already chosen the American F-16s, repeating Carter's exact trick.[66]

The Kfir story had an even more bizarre ending. At the end of the Cold War, IAI exhausted its resources and developed the Lavi, an upgraded Kfir fighter that. used an American Pratt & Whitney turbo engine and thus fell under US export controls. Then, in the 1990s, the near-bankrupted IAI made a last-minute secret deal with mainland China, and the Lavi blueprint became the base design for the PLA Air Force's Chengdu J-10 fighter (Vigorous Dragon). IAI and Israeli diplomats denied this even though it was common knowledge in the Chinese aerospace industry.[67] However, when the J-10 made its first flight in 1998, observers were amused by how much this "indigenously designed Chinese fighter" looked like the Israeli original from every angle except for the oversized Russian Salyut AL-31 engine.[68]

GREAT AMBITION, LIMITED CAPABILITIES

On December 17, 1978, just two days after the Carter administration announced its decision to normalize relations with the PRC, General Wang Shen, director of the KMT Army General Political Warfare Department and Chiang's longtime confidant, was sent to the Philippines in a desperate attempt to secure diplomatic support for Chiang Ching-kuo's dream of building an anti-Communist league in Asia. Wang found an eager audience in President Ferdinand Marcos, a dictator notorious for his neofascist ideology and rampant corruption and for the brutal murders of political dissidents.[69] Even though the Philippines opened diplomatic relations with the PRC in 1974, attracted by its promise of trade, a significant part of the country's establishment, especially the military, remained anti-Communist and anti-Chinese. Most crucially, the Philippines had been a shadow battleground in the Sino-Soviet rivalry in the Third World. For a decade, the Soviet Union supported Marcos's dictatorship, while the Chinese-supported Communist insurgency tried to overthrow it.[70] The United States, on the other hand, was disgusted by Marcos's human rights abuses but still supported him because of his anti-Communist stance.[71] The visit was a classic balance-of-power act on both sides: Marcos wanted Taiwan as insurance against the PRC, while Taiwan wanted another ally after the loss of the United States.

Marcos, according to Wang's account, "seriously expressed the Filipino people's resolute anti-Communism stance, which will not be affected by any external international political forces." Later Wang, being a military man, talked extensively with Philippines Defense Minister Juan Ponce Enrile about "experiences on suppressing the Communists," and Enrile asked Taiwan to "provide the Filipino army with weapons and ammunition." The Philippines' government was especially worried about political instability in the large Chinese communities, and wanted intelligence support from the KMT to track down suspected Chinese Communist infiltrators who came into the Philippines through Hong Kong and who "disappeared as soon as they landed on our shores."[72] On the one hand, Wang reported that Taiwan should engage in more trade with the Philippines to "make them more dependent on Taiwan as a way to gain their political support" and "to increase our propaganda to increase our effort to fight for an anti-Communist alliance." On the other hand, he was aware who Marcos was: inept, brutal, and corrupt. "[Marcos's] wife and those oligarchs connected to high officials controlled the whole economy. Especially—the friends of the First Lady," Wang reported, with a clear sense of contempt. "Oil industry, electricity, ship-building, casinos, were all controlled by the first lady's family clans."[73]

This was just one of the many trips that General Wang and other Taiwanese diplomats made to engage dictators in a desperate effort to shore up Taiwan's global influence after the US-PRC normalization. Wang himself would visit Cambodia's the apartheid regime in South Africa in the same year to enlist more support for his anti-communist cause. "We must support South Africa, or it will bow to the Communists," Wang reported to Chiang Ching-kuo after that trip.[74] It seemed that Chiang and his generals would accept any friend at any cost, and the KMT's flirting with morally dubious regimes would continue until the end of the Cold War. However, those attempts had limited results, as one after another of the ROC's diplomatic partners cut ties with it and instead established relations with the PRC. In addition, Taiwanese politics in the early 1980s was troubled by political infighting among the KMT factions and by increased domestic opposition, further compounded by Chiang's deteriorating health. General Wang, too politically ambitious in Chiang's eyes, eventually aroused suspicion, and Chiang named him the ROC ambassador to Paraguay, a post as distant as possible from Taiwan. This political exile essentially ruined his domestic career and ended his own ardent effort, as well as that of the KMT, to create an anti-Communist alliance in Asia.[75]

CONCLUSION

From secret attempts to acquire nuclear weapons, to a daring adventure to acquire Israeli fighters under close U.S. scrutiny, to the final yet less than satisfactory attempts to build an anti-Communist alliance with the world's last right-wing authoritarian regimes, Chiang Ching-kuo had engaged in the classical realist international politics that everyone did. However, because of the ROC's limited capability and its low ranking on the Carter administration's priority list, the greater Cold War players constantly infringed on its interests. This, however, was not the end of the story of Taiwan's Cold War. In the last part of the book, we will learn about the political and ideological dimension of Taiwan's Cold War, as the discouraged but not defeated Taiwanese leader was determined to utilize his personal ties with members of the US Congress to reverse the damage Carter had done to the ROC's security.

III

IDEOLOGY

5

FROM CLASSMATES TO ENEMIES

Deng Xiaoping and Chiang Ching-kuo

Despite their shared Soviet education and Chinese identity, the two rival Chinese leaders, Deng Xiaoping and Chiang Ching-kuo, pursued different strategies to win the Carter administration's support. Deng's focus on the CCP's geopolitical alignment against the Soviet Union and Chiang's emphasis on the KMT's anti-Communist ideology created a complex rivalry that significantly influenced the development of the Taiwan Relations Act, the challenges in cross-strait relations, and US domestic support for Carter's policy toward the two competing Chinese regimes.

In the third part of this book, I deal with the ideological dimension of the United States' complex relations with the two Chinese regimes in mainland China and Taiwan. This chapter, in which I focus on the competing political influence campaigns launched in the United States by Deng Xiaoping, the leader of the CCP regime in mainland China, and by Chiang Ching-kuo, the leader of the KMT regime in Taiwan. The competition between Deng and Chiang in the United States raised a fundamental question about the nature of the American Cold War. For Deng, the Cold War was about a *geopolitical* and *military* struggle against the Soviet Union. Thus, mainland China should be the ideal partner. Many in Jimmy Carter's administration agreed. In Chiang's rhetoric, the Cold War was a *political* and *ideological* struggle to defend the world against the threat of Communism—and as the last anti-Communist bastion in the Chinese-speaking world, Taiwan, instead of mainland China, should be America's best friend. Because each view had a selling point for the American audience, Deng's and Chiang's lobby and counterlobby campaigns often spread beyond the foreign policy establishment into much broader domestic political debates. This further complicated the Carter administration's attempt to maintain a balanced policy toward Taiwan and mainland China.

FROM SHARED SOVIET ORIGIN TO DIVERGING REVOLUTIONARY PATHS

Despite leading two opposing regimes, Deng and Chiang had quite a few things in common. Both studied in the Soviet Union in their early years and were, in fact, classmates briefly in 1926 at Moscow Sun Yat-sen University, the special institution set up to indoctrinate young Chinese intellectuals and turn them into Communist revolutionaries. According to Chiang's recollection, the three classes they took, aside from Russian language courses, were quite basic: sociology, economics, and geography. These were taught from a strict Marxist-Leninist viewpoint and were complemented by discussion sessions such as "The Chinese Revolution and Our Duties."[1] When Chiang joined the Soviet Communist Party Youth League, he served in the party cell led by Deng, and according to many contemporary accounts, the two were very close. Deng, who had studied in France earlier, was the senior big brother and more politically mature, while Chiang was the more studious younger brother who spoke far better Russian.[2]

Their career paths were similar too: Both served under dangerous, murderous leaders and survived because of a keen sense of self-preservation. In 1926, Deng returned to China, worked under Mao, and survived waves of purges. For twelve years, Chiang was a hostage under Stalin. When Stalin was on bad terms with Chiang Kai-shek in the early 1930s due to the KMT's constant attacks on Chinese Communists, Chiang Ching-kuo openly renounced his biological relationship with his father and penned several articles in the Moscow-controlled newspaper *Pravda* denouncing his father's policy to appease Stalin. On November 16, 1936, at the height of Stalin's purge, Chiang Ching-kuo formally joined the Soviet Communist Party, another act demonstrating his apparent loyalty to the Soviet leader. However, in 1937, Stalin sent Chiang, along with his Belorussian wife, Faina Chiang Fang-Liang, and his infant son, back to China as part of an effort to repair Soviet-ROC relations in the face of the common threat to the Soviet Union and the ROC from imperial Japan. The moment Chiang arrived he ditched his Soviet identity and instead started to denounce Stalin in public. He even published a small pamphlet in 1937, *My Days in the Soviet Union*, in which he listed all the crimes and evil in the Soviet system:

> An old friend who went to study in the Soviet Union at the same time as me talked about our life in the Soviet Union. We all said in unison at the time: "That was really a nightmare!" But now that we think about it more carefully, we realize that the word "nightmare" is inappropriate to describe the situation at that time. The pain we experienced back then was not a dream but the cruelest and most painful reality.
>
> Having been tortured for twelve years, I am very aware of the cunning and vicious methods used by the Communists to destroy young people. They first use clever words to deceive young people, attract them, and anesthetize their minds, and then use terrorist methods to manipulate and destroy their personalities. Their goal is to remove personal free will and turn people into shackled slaves who obey orders.[3]

To regain his father's favor as heir apparent to the KMT regime, Chiang penned several rather cringeworthy and overly flattering books praising his father's virtues; at one point, he even compared the elder Chiang to Jesus Christ, who "sacrificed his personal life for the salvation of the nation."[4] Comparing Chiang Ching-kuo's rapid switch of loyalty from Stalin to his father with Deng's apologetic letter to Mao during the Cultural Revolution and his immediate denunciation of the Cultural Revolution after Mao's death, the historian Yu Jie concluded that both men were survivalists, masters at hiding their true nature, suppressing their emotions, and "speaking the language of humans when seeing a human, and speaking the language of devils when seeing a devil."[5] In the late 1970s, Americans also experienced their ideological and rhetorical flexibility. Deng and Chiang's shared Soviet experiences taught them both many things.

In domestic politics, neither admired Western democracy. Instead, both strived to reform their parties into tightly controlled, militant revolutionary parties with oppressive institutions, omnipresent secret police, and informant systems to solidify their rule. It is essential to keep in mind that the competition between the two Chinese regimes in the late 1970s was not a competition between the evil "Communist Red China" and the good "Nationalist Free China," as Taiwanese lobbyists at the time tended to tell their American audiences. Both Chinese regimes were, in fact, not democratic by any modern standard.

After the KMT's defeat on the Chinese mainland, Chiang Ching-kuo played a crucial role in shoring up the KMT remnant's loyalty to his father by overseeing its secret police, military reorganization, and a newly created ideological indoctrination system—consisting of political warfare units modeled after the Soviet political commissar system. Instead of Marxism, however, Chiang utilized his father's political ideology.[6] This new system might have solidified the Chiang family's control over the army, but many critics, including American military advisers, argued at the time that the system severely interfered with the authority of professional army officers and created a long legacy of inefficiency, abuse, and corruption.[7] In fact, the KMT regime had such a bad human rights reputation that it launched a public relations campaign in the 1980s, and as a result, my George Washington University professor Robert Sutter was once invited to Taiwan while he served as a young analyst for the US Congress. General Wang Sheng, the general in charge of the military's political warfare—or in Sutter's words, "Taiwan's Darth Vader"—offered the young American a tour of Taiwan's prison system and showed that all the political prisoners were apparently well clothed, well fed, and not physically abused. "See, we are not the South Koreans," he said, referring to the equally notorious Park Chung Hee regime in South Korea, while patting Sutter's back and smiling.[8]

In 1978, Chiang Ching-kuo was "elected" president of the ROC by the unelected National Assembly members who had been appointed by his father to lifelong terms. It is also worth noting that Taiwan's democratic movement, the Tangtaiw, (or Dangwai) movement, which meant "outside of the KMT Party," became a unified political force only after Chiang decided to cancel the presidential election in 1979 under the pretext of Carter's decision to abandon US-ROC diplomatic ties. Chiang would continue to jail, execute, and assassinate his political opponents well into the 1980s, making mass arrests of journalists during the 1979 Formosa incidents and authorizing the February 1980 massacre of several family members of Lin Yi-Hsuing, a leader of a democratization movement. In a bizarre and daring case, the KMT government, using the KMT intelligence–controlled criminal triad Zhulianbang (United Bamboo Gang), assassinated Henri Liu, the Taiwanese American dissident writer also known by his pen name Chiang Nan, on October 15, 1985, in California, sinking his relationship with Reagan administration to its lowest point.[9] Murdering an American citizen inside the United States was something even Deng would not dare to do. But in terms of the number of casualties, none of the KMT government crimes could compare to the many thousands killed by Deng and his comrades in Tiananmen Square in June 1989.

To understand how difficult it was for Jimmy Carter to deal with the two Chinese regimes, neither of which valued democracy and human rights, it is crucial to recognize the dictatorial nature of both. First, neither of the competing regimes could pretend it was a free democracy, and it was therefore unable to woo Americans with similar domestic political values. Thus, each had to sell Americans on its unique contribution to the Cold War: Deng focused on his *anti-Soviet* position, and Chiang relied on his *anti-Communist* reputation. Second, each knew all too well that the other side was just as brutal and murderous, if not more so; thus, the competition between the two rival regimes was a zero-sum game without mercy, grace, or the slightest chance of compromise.

Deng made his uncompromising position very clear immediately after the normalization of diplomatic relations between the United States and China. Even though the Carter administration had already blocked Taiwan's access to nuclear weapon technology and turned down arms sales, as discussed previously, Deng still thought the Americans were indulging Chiang, and it was not acceptable. On January 1, 1979, Deng spoke to his comrades in the Central Committee and showed his determination to tighten his grip on Taiwan: "The domestic construction has now refocused upon our four modernizations, US-China relations have been normalized, and finally, the return of Taiwan to the motherland is now on the agenda."[10] When Deng met with a US congressional delegation led by Senator Sam Nunn on January 11, he made sure the Americans got the message: The PRC would not renounce the use of force, as that would "tie our hands" on Taiwan. The problem, Deng said, was that if the "Taiwan authorities led by

Chiang Ching-kuo" were promised a peaceful reunification, they "would become reckless and would enter into no talks at all." Even worse, Deng warned, what if the Soviet Union got into Taiwan? "Suppose the Soviet Union were to occupy Taiwan. Then, I assume the US would not oppose China using force. That is why we cannot bind our hands."[11]

CHIANG'S SOVIET RENDEZVOUS

Deng Xiaoping was not entirely making up his Soviet story. Recent scholarship utilizing Russian and Taiwanese sources suggests that a secret Taipei-Moscow "rendezvous" lasted from the late 1960s to the 1970s where joint Soviet-Taiwanese action against the mainland was discussed. It is essential to point out this prelude because, again, it showed Chiang's ideological flexibility and the extent he would go to so he could play a part in the global Cold War and gain the upper hand against the mainland, even at the high cost of his personal relations with several American presidents. Those secret talks were carried out through diplomatic channels in the United Nations in New York, in the ROC's liaison office in Mexico City, and more discreetly in Taipei through a KGB agent, a Russian journalist working for the British newspaper *The Evening News* under the cover name of Victor Louis. Louis worked for Brezhnev's rival, Alexander Nikolayevich Shelepin, a Politburo member and former head of the KGB, and visited Taiwan at least four times—in 1968, 1971, 1974, and 1975. During that period, both sides reached a tacit agreement that the Soviet Union would stay neutral if the ROC and Mao's PRC were to get into an armed conflict.[12]

A recent study by Hsiao-ting Lin shows that this secret Taiwan-Soviet rendezvous was much more expansive than scholars had previously thought. After the Cultural Revolution broke out on the Chinese mainland in 1966, Soviet diplomats contacted Taiwanese diplomats in Mexico City and the United Nations. In 1968, Chiang Kai-shek sent his Russian-speaking confidant Zhu Xinming to Mexico City, and he returned with the news that the Soviets admitted "their previous mistaken policies on China" and promised they would render "aid to Chiang if his armed forces were joined by anti-Mao forces on the mainland."[13]

Chiang Ching-kuo was personally involved, representing his father in the negotiations. Through Louis's KGB channel, the question of Soviet support of a KMT attack on the mainland was seriously discussed, especially after the 1969 Sino-Soviet border conflicts, when an all-out war between the Soviet Union and mainland China looked like a very real possibility. Both Chiang's diary and that of his aide James Wei mentioned that in November 1970, Chiang accepted Louis's offer to purchase Soviet weapons and let Soviet military advisers train Taiwanese troops. In addition, "in return for the Soviet military aid, the Taiwanese army would target PLA military bases in Shanghai, Nanjing, Wuhan, and Guangzhou." Only in the last weeks of 1970 did the Soviet leadership decide this offer was too risky and far-fetched. Instead, Brezhnev decided to sort out the situation directly with Beijing. Sino-Soviet tensions remained high, but an all-out war never happened. Later in the 1970s, Chiang had to tone down his secret pro-Soviet policy, as he realized that Taiwan would further alienate its only committed ally—the United States—by getting too close to the socialist bloc.[14]

Ironically, by 1975, the CIA already knew that Victor Louis was a KGB agent. Hong Kong and Japanese street tabloids even wrote sensational stories about his travels in Taipei; his cover was already blown.[15] Although the Taiwanese-Soviet talks had little real substance at this point compared to talks in previous decades, the widespread rumors led the Ford administration to seriously consider the possibility of a Taiwan-Soviet rapprochement. President Ford also started questioning Chiang's loyalty as a supposedly anti-Communist ally. On January 12, 1976, Ford ordered US Ambassador Unger to warn Chiang face-to-face that if he decided to build relations with the Soviet Union, it would "cause disastrous results to Taiwan."[16]

The message was clear. The Soviets, however, never gave up on Taiwan and continued to send signals until the end of the decade. Finally, on the eve of the US-PRC diplomatic opening, Chiang made up his mind that ignoring the Soviet signals would be "a fundamental ROC policy" and focused solely on salvaging relations with the United States.[17] Nevertheless, the secret talks with the Soviet Union showed the problematic nature of Chiang's anti-Communist rhetoric and how restricted he must have felt by having to stay on the American side of the Cold War when the US policy toward Taiwan was anything but loyal and sincere. Chiang's hatred and mistrust of the Americans was especially strong during the Carter administration, as demonstrated in the diary entry he wrote after hearing the news of the US-PRC opening on January 1, 1979: "Ever since we became an ally of the United States, I cannot count how many times the Americans have done traitorous deeds and screwed the Republic of China over and over. We have countless times exhorted, warned, and exerted ourselves out of the kindness of our hearts, but all turned out to be useless, which led to the situation we have today. [The United States] taking an enemy as a friend, bringing a wolf into his house. What kind of unwise, terrifying, and dangerous behavior is this? I believe one day the Americans will regret today's mistakes."[18]

TAIWAN'S OLD FRIENDS

Already in September 1977, a week after US Secretary of State Cyrus Vance's trip to Beijing, Chiang concluded that the US-PRC normalization of diplomatic relations was inevitable and, worse, that the United States might pressure the ROC to enter into talks with the mainland. He then laid out his strategy to "expand diplomacy towards the common American people, especially [to] increase contacts with the US Congress."[19] People-to-people diplomacy, he believed, was the only path forward to counter President Carter's inevitable betrayal of the ROC.

As Carter and Deng celebrated their new friendship in Washington, D.C., Chiang knew that Deng would coerce him into an unfair negotiation with the threat of force. Even worse, Deng might be free to deal with Taiwan with the United States' help or silent approval. At the moment, Chiang was concerned not about an immediate military invasion but about a massive mainland propaganda campaign that could shake the hearts and minds of the people living in the ROC. "After the US established diplomatic relations with the CCP bandits," Chiang wrote on January 8, "the CCP bandits launched an unprecedented united front campaign based on rumors of 'unification.' They also stopped shelling the offshore islands of Quemoy. Those methods are more toxic and evil than an actual war."[20]

The answer to this campaign, Chiang believed, was to completely insulate Taiwan from any mainland influence and to run a counterpropaganda campaign. On January 11, 1979, he instructed Sun Yun-suan, Taiwan's chief legislator, to officially announce that any invitation to negotiate from Deng would be treated as a "united front conspiracy aimed at confusing the whole world."[21] The following week Chiang laid out his plan "to fight against the Communist bandits' United Front policy." In it, he called for a unification of the Chinese nation based on the KMT's terms, not the ones offered by the CCP. The Chinese nation would be united under the condition that "everyone has equal rights and the rights to freedom and participation in politics," and the unified regime would be based "on Sun Yat-sen's Three-People's Principles rather than Communism." The only way to make the ROC engage in negotiations would be for the mainland to "abandon Marxist-Leninist thoughts and to stop spreading world revolution, to abandon communist dictatorship, and to embrace democracy, to disband people's communes, and to give properties back to the people." Finally, the mainland would have to "renounce the use of force to unify Taiwan and show their sincerity." Those policies were not realistic, achievable goals but rhetorical rejections of Deng's offer that were designed to win over hard-line anti-Communist politicians in the United States. The mainland leader, he knew, would never accept these terms.[22]

Chiang's next step was to bring the fight back to the United States, but he knew that this would require "patience and strategy" and that it might be necessary to "endure humiliation for the sake of national interests." "We are at a severe disadvantage in our diplomatic negotiations with the United States, as we are weak and they are strong," Chiang wrote in his diary while Deng was on his historic tour of the United States. "This negotiation requires us to both endure if necessary and act boldly when it requires."[23] "Deng the bandit's visit to the United States is a grand diplomatic conspiracy with two aims," Chiang concluded. "One is to provoke a US-Soviet war so he could get away with it, and the second is to take over Taiwan without deploying a single soldier." Those aims would not be easy for Deng to achieve, but "the Chinese Communists Bandits are evil and venomous, while Carter, a typical American politician, is shameless, ignorant, and incompetent, who was not a match for the Communist bandits. . . . In this situation, something needed to be done, but there are also things cannot be done."[24]

What Chiang meant was that Taiwan should not be guided by emotional impulses to act in ways that would further damage its relations with the Carter administration but should find smarter means to reverse the White House's policy through the US Congress. On February 2, the same day Deng visited NASA facilities in Houston, Chiang was in Taipei meeting with a group of US legislators led by Representative John M. Ashbrook, a Republican from Ohio. Chiang laid out a vision that the United States and Taiwan should be united in their mutual struggle against communism: "The Congressman's visit, immediately after Carter has terminated US-China [meaning the ROC] diplomatic relations, is a significant gesture which showed the deep friendship between the Chinese people and the American people, and it was a tremendous encouragement for all seventeen million people [in Taiwan] who were fighting against communism in this raging storm." Ashbrook, in return, promised that he would propose new legislation in Congress "to facilitate the people's friendship between the United States and China [the ROC]." "The Americans must be reminded again," Chiang pleaded with the US legislators, that "eight hundred million Chinese are already suffering under communism, and the United States should not push those free Chinese in Taiwan into the burning pit."[25]

This strategy of going after Carter's domestic rivals was further encouraged by Chiang's stepmother, Madame Chiang Kai-shek, who had played a role in American politics since World War II and immediately saw how the abandonment of Taiwan would cause a political crisis for President Carter—perhaps even to Taiwan's advantage. On March 12, 1979, she wrote to Chiang Ching-kuo from her luxury residence in New York:

> Because [Carter's] policy in the Middle East and Soviet Russia had failed to save his face ... [Carter] had to sacrifice the loyal and faithful friendly country [Taiwan] like a lamb. This will not help his re-election in two years, and this action was seen as disgusting and counter-productive to average Americans. Even the pro-Soviet liberals felt contradicted: they thought Carter would not dare to play the "China Card" until the intercontinental missiles issue [SALT II] with Russia concluded. Now, Carter will even be criticized by the pro-Russian liberals. Carter tried to be smart, but instead, he acted like a fool.

Madame Chiang assured Chiang that she would always be there to help, "just like [she] had helped during every critical moment in [their] nation's history."[26]

One such target of Chiang's influence campaign was Senator Barry Goldwater of Arizona. Goldwater was a heavy-drinking, outspoken, hot-tempered conservative who burst onto the national political stage in 1960 with a controversial book titled *The Conscience of a Conservative*, in which he attacked the federal government's erosion of state rights.[27] He was also known as a Cold War hawk and criticized President Kennedy for not invading Cuba during the 1962 missile crisis.[28] During the Vietnam War, Goldwater shocked his peers in both parties with his controversial opinion on nuclear weapons. He argued in 1964 that NATO generals should use tactical nuclear weapons freely without direct orders from the White House.[29] In 1964, when he ran as the Republican candidate against President Johnson in the presidential election, he promoted the idea of dropping nuclear bombs in Vietnam. Terrified journalists rushed the story to the newspapers, contributing to Goldwater's significant defeat.[30]

Goldwater was also an old friend of Taiwan (figure 5.1). In 1969, he had encouraged Congress to withdraw its political support and funding for

FIGURE 5.1 Taiwan's old friends: Chiang Ching-kuo meeting with Senator Barry Goldwater and the future President of ROC, Ma Ying-jeou, who was Chiang's personal English translator. (Academia Historia)

the UN to prevent "Red China" from taking over Taiwan's seat. "If Free China's base in the Far East were undermined at the United Nations," he argued, "the world organization would become an instrument for contracting liberty."[31] Because Carter had selected half of his senior staff from the Trilateral Commission, signed the Panama Canal Treaty, and started cozying up with the PRC, Goldwater firmly believed the whole administration was a world Communist conspiracy backed by the evil Rockefellers.[32] He feared that Taiwan and the U.S.-China mutual defense treaty would be the next thing the Carter liberals would sacrifice. Therefore, in 1977, he wrote a letter to assure the Taiwanese government that "if Carter recognizes the Communist bandits, the President will face enormous opposition."[33]

But Carter went in precisely the direction Goldwater feared. The senator was especially alarmed that Brzezinski had made a deal with Deng behind Congress's back in May 1978, which coincided with Chiang's inauguration as the new president of the ROC. "Dear Doctor Brzezinski: It has come to my attention, and I hope I am wrong, that you are going to be in Red China on the day that the new President of Taiwan is inaugurated," a concerned Goldwater wrote. "I think it would be an insult not to have some official representative of the president to attend the inauguration."[34] "We have designated Ambassador Unger," Brzezinski wrote back. "In fact, all countries with which the ROC has relations will be represented by their Ambassador to Taipei."[35]

On December 15, 1978, when Carter announced his decision to normalize relations with the PRC and to cease official relations with the ROC, letters poured into Goldwater's office demanding action. "How can this President lash us day and night regarding human rights and then totally ignore the human and constitutional rights of our Congressmen who were elected by the people of this country? He has done nothing but uphold and embrace Communism!" wrote Reuben M. Burnham of Sun City, Arizona.[36] "If the International Communist Conspiracy organization planned to get a certain person elected to the Presidency of the United States for the sole purpose of having their devious, evil plans pushed through one way or another, they could not have chosen a more suitable prospect than James Earl Carter," wrote James F. Byrne, another Arizona resident.[37] Others had legitimate economic concerns: "China wants us for our technology only. Twenty years from now, this country will be flooded with cheap imported goods from China. We already suffer from too many cheap Japanese goods and, besides, more imports mean fewer jobs here in the United States," wrote Gary and Joyce Hawkings of Arizona.³⁸

Given his pro-ROC stance, it was no wonder that the senator became a main target of Taiwan's influence campaign. This time Chiang took full advantage of the fact that an authoritarian regime can concentrate far more resources on a single foreign policy cause than a democracy can. Utilizing the KMT's absolute control over Taiwan's educational institutions, he organized students, from elementary schools to universities, to send thousands of letters to members of Congress. For example, a joint letter from Taipei University students addressed to Senator Goldwater and other pro-Taiwan conservatives stated: "We are college students of Taiwan, Republic of China. We respect the Americans and consider them our friends because both American and Taiwanese people are peace-loving, freedom-loving, and righteous people. We hope all Americans will consider this case prudently and urge the President not to be so shortsighted."³⁹ Some correspondence was written by younger students with a personal touch (figure 5.2): "I'm a 15-year-old boy in Taiwan, ROC.

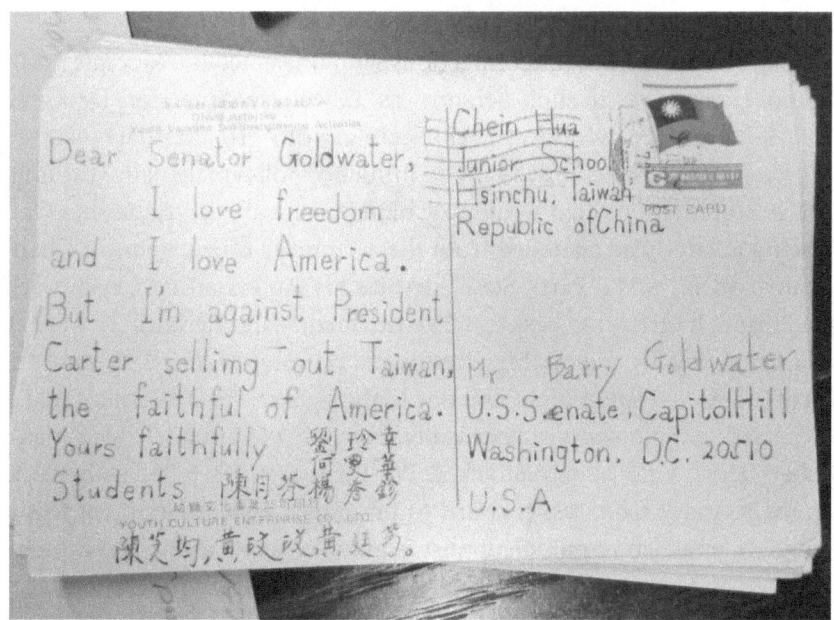

FIGURE 5.2 One of the many cards sent to Senator Goldwater by Taiwanese schoolchildren, asking the United States not to betray Taiwan. (Arizona State University Library)

We are deeply shocked by President Carter's decision to recognize Red China. I hope you will fight in the Senate for the sake of freedom and justice."[40] Another girl wrote, "I'm a schoolgirl. I love my country very much. I know she is in danger now because President Carter recognized Red China."[41]

Supported by his constituency and moved by Chiang's influence campaign, Goldwater went on a personal crusade against Carter in the ROC's defense. He first brought a lawsuit, *Goldwater v. Carter*, in the US District Court for the District of Columbia, alleging that the president illegally abrogated the United States' mutual defense treaty with the ROC. After the court ruled that Carter could not unilaterally terminate the treaty, the well-documented and well-studied case dragged on for a year, with appeals heard by the US Circuit Court of Appeals for the District of Columbia Circuit and the US Supreme Court. The divided Supreme Court did not decide whether President Carter had exceeded his authority by nullifying the treaty. Rather, it returned the case to the district court for dismissal, as four justices found it was a political question that courts should not address and one justice felt the issue was not appropriate for review since Congress had not taken a stance on the treaty. In other words, the Court did not want to meddle in foreign policy.[42]

Chiang also utilized his connections with unelected bureaucrats in the US government. One such person was Taiwanese American Dr. Chen Wen-ke, a senior adviser to the US Secretary of Agriculture, who served as a backdoor channel for Chiang to influence policymakers in Washington. A secret letter Chen wrote to Chiang, ironically in traditional Chinese on a letterhead snatched from the secretary's office, detailed Chen's loyalty to the "KMT Party-State" despite his American citizenship and stated how he tried his best to serve the former motherland. "I want to specify my loyalty to you, Mr. President, and want to do all to serve the Party-State.... I spent night and day lobbying American friends. Finally, I received enough support, especially from my old-time friend, Senator Robert Dole, who openly attacked President Carter's failed policy and agreed to move Congress forward to provide a legal amendment to the situation, and also required support from old friends in the Department of Defense. Many retired generals ... expressed full support to our government," wrote the man currently serving under the US flag. "I wrote the letter hastily and apologize for the bad handwriting. Wish you good health and glory and fortune to our nation." Attached to the letter was an intelligence report Dr. Chen wrote on major American political leaders and their opinions on Taiwan.[43]

THE US CONGRESS AND THE TAIWAN RELATIONS ACT

It was not just the Republicans who felt uneasy about Carter's abandonment of Taiwan. As Madame Chiang Kai-shek correctly predicted, many Democrats also had reasons to oppose Carter's policy. Frank Church, a Democratic senator from Idaho and chair of the Senate Foreign Relations Committee, was the key critic among the liberals who pushed back against Carter's abandonment of Taiwan and who played a major role in shaping the bill that became Taiwan Relations Act (TRA). Church, however, was driven less by anti-Communist zeal than by the belief that congressional oversight should play a role in foreign policy, just as Carter had advocated in his presidential campaign, although he failed to follow through. Church, in fact, had a long track record of advocating congressional oversight in foreign policy: He was among the first US politicians to call for a political settlement for the Vietnam War during the Johnson administration, arguing that it was a civil war rather than a global Communist conspiracy. Later he was a key drafter of the War Powers Act, which ensured, at least in theory, that Congress, not the president, would be responsible for declaring wars.[44] Concerned that the intelligence agencies were getting out of control, he chaired the Senate Select Committee to Study Government Operations with Respect to Intelligence Agencies, often called the Church Committee, which investigated the CIA's unchecked black operations aimed at overthrowing governments and targeting foreign leaders for assassination.[45]

In fact, Church supported Carter's decision to normalize relations with the PRC but disagreed with how the president's action had endangered Taiwan's security. In a letter to a constituent, he wrote, "This final act of diplomatic recognition is the culmination of a series of policy decisions made by three administrations, including Presidents Ford and Nixon. In moving to final recognition of Peking as 'China,' we have at last come to terms with the fact of existence, the power, and the potential of that nation of literally a billion human beings." He further explained why he supported the recognition of the PRC and why this would not contradict his support for the ROC: "The recognition of Mainland China as a fact of life is one matter; the security and well-being of the people of Taiwan is another. I am deeply concerned about the security and future of the Taiwanese. Taiwan has been a good friend, a loyal ally, and a major trading partner. To concede to the reality of recognizing Mainland China does not mean we should turn our back on staunch friends."[46]

However, separating those two issues was not easy for Idaho voters. Church maintained a record of all the angry phone calls he had received regarding his nuanced stance on China, going back to the days after he voted for the PRC's membership in the UN. For example, in a record from the humorously titled "Salter-Sponsored Nut Calls" list, a voter stated that the United States should expel the United Nations and demanded that he, the senator, "stay in Russia." Many others protested his decision in similar ways: "U.S. should get out of U.N.; U.N. should get out of U.S." and "Get Communist organizations out of U.S."[47]

In 1979, hundreds of protest letters poured in from Idaho voters asking Senator Church to do something about Taiwan. Thomas C. Reina of Cottonwood, Idaho, wrote: "You say that you agree with President Carter's betrayal of Taiwan, and you want to make a treaty with China which will leave out any guarantee that Taiwan will be protected from any attempted takeover by China. . . . How you can expect China to keep a treaty when the United States does not keep their treaties? How stupid can we get?"[48] Helan Tsai, a Chinese American, wrote: "We just demonstrated that a treaty signed by the US can be abrogated by the US without any fault of our ally. Are we so desperate that we have to bow to others' demands and forsake our principles? As a naturalized citizen who once admired and cherished American ideals, I became increasingly disenchanted. I cried before, but never have I cried as hard as I did last night over my lost American dreams."[49] Many of the letters expressed strong feelings against Communism. M. I. Wheeler wrote: "It is hard to believe we have a President who talks constantly about Human Rights and then betrays our trusted allies in Taiwan, tossing them to the red butchers in Communist China!"[50]

However, for both Republicans and Democrats, it was easy to oppose Carter vocally but much harder to sit down and work together. Chiang's effort to influence U.S. policymakers seemed to have lost some of its impact when Congress started an endless debate on the TRA, which was supposed to ensure Taiwanese security. Much of the debate concerned US domestic politics—the relations among the presidency, Congress, and US foreign policy—and the real security needs of the ROC were constantly sidelined. Thus, only a few lawmakers lobbied for the position Chiang really wanted: a new, legally binding U.S.-ROC security agreement. According to Zhao Shoubo, Chiang's special envoy to the United States, the only people who fully supported their position were Republican senators like Goldwater, Jacob Javits, and Bob Dole and Democratic senators like Richard Stone.[51]

Some US legislators did not want a security agreement at all. This group included Senator Ted Kennedy of Massachusetts, who believed the United States should only boost Taiwan's self-defense by increasing arms sales and let the two Chinese regimes deal with one another.[52] According to historian Richard C. Bush, the picture got even more complicated when some Democratic senators argued that the United States should add human rights regulations to the TRA to moderate KMT behavior, as they saw the Chiang family as no different from other right-wing dictators who took advantage of the United States' anti-Communist ideology to maintain their hold on power. Taiwanese dissidents persecuted by the Chiang family also jumped into the debate and started their anti-Chiang lobbies.[53]

Beyond contradicting views, those in Congress had to deal with the idea of two Chinas, which caused great confusion during those long congressional debates. Senator Richard Stone, a Democrat from Florida and a longtime friend of the ROC, sent thirty-five questions to the State Department regarding Taiwan's nuclear problem, Taiwanese property rights in the United States, and a range of other difficult questions—including "who ... the People of Taiwan [are]" in legal terms—which Carter administration officials had never clearly thought about.[54] Stone and many other lawyers-turned-legislators also found it mind-boggling that both Chinese governments, the PRC and the ROC, argued that there was only one China, and yet the US government could recognize only the PRC as the one. Here is a strange conversation between Senator Stone and Herbert Hansell, a legal advisor at the State Department:

SENATOR STONE: There is a governing authority [in Taiwan]?
MR. HANSELL: Yes, sir.

SENATOR STONE: Could it be properly called a government?
MR. HANSELL: No, sir, not—
SENATOR STONE: Could it be called a government?
MR. HANSELL: Not for purposes of—
SENATOR STONE: Teng Hsiao-P'ing called it a government, why can't you?
MR. HANSELL: For purposes of U.S. foreign relations, we have acknowledged the position of the Taiwanese [who] believe that there is one government in China.
SENATOR STONE: But not their position that they are it.
MR. HANSELL: Precisely.[55]

The Senate's polarizing debate on the proposed TRA greatly confused Joe Biden, then a thirty-seven-year-old senator from Delaware and later a US president, who was curious, outspoken, and fresh on board the Senate Foreign Affairs Committee. On the one hand, he was very hesitant about supporting the TRA, believing that "constructing a web of ties and obligations would complicate relations with the PRC." On the other hand, he "was mystified that the U.S. could withdraw from the Mutual Defense Treaty, but also insisted that it would not tolerate coercion against Taiwan."[56] Biden did not believe that the TRA would protect the country in the long run, and in an earlier session, he had grilled Secretary of Defense Brown: "The People's Republic of China had three red lines for Taiwan: no declaration of independence, no nuclear weapons, and no close ties with the Soviet Union. What would the People's Republic of China's reaction be if Taiwan took any of these steps? What, realistically, could they [PRC] do [to pressure or punish Taiwan] in light of what Secretary Brown just told us if they don't really have the capability of doing anything for the foreseeable future?" Secretary Brown, neither interested in talking to legislators nor caring much about the Taiwanese, brushed the question away: "I would not want to speculate about what they would do; I would expect a negative political turn rather than military action."[57]

All these concerns and confusions shaped the final version of the TRA, which, according to most studies, had been watered down significantly from the version that Chiang and his Republican Party friends had hoped for.[58] In terms of the security of Taiwan, the TRA ambiguously stated, "It is the policy of the U.S. to consider any effort to determine the future of

Taiwan by other than peaceful means, including by boycotts or embargoes, a threat to the peace and security of the Western Pacific area and of grave concern to the United States." This, in the eyes of constitutional scholars, really meant nothing. The clause regarding arms sales was also watered down from the original draft: It was changed from giving Taiwan "advanced military technology" to allowing Taiwan "a sufficient self-defense capability." What was "sufficient" became an issue for the executive branch to decide.[59]

Scholars have noted that Chiang's voice and concerns were utterly lost in the TRA. The legally binding security guarantee was not there, and the level of arms sales to Taiwan that could be approved was left to the White House to decide—a disaster for Chiang, considering his terrible personal relations with several US presidents, both past and current. Worse, this left a window for Deng to negotiate with the US president behind the scenes regarding what types of weapons Taiwan could get. Taiwanese records did not show whether Chiang knew about it, but this is precisely the position that the Carter administration secretly shared with Deng. For example, when PRC Foreign Minister Huang Hua expressed concerns about the TRA, Deputy Secretary of State Warren Christopher instructed Leonard Woodcock, ambassador to the ROC, to explain to the Chinese that it did not exceed what Deng and Carter had already secretly agreed to and that all major decisions regarding Taiwan would come from the White House: "The final form of the act, as it emerged from Congress, is not in every peculiar what the administration preferred. . . . However, it provides sufficient discretionary authority to enable the President to implement the act in a way fully consistent with normalization. . . . As the Chinese side has noted, our dispute on the Taiwan issue is settled."[60]

AMERICAN LAWMAKERS MEET DENG XIAOPING

In a dramatic turn, on April 21, 1979, just a week after President Carter had reluctantly signed the TRA into law, the men who had written it—Frank Church, Jacob Javits, and a third of the Senate Foreign Relations Committee—flew to Beijing. They needed to talk to Deng about other, much more urgent problems in the global Cold War, particularly the Soviet

Union. After all, the year of crisis had already begun: SALT II was hanging in the balance, an American ambassador had just been brutally murdered in Afghanistan, and Iran—the cornerstone of US Middle East strategy—was descending into chaos after the shah left the country. In January, *Time* magazine even ran a cover with a Russian bear tearing apart the globe.[61] Deng understood why the Americans had come to him, and he took this opportunity to attack the TRA. With the Soviets marching into the Middle East, intervening in Afghanistan, and supporting Vietnamese intervention in Cambodia, Deng warned that the United States needed mainland China more than ever. Yet the TRA was standing in the way of US-PRC Cold War cooperation, and he held the men in the room responsible.

"To be frank," Deng said, "China is dissatisfied with the Taiwan Relations Act. . . . The U.S. is interfering with the basic understanding reached during the normalization of relations. In reality, this act has negated the political basis for normalizing Sino-U.S. relations. I would like to advise the people here to pay attention to these ideas." He then made a vague threat: "You must be very cautious about selling arms [to Taiwan]." The conversation became awkward for the senators. Church thanked Deng for his "frankness." Javits, who had lobbied hard for US military protection of Taiwan in Washington and who was now clearly scared of Deng, did not want to bear any more responsibility if their actions should lead to war: "The Congress was not reactionary. . . . We will be diligent in the U.S. Congress to see that no trace of national sovereignty exists in our commercial and cultural relations with Taiwan." To ensure the Americans understood, Deng again assumed a threatening stance: "China does not agree to the non-use of force. I think the American friends should consider this problem." Biden was also sitting in the room, quietly observing the confrontation. When Deng suddenly turned to him and asked if the United States would sell China F-15s and F-16s, the young senator, like many other legislators, clearly did not wish to bear any more responsibility for foreign policy and politely excused himself: "I'm not the President."[62]

DENG XIAOPING'S NEW OFFER

On August 27, 1979, Deng protested again to US Vice President Walter Mondale while he was in Beijing, demanding that the Americans hand over all Taiwanese government assets in the United States to the PRC and stop giving Chiang any more political support or selling Taiwan any more weapons. "I only want to tell you that in your various dealings with them, it has tended to make Chiang Ching-kuo very cocky. It has caused his tail to rise very high."[63] Meanwhile back in Washington, even the pro-PRC advisers, such as Michel Oksenberg, admitted that US-China relations seemed to be cooling down after the passage of the TRA. Deng was not getting the military and technological items he wanted, and at the same time, Chiang still had his access. According to Oksenberg, Deng felt that we were "simply using our relationship with China to improve our relations with the Soviet Union." In addition, Oksenberg urged, the United States has an obligation to protect their new friends in China: "Several Chinese leaders, particularly Deng Xiaoping, exposed themselves in pursuit of the Sino-American opening, for other reasons, such as their Vietnam conflict, these people have come under some attack, but we are handing their opponents an additional weapon to club them by not being meticulous in our management of the Sino-American relationship."[64]

After his frustration with the United States over the TRA, Deng realized that he had to find a better way to deal with Chiang despite American meddling. Deng's desire to directly negotiate with Chiang was first openly expressed in 1979 when Deng met with *Time* magazine editor Hedley Donovan. "Our policy is reasonable, and it respects the reality in Taiwan. The current Taiwanese regime could keep its power, which means they can keep their own military, trade, business connections, and people-to-people relations with foreign countries. The current policies and ways of life do not have to change, but only under the condition of 'One-China.' This could be solved in the long run. The main body of China should be the mainland, and this will eventually be developed. There is only one main demand, one China, not two Chinas, and that we both love the same homeland."[65] When Deng met Japanese Prime Minister Masayoshi Ōhira on December 6, 1979, he promised that in addition to its own foreign relations, way of life, and political system—what Deng called "three no-changes"—Taiwan would be allowed to keep its military as long as it enjoyed its autonomy as a part of China, which, of course, was represented by the PRC.[66]

Instead of luring Chiang into negotiations, Deng's announcements ignited another round of long and bitter propaganda fights. "Our goal of sustaining our democracy and freedom, of fighting against communism, of recovering the mainland has never changed and will not change under any pressure," Chiang explained his position in the *Washington Post* on April 5, 1980. Further, he assured the Americans that "Taiwan will never reach out to the Soviet Union," since "not to have any contact with Soviet Russia" remained one of the ROC's national founding principles and "will not change even if America's position has changed."[67]

When his open polemics failed, Deng resorted to a back channel directly connected to Chiang. He contacted a Hong Kong–born Chinese American named Eric Hotung, who then reached out to Ray S. Cline, a retired CIA analyst who at the time worked at the Center for Strategic and International Studies, then still a part of Georgetown University in Washington, D.C. Cline had some prior connections with the Chiang family, and sometime in late 1981, he passed Deng's private message to Chiang that the CCP was ready for informal, low-profile negotiations directly with the KMT, which could possibly take place in the neutral city of Hong Kong, outside the great powers' radar.[68] This move, however, made Chiang even more agitated about Deng. Chiang banned Cline from ever seeing him again and confessed his anger and resolution to Madame Chiang Kai-shek, promising never to pay attention to "the Communist bandits and their little game of 'united front policy.' "[69]

As for Deng, the reunification he wished for never arrived, and he was not successful in cutting off US military aid to Taiwan. The new president, Ronald Reagan, stated very clearly that the United States would not stop selling arms to Taiwan in an US-PRC joint communiqué on August 17, 1982. Instead, US arms sales to the ROC would be "correlated to mainland China's peaceful policy towards Taiwan."[70] Even though Deng officially agreed to this communiqué for the sake of maintaining US-PRC relations, he saw the United States' statement on Taiwan as a personal humiliation.[71] Thus, in the 1980s, a self-contradictory phenomenon occurred, as US military and dual-use technologies and finished military products continued to flow to both the PRC and the ROC, fueling the cross-strait arms race between Deng and Chiang. Reagan, however, was quite proud of this policy and called it the "balanced approach" when questioned by members of Congress.[72] Meanwhile, US legislators continued to flock to both sides, complaining about the Soviet Union with Deng while talking about the great achievement of Taiwan's anti-Communist policy and economic miracle with Chiang. At this point, US politicians were also learning how to be masters of "speaking the language of humans when seeing a human, and speaking the language of devils when seeing a devil."[73]

MADAME CHIANG KAI-SHEK STRIKES BACK

Deng Xiaoping and Chiang Ching-kuo used all the tricks in a long propaganda fight over the hearts and minds of the people in the broadly defined "Chinese nation" that lasted through much of the 1980s Cold War. Most of the exchanges were mere slogans that used rather crude propagandistic language, but in one case, Deng borrowed the delicate pen of the well-educated son of a former KMT official and engaged in a bizarre literati exchange with Madame Chiang Kai-shek that almost took the form of a poetry contest in the old Chinese imperial court. This is a textbook case of how manipulative both the CCP and the KMT could be in their efforts to win over the other side, as they followed the classical Chinese art of persuasion and manipulation that can be best described in Chinese idioms such as "a sharp knife is hidden behind the smile" and a "needle is buried in soft cotton."

Liao Zhongkai was a well-respected financer at the turn of the century and one of the early founding fathers of the KMT, as well as the architect of the controversial united front policy that resulted in a temporary truce between the KMT and the CCP in the 1920s.[74] In October 1982, his son, Liao Cheng-chih, a member of the PRC's rubber-stamp People's Congress, used his family reputation and penned a poetic open letter in a classical style to "Dear brother Ching-kuo," who was now separated from him by "a strip of water" and "who never thought ... should have become so vast a distance." In that letter, Liao used every trick—emotional blackmail, public shaming, and emotional manipulation. He opened the letter by calling Chiang to come to the negotiating table "to accomplish the great cause of national reunification" and put an end to the separation so that "compatriots in Taiwan would be able to live in peace and happiness, [and] the people of all nationalities on both sides of the Taiwan Straits would no longer have to endure the pains of separation from their kith and kin." Reunification, Liao further argued, is not just good for the people of Taiwan or those elderly Chinese whom Chiang had a personal responsibility to reunite with their mainland families; it also "would contribute to the stability of Asia and the Pacific region as well as to world peace." "Putting up in that tight eastern corner is not a long-term solution," Liao reminded his "brother." "This is, of course, quite clear for a man as intelligent as you." Lastly, Liao evoked Chiang's filial duty as a good Chinese son and promised to allow his father, Chiang Kai-shek, to be reburied in his ancestral home on the mainland. Thus, Chiang would be fulfilling his duty as a son by accepting reunification. "This would be an answer to the two generations of the changes to history ... otherwise, how could you account for yourself after your passing away?" Chinese unification, in Liao's letter, was never about Deng's or any other CCP leader's ambition or the Cold War; it was instead a matter of the Taiwanese people's desire for family reunion, a contribution to world peace, and Chiang's family responsibility.[75]

Chiang Ching-kuo, abiding by his no contact policy and knowing he was never a poetic writer, delegated the response to Madame Chiang Kai-shek, who was an even better classical essay writer and master manipulator (figure 5.3). She wrote an equally eloquent yet even more bitingly sharp and sarcastic response. "Dear Nephew Cheng-chih," Madame Chiang opened, reminding him that she held seniority over him and that it was not Chiang Ching-kuo's duty to respond to his letter because of the "no contact, no negotiation, no compromise" policy and the much greater duty of the KMT president. "When I read your cable letter, I could have laughed at it and ignored it," she wrote. "I remembered what took place 56 and 57 years ago when you were very young." Madame Chiang then reminded Liao of the entire history of KMT, from the founding of the party to the creation of the Whampoa Military Academy, the northern expedition, and the sad event of the assassination of Liao's father, Liao Zhongkai, which ironically allowed Chiang Kai-shek's rise in the KMT; "although you were still a child, I think that you already felt the pain of losing your father." Then she turned 180 degrees and started to question the elder Liao's loyalty due to his sympathy toward the Communists.

> I think that, from the beginning to the end, your father was a faithful disciple of Dr. Sun. As you mentioned to me, a person should be "both loyal and filial." So, if one imagines that your father only pretended to be loyal

FIGURE 5.3 Madame Chiang Kai-Shek. (Academia Historia)

to the three principles and Dr. Sun but, in actuality, had been planted in the KMT [by the communists], how could one say he was loyal? If your father was actually loyal to the KMT, would you be unfilial to say something to the contrary? If the two generations, your father and yourself, were neither loyal nor filial, wouldn't that make you look bad in history? Please give it some thought.

Madame Chiang next turned the younger Liao's own horrific experiences on the mainland into a weapon of attack. "I would also like to call your attention to the time during the peak of the Cultural Revolution when I heard that you had suffered severely in the power struggle and had been lucky to escape death from the mouth of the tiger. You may consider this a lucky thing for you, among a great number of unlucky matters [death]." She listed all the mortality numbers, suicides, and deaths of "high-level CCP officials, such as Liu Shao-Chi, Peng De-Huai, and He Long, who died because they were exiled or starved." She asked him, "If they could express their views after death, how would they evaluate the ways used by your party to incite large numbers of cadres to their mutual destruction? Mao Tse-tung was a wicked old person. In the style of the bandits, he had many people killed for his personal glory."

In the next two pages, Madame Chiang went deeper into Chinese and world history and mentioned mass murders by Hong Xiuquan, leader of the Taiping rebellion who killed eight million people in the late Qing dynasty, and by Stalin, who notoriously said, "One mourns about one person's death but the deaths of hundreds and thousands of people are nothing but statistics." Yet she reminded him that the CCP had killed "some 50 million people," a number that "pales that of even the most ruthless and evil totalitarian killers in world history." She then went on to ask who the real traitor to China was that Liao had accused in his earlier letter: Was it the KMT, which "never tried to do anything to seek favors from foreigners by being sycophantic," or the "CCP, who put huge portraits of Marx in the prominent places all over the nation and worships him as their ancestor . . . ? This shameless act reminds me of what Ko Mo-jo once said: 'Stalin is my father.' And this makes me feel like vomiting for three days."[76]

Madame Chiang went on for three more pages about the Communists and their sins and the "brink of disaster" yet to come to the Chinese mainland. "If you treasure your own life and come to join us so that you can carry out your father's will, you could have a peaceful life toward the end. If you still refuse to wake up, in the future, when we recover the mainland, you could still be spared. There is no need for you to become a monk in order to redeem yourself. . . . You must know that the shore is behind you." She used a classic Chinese idiom about repentance and redemption: "I hope that you will give this serious thought."[77] Liao never wrote any response, perhaps because the letter was so damaging to his reputation and inner psyche.

Deng Xiaoping, on the other hand, refused to give up. After Chiang Ching-kuo's death on January 13, 1988, Deng again offered the one-China, two-systems option to get Chiang's successor, Lee Teng-hui, to come to the negotiating table. However, by the late 1980s, Taiwan's economic development and living standards were already far ahead of those of the mainland. Thus, Deng's offer was hardly attractive to the Taiwanese people. His own domestic policies also contributed to his failure: The economic reform he initiated a decade before had not yet improved the lives of most of the people living in mainland China. My province, Yunnan, was far away from the Special Economic Zones Deng established and remained poor. My family relied on government-issued food coupons for basic grocery items such as rice, milk, and meat until the early 1990s. We had to share a public toilet with a dozen other families in a commune apartment building provided by the university where my father worked, and everything was in short supply. Also, in 1987, when I was born, Taiwanese were allowed to visit the mainland as tourists and for family reunions. In that year, Taiwan's average GDP per capita reached US$7,480, whereas that of the mainland remained a mere US$754.[78] Taiwanese visitors who witnessed mainland China's poverty—especially in inland provinces such as mine—and its lack of political freedom further convinced the Taiwanese people that the two countries should stay on their separate paths.[79]

On May 16, 1989, Deng achieved another of his major Cold War goals when he normalized Sino-Soviet relations with Mikhail Gorbachev. Yet Taiwan remained a lasting regret. He even confessed this to Gorbachev: "There is only one more thing left in my life, and that is the problem of Taiwan. I am afraid that I won't be able to see it myself."[80] But Deng only had himself to blame. The massacre of students in Tiananmen Square that followed on June 4, 1989, horrified and further antagonized the Taiwanese people. Mainland China's disastrous image after Tiananmen contributed

FIGURE 5.4 A famous poster of a delighted Deng Xiaoping after the end of the Cold War. In 1990, he relinquished all his official positions except that of president of a poker club in Beijing.

to the fact that after the Cold War, more and more Taiwanese youths self-identified as Taiwanese rather than Chinese and wanted absolutely nothing to do with the scary Communist regime on the other side of the Taiwan Strait. Even the Chineseness shared across the strait—a main justification for Deng's reunification goal—was at this point splitting apart.[81]

CONCLUSION

In this chapter, I examined the intricate interplay of diplomacy, ideology, and domestic politics that defined US-China-Taiwan relations during the late 1970s Cold War and how this affected the making of the TRA, Deng's one-China, two-systems strategy, and long-term US relations with the two competing Chinese regimes. From the CCP's perspective, the inability to convince or blackmail Chiang into negotiating on possible reunification was a major disappointment and policy failure for their leader, Deng. The competition between the two Chinese regimes has continued to destabilize the United States' relations with both Chinese regimes. At the same time, a new factor—Taiwan's democratization in the late 1980s and early 1990s—has offered another significant challenge to the CCP's rule on the Chinese mainland.

6

THE GLOBAL RESPONSE TO CARTER'S CHINA POLICY

Unheeded Warnings from Moscow to Washington

The US-China security collaboration emerged as a significant obstacle in the Soviet Union's efforts to stabilize relations with China after Mao's death. Beijing and Washington's anti-Soviet hard-liners continued to push for closer security collaboration despite its destabilizing impact on US-Soviet détente and the overall dynamic of the global Cold War. This effort attracted criticism not just from the Brezhnev regime but also from other high-level Chinese and US officials who, for various reasons, advocated a more balanced foreign policy in their respective capitals.

MAO AND THE LEGACY OF THE SINO-SOVIET SPLIT

The year 1976 was a landmark in Soviet foreign policy and Brezhnev's political career. The Twenty-Fifth Congress of the Communist Party of the Soviet Union (CPSU), held from late February to early March 1976, confirmed that détente was a success and urged the Soviet Union to further pursue the spread of socialism internationally. This was a major departure from—and expansion of—the earlier Brezhnev doctrine, which justified the military intervention of any threat to "the socialist system" within Eastern and Central Europe, such as during the military invasion of Czechoslovakia in 1968. The new interventionists policy, now targeted not just Soviet Union's immediate periphery but the whole world as the Soviet-Cuban intervention in Angola already demonstrated, was enshrined in the new Soviet constitution the following year.[1] The Soviet Union's continued hostile relations with neighboring Communist China, however, offered few things for the general secretary to celebrate. Officially, the CPSU Congress allowed Brezhnev to declare that the Soviet Union had successfully fought off China's "Maoist influence" within the socialist world, which was "aimed against the majority of the socialist states and directly allied with its most extreme reaction worldwide" and was "not just alien to socialist principles and ideals but essentially ... an important reserve of imperialism."[2] However, for Soviet officials who were involved in relations with China, that description was far from reality.

The Sino-Soviet split that started in the early 1960s was still unresolved. For many of Brezhnev's advisers, the Soviet Union's bad relations with the PRC were mainly, if not solely, Mao Zedong's responsibility: Mao's criticism of Khrushchev's 1956 secret speech against Stalinism, Mao's decision to sever the PRC's institutional links with the Warsaw Pact nations and withdraw from the Soviet-led Council for Mutual Economic Assistance in 1961, and the PRC's war with India—a country close to the Soviet Union at the time of the Cuban missile crisis in 1962—were all reasons the PRC and the Soviet Union turned from allies into rivals in the 1960s.[3] Furthermore, the purge of pro-Soviet CCP members like Liu Shaoqi during the Great Cultural Revolution, the bloody border conflict in 1969, Mao's flirtation with Nixon and Kissinger since 1972, and increased Sino-Soviet competition within the socialist world caused tremendous concern among the new Soviet leaders around Brezhnev.[4] Andrei A. Kokoshin, Russia's first deputy minister of defense from 1992 to 1996, recalled, "In the 1970s ... the People's Republic of China was included among the Soviet Union's potential adversaries." The Soviet leadership believed "a war between the Soviet Union and China would involve nuclear weapons since China was by now also a nuclear power and the 'Peking leadership,' like the forces of imperialism, was preparing for nuclear war."[5]

During 1976, the last year of his life, Mao suffered from three heart attacks and was diagnosed with Parkinson's disease and a rare motor-neuron condition called amyotrophic lateral sclerosis, which caused him to lose much of his ability to move and speak.[6] Still, the chairman remained bitterly anti-Soviet till the end. In the Soviet foreign policy community, frustrated diplomats sometimes gleefully circulated gossip about Mao's declining health to pass the time. On May 20, 1976, for example, Boris N. Ponomarev, the head of the International Department of the CPSU Central Committee, passed his aides a ciphered telegram from Beijing recounting a discussion between New Zealand Prime Minister Robert Muldoon and the PRC Chairman, which had been retold to the Soviet ambassador to China Vasily S. Tolstikov in Beijing by the loudmouthed Australian ambassador Stephen FitzGerald:

> The Helmsman was escorted in and supported on both sides. Muldoon was brought over to him. Mao stretched out his hand but looked sideways (he had a loss of coordination). Chinese ceremonies, seating. To play along, Muldoon started the conversation with almost a quote, "There is great excitement in the Celestial Empire. The people of the world are rising to fight for independence. And they will certainly win!"
> Mao was quiet for a while, then said, "No!"
> Muldoon, "Of course, if they have real leaders!"
> Mao: "No!"
> Muldoon wouldn't give up, "And if they unite."
> Mao: "There is still the Soviet Union."
> With that, the reception was over, as the Helmsman became tired and was escorted away. The philosophical debate lasted ten minutes.[7]

Mao's death on September 9, 1976, led to a brief period of uncertainty but also a long-awaited opportunity for change in the direction of the PRC's foreign policy. Soviet leaders initially wished to take advantage of the PRC's post-Mao political transition to improve relations with Beijing and hopefully to convince the new leaders to support the Soviet Union's latest initiative to create a collective security system under Soviet leadership. Soviet diplomats thus launched a "hundred-day thaw"—intended to influence the new Chinese leaders around Hua Guofeng, Mao's successor. The Chinese historian Shen Zhihua noticed that TASS, the Soviet news agency, announced Mao's death on September 9 without the usual polemic against Maoism. Soviet Foreign Minister Andrei Gromyko also visited the PRC Embassy in Moscow to express his condolences—a story publicly announced by the Soviet press so as to draw Beijing's attention.[8] Gromyko, during his speech at the United Nations on September 28, further emphasized that "the Soviet Union continues, as it has done in the past, to attach great importance to its relations with the People's Republic of China" and that "the normalizations of those relations would undoubtedly have a positive effect on the situation in Asia." Further, the Soviet media stopped their usual anti-Maoism polemics; those gestures, confirmed in Brezhnev's later conversation with the Bulgarian leader, were indeed an attempt to signal goodwill to the post-Mao Chinese leadership.[9]

THE SOVIET CHARM OFFENSIVE IN 1977

A close examination of memoirs, diaries, and archival sources at the State Archive of the Russian Federation suggests that to win the hearts and minds of PRC diplomats stationed in Moscow after Mao's death, the Soviet Union launched an intense charm offensive that continued throughout 1977 and even until the mid-1980s. Evidence of this can be found in the Soviet-Chinese Friendship Association activities led by Sergei Tikhvinskii, director of the Soviet Foreign Ministry's Diplomatic Academy and a well-trained sinologist. With detailed written instructions from Tikhvinskii's colleagues Oleg B. Rakhmanin, director of the Department for Relations with Fraternal Countries, and Mikhail Sladkovskiĭ, director of the Far East Institute of the Academy of Sciences, the association carefully choreographed a series of Chinese-themed celebrations in Moscow in the first half of 1977. With titles such as "Great October Revolution and China," "50-Year Shanghai Uprising," "Jubilee of the Funding of the Chinese Communist Party," "Cartoon Commune," "Nanchang Uprising," and "Funding of the PLA. Liberation of Manchuria," these events tried to present a nostalgic view of Sino-Soviet friendship back in the good old days when many of the Soviet sinologists themselves were engaged in the revolutionary activities in China. In all such celebrations, the association emphasized the Soviet Union's contribution to the Chinese Communist Revolution and the debts the Chinese people supposedly owed to their big Soviet brothers. All the proceedings and records of the celebrations were distributed in the PRC through Soviet-sponsored Chinese-language journals, *The Soviet Union*, and *Soviet Woman* and to the global news network through TASS.[10]

For example, during the May 1977 celebration of "Soviet Military Adviser's Participation and Assistance During the Fight for the First Chinese Revolutionary Base in the South from 1925–1927," Tikhvinskii delivered a speech prepared by Rakhmanin and Sladkovskii in which he pointedly called the event "one of the activities to inform the public about our Leninist Internationalist politics towards China." He also reminded the audience that "the Soviet Union had provided brotherly help to all stages of the Chinese people's struggle for unity and the creation of Socialism."[11]

It was routine at such events to praise the "Friends of the Soviet Union" and to denounce the "Enemies of Socialism and Brotherly Socialist Countries"—namely, Mao and his anti-Soviet followers. "For fifty years during the history of the People's Liberation Army of China, the Army has always been guided by Marxist-Leninist principles, which achieved a series of great victories." Another speaker at the celebration of the funding of the PLA stated, "[The PLA] protected the People's Republic of China from aggression, and was an ally of the Soviet Union, and a friend of the socialist nations. . . . It was from the Army that came brave and principled political figures like Peng De-Huai [who was purged by Mao] who already in 1958 [when he was still minister of defense] vocally protested against Maoist politics."[12]

Not all events seemed to be convincing from the Chinese perspective: On April 16, for example, the association invited Meng Qingshu, the widow of the late pro-Soviet Chinese Communist Wang Ming who had adopted the Russian name Rosa Vladimirova Ostrova, to the seventy-fifth anniversary remembrance of her late husband. Sladkovskii read a rousing eulogy: "Comrade Wang Ming! Bright example of indestructible faith in Marxism-Leninism and Proletarian Internationalism" who fought "for the friendship between the Chinese and the Soviet People, and for the Unity of the International Communist movement."[13] It is not hard to imagine this type of propaganda having a counterproductive effect on the post-Mao Chinese leaders if they even noticed it at all, especially considering that the dogmatic pro-Soviet Wang Ming was Deng's political rival during the early Communist movement in the late 1930s. From the perspective of the CCP's official historians, Wang Ming was considered a dangerous Comintern puppet who had little understanding of Chinese local reality. It was Deng, according to official CCP historians, who "saved the Party from Wang Ming's false and right-wing policies" in

1938 during the worst year of the Communists' military campaign against Chiang Kai-shek.[14]

Despite the lack of clear impact on Sino-Soviet relations, the Soviet-Chinese Friendship Association continued to host such activities, including events on classic Chinese culture, into the 1980s. At many of those events, Soviet sinologists and Chinese émigrés—or more precisely, political refugees from Mao's purges—read poems and classical texts along with Russian translations and lamented the destruction of classic Chinese culture under Mao's Cultural Revolution. Records suggest that Chinese Embassy staff occasionally attended such events and had unofficial conversations with their Russian counterparts. Some Chinese diplomats certainly were touched. For example, at one of the association events held in Moscow in September 1979, a saddened Chinese diplomat named Shi Huyao privately admitted to Ilyá S. Shcherbakov, the Soviet Ambassador to China, that "you in your country know our culture better than us, all because of the fact of the Gang of Four."[15] However, the association's activities had little to no effect in terms of improving Sino-Soviet relations at the end of the decade.[16]

THE LONG AND DISAPPOINTING WAIT FOR DENG XIAOPING

Soviet and China watchers' unwarranted expectations added to their disappointment after Mao's successor, Hua Guofeng, confirmed that Mao's thoughts were "powerful weapons" to fight against "imperialism and socialist-imperialism"—the latter a euphemism for the Soviet Union, which was considered "a bigger threat" to world peace in the superpower struggle. Hua called the Soviets "revisionists" and the Brezhnev regime "a capitalist-turned-bureaucrats elite class who dominated the party," and he compared the Soviet leaders to the Chinese Gang of Four. Responding indirectly to the Soviet Union's charm offensive, Hua suggested, "If the Soviet Union truly wanted to improve relations, they must act to prove their sincerity."[17] In September 1977, a frustrated Sladkovskiĭ wrote to the Central Committee that the post-Mao Chinese leader "continued Mao's anti-Soviet, pro-American foreign policy" as "a way to fulfill Mao's will" in foreign policy. Summarizing the Eleventh CCP Congress, Sladkovskiĭ said, "The Chinese changed from fighting two fronts—the USSR and the US—into blockades with all forces, whoever they can exploit, against the Soviet Union, under the disguise of fighting against [Soviet] superpower hegemony.... The Eleventh Party Congress preserved all the basic Maoist ideological and theoretical concepts and [Mao's] evaluation of international conditions."[18]

Soviet scholars found the Eleventh CCP Congress's decision to base the Chinese path to socialism on "practice and reality" incomprehensible, as the Soviet Union already provided a perfect example for such development, a process that was well described in the voluminous works of Mikhail Suslov, their ideological tsar and longtime Politburo member.[19] Thus, they concluded that the new Chinese leadership was "in [a] deep crisis of ideology." "Mao was a revisionist under cover of 'developing Marxism-Leninism,'" and Deng was even worse; on the one hand, he was "apologetic toward Maoism," but on the other, he had "discarded all socialist theories" and "given up Maoism and replaced it with his nationalistic and hegemonic doctrine of 'seeking truth through practice.'"[20]

From an ideological standpoint, Deng, who became the leader of the PRC in December 1978, naturally came under suspicion, as he and his close associates often justified their policy with Mao's words. After a year of observation, the Far East Institute published a summary of the "ideological problems" that they had observed from the new Deng Xiaoping leadership, cherry picking speeches such as Ye Jianying's "Mao's ideas were the foundation of the CCP," and reached the conclusion that despite the "ideological battle" between those who "wanted to dogmatically preserve Mao's ideas" and those who believed in pragmatical adaptation of this ideology, Deng and his associates, nevertheless, "are still Maoists!"[21] Ironically, the Soviet scholars saw Deng's effort to rein in Mao's policy of exporting revolution in Africa as a betrayal of the world communist revolution. This view blatantly contradicted their conclusions a decade before, when they referred to Mao's support of revolutionary groups in Africa as being in direct competition with the Soviet Union's support of similar revolutionary groups and as engaging in a "chauvinistic" adventure that "betrayed Marxism."[22] It was no wonder that when Deng ordered the PLA to invade Vietnam, a fellow Communist country and a close ally of the Soviet Union, the Soviet leadership was deeply traumatized. For

Deng, this attack served several goals: to show Vietnam "who is the boss" in the bilateral relationship, to disrupt the Soviet Union's efforts to encircle China, and to demonstrate to the United States that China's priority lies in Asia.[23] But as the Soviet foreign policy historian Sergei Radchenko has pointed out, China's invasion of Vietnam was extremely worrying to Brezhnev and his comrades: "Much as Brzezinski worried about 'the arc of crises,' so did the Soviets eye with grave suspicion what seemed like Sino-American coordination over China's invasion of Vietnam. Brezhnev accused Carter of complicity in angry letters."[24]

With this significant new development, everything the Chinese did in the developing world was viewed in Moscow with alarm and suspicion. For example, when Chinese Vice Premier Li Xiannian toured Tanzania, Mozambique, and Zimbabwe in early 1980 and promised to stop supporting the local armed Communist revolutionaries, the Far East Institute scholar V. N. Baryshnikov switched his position 180 degrees and claimed China's withdrawal of support for African revolutions and peace-making efforts was "colluding with South Africa and other imperialist, racist colonial regimes, while double-dealing with other representatives of progressive, socialistic nations of Africa." The end goal, the Soviet expert concluded, was "Beijing's standard line with international imperialism, to blockade [the solution] of all current problems, including those regarding national liberation movements."[25]

No matter what the Chinese did, it seems they could not escape the Soviet sinologists' theological fury. When China announced it would open the city of Shenzhen as an experimental Special Economic Zone (SEZ) where foreign direct investment could flow in freely, Fast East Institute economists concluded in a special report in January 1980 that China's SEZ policy was a betrayal of the socialist path of development represented by the Soviet model. They compared Shenzhen's SEZ to the treaty ports in the shameful 1842 Nanking Treaty, signed between the British and the Qing Empire after the First Opium War. The SEZ would make the Chinese leaders "lose their prestige in the Socialist World," the scholars predicted, and make the "People's Republic of China lose its authority in the Third World, where they [the Chinese leaders] see themselves as the leader."[26]

It is unlikely that the Soviet experts were unaware of favorable judgments of the post-Mao Chinese leadership that emerged in the West, given their privileged access to "bourgeois" academic publications. For example, when the Far East Institute scholar Vladimir Alexeyevich Krivzov wrote a letter to the Soviet Central Committee to ask for increased research funds and travel grants, he provided a detailed survey of the current state of "sinologists in the bourgeoisie countries." He admitted that the Western scholars had many advantages, including "better financial support," "modern informatic systems," and "recent access to China, [that the Soviets did not]." However, Krivzov concluded, "All the bourgeoisie China studies scholars' works are inferior to those China studies scholars in the USSR . . . especially here at the Far East Institute." The reason? "They don't understand the true origin of Maoism, and they rarely cited works done by Soviet and other Socialist Scholars," which as he already said, were "superior to those of the bourgeoisie scholars."[27]

THE UNSOLVABLE CHINA PROBLEM IN US-SOVIET RELATIONS

Advised and pushed by those highly ideological advisers, the Soviet leadership grew increasingly hostile toward Deng and especially his pro-American policy. The Carter administration was vaguely aware of Soviet sensitivities regarding any potential US-China military cooperation but never truly comprehended its full psychological impact on those making Soviet foreign policy. For example, President Carter tried to assure Soviet Foreign Minister Andrei A. Gromyko on September 23, 1977, the same day Gromyko spoke about China at the UN, that "we are striving to normalize our relations with China not to create a kind of alliance with it against the Soviet Union but for strengthening peace, developing trade and other relations with that country." Gromyko was immediately alarmed and threw back a warning, using powerful language that one would typically not hear from the Soviet foreign minister:

> Now, about China. From the point of view of the international situation and of the broad interests of the USA and, of course, the Soviet Union, we believe it is correct to emphasize that it would have been a great mistake if a dirty game had been played here, the open or secret conspiracy against the Soviet Union, against its interests. Because sooner or later,

it would have become known, and the appropriate consequences would follow, including those in the area of U.S.-Soviet relations. We would like to hope that the USA does not intend to play the Chinese card against the Soviet Union.[28]

Not all in the Carter administration fully appreciated the warning, while others, like Brzezinski, deliberately tried to add salt to the wounds. Behind Gromyko's back, Brzezinski had already urged Carter to make an exception within the COCOM structure to supply military equipment to the PRC as early as April 5, 1977.[29] And for a second time, on June 14, 1977, he asked Carter to "tacitly permit Third Country sales of defense equipment and technology to China" and to "enhance China's own intelligence capability vis-a-vis the Soviets through sale of intelligence-related technology." Brzezinski specifically recommended that the United States "sell weapons and military technology to China which would enhance Chinese defensive capabilities vis-a-vis the USSR," such as "anti-tank missiles or over-the-horizon radar." Carter must have felt both intrigued and concerned. He wrote a question mark by the first suggestion, wrote "only on an individual case basis" by the second, and wrote "no" by the third.[30]

Brzezinski's moment arrived when Deng began signaling that he was interested in pursuing military cooperation with the Americans and in purchasing US dual-use technologies. In January 1978, for the first time, the Chinese military allowed a US Air Force plane to land in the Chinese province of Guangdong to pick up a visiting congressional delegation, an unprecedented gesture to the US military establishment and a hint of China's openness to further, more substantial military cooperation.[31] Simultaneously, Chinese officials raised the idea of purchasing American petroleum exploitation technology and other items under COCOM restrictions with the US Department of Energy.[32]

Brzezinski was not alone; the two leading Asia experts on the National Security Council also supported dual-use technology transfers to China to sweeten the diplomatic normalization deal. On March 24, 1978, Michel Oksenberg and Michael Armacost suggested that the president allow the Chinese to purchase US technology on Brzezinski's upcoming trip to China: "The Chinese should be encouraged to make substantial purchases of equipment and technology from the U.S. The purchases could embody dual-purpose technology, the license for which would require presidential approval."[33]

In Beijing, the PRC leaders had similar thoughts. On May 21, 1978, Deng probed Brzezinski about the United States' previous interventions in China's attempts to purchase Japanese and European computers and American infrared scanning devices, all of which were rejected by US officials as they fell under COCOM restrictions. Deng wondered if the real reason was US concern over an adverse Soviet reaction. "Perhaps," Deng said carefully, "I think you have the fear of offending the Soviet Union. Is that right?" Brzezinski seized the opportunity to show he was the man to talk to regarding technology transfers. "I can assure you that my inclination to be fearful of offending the Soviet Union is rather limited," he bragged to Deng. "The origin of these restrictions is our policy toward the Soviet Union and other communist countries that at one time were closely associated with the Soviet Union. The policy is, therefore, a legacy of the past, and the rules are not sufficiently flexible and elastic to recognize the new existing political realities." Brzezinski promised Deng that he was personally interested in those cases and bragged again, "As far as being afraid to offend the Soviet Union, I would be willing to make a little bet with you as to who is less popular in the Soviet Union—you or me."[34]

In Moscow, the prospect of future US arms sales to China both vindicated and alarmed Brezhnev's China watchers, who had warned the Soviet leadership of such a danger since Mao's death. Deng, it seemed, had finally proved himself to be an anti-Soviet Maoist. On May 23, 1978, at precisely the time when Brzezinski was in China on his grand dealmaking trip, Mikhail Sladkovskiĭ, citing this trip, advised the Central Committee that the Soviet Union should revert to its pre-Mao confrontational policy toward China: "The 1977 leadership change [in China] in essence allowed Beijing to coordinate with the [American] imperialists openly, use propaganda to attack other socialist countries, to stir up anti-Socialist, anti-revolutionary forces." He was convinced that "Beijing's close relation to the West and NATO, under the disguise of 'mutual security' is a growing threat to world peace." The Soviet Union, he argued, "has to get serious in fighting Maoists for the hope of socialist internationalism, uniting the front of all brotherly parties."[35] Brezhnev, too, was convinced after Brzezinski's trip to Beijing that "Carter is not simply falling under the usual influence of the most shameless anti-Soviet types and ringleaders of the military-industrial complex of the USA, but is intent upon struggling for his election to a new term as President of the USA under the banner of anti-Soviet policy and a return to the 'Cold War.'" On June 8, 1978, he told the Central Committee: "The current creators of American policy, it seems, have already found a common language with the aggressive anti-Soviet rulers of China, who, as it is known, declare peace and detente to be a fraud, and war to be the single realistic prospect."[36]

On July 7, 1978, when there were sufficient rumors to indicate that the normalization of US-China diplomatic relations was inevitable, the Soviet Ministry of Foreign Affairs held an emergency meeting with both sinologists and Americanists from the Institute of Far East, the Oriental Institute, and the Institute of U.S. and Canadian Studies to determine what the Soviet Union should do regarding a possible new US-Chinese military alliance against the Soviet Union. The meeting was attended by many prominent figures in the Soviet foreign policy establishment, including G. A. Arbatov, who was negotiating with the Americans on the SALT II treaty.

In his opening report at the meeting, L. P. Delyusin, the head of the China Department of the Institute of Oriental Studies, said: "Mao's close associates are out, but the new leadership's anti-Soviet voice did not diminish; on the contrary, it had increased globally.... China increased its fight in foreign policy and against the Soviet Union." He warned that the Soviet Union should not be misguided by Deng's opening and reform policy because a stronger China would be even more dangerous for the Soviet Union. Delyusin further lamented: "The Chinese Communist Party brought China out of chaos into great order, which is to create a new and rich China.... This action is to fulfill the true, not fake, testimony of Mao.... The current leaders use American technological potential to serve the same anti-Soviet goal.... The Americans are using China to put pressure on the Soviet Union."[37]

The only person who dared to disagree with this pessimistic view was Vladimir Petrovich Lukin, a young economist at the time and Russia's ambassador to the United States in 1992.[38] In this meeting, he suggested that the older scholars might be overreacting and that China's post-Mao stabilizing political condition might benefit the Soviet Union. "There were two models [in China]: the Soviet Model, now forgotten, and the Cultural Revolution Model, but now a third" under Deng, Lukin suggested. "Maybe it is better than before—as politics is now less brutal, could this be a positive sign? Could this emerge as a positive system in China?" The question was quickly brushed away by another scholar, B. N. Zametin: "China, under the Maoist, is a combination of left-wing small bourgeoisie and militant nationalists, the testament would be this relationship with the USA against the Soviet Union—according to the canon of Mao—Unite with those who are against the main enemy." "Americans are realists," added T. A. Trofimenko, "playing the balance of force on anti-Soviet ground."[39]

The Soviet leadership adopted the hard-liners' approach. On July 25, 1978, Brezhnev told East German leader Erich Honecker that the PRC was a main obstacle in the current US-Soviet détente. "Another tendency within the policy of the American administration has recently become more powerful. I am talking about their efforts to play the 'Chinese card.' The question now is not simply a normalization of relations between the USA and China but attempts at a rapprochement on an anti-Soviet, anti-Socialist basis. This coincides with the efforts of the Chinese to use the 'American card' in the fight against the USSR and the other countries of the Socialist community." To make sure Honecker got the point, Brezhnev warned that the PRC was also a danger to the GDR because PRC diplomats were approaching "revanchists in West Germany" and supporting "the unity of Germany which de facto means the incorporation [annexation] of the GDR [by West Germany]."[40]

Throughout late 1978, at several of their regular "casual lunch talks" over vodka and chess, Soviet Ambassador Anatoly Dobrynin privately expressed to Brzezinski his Kremlin boss's strong displeasure at Carter's China policy. On August 14, 1978, for example, the pair met for a casual lunch, and Dobrynin pointed out that "the Soviet leadership feels rather emotional about the [US-Soviet] relationship." Citing Brezhnev's earlier complaints to Carter, he lamented that "the correspondence between the two leaders has not filled the void." Without being specific, he let Brzezinski know that US-Soviet relations had deteriorated a great deal that year and the Soviet leader knew Brzezinski was the person most accountable for this failure.[41] And finally, during one of those unofficial meetings on the eve of US-China normalization, Dobrynin told Brzezinski frankly that he did not believe Brzezinski's claim that President Carter's move to "establish diplomatic relations with China had no other purpose but to promote the course of world peace."[42]

A post–Cold War interview with Ambassador Dobrynin suggests that the Carter administration's military cooperation with China had a direct negative impact on US-Soviet arms control efforts. He recalled that the Soviet Politburo members became very angry after they were informed as late as December 15, 1978—through the unofficial Brzezinski-Dobrynin channel—that the United States was about to normalize relations with China, while at the same time the US position at the SALT II negotiations became much harsher. Brezhnev thus thought Carter's China policy was being conducted so as to blackmail the Soviet Union. "Everything [about SALT II] was already prepared; you were coming just to finish things off, and then suddenly, after this love affair with the Chinese, he [Vance] received instructions to take a very tough position on [Soviet] encryption [of missile test data]. So, Gromyko was really angry; he, in turn, decided to be tough, too, and for half a year, the treaty was delayed after it was practically ready."[43]

A frustrated Brezhnev wrote to Carter on December 27, 1978, warning him that linking SALT II with China would have severe consequences. The problem, Brezhnev said, was not just that the United States and its allies were sending weapons to China to be used against the Soviet Union; rather, "the question here is of arming a country with the biggest ground forces, a country whose leaders proclaim for all to hear the inevitability of a new world war and are driving in practice at unleashing such a war." Brzezinski commented on the letter before handing it to the president: "It is noteworthy that the Soviet Union armed China when China was hostile to the US, and it has ignored all your expressions of concern regarding Cuban and Soviet arms in Africa as well as elsewhere." He suggested that the president offer Brezhnev "an ambiguous answer" and insist that each state has the right to "acquire defensive weapons."[44]

DÉTENTE STRETCHED TO THE LIMIT: VIETNAM, AFGHANISTAN, AND INTELLIGENCE COOPERATION IN CENTRAL ASIA

On February 17, 1979, the PLA invaded the Socialist Republic of Vietnam, a close ally of the Soviet Union, in what Deng called a "self-defense counterattack," aimed at punishing the Vietnamese government under General Secretary Le Duan for sending troops to Cambodia, which was itself ruled by the genocidal regime of the Khmer Rouge.[45] For Soviet and China watchers, this war only demonstrated Deng's true nature as a violent challenger to Soviet leadership in the socialist bloc. It could not be a coincidence that the invasion happened shortly after Deng visited the United States; they concluded the United States must have been involved. The immediate report provided to the CPSU Central Committee called the war undeniable proof of the "deep-rooted expansionism of Chinese leadership's history," whose eventual goal was to "fight against the international communist movement, and to take control of South East Asia with the support of the Americans."[46] Similar reports poured in to the committee throughout 1979. For example, on September 10, 1979, Sladkovskiĭ wrote a lengthy polemic against Deng, citing Marx, Lenin, and Chinese newspapers but mainly his own works. The whole of PRC foreign policy now, he argued, was a result of "the bourgeoisie and revisionists' attempt to exploit Maoism to undermine the international revolution moment, and to discredit the idea of Scientific Socialism and Proletarian Internationalism."[47] In addition, the Institute of Far East scholars prepared a ninety-page report for the Ministry of Foreign Affairs and the Central Committee forecasting China's dangerous future goals:

1. Strategic Goal: Transform China into an economically and militarily powerful nation capable of becoming a hegemon in Asia and later in the world.
2. Tactical Goal: Attack the Soviet Union and other socialist states
3. Strategic Allies: Imperialism
4. Base for Realization of Strategic Goal: Build up nuclear rocket potentials in China, build a military-political alliance with imperialist powers, and create what Beijing's slogan [writers] would deem a "United Front" with multiple regional powers in the fight against the Soviet Union and other socialist states.[48]

On the diplomatic front, Sino-Soviet talks at the vice-minister level that began on October 17, 1979, failed to yield concrete results. The Soviet side refused the PRC delegation's three demands: reduce troops along the Chinese border, end the Soviet occupation of Mongolia, and cease military aid to Vietnam.[49] Meanwhile, according to a junior PRC diplomat, "The Soviets pretended their one-million-strong military presence near the Chinese border was entirely harmless," and the PRC diplomats "insisted that the Soviet military threat was an 'objective fact.'"[50] These negotiations yielded no result, and on December 3, both sides decided that they had heard enough from one another. The talks were postponed until 1980 and then further delayed after the Soviet invasion of Afghanistan in December 1979. When they resumed in 1982, Deng added the Soviet withdrawal from Afghanistan as another demand.[51]

The PRC's continued confrontation with the Soviet Union certainly gained the attention and, to a certain extent, the approval of the Carter administration, as Brzezinski continued to persuade the president to use Deng's anti-Soviet stance to put pressure on Brezhnev. Before the Carter-Brezhnev SALT II summit, Brzezinski listed all the Soviet activities that endangered US interests and argued that they existed because the Soviets "do not want our economic and technological might mobilized against them. They do not want us to move closer to China." Brzezinski contended that the United States should move closer to the PRC precisely as a reaction to "Soviet insensibility to our concerns in such areas as the Middle East, Southern Africa, Vietnam, or Cuba." The United States' relations with the PRC, he intimated, should therefore be a part of "major, comprehensive, and matching efforts" to meet the "Soviet military buildup, both strategic and conventional," which "has gone beyond the point of legitimate defense needs," unless the Soviet Union showed restraint.[52]

Carter's and Brezhnev's fundamentally different approaches to their Chinese policies were a decisive destabilizing factor during the June 1979 US-Soviet SALT II Summit in Vienna. While the Americans complained about the recently discovered Soviet brigade in Cuba, the Soviets complained about China, all on top of their existing disagreement over which side should keep more and better nuclear weapons. The Soviet delegation was shocked to learn that the Americans had passed their confidential SALT II negotiation records to the Chinese without Soviet consent, which was utterly unacceptable to the Soviet side. An angry Gromyko told Vance: "Now on top of all this [disagreement], there is the question of your transfer of information about the progress of negotiations on SALT [II] to the Chinese leadership. On what basis did you do this? We did not agree that you should do this. . . . What advice could the Chinese give you for the negotiation on SALT? Perhaps only one piece of advice: damn the agreement on SALT!"[53]

In another meeting between Carter and Brezhnev, China again became a significant point of disagreement and, in the eyes of the Soviet leader, a major obstacle to US-Soviet talks on arms reduction, whether nuclear or conventional. Brezhnev complained to Carter that China's continued nuclear weapons testing was endangering nonproliferation and its refusal to join the chemical weapon ban negotiations was setting a dangerous precedent. "What kind of an agreement would that be without the participation of China? Could one really agree to a situation in which the Chinese alone would have a free hand to manufacture chemical weapons?" In Southeast Asia, too, China was the main destabilizing factor: "The threat to peace came from China, which had already carried out blatant aggression against Vietnam and which was now openly threatening to teach Vietnam a new lesson."[54]

Even though the SALT II treaty was signed, the two sides parted with feelings of suspicion and mistrust (figure 6.1). "There is nothing wrong

FIGURE 6.1 Jimmy Carter and Leonid Brezhnev signing the SALT II agreement in Vienna on June 18, 1979, amid heightened US-Soviet tension. (Jimmy Carter Presidential Library and Museum)

with opening diplomatic relations between the US and China," Brezhnev told the Bulgarian dictator Todor Zhivkov, "but the whole thing is taking a negative turn. In my letter to Carter, I clarified that importing anti-Soviet content into American-Chinese cooperation is unacceptable. There is no doubt that Beijing and Washington are using their connections to put pressure on the Socialist countries."[55]

The Soviet Union soon stumbled, making a mistake that offered the anti-Soviet hard-liners in the United States more reasons to arm the PRC. The Soviet invasion of Afghanistan in December 1979 led to a significant overhaul of the US export control policy. The sources at the Jimmy Carter Presidential Library, although only the tip of the iceberg, suggest that US-China military cooperation immediately picked up steam in January 1980. Previously restricted American military technologies started to flow into China in massive quantities, while remaining out of the Soviet Union's reach. For example, on January 6, 1980, Under Secretary of Defense Gerald P. Dinneen frankly told the assistant to PLA Deputy Chief of Staff Admiral Liu Huaqing that the Department of Defense was ready to work around the Department of Commerce's regulations to give China military hardware and technologies that "we would not want to sell to the Soviet Union," including NASA's Landsat earth-monitoring satellite, which served both military and civilian purposes. Liu, the leading proponent of China's military modernization and a navy strategist under Deng, was highly impressed and immediately booked further meetings with the Department of Defense.[56]

Two days later, on January 8, 1980, Secretary of Defense Harold Brown, an MIT-trained technocrat, landed in Beijing to see Deng, his favorite conversation partner regarding anti-Soviet activities.[57] The two men boasted about the achievement of US-China normalization and the "strategic advantages" of this new relationship. Brown, probably with a sense of satisfaction, was glad to see Brezhnev foolishly invade Afghanistan, as it finally vindicated his anti-Soviet views. "Soviet behavior in the last year or more—use of Cuban and Vietnamese proxies for military purposes in the Third World—has affected U.S. public opinion. . . . But most of all, events in Iran and Afghanistan have crystallized in the U.S. mood," Brown told Deng. He boasted: "We were increasing our defense budget, and we will increase it more. We have accelerated our plans to have rapidly deployable military forces. We have planned to increase arms supply to Pakistan." Despite their historical differences, Deng gladly agreed and repeated his earlier vision that the United States, Europe, China, and even Japan should build a global alliance to counter Soviet expansion. The PRC, of course, would play its part in relieving the United States' military burdens. Afghanistan was now the key to halting Soviet expansion. Deng said: "The Afghan people have been fighting fiercely against Soviet aggression. We must turn Afghanistan into a quagmire in which the Soviet Union is bogged down for a long time, engaged in guerrilla warfare." This statement was music to Brown's ears. He responded, "Our actions will have that effect, but we must keep our intentions confidential."[58]

The same month, an early warning radar system—used to detect incoming hostile airplanes and ballistic missiles—was delivered to China. It was a clear reward from the US military establishment to Deng for his anti-Soviet views. The delivery triggered intense interest in Washington, D.C., and curious journalists grilled the Department of Defense spokesperson about it. Did this mean China was now a U.S. ally? Would more military hardware be sold to the Chinese? Was the long-established COCOM system now officially defunct? How would the Soviet Union react, and did this mean that détente was already dead? With a poker face, the department spokesperson tried his best to pretend that this was not a military sale.

> QUESTION: Early warning radar is clearly military, so does that mean you have altered your position from the dual-use concept?
> SPOKESPERSON: Well. We really can't be specific about radar, as you have indicated. But I could just simply point out that there are radars, for example, which are used for air traffic control, and we use those now for air traffic control and for tracking military targets.
> QUESTION: But you don't call them early warning radar.
> SPOKESPERSON: We don't call those early warning radar.
> QUESTION: But the statement says early warning radar. You are clearly trying to make a point here that this is equipment whose primary use is military as opposed to civilian.
> SPOKESPERSON: Well, it's equipment that is also suitable for military use. That's right.[59]

Following Secretary Brown, Under Secretary of Defense William Perry—the intellectual mind behind the US high-tech offset strategy, an ideal that United States' rapid technological advances in modern communication, stealth technology, and aerospace, will render the Soviet military's quantitative superiority useless in the next high-tech war—visited China later in 1980, and their visits were reciprocated by Chinese Vice Premier and Secretary General of the CCP Central Military Commission Geng Biao and Deputy Chief of Staff Liu Huaqing, who visited the United States separately in May and June 1980. In addition, "exchanges of working-level military delegations on subjects such as health and logistics, institutional ties between the American and Chinese national defense universities, and the placement of military attaches in the two countries' embassies opened further communication channels between the two defense establishments."[60]

THE CIA BOYS IN CHINA

The United States and China launched several intelligence operations against the Soviet Union, some of which were so morally dubious that neither government has ever recognized their existence. One such example is Operation Chestnut, a secret deal between Carter and Deng to set up CIA monitoring stations designed to track Soviet missiles in the desert of the autonomous region of Xinjiang. Kissinger first proposed the idea to Deng during his visit to Beijing in October 1975, as "from the mountain ridges of Xinjiang, the Chinese had a clear shot of the Soviet missile-testing area at Semipalatinsk in what was then known as the Kazakh Soviet Socialist Republic." Deng turned down the offer and told Kissinger to wait until after the two countries had normalized their relations.[61]

The issue became more urgent when the CIA lost its monitoring stations in Iran after the 1979 Islamic Revolution and China also wanted to learn about US technology. Deng thus brought this offer up again on April 9, 1979, with a delegation from the US Senate Foreign Relations Committee led by Senator Frank Church. This time, however, the deal had strings attached: The United States had to pass missile monitoring technology to China. Using the Chinese tactic known as "picking the softest persimmon to squeeze," Deng addressed this hard question to the youngest member of the group, Senator Joe Biden: "If you provide monitoring technology and the sovereignty belongs to China, China will accept. I will not do it if the US comes to China to set up monitoring bases." Biden could not provide a direct response.

Nevertheless, in December 1980, Robert Gates, a Georgetown University–trained historian focused on Soviet sinology and CIA analyst who would later serve as secretary of defense, accompanied CIA Director Stansfield Turner to Beijing to agree on the technical details of the operation (figure 6.2). "The visit took place in utmost secrecy," Gates remembered. "Turner even grew a mustache for a visit."[62] Those CIA-operated monitoring stations remained throughout the Cold War and even survived the Tiananmen Square massacre in 1989. Even today, the existence and exact whereabouts of those stations have never been declassified by either side. Only in a 2019 speech at the U.S. Embassy in China did David R. Stilwell, assistant secretary of state and a former Air Force general, mention that an Operation Chestnut was the high point of US-China Cold War cooperation.[63]

Intelligence sharing between the United States and China also expanded into Afghanistan. However, not all players in the new anti-Soviet alliance were decent people. To get weapons to the Afghan Mujahideen while keeping their hands clean, the anti-Soviet hard-liners in Beijing and Washington found a trusted proxy in Pakistani General-President-Dictator Muhammad Zia-ul-Haq, a terrifying man known for his fondness for playing golf and hanging his political opponents, including the previous president whom he had overthrown. General Zia-ul-Haq was on the Carter administration's sanctions list due to his horrendous human rights violations, drug-trafficking crimes, and attempts to build nuclear bombs, all of which were quickly forgiven after the Soviet invasion of Afghanistan.[64] Soon knockoff copies of Soviet weapons of dubious origin, primarily Czech and Chinese, started to flow into Afghanistan through Zia-ul-Haq's drug-trafficking networks.[65] A concerning report appeared in a Canadian newspaper that the Mujahideen were purchasing US weaponry through "Chinese men in Pakistan" identified as "Hong Kong Chinese heroin dealers" and paying with, naturally, Afghan heroin, which was eventually smuggled back into North America and "now reportedly reaching the streets of U.S. cities in massive quantities."[66]

While most politicians in Beijing and Washington wished to stay distant, Brzezinski was eager to meet those dangerous rebels. In February

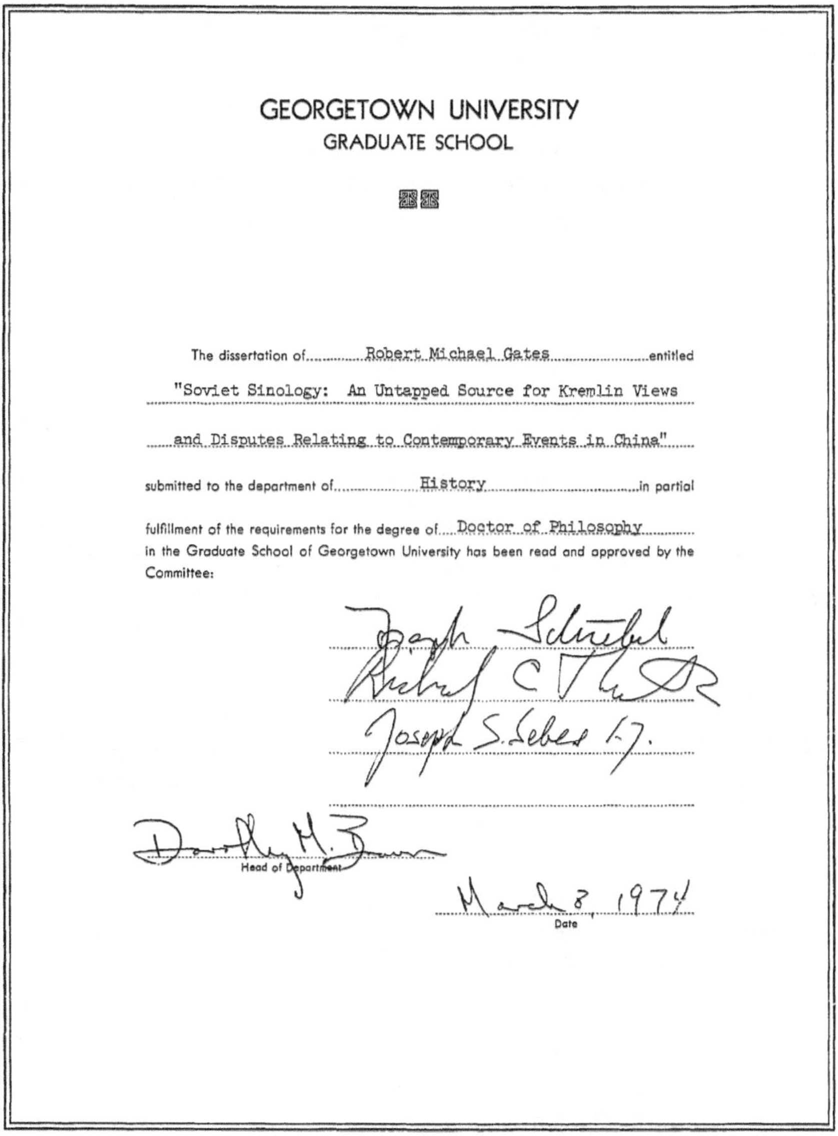

GEORGETOWN UNIVERSITY
GRADUATE SCHOOL

The dissertation of Robert Michael Gates entitled "Soviet Sinology: An Untapped Source for Kremlin Views and Disputes Relating to Contemporary Events in China" submitted to the department of History in partial fulfillment of the requirements for the degree of Doctor of Philosophy in the Graduate School of Georgetown University has been read and approved by the Committee:

Head of Department

March 8, 1974
Date

FIGURE 6.2 Robert M. Gates, a CIA officer and future US secretary of defense, wrote his PhD dissertation on Soviet sinology. (Georgetown University Library)

1980, an excited Brzezinski flew to the Pakistan-Afghanistan border. Stepping out of a helicopter wearing a *Top Gun*–style leather jacket and aviator sunglasses, the fist-waving Brzezinski, a devoted Catholic, rallied a group of bemused—and possibly confused—Afghan Islamic fundamentalist fighters: "That land over there is yours, you will get it back one day because your fight will prevail, and you will have your homes and mosque back again, because your cause is right, and God is on your side!"[67]

DISSENTING VOICES IN WASHINGTON, MOSCOW, AND BEIJING

Brzezinski and Brown's hard push for closer military ties with China, especially in Afghanistan, a region known for violence and organized crime, deeply troubled US arms control officials. What if US or Chinese weapons were passed out of war zones and used in future crimes? Were there any assurances that the Chinese would not pass sensitive US technologies to other bad guys? For example, the arms control officials at the State Department, led by Gerard C. Smith, had been trying hard to isolate Pakistan to stop its nuclear program.[68] With China and US hard-liners openly cooperating with the Pakistanis, US nuclear nonproliferation officials' biggest nightmare was about to happen. On April 21, Gerald C. Smith wrote that if Pakistan got away with developing nuclear weapons, the "Soviet Union might offer the Indians a nuclear guaranty against both Chinese and Pakistan nuclear action against India." Pakistan's nuclear program, Smith thought, could also be a major regional destabilizing factor: "If there were a general war in the area involving Afghanistan, Iran, Pakistan, the Soviet Union and the United States, the Pakistani plants would probably be in great jeopardy of sabotage." Nuclear proliferation, as had been feared, went wild in South Asia.[69]

Conventional proliferation experts at the U.S. Department of Defense also feared that China would pass sensitive weapons technologies to other countries, where they could end up in the hands of notorious terrorist groups, as the Chinese had a very relaxed or near-nonexistent export control policy. On March 28, 1980, the Defense Intelligence Agency issued a warning about possible Chinese knockoff copies of Soviet 9K32 Strela-2 (NATO designation SA-7) shoulder-fired antiair missiles—

similar to the Stinger missiles the Reagan administration later passed to the Mujahideen—ending up in the hands of international terrorists: "The Chinese have apparently completed development of a Soviet SA-7/Grall-type shoulder-fired surface-to-air missile (SAM) and are offering [it] for export.... To date there have been no known foreign contracts for Chinese SA-7s. However, if the Chinese are producing these weapons and their arms sales policies remain lax, it is possible these weapons will eventually find their way into the hands of international terrorist groups. It is also likely that Chinese-backed insurgent groups in Kampuchea, Laos, and Afghanistan will receive them."[70]

American diplomats interested in repairing relations with the Soviet Union disagreed with Brzezinski's policy of playing the China card, fearing it would only make the Soviets more reckless in their global adventures. On February 8, 1980, US Ambassador to the Soviet Union Thomas J. Watson cautioned Secretary of State Vance that US-Soviet relations were on a highly perilous course, as US policy was giving "the old men in the Politburo" the wrong impression that the United States wanted a confrontation with the Soviet Union. Watson's report pointed out the possibility that "the Soviet leader would conclude that the U.S. must be taught a more powerful lesson by being forced to back away from nuclear confrontation as the USSR did in 1962." "Some Soviet leaders want such a confrontation [with the United States], and they may feel that if a confrontation must come, it should be sooner rather than later. We should not give Moscow grounds to believe that the US follows a policy of trying to destroy, fragment, or overthrow the Soviet regime." The report urged that to avoid this, the United States should take measures immediately: "Stop further moves toward China for the remainder of this year because (a) such moves could strengthen inclinations in Moscow to seek a confrontation with us sooner rather than later, and (b) once played, China cards lose their usefulness as leverage and become excuses for Soviet counteractions. We should also obviously not do anything constructive with China when relations [with the Soviets] improve, since such action by us would jeopardize hopeful movement back toward detente."[71]

Brzezinski, however, intercepted the report, threatened the State and Defense Departments not to leak it to the press, discredited the report in the comment section, and then forwarded it back to both agencies: "The cable contains some rather extraordinary statements, which I hope will not be taken seriously by anyone here," he stated. It seemed that Watson's words might be questioning Brzezinski judgment as the self-appointed sole authority on China policy. Thus, he deemed the ambassador to "need some clarification" on "where the president stands" on those issues, almost as if he was the president.[72]

In June 1980, Brzezinski and Watson stood together before Carter, and the president finally gave his ambassador a belated "clarification" on his China policy. "All the actions we have taken toward China are based on our desire to improve relations with that very important country," Carter told him. "We are not normalizing our relations with the Chinese just in order to hurt the Soviets." Ambassador Watson, however, was not convinced: "I am no historian, and Dr. Brzezinski certainly knows more about the subject than I do, but it seems to me that the Chinese have a tendency to jump around from bed to bed. And I think we ought to make sure that they are lashed down to our bed before we undertake actions which we might regret later on." Brzezinski, however, brushed the question away: "You have to remember that we are very sexy people."[73]

The intensified US-China military cooperation offered Brezhnev's advisers fresh ammunition to denounce Deng—and block other, more moderate officials' attempts to advocate for a more realistic and flexible rapprochement toward China. Citing Secretary Brown's visit to China, Sergei Tikhvinskii, the Foreign Ministry diplomat and China specialist, argued in January 1980 that the Americans and the Chinese were orchestrating a global conspiracy against the Soviet Union. "China went on the provocative path of cobbling together an anti-Soviet front, joining the league of Carter's threatening anti-Soviet military-political blockade to destroy political détente." Brown's visit, he wrote, was evidence of "Beijing using the tension in South East Asia to help Americans to expand their military influence in the region . . . and to use closer Chinese-American military relations to modernize China's military forces, now armed with new American equipment and technologies."[74] The sinologists at the Far East Institute also rewrote their conclusions in the new version of the "China After Mao" annual report. Now, in 1980, China's foreign policy goal was no longer "establishing Chinese hegemony in Asia," as they had believed a year earlier; rather, it was "establishing Chinese hegemony in the entire world." The "Maoist Chinese" were now "the enemy of USSR, all socialist countries, and all progressive forces in the world."[75]

In both Washington and Moscow, dissident voices existed on all sides. Just as some US diplomats questioned Carter's approach to China, not all

Soviet sinologists followed the hard-line view on China. In 1979, Vladimir Lukin, the young China expert and economist at the Institute of U.S. and Canadian Studies, published an insightful article titled "Washington-Beijing: Quasi-Alliance?" in the institute's journal, *USA: Economics, Politics, Ideology*, in which he questioned the official viewpoint that "China was on its way to forming a military alliance with the United States, and that there was no hope for improving Sino-Soviet relations." This was not true, Lukin argued, as the United States and China faced far more problems in their relationship and could find no easy solutions in the long run. First, China opposed US disarmament efforts and SALT II, which "fundamentally diverged from the vast majority of states in the world." Furthermore, how could Chinese leaders who were still interested in Mao's vision of world struggle possibly be a part of the US vision of collective security? How could China's "desire to expand its sphere of influence in Asia" be compatible with the United States' strategic influence in Asia, which thus far "was maintained by the US 7th Fleet?"[76]

Later, in 1981, Lukin cited the Republican Party's close connection with Taiwan and President Reagan's criticism of Carter's abandonment of Taiwanese defense in a draft paper in which he predicted that "Beijing will not be able to swallow the bitter pill of 'Two-Chinas' and exclude the possibility of ruining its relations with the new Republican Party government if the U.S. decided to renew military ties with Taiwan. . . . Under friendship and harmony, there are always boiling and difficult, strong feelings that are ready to surface at any moment."[77] "The Taiwan problem," Lukin further predicted, "was for Deng a question of national symbolism and a criterion of patriotism." At the same time, for the Americans, Taiwan was "a part of their Pacific Ocean strategy." Thus, "the Taiwan crisis will not emerge on its own, but more as a symptom of other much bigger chronic problems on both sides."[78] This paper was never published before the dissolution of the Soviet Union, as Lukin was too far ahead of his time.

UNLIKELY DISSIDENTS IN BEIJING

At the time, a state news outlet in Beijing tried to reflect a strong sense of unity behind Deng's decision to switch to the American side of the Cold War—and so did a later generation of CCP-affiliated historians. Deng had made the wise decision, and the other comrades had followed.[79] Anything that went wrong—such as continued US arms sales to Taiwan or the Taiwan Relations Act—was entirely the fault of the Americans, who "betrayed the spirit of the Shanghai Communiqué."[80] For example, the second 1981 issue of *International Studies*, the Chinese Academy of Social Sciences' premier journal on foreign affairs, contained an editorial—which usually presented the collective opinion of the academy's leadership—warning of the possibility of a decline in US-PRC relations due to the United States' continued arms sales to Taiwan. The article was written by an anonymous "special commentator," and the tone was unusually harsh and sarcastic at a time when both countries were still enjoying their postnormalization honeymoon:

> The arms trade between the United States and Taiwan is not a business relationship between people, as the US government has to approve the sale of weapons to Taiwan by American companies. . . . For a long time, the US has sold weapons to Taiwan by treating Taiwan as a "country" and under the US law on selling arms to foreign countries. After the establishment of diplomatic relations between China and the United States, and after the United States recognized that Taiwan is part of China, such transactions should naturally stop. . . . The Americans who advocate the sale of weapons to Taiwan use the Taiwan Relations Act as a basis. . . . They even say that China's opposition to the US selling weapons to Taiwan is to oppose the US enforcing its own laws and interfering in American internal affairs. This is really absurd.[81]

This editorial set the tone for the PRC's official criticism of US policy toward Taiwan. However, the argument that US arms sales to Taiwan were the only problem in early US-PRC relations was a gross simplification of the foreign policy debate among the top leaders of the CCP. High-level party members, in fact, raised much deeper and more profound questions about Deng's decision to build US-PRC relations solely on the basis of his anti-Soviet policy.

The PRC Foreign Ministry has never declassified the files from the 1970s. Still, some rare copies of papers as well as documents that have been smuggled out suggest Deng's policy was questioned by at least two top CCP leaders—Hu Yaobang and Zhao Ziyang, the two leaders often seen as Deng's lieutenants and reformers until their purges—Hu in 1987 and then Zhao in 1989 after the Tiananmen Square massacre. Hu Yaobang was a dedicated Communist who firmly believed in Marxism and Leninism. With Deng's blessing, he became the general secretary of the CCP on February 29, 1980. Shortly thereafter, on March 9, 1981, Hu gave a rare talk on foreign policy at his party office, in which he insisted that the PRC opposed only the Soviet Union's hegemony; it never intended to oppose everything the Soviet Union represented. He specifically wanted to make three points clear:

(1) We are only, but resolutely opposing their [Soviet] hegemony, and normally we do not oppose their domestic policy. The phrase "United the Americans to Oppose the Soviets" should never be used, as the Soviets have never mentioned that they are anti-Chinese.
(2) We should not equate political struggle and fight against hegemony with equal and mutually beneficial economic exchanges. Comrades from Xinjiang told me that the province can then import riding boots and export some of their sweet melons. As long as it benefits us, a small amount of trade is fine, and a medium amount of trade is also fine; I don't see the problems.
(3) We should not let the people misinterpret that we oppose everything about the Soviet Union. On the contrary, we should build exchanges with the wider average Soviet people, have good relations with their social elites, respect their national feelings and their glorious revolutionary history and cultural heritage.

Hu further stated that an "independent foreign policy" is "beneficial to the people of our nation and the people in the world." However, "a few comrades lacked a clear head in this or that problem." To solve this problem, the PRC should

(1) Never at any moment affiliate our foreign policy with another country's foreign policy.
(2) Never be dictated by the momentum of an international event.
(3) Not be blinded and angered by any domestic feelings. Don't jump up when we get checkmated, and thus be blinded and dominated by seemingly terrifying environment and emotions.

All of this, Hu insisted, required a "procession of the absolute principles of Marxism and the clear, cool head of a Proletarian Party Member."[82]

Was this a vague criticism of Deng's one-sided anti-Soviet cooperation with the United States? It could be, as in mid-March 1981, Hu not only gave a speech opposing "Unifying the Americans to oppose the Soviet"—Deng's signature foreign policy—but also printed it out and distributed it among the leaders. According to Hu, this criticism was considered by many as a "highly responsible act" and received approval and praise from PLA General Ye Jianying and Premier Zhao Ziyang. "You are fearless," Zhao said. "You dare to print this speech out."[83]

According to Zhao's papers that were smuggled out and printed in Hong Kong and the United States, his opposition to Deng's policy was based more on his distrust of the United States and his Marxist-Leninist worldview of anti-imperial struggles, causing him to see American imperialism as being just as immoral as Soviet imperialism. This is curious, as Zhao is often remembered in the West as a pro-American liberal reformer. However, a close examination of his papers suggests that he also had a Marxist-Leninist way of thinking and a deep anti-American worldview. Zhao, despite his celebratory legacy in the West, was not a friend of "American hegemony." On April 19, 1982, when Zhao met with state visitors from Ghana, he said that, of course, the PRC opposed Soviet imperialism and its pursuit of hegemony, but "China also opposed US imperialism." He went on to provide examples:

> The United States is still pursuing hegemony, as in South Africa, where the US supported South Africa and opposed Namibia's independence and made itself the enemy of the African countries; in the Middle East, the United States supported Israel and made an enemy of the Arab people; in Latin America. It supported counter-revolutionary dictatorship . . . in Korea, it opposed the withdrawal of troops from South Korea and opposed the unification of the Koreans; the US, in fact, still practiced hegemony and still sold weapons to Taiwan, making Taiwan an unsinkable aircraft carrier in the Pacific Ocean. While China opposes Soviet hegemony, we also oppose American hegemony; wherever America does it, we oppose it resolutely.[84]

In another meeting with fellow Chinese diplomats, Zhao warned that the PRC should not get too close to countries based on an anti-Soviet stance without discernment and should not "use their anti-Soviet policy as a line" to categorize them. First, some countries have engaged in anti-imperial struggles with both the Soviet Union and the United States, and as a result, "they have great problems with the American imperialists." Zhao insisted that the PRC diplomats understand the nuances and not distance themselves based only on those countries' Soviet policy. Second, "Some third world rulers oppose the Soviet Union not because they oppose Soviet hegemony, but because they oppose Communism and the Socialist System." Those rulers, Zhao said with disgust, "are counter-revolutionary, corrupt, and notorious ruling cliques such as Emperor Haile Selassie I of Ethiopia or Shah Pahlavi of Iran," who "will eventually be overthrown by their own people." Thus, the PRC should "stay some distance from them . . . not creating an illusion among the people of the world that we are too close to the rulers of those countries while the Soviet imperials were much closer to their people, and thus making the Soviets look like the progressive force in the world, while we are supporting the corrupted ruling classes."[85]

Did Hu's and Zhao's criticisms of Deng's anti-Soviet policy create a rift between them and Deng, thus having an impact on their later downfall toward the end of the Cold War? There is no evidence, but those rare documents suggest a polarization in internal foreign policy debates that coincided with diversifying opinions in domestic and economic policies, an unusual occurrence in the PRC's high-level politics in the 1980s. Yet both politicians supported their dissenting views with strict Marxist-Leninist arguments and Mao's principles of anti-imperial struggles, the main targets of which were the United States and the Soviet Union. Regardless of how US officials wish to remember those two politicians, their worldview, in fact, was profoundly and orthodoxically Communist.

PATH OF NO RETURN: US ARMS SALES TO THE PRC

Hu's and Zhao's dissenting views unfortunately had little impact at the time. US-PRC anti-Soviet cooperation moved ahead at full speed in the early 1980s despite warnings from both Carter's advisers and the Soviet leadership. In May 1980, the State Department added six military systems to the list of items available for China to purchase—ranging from "surveillance radar" to an "air navigational system" to a "mobile tactical reconnaissance facility."[86] In the following days, the list kept growing longer and longer: "H.R. 30 Air Defense Radar, Aircraft equipment—Temperature sensors, pressure sensors, pilot-static tubes, Air ATA sensors."[87] Even a "Boeing 737-200 as troop transport" was added.[88] Most items on the list were high-technology items that could be integrated into China's outdated systems to give the Chinese an advantage—or at least a chance—in its efforts to counter the weapons made in the Soviet Union. The Chinese were undoubtedly encouraged by the United States' change of policy. On June 14, 1980, before PLA General Geng Biao's visit to the United States, the advance team told Ambassador Woodcock that the "PRC was viewing this preliminary trip as a shopping visit." The Chinese were interested in "a variety of American weapons and technology, including tanks, armored personnel carriers (APCs), communications equipment, rockets, the F-16, and they would like to have the same arms relationship with the United States as Egypt," another of the United States' Cold War allies.[89]

Thus, from 1980 onward, military delegations from the PRC on the mainland and the ROC in Taiwan took turns visiting the same US military sites and arms manufacturers, checking out similar weapons and making deals while carefully trying to avoid one another. For example, a week after PLA General Geng Biao bought radar equipment in the United States, a Taiwanese delegation arrived to test-fly F-104G fighters, which would be used to fend off the PLA Air Force's new J-8 fighters codesigned with the United States or its J-7 tactical bombers upgraded by the British.[90] While Brzezinski and other anti-Soviet hard-liners were urging President Carter to approve weapons deliveries to the PRC, US officials sympathetic to Taiwan were advising the same president to speed up delivery of heavy artilleries to the Taiwanese army to help with "modernizing their obsolescent artillery forces . . . consistent with our policy of making available equipment to meet Taiwan's legitimate defense requirements."[91] Ironically, the United States' effort to rearm the PRC against the Soviet Union triggered a secondary arms race across the Taiwan Strait.

CONCLUSION

President Carter and his hardline anti-Soviet advisers' singular goal of bringing Deng's PRC into the anti-Soviet alliance brought the Soviet Union's attempt to repair relations with the PRC to a standstill. In particular, US arms sales and technology transfers to the PRC significantly worsened the already fragile US-Soviet détente before its final collapse on December 24, 1979, when Soviet troops entered Afghanistan. However, this period was marked not only by high-level diplomatic maneuvers but also by intense internal debates and dissenting voices within each country. Not all policymakers in Washington, Moscow, and Beijing agreed with their respective governments' singular and stubborn policies. Those original ideas, immature as they seemed then, nevertheless identified some crucial emerging themes and potential crises in the rapidly changing late 1970s and early 1980s Cold War. As I will show in the conclusion, those ideas and the hidden issues they had failed to address at the time have profoundly and permanently reshaped our world following the end of the global Cold War.

CONCLUSION

Multilateral Competition Beyond the Cold War

The independent ambitions of the two competing Chinese regimes fundamentally complicated the strategic, technological, and ideological aspects of US Cold War policy. By examining these themes through a multilateral lens, I challenge the simplistic Cold War narratives and highlight the intricate nature of international relations during this critical period. In the post–Cold War world, those analytical themes, with new developments and variations, are still relevant in understanding the renewed competition between the US and China centered around Taiwan's sovereignty and security.

REVISITING CARTER'S CHINA LEGACY

People close to the Carter family, including those who work at the Jimmy Carter Presidential Library and Museum in Atlanta, know how hard Jimmy and Rosalynn Carter tried to help China develop grassroots democracy after the end of the Cold War, a goal Jimmy Carter had already set when he took the oath of office. The Carter library holds detailed records of the Chinese Village Elections Project, an expansive program the Carter family sponsored in 1998 to guide and monitor village elections in China, including in my home province of Yunnan.[1] However, in

2011, prodemocratic protests, inspired mainly by the Jasmine Revolution in Tunisia and by environmental crises at home, took place in several major Chinese cities leading to a swift crackdown by the CCP. Shortly afterward, the Chinese government halted the village elections project, and the Carters were no longer welcome in China despite all they had done to improve US-China diplomatic relations during the Cold War.[2] In September 2014, Jimmy and Rosalynn visited mainland China as private individuals to "enhance understanding between the two countries."[3] Unfortunately, this final trip was heavily censored in the state-controlled Chinese media. Jimmy Carter's speech at Renmin University in Beijing was overshadowed by an unrelated business conference. During their visit to Shanghai, Chinese officials at the last minute relocated the former president's meeting with local scholars from Jiao Tong University to a remote suburban hotel so they could hide the Carters away from curious students and pro-Western local media, which still existed in the cosmopolitan coastal city. Finally, on the last night, there was a sense of personal warmth when Carter, then ninety years old, met Deng Xiaoping's daughter, Deng Rong, and many other retired officials who had worked closely with the Americans during the Cold War. Together, they had a lovely traditional Chinese dinner, drank rice wine, and reminisced about the "good old days" of US-PRC relations. "The former president and his wife were said to be extremely gratified to see so many old friends," who now, like Jimmy Carter himself, were out of office and out of power.[4]

The Carter family's cold treatment in Shanghai reflected the general deterioration of US-PRC relations during the Obama years—and later the Trump and Biden years. This renewed tension also sparked the interest among academics as well as the public in revisiting the Carter years and the United States' relations with the two competing Chinese regimes, which, due to their diverging political and cultural identities, are more often referred to as simply China and Taiwan in today's media. Unlike critics during Carter's time, who were mainly concerned about the détente and Taiwan's immediate security, today's critics, armed with hindsight, questioned the long-term consequences of Carter's decision to engage with China through trade, diplomacy, and technological exchanges. Carter chose to partner with China, yet China refused political change. Taiwan was abandoned, yet it turned into a democracy. Michael Pillsbury, for example, argued that the Carter administration failed to see the Chinese leadership's long-term strategic ambition to replace the United States as the world's leading great power. Its decision to allow China to access the Western market and its technology, Pillsbury further contended, opened the path for China's rise as the only military power that could pose a significant challenge to the United States in the twenty-first century.[5] Without directly blaming Carter, many other scholars questioned the wisdom of the engagement policy initiated by his administration, which the subsequent US administrations faithfully followed. They pointed out that the United States' diplomatic, economic, and cultural interaction with China had failed to change the authoritarian nature of the CCP regime and had aided China's global ambitions in the twenty-first century. As Kurt Campbell and Ely Ratner wrote in 2018, in the midst of the US-China trade war during the first Trump administration, China repeatedly "defied American expectations" over the past four decades and failed to liberalize as Americans had wished.[6] During the Biden administration, experts from both the conservative and the liberal wings of the US foreign policy establishment reached the painful conclusion that the policy of engagement with China, followed for the past forty years by Democratic and Republican administrations alike, had failed. Their only disagreement regarded how to correct the situation: For example, in a heated debate carried out in *Foreign Affairs* in 2024, Matthew Pottinger, deputy national security adviser during the first Trump administration, called for a full confrontational policy toward China to force the CCP's collapse, while Rush Doshi, President Biden's deputy senior director for China and Taiwan, preferred a less radical "managed competition" without the risk of escalation.[7] None of them, however, believed open-arms engagement was still the right thing to do.

President Carter's abandonment of Taiwan was a traumatic, unforgivable act in the minds of the Taiwanese people. A whole school of literature emerged in Taiwanese academia to reflect on the lessons of the Carter administration's betrayal and to remind readers that the nonbinding nature and strategic ambiguity of the 1979 Taiwan Relations Act left Taiwan in a security limbo, as it provided no legally binding guarantee that the United States would come to its aid when China launched an attack.[8] Since Tsai Ing-wen took office as president of Taiwan in 2016, the Democratic Progressive Party (DPP) of Taiwan has implemented a series of defense policy reforms, including increasing the defense budget, increasing domestic production of weapons systems, promoting civilian mobilization, and restoring one-year military conscription.[9] Those reforms echoed the words of the DPP's historical archrival, KMT leader Chiang Ching-kuo, who called for self-reliance in Taiwanese defense after repeated American betrayals. It was no wonder that, on April 14, 2024, at ceremony commemorating the forty-fifth anniversary of the passage of the Taiwan Relations Act, Taiwan's Vice President Hsiao Bi-Khim, a member of the DPP, quite bluntly pointed out that when it comes to the island's self-defense, "self-help" must come before "getting help from the others." Hsiao reminded her audience: "The Taiwanese people must demonstrate our determination to defend our freedom, democracy, and sovereignty; we must increase the defense budget and accelerate our military reforms to gain more support from our international friends."[10]

GREAT POWER COMPETITION: FROM COLD WAR PARTNERS TO STRATEGIC RIVALS

I did not write this book on the Carter administration's handling of the two competing Chinese regimes to, shall we say, save Taiwan from its peculiar security situation or magically change China into that democracy that many past US officials had expected. My intention is also not to criticize the policies of any past or current US administration. However, I believe in this book I offer powerful analytical tools that illuminate how and why US relations with the two Chinas are at a crisis point today. My study's three major themes—multilateral strategic competition, technology transfer, and ideological differences—are still highly relevant to understanding today's dynamic relations among the three players.

I have demonstrated that the late 1970s and early 1980s marked a pivotal shift in Cold War dynamics, turning the Kissinger era's delicate twin policies of US-China rapprochement and US-Soviet détente into a de facto US-China military alliance against the Soviet Union. The US-China military collaborations and China's hostile attitude toward US-Soviet efforts at arms control, coupled with the Soviet Union's failure to improve relations with China and to stop the United States' NATO allies from arming China, reshaped global power balances and contributed significantly to the collapse of détente. Furthermore, the Carter administration first ignored and then was forced by the Taiwan lobby and the US Congress to reconsider its relations with Taiwan, leading to a complex policy of arming both China and Taiwan, fueling the political, ideological, and military competition between the two hostile Chinese regimes, that of the Communists led by Deng Xiaoping and that of the Nationalists led by Chiang Ching-kuo. These developments had far-reaching consequences, influenced the eventual collapse of the Soviet Union, and shaped the multilateral geopolitical, technological, and ideological competitions that continued beyond the Cold War.

While their fundamental logic remains, these themes are playing out in the 2020s, which is a much different world than that of the late 1970s Cold War. The most important change is the transition of US-PRC relations from anti-Soviet partners to competitors after the collapse of the Soviet Union. The end of the Cold War did not mean that post-Soviet Russia ceased to be a security threat to Europe, although the front line moved eastward from the center of Berlin to the newly independent former Soviet republics. However, China now stood by Russia's side. In the 1990s and 2010s, the Jiang Zemin and the Hu Jintao administrations in China played a carefully balanced game, a "marriage of convenience" with Yeltsin's and later Putin's Russia.[11] While expanding trade with the West, post–Cold War CCP leaders Jiang and Hu resisted domestic nationalist pressure and slowly but steadily resolved China's borders dispute with Russia. From 1991 to 2008, they signed a series of resolution agreements with Russia and, at least on paper, solved the century-old border problems that plagued Sino-Soviet relations during the Deng Xiaoping and Brezhnev years.[12]

Russia, too, at this point, carefully balanced its relations with the West and China. After the terrorist attack in New York City on September 11, 2001, Putin acquiesced to the George W. Bush administration's plan to establish military bases in Central Asia as part of the Global War on Terrorism, while entertaining a vague "strategic partnership" with China both bilaterally and within the loosely formed Shanghai Cooperation Organization.[13] No partnership, either during the Cold War or today, is without nuisances and potential problems. Russia's officials, intelligence services, and mafia organizations constantly kept a watchful eye on potential Chinese economic, social, and cultural incursions in the Russian Far East, where about ninety million Chinese in the bordering provinces faced fewer than eight million Russian citizens of various ethnicities. Especially in the late 2000s, the increased number of Chinese immigrants and mixed marriages caused Sinophobia among Russian nationalists, and crimes against Chinese immigrants increased. As a local Russian journalist explained it, "The lazy, wife-beating, alcoholic Siberian man hates to see another beautiful Russian girl running into a Chinese man's arms."[14]

However, China's geopolitical and military cooperation with Russia became much more comprehensive after Xi Jinping came to power in 2012, despite the racism, nationalism, and anxiety of Russian political elites over China's future role in the Russian Far East.[15] This was demonstrated by the fact that the two strongman-type leaders of these authoritarian regimes backed one another against the West in two major geopolitical crises. First, during Russia's annexation of Crimea in 2014, China abstained from the UN Security Council's attempt on March 15, 2014, to invalidate the Russia-supported Crimea referendum and again abstained from the UN General Assembly's March 27 successful vote to discourage Crimea's international status. Both were seen as Xi's encouragement of Putin's behavior.[16] Second, during the 2018–2019 Hong Kong prodemocratic protests, when the Chinese leaders' decision to crack down on the protesters led to strong criticism from the West, Russian diplomats and media sided with the CCP propaganda machine and blamed the West and its intelligence agencies for "meddling in China's domestic issues," claiming they had "directly participated and organized unrest" in Hong Kong.[17]

Michael Beckley, an expert on US-China relations at Tufts University, noted that public opinion outside China has also changed in response to China's increased domestic oppression and international assertiveness: "A 2021 survey by the Pew Research Center found that roughly 75 percent of people in the United States, Europe, and Asia held unfavorable views of China and had no confidence that President Xi Jinping would behave responsibly in world affairs or respect human rights. Another survey, a 2020 poll by the Center for Strategic and International Studies, revealed that about 75 percent of foreign policy elites in those places thought that the best way to deal with China was to form coalitions of like-minded countries against it."[18] China has seemingly replaced the Soviet Union as the main rival in the United States' coalition-building efforts.

When Putin invaded Ukraine in 2022, Chinese firms and state-owned banks, often using hastily established shell companies in Hong Kong, were Russia's primary source of advanced Western technology, critical materials, and hard currencies in support of its war machine. According to a study by Nikkei, the Russian military evaded Western sanctions and managed to access 75 percent of Western-made advanced semiconductors through shadow companies set up in mainland China and Hong Kong.[19] In addition, according to a study by the Kyiv School of Economics, mainland China, Hong Kong, and Turkey were Russia's main sources of Western-sanctioned critical components used in the war industry during the first year of the fighting. Ukrainian scholars also found something rather absurd: Not only did China provide Russia with 63.1 percent of its war materials and 58.7 of its critical components, but also Taiwan, in 2023, provided Russia with 8 percent of its war materials and 5 percent of its critical components—most likely advanced semiconductors. Even now, Taiwanese companies and rogue traders aggressively take advantage of the international crisis and make a profit at the cost of the United States' and Europe's security—and perhaps their own.[20] Meanwhile, on the front lines, Ukrainian soldiers and engineers, after taking apart captured Russian war equipment, found Chinese navigation gear in Russian killer drones and Chinese fire-control systems in Russian tanks, further demonstrating the complex, multilateral nature of technology transfer in modern conflict.[21]

Even though Taiwan is rather far from Russia geographically and the ROC has no official diplomatic relations with it today, Russia's military cooperation with China has an indirect yet tremendously grave impact on Taiwan's security and sovereignty. Many of the weapons systems the PLA purchased from Russia are directly aimed at Taiwan or are intended to be used as a deterrent against US intervention in a future conflict across the Taiwan Strait, making Taiwan's 5 percent high-tech contribution to the Russian arms industry even more absurd. Furthermore, Putin's invasion of Ukraine in 2022 has taught many lessons to the PLA military planners who are determined to take Taiwan by force. Ironically, some of these lessons are pretty embarrassing. For example, the expensive Russian Sukhoi fighters China imported did not perform as advertised when in the hands of Russian pilots. The sinking of the Russian flagship *Moskva* in the Black Sea by Ukraine, a country without a navy, also embarrassed Chinese naval planners, who relied heavily on Russian-made combat ships, submarines, and maritime technologies.[22]

Putin's aggression in Europe and China's increasingly disruptive role in that aggression, reflecting their close military cooperation, prompted US officials to rethink their global strategy. Renewed multilateral thinking was reflected in the Biden administration's 2022 National Defense Strategy, which, for example, clearly connected the security of Taiwan with China's ambitions in the East China Sea and South China Sea and along the PRC-India border and thus required renewed efforts to rebuild the United States' alliance with countries in those regions. In other words, the United States had to have a multilateral response to the new challenges posed by the close cooperation between Xi's PRC and Putin's Russia—a reversal of the scenario seen in the Cold War when Deng Xiaoping and the Carter administration wove together an anti-Soviet alliance on the Eurasian continent. Further, in April 2024, two years after Russia's invasion of Ukraine, Biden signed a law that made Taiwan, Ukraine, and Israel the top three recipients of a $95 billion military aid bill, demonstrating US determination to boost its most vulnerable partners around the world in response to the global challenge posed by China and Russia.[23] Donald Trump, who won the 2024 presidential election and took office in 2025, will also face significant difficulties in trying to play the "reverse Kissinger card"—to peel China and Russia apart—in his administration's efforts to negotiate an end to the Ukrainian War.[24]

A NEW ARMS RACE

In the first part of this book, I examined China's role in the US-Soviet strategic arms race, as both Deng Xiaoping's hostile attitude toward the superpowers' dominant role in global nuclear affairs and China's independent ICBM ambitions seriously disrupted US-Soviet détente before its final collapse. By refusing to join any US- and Russia-led arms control process, China continued to play a disruptive role in the post–Cold War world, just as it had done during the Cold War, even though China was now a major player in the field instead of a minor one. In October 2019, President Trump announced that the United States would withdraw from the Intermediate-Range Nuclear Forces Treaty (INF), which had been signed by Russia and the United States in 1987. This announcement raised serious concerns among nonproliferation officials in the West and handed Putin's propaganda machine plenty of ammunition for its anti-American campaigns. Russian Foreign Ministry spokesperson Maria Zakharova called the United States' unilateral withdrawal from the INF "a destructive act that had created a vacuum and stoked additional security risks."[25] After US and Russian officials accused one another of violating the treaty, President Putin officially ended Russia's participation in the treaty in March 2019, and the United States did the same in August.[26] The US and Russian decisions to withdraw from the INF sent shockwaves through the international community. On the surface, Russia's development of ground-launched cruise missiles in a range prohibited under the INF treaty was the center of the official debate (table C.1). Yet the issue became much more complicated, considering China's position and missile development programs. Officially, the Chinese Foreign Ministry denounced the US

TABLE C.1 Estimate of how the PRC's strategic rocket forces would be restricted if it was a signatory to the INF Treaty (2019 data).

Type of missile	Would it be restricted under the INF Treaty?	Estimated range	Launchers (mechanisms for moving and firing missiles)	Number of missiles
Intermediate-range ballistic issile	Yes	3,000+ km	16–30	16–30
Medium-range ballistic missile	Yes	1,500+ km	100–125	200–300
Ground-launched cruise missile	Yes	1,500+ km	40–55	200–300
Short-range ballistic missiles	Yes, for a significant percentage of China's short-range missiles with ranges beyond 500 km	300–1,000 km	250–300	1,000–1,200
Intercontinental ballistic missile	Yes, for the small number of missiles with ranges under 5,500 km	5,400–13,000+ km	50–75	75–100

Source: Jacob Stokes, *China's Missile Program and U.S. Withdrawal from the Intermediate-Range Nuclear Forces (INF) Treaty* (U.S.-China Economic and Security Review Commission, 2019).

decision and called it "another negative move" that "ignores its international commitment and pursues unilateralism." However, a closer examination of China's behavior provides some credibility to Trump's claim that "unless Russia comes to us, and China comes to us, and they all come to us," the United States would have to withdraw; unilaterally adhering to the agreement would be "unacceptable."[27]

There are, of course, significant differences between the 1970s and the present. During the Cold War, China was a latecomer to the ICBM club and had the weakest nuclear force among the superpowers, but since the mid-1990s, the PLA has built up one of the world's largest and most diverse arsenals of ground-launched missiles and has a distinct advantage in intermediate-range ballistic missiles—the precise kind of weapon that was banned by the INF. The US Department of Defense estimated in 2024 that China had nearly six hundred operational nuclear weapons and was in the process of constructing new solid-propellant silo fields for at least three hundred new ICBMs. According to the same report, the PLA, as of 2024, possessed 3,500 ballistic and cruise missiles, armed with both nuclear and conventional warheads, that could be used to target US military bases in the Pacific.[28] In addition, as a part of its antiaccess strategy to push the US military out of East Asia, China had since the early 2010s been developing and refining a type of antiship ballistic missile that could target the US fleet if it was to intervene during the PLA's invasion of Taiwan, as well as hypersonic glider missiles that could be very hard for current US missile defense systems to intercept.[29] China's hyperglide missile technology, according to US experts, was "much more advanced than the US program" and possibly also more advanced than that of Russia.[30] Nonclassified publications from Chinese military analysts generally have avoided the question of China's missile development and observed that the US desire to maintain hegemony was the main reason for the INF Treaty's demise.[31]

TECHNOLOGY TRANSFER: A NEW HIGH-TECH ARMS RACE

In the late 1970s and 1980s, the United States provided mainland China with investments, weapons, and intelligence in their mutual struggle against the Soviet Union. At the same time, US allies in Western Europe offered China additional, and sometimes even more sensitive, technologies that the US government was reluctant to sell. Now the roles have reversed. Russia became a major producer of weapons and military technologies for mainland China after the First Persian Gulf War in 1990–1991, when the US-led coalition force's quick victory demonstrated the technological gap between the PLA and the high-tech military of the West. To close this gap, China turned to post-Soviet Russia. In 1993, the PLA bought an S-300 air defense system, twenty-six Sukhoi SU-27 multirole fighters, and a Kilo-class submarine from Russia.[32] After the United States intervened in the third Taiwan Strait Crisis with the carrier-centered 7th Fleet in 1996, the PLA began negotiations with Russia and eventually bought four Sovremenny-class destroyers, which entered service from the late 1990s to 2004. Furthermore China purchased 76 Su-30 fighters from 1999 to 2001, and further purchased 24 Su-35 fighters and received all deliveries in 2019.[33] Those ships were specifically designed to take down US carriers with their hypersonic antiship missiles—at least, in theory.[34] Those Russian warships and the Russian Su-30 and Su-35 fighters would do the heavy lifting in a potential conflict with the United States in the Taiwan Strait.[35]

The end of the Cold War and the deterioration of US-China relations also led US officials to reevaluate Taiwan's role in US security and the security of the Asia-Pacific region. As a result, the United States not only continued to sell arms to Taiwan but also increased the quantity and quality of the arms it sold; in particular, the George H. W. Bush administration delivered 150 F-16 fighters to Taiwan in 1992, and the Clinton administration delivered 300 M60 main battle tanks; thousands of antitank, antiship, and antiair missiles; and other military technologies after the 1996 Taiwan Strait Crisis.[36]

Even though Taiwan's economic development and democratization offered new financial incentives and humanitarian justification for foreign defense companies to enter its market, Western Europe's post–Cold War arms sales to Taiwan remained a small fraction of those from the United States. During the Cold War, US export control and competition were the two main factors that inhibited European defense firms from playing a more significant role in Taiwanese defense. Now China's increasing diplomatic and economic pressures became the new obstacle for European firms wanting to enter Taiwan, especially after China sanctioned France, in addition to closing the French Consulate in Guangzhou, after it sold sixty Mirage fighters to Taiwan in 1993. Thus, France and Germany, the two major continental European military powers, exported only US$193 million worth of weapons and military technology to Taiwan in the first decade after the Cold War. Ironically, the same two countries exported US$1.9 billion worth of arms to China during the same period despite post–Tiananmen Square massacre sanctions.[37]

With the collapse of the Soviet Union, many cash-strapped former Soviet republics were left with piles of weapons. The former Soviet republic of Ukraine became a primary target of China's aggressive military technology acquisition strategy, an ironic situation considering China's current role in Russia's invasion of Ukraine. Like Nicolas Cage in the 2005 Hollywood crime drama *Lord of War*, Xu Zengping, a former PLA basketball team player and self-proclaimed Hong Kong businessman, managed to purchase the unfinished Soviet Kuznetsov-class aircraft carrier *Varyag* in 1998 from corrupt, vodka-wielding Ukrainian officials to use as a floating casino in Macau. After the deal was sealed in Kyiv and enough bribes were paid to Turkish officials to let the *Varyag* pass through the Dardanelles and Bosphorus Straits, Xu conveniently declared bankruptcy and "gifted" the supposed floating casino, along with eight truckloads of the original blueprints, to the PLA naval shipyard in the port city of Dalian in northern China. The *Varyag* was eventually retrofitted and launched in 2012 as the *Liaoning*, China's first aircraft carrier, while Xu retired as a modern Chinese internet legend.[38] He later admitted to the *South China Morning Post* that the deal with Ukraine was, in fact, a rogue operation of the PLA Navy, conducted behind President Jiang's back.[39] However, the truth remained elusive to the public.

Into the 2000s, China utilized a mix of technology imports and military-industrial espionage, combined with increased domestic R&D investments in the modernization of PLA war-fighting capabilities, to overcome the targeted sanctions of the United States.[40] As in the Cold War, Western Europe remained a loophole, despite the post-1989 Tiananmen Square massacre sanctions. This was especially true after China entered the World Trade Organization. Because EU countries lacked a coordinated and careful approach to the identification of military-end users, they became China's primary points of access to advanced Western technologies, particularly through trade and investment where Chinese investors shore up shares of European companies and invest seed funds into tech start-ups. Those state backed Chinese investors were especially interested in the areas of "commercial aviation, space technology, information and communications technology, material science, mechanical engineering, nuclear physics, and others." In addition, China resorted to commercial espionage for obviously military-related technologies that EU countries refused to sell.[41] In the short run, the EU's decision to cooperate with China in defense-related technology—especially aerospace, telecommunication, and information technology—served European countries' desire to exploit new markets and become more independent from US competitors. At the same time, Europe's lackluster export control mechanism benefited China's long-established tradition of countering the technological supremacy of hegemonic powers: "the United States and the Soviet Union during the Cold War, the United States alone afterward."[42]

The methods of technology transfer also changed to the benefit of the end user at the expense of the innovator. During the Cold War, technology acquisition was more civilized: Gentlemen from both sides had to sit down, light the cigars, negotiate the deals, and then pop the champagne and ship the equipment or blueprints in large boxes physically. The subsequent spread of the internet allowed rogue actors to use cyberattacks to acquire technologies illegally and quite quickly. China, Russia, and, increasingly, North Korea became quite proficient at this craft, which forced recent US administrations to employ ever stricter measures to slow down—if not prevent—their cyberattacks against its military and industrial assets. In September 2015, for example, the Obama administration tried to protect US firms from intellectual property theft by Chinese companies, often with the backing of the mainland's vast military and intelligence cyber warfare institutions, by reaching a cybersecurity agreement with Xi during a face-to-face summit in California.[43] The agreement only temporarily halted such actions. In addition to cyberattacks, the hostile purchase of advanced US tech firms by the CCP's state-owned enterprises—another "innovative" way for mainland China to acquire American technology—became central to the two countries' trade disputes during the first Trump administration, continued during the Biden administration, and returned at an even higher level in the second Trump administration.[44]

Europe has remained the Wild West in China's technology acquisition strategy, as shown in this anecdote. Professor Anton Zeilinger from Vienna University, where I worked as an economic historian, won the 2022 Nobel Prize in Physics.[45] He represents the best of Austria's intellectual tradition and Europe's strong leadership role in fundamental scientific research. Zeilinger's research focuses on the fundamental question and application of quantum entanglement, the strange phenomenon in which fundamental particles can be intimately linked with one another and share the same measurement simultaneously so that one is affected by a change in the other, even if vast distances separate them.[46] This phenomenon breaks down what scientists know about classic physics and challenges the assumption that information cannot be transmitted faster than light. A century ago scientists thought quantum entanglement was so counterintuitive to the reality described by the theory of general relativity that even Alfred Einstein called it the "spooky action at a distance"; today it has been proven by experiments conducted jointly by Austria and China.

In 2001, Zeilinger and other theoretical physicists pushed the European Space Agency hard for funding to test the possibility of quantum entanglement, but their proposal was lost in the agency's bureaucratic labyrinth. However, Chinese physicist Pan Jianwei, Zeilinger's former student, contacted his Vienna mentor and offered generous funding from the Chinese Academy of Sciences. The collaboration among Vienna University, the Austrian Academy of Sciences, and the Chinese Academy of Sciences resulted in the first quantum-enabled satellite in 2015.[47] After two years of testing, on September 29, 2017, the satellite, named after ancient Chinese philosopher Micius, beamed down a small data packet to a ground station in Xinglong, a couple of hours' drive to the northeast of Beijing. Less than an hour later, the satellite passed over Austria and dispatched another data packet to a station near Graz. The two packets were encryption keys made from quantum-entangled photons that would secure data transmissions. Due to both quantum entanglement and another equally bizarre phenomenon called the observation effect, any attempt to intercept one of two packets would collapse the state of measurement of both packets in China and Austria, thus immediately destroying the information and notifying both research stations of the presence of a hacker. This is a genuinely cutting-edge experiment, as the two keys are like self-conscious twins who know—and inform one another across vast distances—when one of them has been hacked.[48] As stated by Zeilinger, "Quantum communication is absolutely secure against eavesdropping and also works on a global scale."[49] Zeilinger and Pan's project is a classic case of China's post–Cold War technology transfer strategy: Instead of purchasing existing technology or outdated equipment, China is using academic cooperation—often backed with lavish state funding—to attract the best international talents to develop those technologies within China. The Mucius satellite was no doubt a tribute to humanity's understanding of quantum mechanics, but it was also a dual-use technology that attracted anxious attention from US national security officials.

No wonder the 2017 Zelinger-Pan experiment was the center of discussion at the NATO-sponsored international conference on cyber conflict, held in Washington, D.C., in 2017. One US researcher called China's development of quantum communication a "disruptive technology" and "theoretically unhackable."[50] At the same time, a much longer Brookings report noted that China's determination to pursue secure quantum communication followed the 2013 leaks of US classified information by Edward Snowden, a situation that "caused deep concern in Beijing." Nevertheless, the recent developments in China were "a loss for American intelligence organizations." They also raised serious questions about how the United States and China would manage their scientific competition in outer space.[51] In addition, US Military analysts were alarmed by how heavily China had invested in quantum computer (QC) technology, as "seven of the top ten universities with QC patents ranked globally are Chinese." Because this technology "can break through cyber security measures once thought almost impossible to breach," China's efforts to utilize "the entirety of its government, academia, and industry" in its development made sure "the United States and its allies will find it harder to protect vulnerable information systems, compromising their pursuit of national and global interests."[52]

Curiously, it was only in 2023 that the German federal media outlet Deutsche Welle (DW) finally launched an investigation into Zeilinger's Chinese partner Pan and found out he was working for China's Thousand Talent Program, which channeled Chinese state funding abroad to acquire foreign talents and cutting-edge military and dual-use technologies. DW also discovered that Pan was involved in a parallel program in Germany as the director of Heidelberg University's new quantum research center in China. To the shock of German journalists, the Chinese partner was none other than the Chinese National University of Defense Technology (NUDT)—China's top military research university, which reports directly to the CCP Central Military Commission, of which Xi was the chairman. In a last-minute effort to clean up its reputation, Heidelberg University stated that the NUDT played no role in planning the joint research center. However, admittedly, it "would not have entered into a cooperation if the military connection had been examined more closely."[53] As they did during the Cold War, European institutions and their near-absent security measures created serious loopholes through which Chinese military end users could easily access the best research in the West.

A NEW BATTLE FOR IDEOLOGY: AUTHORITARIANISM VERSUS DEMOCRACY

In much of this book, I have focused on the ideological bickering and diplomatic maneuvering between Deng Xiaoping and Chiang Ching-kuo and how these complicated their cross-strait relations and their respective relations with the United States. I hope attentive readers have already noticed a common tacit agreement between the two Chinese leaders despite their other differences: Both firmly believed that China's future lay in its close relationship with the United States, even though they fiercely disagreed on which China should be part of the relationship. It took tremendous effort for both men to come to this conclusion and act as they did. Deng, for example, was at heart a Communist and shared many of Mao's anti-imperial and anti-American views. The threat the Soviet Union posed to the PRC, however, was a much stronger motivation for Deng, and he had to make friends with the United States. Chiang, on the other hand, was fed up with the United States' repeated betrayals: Truman's withdrawal of US troops from mainland China on the eve of the Chinese Civil War, Nixon's secret diplomacy with Mao without his or his father's knowledge, and Carter's sudden switch of diplomatic allegiance. In his diary, Chiang clearly documented how he lost faith in the United States because of the constant betrayals.

This mistrust and disappointment, however, did not prevent Chiang from tying Taiwan's fate firmly to the United States, even to the point of allowing much belated, albeit fruitful, democratization efforts in his final years of life. On behalf of their leaders, PRC and ROC diplomats pursued bold initiatives in the Cold War that undermined the United States' global influence in one way or another. Still, none were damaging enough to destroy their respective regimes' relations with the United States. These shared pro-US attitudes, however, started to change after the end of the Cold War. With the collapse of the Soviet Union in 1991, the anti-Soviet basis for US-PRC relations was gone, and the problems with China's political identity—its authoritarian rule, its terrible human rights record, and the increased anti-American propaganda sanctioned by the CCP—moved to the center of US-PRC relations. Today's mainland China is nowhere near anything appearing to be the democracy Americans had hoped for, especially after Xi amended the constitution in 2018 to allow himself to serve unlimited terms as the head of state.[54]

Therefore, the ideological competition between the two competing Chinese regimes became less about *which* regime should represent China and more about *what* that regime should be, regardless of its political self-identification: an increasingly oppressive, inward-looking dictatorship or a democracy that enjoyed friendly relations with the West. Unlike mainland China, Taiwan experienced political democratization during the final years of Chiang's rule. When those opposing his one-party rule, a loosely associated group called the Tangwai movement, became a unified political party, the Democratic Progressive Party (DPP) in 1986, Chiang, under heavy pressure from the Reagan administration, acted against his own generals' advice and decided not to arrest and murder the opposition, as Deng had done during the student protests in 1989. Instead, Chiang opened the media for free discussion and allowed the members of the DPP to run for seats in the National Assembly—the ROC's legislative body.[55] After this, politics in Taiwan diverged from politics in mainland China and progressed on a slow but steady path to democracy.

Thus, another significant variation between our current time and the Cold War is found in the ideological dimension: today Taiwan is no longer a right-wing military dictatorship but a democracy. In 1996, the ROC had its first democratic presidential election and grew into a thriving democracy with a world-class, innovation-based economy in the twenty-first century. When the Carter family visited mainland China in 2014, Taiwan had just experienced one of the largest post–Cold War student protests, the Sunflower movement, during which students and academics led widespread demonstrations against a proposed trade agreement between mainland China and Taiwan. According to the protestors, the agreement proposed by President Ma Ying-jeou, a member of the KMT, would further compromise Taiwan's economic independence and lead to increased political pressure from the mainland in Taiwanese politics.[56] If Xi's concentration of power marked the return of strict authoritarianism and a cult of personality to the Chinese mainland, then the Sunflower movement, in contrast, marked the maturity of Taiwan as a democracy. The KMT eventually compromised with the students, which further led to a change in government and the return of the DPP to power in early 2016. The 2016 election also made Dr. Tsai Ing-wen, educated at Cornell and the London School of Economics, the first female president of Taiwan.[57]

Taiwan's democratic political system and free-market economy allowed technology transfer to play a very different and much more important role in its relations with the United States. Unlike what China had done, Taiwan's integration into the US-led economic and technological ecosystem joined the fates of the US and Taiwanese tech sectors in a mutually beneficial and constructive manner. In Chiang's time, the KMT had to beg the United States to sell advanced technology. Today the two sides are equal partners. The Taiwanese economy is now deeply integrated into the global high-tech economy and is an indispensable security and innovation partner of the United States. Working closely with American high-tech firms such as AMD, IBM, Apple, Cisco, and Intel, Taiwanese microchip producers help Americans manufacture their most advanced semiconductors, many of which are used in the US defense industry. Furthermore, by allocating design to the United States and manufacturing to Taiwan, both sides avoided toxic competition and thrived on one another's success, further increasing mutual interdependence.[58] In March 2025, Taiwanese chipmaker TSMC announced a plan to invest US$100 billion in factories in the United States, further facilitating mutual economic dependence and increasing Taiwan's influence in US politics.[59]

Overall, Taiwan's transparent political system and adherence to the rule of law allowed it to produce goods superior to those made on the mainland in various sectors and indirectly enhanced its international attractiveness, or "soft power." With a highly advanced agriculture sector and well-implemented environmental regulations, Taiwanese fruits, tea, and other organic products are considered the best and safest to consume in Asia. When the CCP sanctioned Taiwanese fruit and seafood products to protest US Representative Nancy Pelosi's visit to Taiwan in 2022, other Asian countries encouraged their citizens to "eat Taiwanese" to show solidarity and support.[60] In contrast, the mainland was plagued with food poisoning scandals, from poisonous baby formula and gutter oil to heavy metal pollution in cooking oils, as they were transported in the same trucks that carried fuel.[61] I accidentally ate some of China's fake beef in 2017. It was not the "beyond meat" type of vegan food you could buy in upscale American grocery stores but low-quality beef scraps that had been ground, glued together with chemicals, and resold as "Californian beef steak" in a shopping mall in my hometown of Kunming.

Before I end my story, I wish to point out that the diverging natures of the relations the two Chinese regimes have with the United States have also changed personal relations and day-to-day interactions among their people. Unlike Chiang and his generals, who ruled Taiwan with an iron fist, the civilian officials that govern Taiwan today are charming, easygoing, and democratically elected. I have noticed that ROC politicians carry a special charisma that their mainland peers cannot match. Many prominent political figures in the ROC—including three of its presidents: Tsai Ing-wen, Ma Ying-jeou, and Lee Teng-hui—were educated in the United States. All speak fluent English and are sincerely well treated by their US counterparts, like old friends. Lai Ching-te, elected president in 2024, also studied at Harvard for his master's in public health. I had the honor of meeting and speaking to then–Vice President Annette Lu Hsiu-lien, a DPP member, in 2012 when I was a student at George Washington University. She also studied abroad and obtained two master of laws degrees, one from the University of Illinois at Urbana–Champaign and the other from Harvard. When she arrived at George Washington's Elliott School of International Affairs, across the street from the US State Department, she was smiling and waving and had just one young assistant. She gave a fantastic lecture, answered all sorts of questions in flawless English, and gladly welcomed "selfies" with American and international students. During my friendly encounters with Taiwanese officials, the only US policymaker they obviously took issue with was President Carter. In 2016,

FIGURE C.1 The "good old days," with Jimmy Carter (*left*), Richard Nixon (*second from left*), and Deng Xiaoping (*right*) at the White House on the eve of the normalization of US-PRC diplomatic relations. (Jimmy Carter Presidential Library and Museum)

I shared an office at George Washington with a young Taiwanese diplomat, and when I told her that I was researching the Carter administration, she was immediately intrigued. "Jimmy Carter? The president who dumped us?" "That is right," I half-joked. "The president who threw you under the bus."

In contrast, the only Western-educated politician in mainland China who served in Xi's administration was Liu He, the economic expert and former vice premier who studied public policy at the Harvard Kennedy School, where I am currently a associate fellow with the Belfer Center's Applied History Project. Liu, popular abroad but heavily criticized at home by hard-line nationalists for being too soft toward the Americans and "raising too many questions about the president's policies," was never at the center of power despite his Harvard résumé. In October 2023, Liu was replaced by a more conservative and seemingly loyal He Lifeng, who, unlike Liu, never studied abroad and does not speak English.[62] Instead of engaging Westerners personally through people-to-people diplomacy, the CCP spends billions of dollars each year trying to promote its image and downplay international criticism of its policies through controlled overseas media sources such as the China Global Television Network and carefully choreographed political events.[63]

Mainland officials have also tried their best to block Western visitors from interacting with average Chinese people. On March 22, 2014, US First Lady Michelle Obama visited Beijing University during an unofficial trip she made in a well-intended attempt to help President Barack Obama improve the United States' image with young people in mainland China. The "students" Michelle met and interacted with were, in fact, actors—young Communist Party Youth League members handpicked for the special occasion.[64] In 2023, when Xi visited California, the city of San Francisco—at the urging of the PRC Consulate—cleaned up several blocks of drug-dealer-infested neighborhoods and bussed homeless people away from Xi's travel route.[65] When visiting the United States, mainland leaders never had the intimate and relaxed interactions that Taiwanese leaders enjoyed with their hosts and the American people. The "good old days" when a Chinese Communist leader like Deng Xiaoping could skillfully play a cowboy and entertain Americans at a Texas rodeo seemed ever so far away, buried in the distant memories of the Cold War.

NOTES

INTRODUCTION

1. Ray Takeyh and Gideon Weiss, "The Legacy of Jimmy Carter's Foreign Policy," Council on Foreign Relations, December 29, 2024, https://www.cfr.org/article/legacy-jimmy-carters-foreign-policy. Also see Robert A. Strong, "Jimmy Carter: Foreign Affairs," Miller Center, accessed March 19, 2025, https://millercenter.org/president/carter/foreign-affairs.
2. "Read Trump's Statements on Jimmy Carter's Death," CBS News, December 30, 2024, https://www.cbsnews.com/news/jimmy-carter-death-donald-trump-statement/.
3. Irie Sentner. "Trump Slams Carter's Panama Canal Deal As He's Set to Lie in State," *Politico*, January 7, 2025, https://www.politico.com/live-updates/2025/01/07/congress/trump-jimmy-carter-panama-canal-00196862.
4. Leila Fadel, "A Review of Carter's Foreign Policy and Views on Global Affairs Post Presidency," NPR, December 30, 2024, https://www.npr.org/2024/12/30/nx-s1-5241005/a-review-of-carters-foreign-policy-and-views-on-global-affairs-post-presidency.
5. Two important studies by the economic historian Julian Gewirtz deal with the question of Western support in the economic transition of the PRC at the end of the Cold War period: Julian Gewirtz, *Unlikely Partners: Chinese Reformers, Western Economists, and the Making of Global China* (Harvard University Press, 2017); Julian Gewirtz, *Never Turn Back: China and the Forbidden History of the 1980s* (Harvard University Press, 2022). Other scholars, such as David Shambaugh, pointed out the CCP's internal adaptation as the key to its continued survival: David L. Shambaugh, *China's Communist Party: Atrophy and Adaptation* (Woodrow Wilson Center Press and University of California Press, 2008).
6. Zbigniew K. Brzezinski, *Power and Principle: Memoirs of the National Security Adviser 1977–1981* (Farrar, Straus & Giroux, 1985): Cyrus R. Vance, *Hard Choices: Critical Years*

in America's Foreign Policy (Simon & Schuster, 1983). Vance did question whether Carter and Brzezinski had acted too quickly in recognizing the PRC; however, he believed the decision to normalization relations with the PRC was generally correct. See Vance, *Hard Choices*, 32, 41.

7. Jimmy Carter, *Keeping Faith: Memoirs of a President* (University of Arkansas Press, 1995), 216.

8. The literature that covered the Jimmy Carter period in a more critical manner includes Patrick Tyler, *A Great Wall: Six Presidents and China; An Investigative History* (PublicAffairs, 2000); and James Mann, *About Face: A History of America's Curious Relationship with China from Nixon to Clinton* (Vintage, 2000). On Taiwanese domestic factors, see Kerry Brown and Kalley Wu Tzu-Hui, *The Trouble with Taiwan: History, the United States and a Rising China* (Bloomsbury Academic, 2022).

9. Nancy Bernkopf Tucker, *Strait Talk: United States–Taiwan Relations and the Crisis with China* (Harvard University Press, 2011).

10. Robert S. Ross, ed. *China, the United States and the Soviet Union: Tripolarity and policy making in the Cold War* (London: M. E. Sharpe, 1993).

11. Gong Li 宫力, *Deng Xiaoping Yu Zhong Mei Waijiao Feng Yun* 邓小平与中美外交风云 (红旗出版社, 2015). Another work with an official "orthodox" view is Tao Wenjian, 中美关系史: 1972–2000 [US-China relations: 1972–2000] (Shanghai Renmin Chubanshe, 2004). Also see a more critical account of both Deng and Chiang: Yu Jie 余杰, 偽裝的改革者：破解鄧小平和蔣經國神話 [Reformers in disguise: Deciphering the myths of Deng Xiaoping and Chiang Ching-kuo] (Ba qi wen hua chu ban, 2022); Hsiao-ting Lin, *Accidental State: Chiang Kai-shek, the United States, and the Making of Taiwan* (Harvard University Press, 2016); Hsiao-ting Lin, 蔣經國的台灣時代, 中華民國與冷戰下的台灣 [The Chiang Ching-kuo era: The Republic of China on Taiwan in the Cold War] (Yuan zu wen hua, 2021).

12. Nancy Mitchell, "The Cold War and Jimmy Carter," in *The Cambridge History of the Cold War*, ed. Melvyn P. Leffler and Odd Arne Westad (Cambridge University Press, 2010), 67.

13. One such effort is William C. Kirby, Robert S. Ross, and Li Gong, eds., *Normalization of U.S.-China Relations: An International History* (Harvard University Asia Center, 2007). Also see Lorenz M. Lüthi, *Cold Wars: Asia, the Middle East, Europe* (Cambridge University Press, 2020), 520, 524.

14. Edward C. Keefer, *Harold Brown: Offsetting the Soviet Military Challenge 1977–1981* (Historical Office, Office of the Secretary of Defense, 2017), 396.

15. K. G. Lieberthal and Michel Oksenberg, *Policy Making in China: Leaders, Structures, and Processes* (Princeton University Press, 1988); John King Fairbank, *The United States and China*, 4th ed. (Harvard University Press, 1983), 462–65.

16. Harry Harding, *A Fragile Relationship: The United States and China Since 1972* (Brookings Institution, 1992); Robert S. Ross, *Negotiating Cooperation: The U.S. and China, 1969–89* (Stanford University Press, 1997). Also see David L. Shambaugh "Patterns of Interaction in Sino-American Relations," in *Chinese Foreign Policy: Theory and Practice*, ed. Thomas

W. Robinson and David L. Shambaugh. (Clarendon, 1995); Richard H. Solomon, *Chinese Political Negotiating Behavior, 1967–1984* (RAND, 1995); and Rosemary Foot, *The Practice of Power: US Relations with China Since 1949* (Oxford University Press, 1995).

17. John W. Garver, *China's Quest: The History of the Foreign Relations of the People's Republic of China* (Oxford University Press, 2018); Kirby, Ross, and Gong, *Normalization of US-China Relations*; Odd Arne Westad, "China and the End of the Cold War in Europe," *Cold War History* 17, no. 2 (2017): 111–13.

18. Martin Albers, *Britain, France, West Germany and the People's Republic of China, 1969–1982: The European Dimension of China's Great Transition* (Palgrave Macmillan, 2016); Frank Bösch, *Zeitenwende 1979: Als Die Welt von Heute Begann* (Beck, 2019).

19. Jay Taylor, *The Generalissimo's Son: Chiang Ching-kuo and the Revolutions in China and Taiwan* (Harvard University Press, 2000); Tucker, *Strait Talk*; Hsiao-ting Lin, *Taiwan, the United States, and the Hidden History of the Cold War in Asia: Divided Allies* (Routledge, 2023).

20. Martin B. Gold, *A Legislative History of the Taiwan Relations Act: Bridging the Strait* (Lexington Books, 2017); Kuang Ger Yeong, "Cross-Strait Relations and the Taiwan Relations Act," *American Journal of Chinese Studies* 22, special issue no. 2 (2015); David Tawei Lee, *The Making of the Taiwan Relations Act: Twenty Years in Retrospect* (Oxford University Press, 2000) (Lee served as President Tsai Ing-wen's foreign minister and national security adviser).

21. Odd Arne Westad, *The Global Cold War: Third World Interventions and the Making of Our Times* (Cambridge University Press, 2005); Raymond L. Garthoff, *Detente and Confrontation: American-Soviet Relations from Nixon to Reagan* (Brookings Institution, 1994); Nancy Mitchell, *Jimmy Carter in Africa: Race and the Cold War* (Woodrow Wilson Center Press, 2016); Elizabeth Wishnick, *Mending Fences: The Evolution of Moscow's China Policy from Brezhnev to Yeltsin* (University of Washington Press, 2014).

22. Hugo Meijer, *Trading with the Enemy: The Making of US Export Control Policy Toward the People's Republic of China* (Oxford University Press, 2018); Frank Cain, "The US-led Trade Embargo on China: The Origins of CHINCOM, 1947–52." *Journal of Strategic Studies* 18, no. 4 (1995): 33–54; Jing-dong Yuan, "The Politics of the Strategic Triangle: The U.S., COCOM, and Export Controls on China, 1979–1989," *Journal of Northeast Asian Studies* 14, no. 1 (1995); Brian J. Auten, *Carter's Conversion: The Hardening of American Defense Policy* (University of Missouri Press, 2008); Xiaoming Zhang, *Deng Xiaoping's Long War: The Military Conflict Between China and Vietnam 1979–1991* (University of North Carolina Press, 2018); Zhihua Shen and Danhui Li, *After Leaning to One Side: China and Its Allies in the Cold War* (Woodrow Wilson Center Press, 2011); Yang Kuisong 杨奎松 et al., eds., 中苏关系史纲 [Survey of Sino-Soviet relations] (Shehui Kexue Chubanshe, 2016).

23. Yang Zhong, "Explaining National Identity Shift in Taiwan," *Journal of Contemporary China* 25, no. 99 (2016).

24. Hui-ching Chang and Richard Holt, *Language, Politics and Identity in Taiwan: Naming China* (Routledge, 2015), 6–11.

1. THE DECLINE OF DÉTENTE AND THE NORMALIZATION OF US-CHINA DIPLOMATIC RELATIONS

1. H. W. Brands, "Vietnam and the Origins of Détente," in *The Search for Peace in Vietnam, 1964–1968*, ed. Lloyd C. Gardner and Ted Gittinger (Texas A&M University Press, 2004), 378–79.
2. Chen Jian, "China, the Vietnam War, and the Sino-American Rapprochement, 1968–1973," in *The Third Indochina War: Conflict Between China, Vietnam and Cambodia, 1972–79*, ed. Odd Arne Westad and Sophie Quinn-Judge (Routledge, 2006).
3. Jian, "China, the Vietnam War, and the Sino-American Rapprochement," 47–50.
4. Robert Jervis, "Mutual Assured Destruction," *Foreign Policy*, no. 133 (2002); Edward Kaplan, *To Kill Nations: American Strategy in the Air-Atomic Age and the Rise of Mutually Assured Destruction* (Cornell University Press, 2020), 172–73, 179–83.
5. James Cameron, "Moscow 1972," in *Transcending the Cold War: Summits, Statecraft, and the Dissolution of Bipolarity in Europe*, ed. Kristina Spohr and David Reynolds (Oxford University Press, 2020), 83.
6. Vladislav M. Zubok, *A Failed Empire: The Soviet Union in the Cold War from Stalin to Gorbachev* (University of North Carolina Press, 2010), 230.
7. Raymond L. Garthoff, *A Journey Through the Cold War: A Memoir of Containment and Coexistence* (Brookings Institution, 2002), 284.
8. Robert Michael Gates, *From the Shadows: The Ultimate Insider's Story of Five Presidents and How They Won the Cold War* (Pocket, 2008), 49.
9. Some excellent literature exists on the collapse of détente, including Raymond L. Garthoff, *Detente and Confrontation: American-Soviet Relations from Nixon to Reagan* (Brookings Institution, 1994); Robert S. Ross, ed., *China, the United States and the Soviet Union: Tripolarity and Policy Making in the Cold War* (Sharpe, 1993); and Strobe Talbott, *Endgame: The Inside Story of SALT II* (Harper & Row, 1980). For the Horn of Africa, see Nancy Mitchell, *Jimmy Carter in Africa: Race and the Cold War* (Woodrow Wilson Center Press, 2018). China's position on SALT II has barely been studied except in an essay from 1979: William V. Garner, "SALT II: China's Advice and Dissent," *Asian Survey* 19, no. 12 (1979).
10. Barbara Zanchetta, "Re-Creating the Strategic Triangle: Normalization with China and SALT II," in *The Transformation of American International Power in the 1970s* (Cambridge University Press, 2014).
11. November 8, 1976, *Chiang Ching-kuo Diary: 1976*, Academia Historica, Taipei (hereafter cited as *Chiang Ching-kuo Diary*).
12. Campaign Notes, "1976 Campaign," Box 2, Folder: Arms Control, 2/75–9/76, Stuart Eizenstat Files, Jimmy Carter Presidential Library, Atlanta (hereafter cited as JCPL).
13. Jimmy Carter, *The Presidential Campaign 1976*, vol. 1, pt. 1 (GPO, 1979), 695.
14. "Intelligence Community Experiment in Competitive Analysis: Soviet Strategic Objectives and Alternative View, Report of Team 'B,'" CIA, December 1976, National Security Archive, https://nsarchive2.gwu.edu/NSAEBB/NSAEBB139/nitze10.pdf.
15. Brian J. Auten, *Carter's Conversion: The Hardening of American Defense Policy* (University of Missouri Press, 2008), 143.

1. THE DECLINE OF DÉTENTE AND NORMALIZATION   247

16. Anne Hessing Cahn, "Team B: The Trillion Dollar Experiment," *Bulletin of the Atomic Scientists* 49, no. 3 (1993).
17. M. Todd Bennett, ed., *National Security Policy, 1973–1976*, vol. 35 of *Foreign Relations of the United States, 1969–1976* (GPO, 2014), 6.
18. Erin R. Mahan, ed., *SALT II, 1972–1980*, vol. 33 of *Foreign Relations of the United States, 1969–1976* (GPO, 2013), 665–67.
19. Melissa Jane Taylor, ed., *Soviet Union*, vol. 6 of *Foreign Relations of the United States, 1977–1980* (GPO, 2013), 34–35.
20. Anatoly Dobrynin, *In Confidence: Moscow's Ambassador to America's Six Cold War Presidents* (Random House, 1995), 444–45.
21. Edward C. Keefer, *Harold Brown: Offsetting the Soviet Military Challenge 1977–1981* (Historical Office, Office of the Secretary of Defense, 2017), 152–53.
22. April 3, 1977, *Chiang Ching-kuo Diary*.
23. Deng Xiaoping 邓小平, "Mei su jiang caijun yue lihai, yue shi yangai geng da de kuojun" 美苏讲裁军越厉害，越是掩盖更大的扩军 [The more America and USSR talk about arms reduction, the more they cover up their military expansion], in *Deng Xiaoping Junshi wenji III* 邓小平军事文集 III [Deng Xiaoping Military Papers III] (Zhongyang Wenxian Chubanshe, 2014), 14–17.
24. Cable, PEIKING to STATE, April 14, 1977, National Archives, https://aad.archives.gov/aad/createpdf?rid=84044&dt=2532&dl=1629.
25. Hua Guofeng 华国锋, "Shiyi da shang de zhengzhi baogao" 十一大上的政治报告 [Report on the Eleventh People's Congress], Central People's Government of the People's Republic of China, August 18, 1977, http://www.gov.cn/test/2007-08/28/content_729705.htm.
26. David Paull Nickles, ed., *China*, vol. 13 of *Foreign Relations of the United States, 1977–1980* (GPO, 2013), 26–27.
27. Svetlana Savranskaya and David A. Welch, eds., "Transcript, Global Competition and the Deterioration of U.S.-Soviet Relations, 1977–1980," The Carter-Brezhnev Project, June 8, 1995, https://nsarchive2.gwu.edu/carterbrezhnev.
28. Paul Nitze had fundamental differences with the more moderate group of advisers, including George F. Kennan, his predecessor as director of policy planning at the State Department. Kennan believed the Soviet Union could be satisfied with the consolidation of its power within the socialist bloc and therefore argued for a containment policy. In contrast, Nitze believed that the Soviet Union wanted global dominance. Secretary of State Dean Acheson sided with the hard-liners and replaced Kennan with Nitze in January 1950. John Lewis Gaddis, *George F. Kennan: An American Life* (Penguin, 2012), 361–65.
29. Very few studies have been dedicated to the committee itself. See Jerry W. Sanders, *Peddlers of Crisis: The Committee on the Present Danger and the Politics of Containment* (South End Press, 1983); Beth Ingold, "The Committee on the Present Danger: A Study of Elite and Public Influence, 1976–1980" (PhD diss., University of Pittsburgh, 1989); and Patricia L. Dunmire, "'Alerting America': The Committee on the Present Danger and the Re-Securitization of the Soviet Union," in *The Great Nation of Futurity: The Discourse and Temporality of American National Identity* (Oxford University Press, 2023).

30. Nicholas Thompson, *The Hawk and the Dove: Paul Nitze, George Kennan, and the History of the Cold War* (Picador, 2010), 272.
31. Heavy drinking and toasting at banquets were frequently mentioned. Personal Journal, "Notes, November 28, 1977," Box 18, Folder 3, Paul Nitze Papers, Library of Congress.
32. A curious document at the Library of Congress revealed this was an intelligence gathering mission: "Nitze's Mission with Defense Intelligence Agency"; see section "Approval for Travel to Denied Areas," November 11, 1977, Department of Defense, Box 18, Folder 3, Paul Nitze Papers, Library of Congress.
33. Cable, PEIKING to STATE, December 1, 1977, National Archives, https://aad.archives.gov/aad/createpdf?rid=305371&dt=2532&dl=1629. The version in Nitze's own notes is slightly different from the Department of State copy: "The most important question is to fight against the appeasement trend and fight against the illusion of peace so that people will be rid of any illusions about 'peace.'" Note, Tuesday, November 28, 1977, Box 18, Folder 3, Paul Nitze Papers, Library of Congress.
34. Letter, Henry Jackson to President Carter, August 22, 1977, Box 40, Folder: SALT 8/77–11/77, Brzezinski Collection, NSA Files, JCPL.
35. Memorandum, "Brown Memo to the President on Senator Jackson's Memo," March 28, 1977, Box 40, Folder: SALT 8/77–11/77, Brzezinski Collection, NSA Files, JCPL.
36. Letter, President Carter to Henry Jackson, August 22, 1977, Box 40, Folder: SALT 3/77–4/77, Brzezinski Collection, NSA Files, JCPL.
37. Garthoff, *Detente and Confrontation*, 627. Later Paul Warnke recalled, "Well, I think it's quite clear that people like the late Senator Jackson and his former aide, now Assistant Secretary of Defense Richard Perle, do not believe you can do business with the Soviet Union. They assume that the Soviet Union is bound to world conquest and that, accordingly, any deal they make with the United States on strategic arms is bound to be one that advances that objective. I think they're absolutely wrong, but they are sincere." Paul Warnke, "War and Peace in the Nuclear Age; Interview with Paul Warnke, 1986," November 19, 1986, https://openvault.wgbh.org/catalog/V_12C9C3E486D44769A6AF4B243D6D5E4E.
38. Andreĭ Andreevich Gromyko, *Памятное: Новые Горизонты* [Memoir: New horizons], vol. 2 (Памятное. Новые горизонты, 2015), 319–20.
39. Robert Gordon Kaufman, *Henry M. Jackson: A Life in Politics* (University of Washington Press, 2000), 379–80.
40. The only translated biography of Brzezinski available is Justin Vaïsse and Catherine Porter, *Zbigniew Brzezinski: America's Grand Strategist* (Harvard University Press, 2018).
41. Zbigniew K. Brzezinski, *The Permanent Purge: Politics in Soviet Totalitarianism* (Harvard University Press, 1956).
42. Zbigniew K. Brzezinski, *The Soviet Bloc: Unity and Conflict*, rev. ed. (Harvard University Press, 1967).
43. Zbigniew K. Brzezinski, *Between Two Ages: America's Role in the Technetronic Era* (Viking, 1970).
44. Joint Statement, June 25, 1974, Box 7, ZB Correspondence 7/74, Brzezinski Collection, Trilateral Commission Files, JCPL.

1. THE DECLINE OF DÉTENTE AND NORMALIZATION 249

45. Milo G. Goerper, "The Trilateral Commission, a Private American-European-Japanese Initiative on Matters of Common Concern," *German American Trade News*, April 1974, sent from Brzezinski to President Carter, July 31, 1975, Box 7, ZB Correspondence 7/74, Zbigniew Brzezinski Collection, Trilateral Commission Files, JCPL.
46. Brzezinski to President Carter, July 31, 1975, Box 8, ZB Correspondence 6/75, Brzezinski Collection, Trilateral Commission Files, JCPL.
47. Brzezinski to David Rockefeller, January 9, 1974. Box 8, ZB Correspondence 1/75, Brzezinski Collection, Trilateral Commission Files, JCPL.
48. Odd Arne Westad, *The Global Cold War, Third World Interventions and the Making of Our Times* (Cambridge University Press, 2005), 250.
49. Helen Lackner, "The People's Democratic Republic of Yemen: Unique Socialist Experiment in the Arab World at a Time of World Revolutionary Fervour," *Interventions* 19, no. 5 (2017).
50. Myra F. Burton, ed., *Middle East Region; Arabian Peninsula*, vol. 18 of *Foreign Relations of the United States, 1977–1980* (GPO, 2015), 530.
51. Memorandum, "Soviet Naval Ships and Arms Shipments at Aden, South Yemen, April 1978–April 1979," CIA CREST, https://www.cia.gov/library/readingroom/docs/CIA-RDP79T01819A000100610001-7.pdf.
52. The current Ethiopian government gives the number as 55,000, although others connected with the EPRP claim it is much higher. Pietro Toggia, "The Revolutionary Endgame of Political Power: The Genealogy of 'Red Terror' in Ethiopia," *African Identities* 10, no. 3 (2012).
53. Richard J. Reid, *Frontiers of Violence in North-East Africa: Genealogies of Conflict Since C. 1800* (Oxford University Press, 2011), 174–75.
54. Mitchell, *Jimmy Carter in Africa*, 348.
55. "The Ethiopian Revolution and Its Implications," March 28, 1977, CIA, CIA CREST, https://www.cia.gov/library/readingroom/docs/CIA-RDP97S00289R000100170015-5.pdf.
56. Memorandum, "Closing Kagnew Station," NSA, March 28, 1977, Box 1, Folder: 3/77, NSA Horn of Africa Files, JCPL.
57. Mitchell, *Jimmy Carter in Africa*, 271.
58. Mitchell, *Jimmy Carter in Africa*, 272, 278–79.
59. Gebru Tareke, "The Ethiopia-Somalia War of 1977 Revisited," *International Journal of African Historical Studies* 33, no. 3 (2000).
60. Transcript of Meeting Between East German Leader Erich Honecker and Cuban Leader Fidel Castro, East Berlin, April 3, 1977, Wilson Center Digital Archive, https://digitalarchive.wilsoncenter.org/document/111844.pdf?v=f309df8815718e8037fc161211b6679e. Also see Mitchell, *Jimmy Carter in Africa*, 197.
61. Robert G. Patman, *The Soviet Union in the Horn of Africa: The Diplomacy of Intervention and Disengagement* (Cambridge University Press, 2009), 217.
62. Patman, *Soviet Union in the Horn*, 286–87.
63. Patman, *Soviet Union in the Horn*, 218–19.

64. Anne Hessing Cahn, "Team B Panel Report on Soviet Strategic Objectives," in *Killing Detente: The Right Attacks the CIA* (Pennsylvania State University Press, 1998); Anne Hessing Cahn, "Team B: The Trillion Dollar Experiment," *Bulletin of the Atomic Scientists* 49, no. 3 (1993). Post–Cold War interviews with Soviet military officials, however, revealed that since the 1970s US intelligence has constantly overestimated the Soviet Union's ambition and underestimated its fear of a US first strike. See William Burr and Svetlana Savranskaya, eds., "Previously Classified Interviews with Former Soviet Officials Reveal U.S. Strategic Intelligence Failure Over Decades," September 11, 2009, National Security Archive, https://nsarchive2.gwu.edu/nukevault/ebb285/.
65. Chris Tudda, ed., *Arms Control and Nonproliferation*, vol. 26 of *Foreign Relations of the United States, 1977–1980* (GPO, 2015), 27.
66. Auten, *Carter's Conversion*, 165.
67. Post–Cold War interviews with US officials and their Russian counterparts, including Dobrynin, suggested that the Soviet Union relied heavily on land-based missiles and thus saw the US demand to reduce their number as unfair. Svetlana Savranskaya and David A. Welch, eds., "SALT II and the Growth of Mistrust," The Carter-Brezhnev Project, February 5, 1995, https://nsarchive2.gwu.edu/carterbrezhnev/salt_i_intro.html.
68. *Pravda*, "Задача Ограничения Стратегических Вооружении: Перспективы И Проблемы" [The task of limiting strategic weapons], February 11, 1978.
69. Raymond L. Garthoff, "Soviet Perspective," in *Cruise Missiles: Technology, Strategy, Politics*, ed. Richard K. Betts (Brookings Institution, 1981).
70. Cable, MOSCOW USSALTTWO to STATE, February 14, 1978, National Archives, https://aad.archives.gov/aad/createpdf?rid=37788&dt=2694&dl=2009.
71. The Soviet breach of the SALT II agreement with a "rapid reload" system was discovered only in 1980 *after* the signing of the treaty. Edgar Ulsamer, "Alarming Soviet Developments," *Air & Space Forces Magazine*, November 1, 1980.
72. Gregg Brazinsky, *Winning the Third World: Sino-American Rivalry During the Cold War* (University of North Carolina Press, 2017), 335–36.
73. Memorandum, "Weekly National Security Report 62," Zbigniew Brzezinski to President Carter, February 26, 1977, Box 41, Folder: Weekly Reports 2/77–6/77, Brzezinski Collection, NSA Files, JCPL.
74. Cable, SECSTATE WASHDC to AMEMBASSY MOGADISCIO, June 3, 1977, National Archives, https://aad.archives.gov/aad/createpdf?rid=127228&dt=2532&dl=1629.
75. David P. Nickles, ed., *China*, vol. 13 of *Foreign Relations of the United States, 1977–1980* (GPO, 2013), 159, 161, 167.
76. Nickles, *China*, 182.
77. On Deng's similar demand of Japan, see Robert Hoppens, "Deng Xiaoping Visits Tokyo, October 1978 and February 1979," Wilson Center, May 18, 2020, https://www.wilsoncenter.org/blog-post/deng-xiaoping-visits-tokyo-october-1978-and-february-1979.
78. Nickles, *China*, 192–204.
79. John H. Holdridge, *Crossing the Divide: An Insider's Account of Normalization of US-China Relations* (Rowman and Littlefield, 1997), 173.
80. Mitchell, *Jimmy Carter in Africa*, 285.

1. THE DECLINE OF DÉTENTE AND NORMALIZATION   251

81. State Dinner Menu, Box 8, Folder: Group no. 1664, Series no. 2, Cyrus Vance Papers, Yale University Library.
82. Mengrui Wang, "1972 年欢迎尼克松的神秘晚宴" [Nixon's secret state dinner in 1972], June 4, 2019, http://zhouenlai.people.cn/n1/2019/0604/c409117-31119591-2.html.
83. August 25, 1977, *Chiang Ching-kuo Diary*.
84. August 26, 1977, *Chiang Ching-kuo Diary*.
85. Patman, *Soviet Union in the Horn*, 228.
86. Michael T. Kaufman, "Ogaden Conflict Termed Threat to Africa's Stability," *New York Times*, October 9, 1977.
87. Louise P. Woodroofe, ed., *Horn of Africa*, vol. 17, pt. 1 of *Foreign Relations of the United States, 1977–1980* (GPO, 2016), 77.
88. Woodroofe, *Horn of Africa*, 81.
89. Woodroofe, *Horn of Africa*, 81, 87.
90. Kenneth M. Pollack, *Armies of Sand: The Past, Present, and Future of Arab Military Effectiveness* (Oxford University Press, 2020), 88–89.
91. Patman, *Soviet Union in the Horn*, 219–220.
92. Taylor, *Soviet Union*, 85.
93. Zbigniew K. Brzezinski, *Power and Principle: Memoirs of the National Security Adviser, 1979–1981* (Farrar, Straus, & Giroux, 1985), 189.
94. Record of Conversation, "The Horn of Africa," Special Coordination Committee, February 22, 1978, Box 11, Folder: Ethiopia-Somalia 4/77–2/22/78, Brzezinski Collection, NSA Files, JCPL.
95. Nickles, *China*, 302, 304.
96. Brzezinski, *Power and Principle*, 149–50.
97. NSC Weekly Report #51, Brzezinski to President Carter, March 10, 1978, Box 41, Folder: 1/78–3/78, Brzezinski Collection, NSA Files, JCPL.
98. Nickles, *China*, 309.
99. Memorandum, "Recent Soviet Ground Force Activity on the Sino-Soviet Border," November 9, 1977, CIA CREST, https://www.cia.gov/library/readingroom/docs/DOC_0000969745.pdf.
100. "National Intelligence Estimate: Soviet Strategic Objectives," January 12, 1977, CIA CREST, https://www.cia.gov/library/readingroom/docs/DOC_0005289044.pdf.
101. Memorandum, "Sino-Soviet Relations," February 27, 1978, CIA, CIA CREST, https://www.cia.gov/library/readingroom/docs/CIA-RDP81B00401R002400020022-3.pdf.
102. Special Report, "The Men in the Sino-Soviet Confrontation," July 5, 1963, CIA CREST, https://www.cia.gov/library/readingroom/docs/CIA-RDP79-00927A004100040002-3.pdf.
103. Memorandum, "State of the World," January 12, 1976, CIA CREST, https://www.cia.gov/library/readingroom/docs/CIA-RDP83B00100R000100130068-8.pdf.
104. "Presidential Briefing China—Outline," April 10, 1978, CIA, CIA CREST, https://www.cia.gov/readingroom/document/cia-rdp83b00100r000100050017-2.
105. "Chinese Foreign Policy," CIA, undated, Box 8, Folder: China [PRC] 10/77–1/78, NSA Files, JCPL.

106. Lin Xiaoguang 林晓光 and Sun Hui 孙辉, "Zhongri heyue de qian ding yu 20 shiji 70 niandai de zhongri guanxi" 中日和约的签定与20世纪70年代的中日关系 [Sino-Japanese Friendship Treaty and the 1970s Sino-Japanese relations], *Riben yanjiu jilin* 日本研究集林 [Fudan University Center for Japanese Studies Collection] 2 (2008).
107. Niu Dayong 牛大勇, "Zhong mei jiedong guanxi shi dui riben wenti de kaoliang yu jueli" 中美解冻关系时对日本问题的考量与角力 [The consideration and trial of strength over the issue of Japan in the period of the thawing of relations between China and the United States], *Meiguo yanjiu* 美国研究 [The Chinese journal of American studies] 5 (2014).
108. Memorandum, "Jackson's Conversation with Chinese," From Oksenberg to Brzezinski, February 28, 1978, Box 8, Folder: China [PRC] 10/77–1/78, NSA Files, JCPL. On Wu's role during the special trial of the Gang of Four, see Wu Xiuquan 伍修权, *Wang Shi Cang Sang* 往事沧桑 (Shanghai wen yi chu ban she, 1986), 306, 326.
109. Memorandum, "Noon Notes," from the Situation Room to Brzezinski, April 11, 1978, Box 5, Folder: 4/1/78–4/12/78, President Daily Report Files, NSA Files, JCPL.
110. Memorandum, "The People's Republic of China and NATO," from Secretary of Defense Brown to Brzezinski, October 4, 1977, Box 8, Folder: China [PRC] 10/77–1/78, NSA Files, JCPL.
111. "White House Evening Report," April 12, 1978, Box 6, Folder: 2–5/78, Staff Material, Horn/Special, NSA Files, JCPL.
112. *New York Times Magazine*, May 7, 1978.
113. Nickles, *China*, 357–65.
114. Nickles, *China*, 378–79.
115. Nickles, *China*, 394.
116. Nickles, *China*, 404.
117. Nickles, *China*, 410.
118. Nickles, *China*, 432–47.
119. Memorandum, "More on Daedalus," from Oksenberg to Brzezinski June 1, 1978, Box 8, Folder: China [PRC] 10/77–1/78, NSA Files, JCPL.
120. Brzezinski, *Power and Principle*, 405.
121. Nickles, *China*, 747.
122. "Vice Premier Deng Xiaoping at the Tomb of Martin Luther King Jr. After a Wreath-Laying Ceremony, Atlanta, Georgia, February 2, 1979," *Atlanta Journal-Constitution*, http://digitalcollections.library.gsu.edu/cdm/ref/collection/ajc/id/7198.
123. Fox Butterfield, "Teng Takes Quest for U.S. Technology to Atlanta," *New York Times*, February. 2, 1979, https://www.nytimes.com/1979/02/02/archives/teng-takes-quest-for-us-technology-to-atlanta-teng-takes-quest-for.html.
124. Butterfield, " Teng Takes Quest."
125. Adam Taylor, "How a 10-Gallon Hat Helped Heal Relations Between China and the United States," *Washington Post*, September 25, 2015.
126. "1979 年邓小平访美：在休斯顿宇航中心进行模拟飞行," Ifeng, February 23, 2021, https://news.ifeng.com/c/846L5rXodRO

2. THE CHINA-FRANCE NUCLEAR ALLIANCE   253

127. Leslie Wayne, "Visiting Boeing, China's President Praises Planes and Trade," *New York Times*, April 19, 2006; Jane Perlez, "President Xi Jinping of China Arrives in Seattle," *New York Times*, September 28, 2015.
128. "U.S.-China: Thirty Years of Science and Technology Cooperation," US Department of State, October 15, 2009, https://2009-2017.state.gov/e/oes/rls/fs/2009/130625.htm. Whether or not to continue the agreement would be hotly debated during the 2024 US presidential campaign. "Expired US-China Science Treaty Signals Deep Uncertainty Amid High Tensions," *South China Morning Post*, August 30, 2024, https://www.scmp.com/news/china/diplomacy/article/3276479/expiration-major-us-china-science-treaty-signals-deep-uncertainty-amid-high-tensions.
129. Sergey Radchenko, *To Run the World: The Kremlin's Cold War Bid for Global Power* (Cambridge University Press, 2024), 460.
130. Jimmy Carter, *Keeping Faith: Memoirs of a President* (University of Arkansas Press, 1995), 207.
131. This will be the main topic of chapter 5.
132. May 6, 1978, *Chiang Ching-kuo Diary*.

2. THE CHINA-FRANCE NUCLEAR ALLIANCE AND THE FAILED COMPREHENSIVE TEST BAN NEGOTIATIONS

1. Evan S. Medeiros, *Reluctant Restraint: The Evolution of China's Nonproliferation Policies and Practices, 1980–2004* (NUS Press, 2009), 30; Ann Kent, *Beyond Compliance: China, International Organizations, and Global Security* (Stanford University Press, 2010). Others argued that China did not believe in the effectiveness of the CTBT, which was the main reason for rejecting it. See Wendy Frieman, *China, International Arms Control and Non-Proliferation* (Routledge, 2004), 39–40.
2. Nicola Horsburgh, *China and Global Nuclear Order: From Estrangement to Active Engagement* (Oxford University Press, 2015), 76–95.
3. Raymond L. Garthoff, *Detente and Confrontation: American-Soviet Relations from Nixon to Reagan* (Brookings Institution, 1994), 626.
4. Kosta Tsipis et al., "Thirty-Seven Years of Nuclear Weapons," *Bulletin of the Atomic Scientists* 38, no. 10 (1982). Also see Andrew Futter, *The Politics of Nuclear Weapons* (Sage, 2015), 70–129. Early studies of such concepts include Nance W. Gallagher, *Arms Control: New Approaches to Theory and Policy* (Routledge, 1998).
5. Strobe Talbott, *Endgame: The Inside Story of Salt II* (Harper & Row, 1980).
6. John B. Rhinelander, "The Comprehensive Test Ban Treaty as a Prelude to SALT II," *Arms Control Today* 8, no. 4 (1978).
7. John J. Politi, "Concerning a Comprehensive Nuclear Test Ban," *US Army War College Quarterly: Parameters* 8, no. 1 (1978).
8. Statement of Rear Admiral Thomas Davies, Assistant Director, Bureau of Multilateral Affairs, Arms Control and Disarmament Agency, *Current Negotiations on the*

Comprehensive Test Ban Treaty: Hearings Before the Intelligence and Military Application of Nuclear Energy Subcommittee of the Committee on Armed Services, House of Representatives, 95th Congress, 2nd Session (March 15 and 16, 1978) (GPO, 1978).

9. Roland M. Timerbaev, *Рассказы О Былом. Воспоминания О Переговорах По Нераспространению И Разоружению И О Многом Другом* [Tales of the past: A memoir on the negotiation of nonproliferation and disarmament] (PIR-Center, 2007), 81.
10. Horsburgh, *China and Global Nuclear Order*, 80.
11. "The Nuclear Testing Tally 1945–2017," Arms Control Association, last reviewed January 2024, https://www.armscontrol.org/factsheets/nucleartesttally.
12. Edward C. Keefer et al., eds., *Northeast Asia*, vol. 22 of *Foreign Relations of the United States, 1961–1963* (GPO, 1996), 174.
13. William Burr and Jeffrey T. Richelson, "Whether to 'Strangle the Baby in the Cradle': The United States and the Chinese Nuclear Program, 1960–64," *International Security* 25, no. 3 (2001).
14. Nina J. Noring, ed., *Near East*, vol. 18 of *Foreign Relations of the United States, 1961–1963* (GPO, 1995).
15. Vladislav M. Zubok, "Look What Chaos in the Beautiful Socialist Camp: Deng Xiaoping and the Sino-Soviet Split, 1956–1963," *Cold War International History Project Bulletin* 10 (1998).
16. Kendrick Oliver, *Kennedy, Macmillan and the Nuclear Test-Ban Debate, 1961–63* (Macmillan, 1998), 145.
17. William Burr and Hector L. Montford, eds., "The Making of the Limited Test Ban Treaty, 1958–1963," August 8, 2003, National Security Archive, https://nsarchive2.gwu.edu/NSAEBB/NSAEBB94/#29.
18. Viktor Adamsky and Yuri Smirnov, "Moscow's Biggest Bomb: The 50-Megaton Test of October 1961," *Cold War International History Project Bulletin* 4 (1994).
19. Jeffrey Lewis, "Point and Nuke," *Foreign Policy*, September 12, 2018, https://foreignpolicy.com/2018/09/12/point-and-nuke-davy-crockett-military-history-nuclear-weapons/.
20. Robert Powell, "Nuclear Brinkmanship, Limited War, and Military Power," *International Organization* 69, no. 3 (2015); Jan Hanska, "Rethinking the Unthinkable—Revisiting Theories of Nuclear Deterrence and Escalation," *Journal of Military Studies* 9, no. 1 (2018).
21. John Pike, "Atomic Artillery," Global Security, accessed December 30, 2022, https://www.globalsecurity.org/military/world/russia/atomnaya-artilleriya.htm.
22. "中国政府关于全面禁止和彻底销毁核武器的声明" [Chinese government's statement regarding the total ban and elimination of nuclear weapons], *People's Daily*, October 21, 1964.
23. "在战争与和平问题上的两条路线五评苏共中央的公开信" [Five comments to the Soviet Central Committee on the two paths of peace and war, an open letter], *Renmin Ribao*, November 19, 1963. For Deng's role in drafting those statements, see Alexander V. Pantsov and Steven I. Levine, *Deng Xiaoping: A Revolutionary Life* (Oxford University Press, 2015), 231.
24. Li Danhui 李丹慧, "走向分裂：从暗中斗争到公开论战, 1960 年代中苏关系研究之二" [Toward the split: From intrigues to polemics, 1960's Sino-Soviet relations, Study 2], *Shixue jikan* 史学集刊 [Collected papers of history studies], no. 6 (2006).

2. THE CHINA-FRANCE NUCLEAR ALLIANCE   255

25. Deng was instrumental in Mao's propagandist war against Moscow. See Pantsov and Levine, *Deng Xiaoping*, 228–29, 231.
26. Lorenz M. Lüthi, "Rearranging International Relations? How Mao's China and de Gaulle's France Recognized Each Other in 1963–1964," *Journal of Cold War Studies* 16, no. 1 (2014).
27. Harriet Dashiell Schwar, ed., *China*, vol. 30 of *Foreign Relations of the United States, 1964–1968* (GPO, 1998), 225.
28. Xi Qixin 奚启新, *Qian Xuesen zhuan* 钱学森传 [Qian Xuesin biography] (Renmin Chuban She, 2011), 381.
29. Xi Qixin, *Qian Xuesen zhuan*, 385.
30. Yafeng Xia, *Negotiating with the Enemy: US-China Talks During the Cold War, 1949–1972* (Indiana University Press, 2006), 119–24.
31. "1949 年后大陆科学家景况一览" [Overview of the situation of scientists in mainland China after 1949], Qiushi.org, January 2012, http://www.qiushi.org/index.php?m=content&c=index&a=show&catid=30&id=197.
32. Survey of returning scientists.
33. Hua Xinmin 华新民, "文革中的钱学森" [Qian Xuesen during the Cultural Revolution], *Ji Yi* 记忆 32, no. 3 (2010).
34. "周恩来生平和思想研讨会在京开幕" [Zhou Enlai life and thoughts conference opens in Beijing], *Renmin Ribao*, February 18, 1998.
35. "National Intelligence Estimate 13-8-69, 'Communist China's Strategic Weapons Program,'" Director of Central Intelligence, February 27, 1969, CIA CREST, https://www.cia.gov/library/readingroom/docs/DOC_0001098205.pdf.
36. M. Todd Bennett, ed., *National Security Policy*, vol. 35 of *Foreign Relations of the United States, 1969–1976* (GPO, 2014), 285.
37. Steven E. Phillips, ed., *China, 1969–1972*, vol. 17 of *Foreign Relations of the United States, 1969–1976* (GPO, 2006), 23.
38. For the US-China opening, see Chris Tudda, *A Cold War Turning Point: Nixon and China, 1969–1972* (Louisiana State University Press, 2012).
39. Xin Zhan, "Prelude to the Transformation: China's Nuclear Arms Control Policy During the U.S.-China Rapprochement, 1969–1976," *Diplomatic History* 41, no. 2 (2017).
40. Xin Zhan, "Prelude to the Transformation."
41. Zhang Aiping 张爱萍, 张爱萍军事文选 [Zhang Aiping military papers] (Changzheng Chuban She, 1994), 317.
42. Wang Wenhua 王文华, 钱学森实录 [Qian Xuesen chronology] (四川文艺出版社, 2001), 265.
43. Xi Qixin 奚启新, 钱学森转 [Qian Xuesen biography] (Jiao Tong University Press, 2011), 455–56.
44. Zhang Aiping, Zhang Aiping military papers, 335–36.
45. Deng Xiaoping 邓小平, "美苏讲裁军越厉害, 越是掩盖更大的扩军" [The more America and USSR talk about arms reduction, the more they cover up their military expansion]," in 邓小平军事文集 III [Deng Xiaoping Military Papers III] (Zhongyang Wenxian Chubanshe, 2014), 14–17.

46. Chris Tudda, ed., *Arms Control and Nonproliferation*, vol. 26 of *Foreign Relations of the United States, 1977–1980* (GPO, 2015), 328–29.
47. Memorandum, "Your Meeting with Huang Chen," Brzezinski to President Carter, Box 8, Folder: China (People's Republic of, 1–2/77), NSA Country File, JCPL.
48. "Official Biography of Huang Zhen," Ministry of Foreign Affairs, PRC, January 15, 2009, http://www.mfa.gov.cn/chn//pds/ziliao/wjrw/lrfbzjbzzl/t9071.htm.
49. Tudda, *Arms Control and Nonproliferation*, 22–23.
50. David P. Nickles, ed., *China*, vol. 13 of *Foreign Relations of the United States, 1977–1980* (GPO, 2013), 57–60.
51. DEFE 13/350, PS to S of S, "The Case for 5 SSBNs," October 19, 1964, Kew, National Archive, quoted in David Owen, *Nuclear Papers* (Liverpool University Press, 2009), 7–11.
52. Peter Hennessy, *Cabinets and the Bomb* (Oxford University Press, 2007), 232–40; John Baylis and Kristan Stoddart, *The British Nuclear Experience: The Role of Beliefs, Culture, and Identity* (Oxford University Press, 2015), 129–132.
53. Memorandum, "Consultations with Key NATO Allies on the Impact of a Comprehensive Test Ban," Brzezinski to President Carter, July 7, 1977, Box 13, Folder: Comprehensive Test Ban, 3–12/77, NSA Brzezinski File, JCPL.
54. The Soviet delegation representative Roland Timerbaev remembered that verification should not be necessary because each country should trust the other; building verification would destroy such trust. Of course, Americans did not buy into this argument. Warren Heckrotte, "A Soviet View of Verification," *Bulletin of the Atomic Scientists* 42, no. 8 (1986).
55. Memorandum, "Soviet High Yield Testing," Cyrus Vance to Zbigniew Brzezinski, October 31, 1979, Box 59, Folder 4, Herbert York Papers, University of California San Diego.
56. Aleksei Fenenko, "Ядерные Испытания В Системе Стратегической Стабильности" [Nuclear testing and system strategic balance], *Mezhdunarodnaia Zhizn'* 12 (2009), https://interaffairs.ru/jauthor/material/161.
57. Cable, GENEVA to SECSTATE, "Soviet Views on Duration and PNE Protocol—Treaty Linkage," December 15, 1977, National Archives, https://aad.archives.gov/aad/createpdf?rid=293362&dt=2532&dl=1629.
58. Bruno Tertrais, "France and Nuclear Non-Proliferation: From Benign Neglect to Active Promotion," in *Nuclear Proliferation and International Order: Challenges to the Non-Proliferation Treaty*, ed. Olav Njølstad (Routledge, 2010), 218–19.
59. William Burr, "The United States and Pakistan's Quest for the Bomb," The Nuclear Vault, December 21, 2010, National Security Archive, https://nsarchive2.gwu.edu/nukevault/ebb333/index.htm.
60. Cable, Peking LE to Diplomatie Paris, Ministères des Affaires Étrangères, March 1, 1977, Asie-Oceanie, Les centres des archives diplomatiques, La Courneuve.
61. Memorandum, "Questions Atomiques," AMBAFRANCE PRKING, October 23, 1978, Asie-Oceanie, Les centres des archives diplomatiques, La Courneuve.
62. Memorandum, "Cooperation franco-chinoise dans le domaine nucleaire," Affaires Étrangères, September 13, 1979, Asie-Oceanie, Les centres des archives diplomatiques, La Courneuve.

2. THE CHINA-FRANCE NUCLEAR ALLIANCE   257

63. Cable, Paris to DSMT Genève, Ministere des Affaires Étrangères, "Entree de la Chine Au Comité Du Désarmement," January 21, 1980, Asie-Oceanie, Les centres des archives diplomatiques, La Courneuve.
64. Cable, Ministère Des Affaires Étrangères, Télégramme A L'arrivée, to DSMT Genève, CQ Peking, March 20, 1980, Asie-Oceanie, Les centres des archives diplomatiques, La Courneuve. Emphasis added.
65. Aide—Memoire, Ministere des Affaires Étrangères, Paris, October 10, 1978, Asie-Oceanie, Les centres des archives diplomatiques, La Courneuve.
66. Cable, Ministere des Affaires Étrangères, Washington, "Objet: Vente de Centrales Nucleaires a La Chine," December 4, 1978, Asie-Oceanie, Les centres des archives diplomatiques, La Courneuve.
67. Memorandum, "Comprehensive Test Ban Negotiations," George M. Seignious II to Secretary Vance, January 16, 1979, Box 29, Folder 5, Herbert York Papers, University of California San Diego.
68. Nickles, *China*, 763–65.
69. Or Rabinowitz and Nicholas L. Miller, "Keeping the Bombs in the Basement: US Nonproliferation Policy Toward Israel, South Africa, and Pakistan," *International Security* 40, no. 1 (2015).
70. Nickles, *China*, 780.
71. After his summit meeting with Brezhnev, Carter approved the option of starting to "proceed very cautiously to implement a modest program of cooperation" with China on nuclear test technologies. Nickles, *China*, 791.
72. Nils-Olov Bergkvist and Ragnhild Ferm, "Nuclear Explosions 1945–1998," International Atomic Energy Agency, January 1, 1970, https://inis.iaea.org/search/search.aspx?orig_q=RN%3A31060372.
73. Paul Warnke and Walter Pincus, "Pass the SALT: An Interview with Paul Warnke," *New York Review of Books*, June 14, 1979.
74. CIA National Foreign Assessment Centre Office of Political Analysis, "A Review of the Evidence of Chinese Involvement in Pakistan's Nuclear Weapons Program," December 7, 1979, National Security Archive, http://nsarchive.gwu.edu/nukevault/ebb423/docs/3a.%20Chinese%20involvement%20in%20Pakistan%20nuke%20program%201979.pdf.
75. Cable, US MISSION GENEVA to SECSTATE, February 23, 1979, National Archives, https://aad.archives.gov/aad/createpdf?rid=98689&dt=2776&dl=2169.
76. Cable, US MISSION GENEVA to SECSTATE, February 26, 1979, National Archives, https://aad.archives.gov/aad/createpdf?rid=100634&dt=2776&dl=2169.
77. Timebaev, Tales of the past, 88.
78. Cable, US MISSION GENEVA to SECSTATE, March 13, 1979, National Archives, https://aad.archives.gov/aad/createpdf?rid=188318&dt=2776&dl=2169.
79. York, *Making Weapons, Talking Peace*, 310. In addition, a discussion can be found in the following report and its attached cable: Memorandum, "CTBT: NSS on UK Territory" May 27, 1980, J. C. Edmonds to Cabinet Office and Ministry of Defense, FC066/1467, UK National Archives.

80. Memorandum, "Comprehensive Test Ban: Prototype National Seismic Station (NSS) on UK Territory," Foreign and Commonwealth Office to 10 Downing Street, July 30, 1980, PREM 19/693, UK National Archives.
81. Cable, USMISSION GENEVA to SECSTATE WASHDC, September 27, 1979, National Archives, https://aad.archives.gov/aad/createpdf?rid=320364&dt=2776&dl=2169.
82. Cable, US MISSION GENEVA to SECSTATE, December 6, 1979, National Archives, https://aad.archives.gov/aad/createpdf?rid=55475&dt=2776&dl=2169.
83. Legal Memorandum, Department of Defense, Office of General Counsel, May 22, 1979, Box 59, Folder 9, Herbert York Papers, University of California San Diego.
84. Timebaev, Tales of the past, 91.
85. Soviet and UK positions did not change until the end of 1980. The Soviet team blamed the Americans for fooling them into believing the UK was more flexible than it was. Cable, US MISSION GENEVA to SECSTATE, July 2, 1980, Box 57, Folder 10, Herbert York Papers, University of California, San Diego.
86. This is according to the US Naval Institute's official history: Norman Polmar and Robert S. Norris, *The US Nuclear Arsenal: A History of Weapons and Delivery Systems Since 1945* (Naval Institute Press, 2009), 238.
87. Tudda, *Arms Control and Nonproliferation*, 375–77.
88. Memorandum, "Technical Assistance to China for Underground Nuclear Testing," Department of State, March 15, 1979, National Security Archive, https://nsarchive2.gwu.edu/nukevault/ebb323/doc11a.pdf.
89. Cable, US MISSION GENEVA to SECSTATE, "CTBT Negotiations: USSR, Plenary Statement," November 12, 1980, Box 58, Folder 14, Herbert York Papers, University of California San Diego.
90. Judith Miller, "US Said to Decide Against New Talks to Ban All A-Tests," *New York Times*, July 20, 1982.
91. Bergkvist and Ferm, "Nuclear Explosions 1945–1998."
92. Xi Qixin, *Qian Xuesen zhuan*, 458–60.
93. Lu Qiming 陆其明 and Fan Minruo 范敏若, 张爱萍与两弹一星 [Zhang Aiping and the "two missiles," "one satellite"] (Jiefangjun Chuban She, 2011), 394.
94. The United States wanted China to accept international nonproliferation practices and norms, which was a major reason for the 1985 US-China Nuclear Energy Cooperation Agreement. See Qingshan Tan, "U.S.-China Nuclear Cooperation Agreement: China's Nonproliferation Policy," *Asian Survey* 29, no. 9 (1989). Also see *Nuclear Energy Cooperation with China, Hearing Before the Special Subcommittee on US–Pacific Rim Trade of the Committee on Energy and Commerce*, House of Representatives, 99th Congress, 1st Session (GPO, 1986).
95. Medeiros, *Reluctant Restraint*, 30–41.
96. "张军大使在安理会《全面禁止核试验条约》问题公开会上的发言" [Ambassador Zhang Jun's speech at the UN Security Council public meeting on the Comprehensive Nuclear Test Ban Treaty], Permanent Mission of the PRC to the UN, September 27, 2021, http://un.china-mission.gov.cn/zgylhg/jjalh/alhzh/qita1/202109/t20210928_9579278.htm.

97. United Nations. "Chapter XXVI, Disarmament, 4. Comprehensive Nuclear-Test-Ban Treaty, September 10, 1996, Accessed September 11, 2025. https://treaties.un.org/pages/ViewDetails.aspx?src=TREATY&mtdsg_no=XXVI-4&chapter=26
98. Chandelis Duster, "Top Military Leader Says China's Hypersonic Missile Test 'Went Around the World,'" CNN, November 18, 2021, https://edition.cnn.com/2021/11/17/politics/john-hyten-china-hypersonic-weapons-test/index.html.

3. WESTERN EUROPEAN MILITARY AND DUAL-USE TECHNOLOGY TRANSFERS TO CHINA

A shortened version of this chapter was published under the title "A 'Gentleman's Understanding': British, French, and German Dual-Use Technology Transfer to China and America's Dilemma During the Carter Administration, 1977–1981," in *Diplomacy & Statecraft* 32, no. 1 (2021).

1. Angela Romano and Valeria Zanier, "Circumventing the Cold War: The Parallel Diplomacy of Economic and Cultural Exchanges Between Western Europe and Socialist China in the 1950s and 1960s: An Introduction," *Modern Asian Studies* 51, no. 1 (2016); Martin Albers and Zhong Chen, "Socialism, Capitalism, and Sino-European Relations in the Deng Xiaoping Era, 1978–1992," *Cold War History* 17, no. 2 (2017).
2. Oliver Bräuner, "Beyond the Arms Embargo: EU Transfers of Defense and Dual-Use Technologies to China," *Journal of East Asian Studies* 13, no. 3 (2013).
3. David L. Shambaugh, *Modernizing China's Military: Progress, Problems, and Prospects* (University of California Press, 2004), 229.
4. Hugo Meijer, *Trading with the Enemy: The Making of US Export Control Policy Toward the People's Republic of China* (Oxford University Press, 2018), 17.
5. Frank Cain, "The US-Led Trade Embargo on China: The Origins of CHINCOM, 1947–52," *Journal of Strategic Studies* 18, no. 4 (1995), 33–54.
6. Cain, "The US-Led Trade Embargo on China."
7. Chi-kwan Mark, *The Everyday Cold War: Britain and China, 1950–1972* (Bloomsbury Academic, 2017), 103.
8. Frank Cain, *Economic Statecraft During the Cold War: European Responses to the US Trade Embargo* (Routledge, 2007), 177–78.
9. Huang Wenjiang 黄文江, "国际关系, 商贸机会, 科技转移对1975年中英'斯贝202'发动机专利合同及其时代意义的解读" [International relations, trade opportunities, and the interpretation of the "British Spey 202" engine technology transfer to China in 1975], 外交评论 [Foreign affairs] 1 (2010).
10. Dennis M. Gormley et al., "A Potent Vector: Assessing Chinese Cruise Missile Developments," *Joint Force Quarterly* 75 (October 2014): 101.
11. Romano and Zanier, "Circumventing the Cold War," 8.
12. Garret Martin, "Playing the China Card? Revisiting France's Recognition of Communist China, 1963–1964," *Journal of Cold War Studies* 10, no. 1 (2008).

13. Memorandum, "Gaullist France, and Communist China," October 23, 1963, CIA CREST, https://www.cia.gov/library/readingroom/docs/CIA-RDP79R00904A001000020021-8.pdf.
14. William Burr, "The Limited Test Ban Treaty—50 Years Later: New Documents Throw Light on Accord Banning Atmospheric Nuclear Testing," The Nuclear Vault, August 2, 2013, https://nsarchive2.gwu.edu/nukevault/ebb433/.
15. Mao Zedong 毛泽东, "Zhongjian didai you liangge" 中间地带有两个 [On the two intermediate zones], in *Mao Zedong waijiao wenxuan* 毛泽东外交文选 [Mao Zedong foreign affairs papers] (Zhongyang Wenxian Chuban She, 1994), 506–9.
16. Bernd Schaeffer, "Ostpolitik, 'Fernostpolitik,' and Sino-Soviet Rivalry: China and the Two Germanys," in *Ostpolitik, 1969–1974: European and Global Responses*, ed. Carole Fink and Bernd Schaefer (Cambridge University Press, 2008).
17. Bernd Schaefer et al., "Sino-West German Relations during the Mao Era," Wilson Center, March 10, 2025, https://www.wilsoncenter.org/publication/sino-west-german-relations-during-the-mao-era.
18. Memorandum, "Lieferung von Spey 512 und Spey 202 Jet-Turbinen der britischen Firma Rolls Royce and die VR China," July 13, 1973, B63 ZA 117660, Folder: 410.55 CHN, File: COCOM Ausfuhr von Düsentriebwerken 1973–1974, Politisches Archiv des Auswärtigen Amts.
19. Frank Bösch, *Zeitenwende 1979: Als Die Welt von Heute Begann* (Beck, 2019), 172.
20. Martin Albers, *Britain, France, West Germany and the People's Republic of China, 1969–1982: The European Dimension of China's Great Transition* (Palgrave Macmillan, 2016), 254.
21. "华国锋等中央领导同志在中央工作会议上的讲话等" [Hua Guofeng and other central party leaders' speech], File SZ 1-4-791, Hubei Provincial Archives.
22. Zhang Aiping 张爱萍, 张爱萍军事文选 [Zhang Aiping military papers] (Changzheng Chuban She, 1994), 335.
23. Memorandum, "China," from Brzezinski to the Secretary of State, the Secretary of Energy June 19, 1978, Box 8, Folder: China [PRC] 10/77–1/78, NSA Files, JCPL.
24. Memorandum, "Draft Scope Paper for Frank Press's Visit to China," June 30, 1978, From Michel Oksenberg to Zbigniew Brzezinski, Box 8, Folder: China [PRC] 10/77–1/78, NSA Files, JCPL.
25. Xiong Chenxi 熊晨曦, "卡特政府对华科技交流与合作政策研究" [The study of the Carter administration's policy of S&T exchange and cooperation toward China] (Diss., East China Normal University, 2021), 50.
26. Zhang Jing 张静, "邓小平与中美科技合作的开展（1977–1979）" [Deng Xiaoping and the beginning of US-China S&T cooperation, 当代中国史研究 [Contemporary Chinese history studies] 3 (2014).
27. Zhang Jing, Deng Xiaoping and the beginning of US-China S&T cooperation, 16.
28. David P. Nickles, ed., *China*, vol. 13 of *Foreign Relations of the United States, 1977–1980* (GPO, 2013), 720–21.
29. Memorandum. "Third Country Sales to China," NLC-21-15-10-23-6, Carter Library CREST.

3. WESTERN EUROPEAN MILITARY AND DUAL-USE TECHNOLOGY   261

30. Intel, Oversees Economic Intelligence Committee: China: Future Import Policies, August 22, 1978, DEFE11/977, UK National Archives.
31. Li Qiang, military engineer and diplomat (1905–1996), should not to be confused with Li Qiang (1959–), eighth premier of the PRC. Policy Paper, "Harrier for China," Foreign and Commonwealth Office to 10 Downing Street, January 1, 1973, FCO1H/1003, UK National Archives. The folder also contains another internal British discussion of the 1972–1973 proposed Harrier sales to China, which mostly had negative responses.
32. Cable, "My Two Immediate Preceding Telegrams: Defence Sells: Harrier," Peiking to Ministry of Defencex, October 23, 1978, DEFE11/977, UK National Archives. For Li Qiang's biography, see 李强同志生平 [Biography of comrade Li Qiang], 人民日报 [People's daily], October 10, 1996.
33. Memorandum, "Defense Sales to China," Eric Varley to Prime Minister, November 30, 1978, FCO IH/1003, UK National Archives.
34. Transcript, "Record of a Discussion Between the Secretary of State and the United States Secretary of Defense at the Palais D'Egmont, Brussels, on 18th October 1978 at 2pm," 2/2580, DEFE11/977, UK National Archives.
35. Cable, TELNO to Bonn, "Defense Sale to China," November 17, 1978, FCO 14/1003, UK National Archives.
36. Cable, TELNO to Bonn, "Defense Sale to China."
37. For the Foreign Office comment on the agreement and the French decision not to attend the meeting, see Letter, "Defense Sales to China," Foreign and Commonwealth Office, G. H. Walden to 10 Downing Street, November 23, 1978, FCO 14/1003, UK National Archives.
38. For the history of US fighter aircraft development, see Mark A. Lorell and Hugh Levaux, *The Cutting Edge: A Half Century of U.S. Fighter Aircraft R&D* (RAND, 1998).
39. Letter, Roy A. Granthan to James Callaghan, August 21, 1978, FCO21/1629, UK National Archives.
40. Letter, Michael Foot to Prime Minister, August 4, 1978, FCO21/1629, UK National Archives.
41. Memorandum, "UK/Chinese Trade and Harrier," Foreign Office, January 10, 1979, FCO21/1630, UK National Archives.
42. Telegram, Washington to Foreign and Commonwealth Office, December 4, 1978, FCO21/1630, UK National Archives. Another attached document, dated in 1972, stated that the Harrier was, in fact, already ten years old.
43. Memorandum, "Trade with China," Department of Trade to Prime Minister, December 20, 1978, FCO21/1630, UK National Archives.
44. Telegram, FCO to Peiking, "Your TELNO 500 of 11 August: Harrier," Foreign and Commonwealth Office, August 24, 1978, PREM16/1546, UK National Archives.
45. Letter, Andrew Duguid to Prime Minister, "UK/Chinese Trade in Harriers," December 2, 1978, FCO 21/1630, UK National Archives.
46. Letter, Ewan Fergusson to Private Secretary, December 28, 1979, FCO 21/1630, UK National Archives.
47. Telegram, "Visit by Mr. Li Ch'iang: Harriers," Far Eastern Department to Foreign and Commonwealth Office, December 22, 1978, FCO 21/1630,UK National Archives.

262 3. WESTERN EUROPEAN MILITARY AND DUAL-USE TECHNOLOGY

48. Li Xiannian 李先念, *Li Xiannian wenxuan* 李先念文选 [Li Xiannian papers] (Zhonggong Zhongyang Dangshi He Wenxian Yanjiu Yuan, 1989), 238.
49. Li Xiannian, *Li Xiannian wenxuan*, 257.
50. Li Xiannian, *Li Xiannian wenxuan*, 325.
51. Li Xiannian, *Li Xiannian wenxuan*, 315.
52. Telegram, R. C. Samuel to Lord Goronwy-Roberts, date redacted but from the content it should be from June 1978, FCO21/1629, UK National Archives.
53. Memorandum, "Sale of Sea Harrier to India," Foreign and Commonwealth Office, April 25, 1979, FCO21/1722, UK National Archives.
54. Memorandum, "Arms Sales to China: Harrier and BL 755," Defense Department, August 9, 1979, FCO21/1723, UK National Archives.
55. For the Chinese response, see Memorandum, "BL 755 for China," Ministry of Defense, July 11, 1979, FCO21/1722, UK National Archives.
56. Transcript of David Owen Interview, Foreign and Commonwealth Office, March 8, 1979, FCO21/1722, UK National Archives.
57. Memorandum, "Labour Party International Committee," February 13, 1979, FCO21/1722, UK National Archives.
58. David Crane, "The Harrier Jump-Jet and Sino-British Relations," *Asian Affairs: An American Review* 8, no. 4 (1981).
59. Xiao Donglian 蕭冬連, 歷史的轉軌: 從撥亂反正到改革開放, 1979–1981 [The transition of history: From bringing order out of chaos to reform and opening up, 1979–1981] (香港中文大學當代中國文化研究中心, 2009), 722.
60. Xiao Donglian, The transition of history, 723.
61. 李先念年谱 VI [Li Xiannian Yearbook VI] (中央文献出版社, 2011), 24.
62. Li Xiannian, *Li Xiannian wenxuan*, 333.
63. Li Xiannian, *Li Xiannian wenxuan*, 333.
64. Li Xiannian Yearbook VI, Entry: June 24, 1979.
65. Li Xiannian Yearbook VI, Entry: June 26, 1979.
66. "China's CITIC Group Corp Executive Probed for Suspected Corruption," Caixin Global, June 10, 2024, https://www.caixinglobal.com/2024-06-10/chinas-citic-group-corp-executive-probed-for-suspected-corruption-102204792.html.
67. Memorandum, "Defense Sales to China: Harrier," Foreign and Commonwealth Office, July 12, 1979, FCO21/1722, UK National Archives.
68. Memorandum, "BL 755 for China, Ministry of Defense," July 11, 1979, FCO21/1722, UK National Archives.
69. Morning Summary, "Chinese Arms Policy Evolving on Chinese Lines," Department of State, July 30, 1979, NLC-21-15-10-14-6, Carter Library CREST.
70. Memorandum, "DOD Briefing on Sales of Military Technology to China," From SECSTATE WASDC to Embassy Beijing, January 20, 1980, NLC 21-15-11-28-0, Carter Library CREST.
71. US Embassy Bonn, "Controls on Exports to China," March 13, 1980, File 141445, Folder 421–410.55CHN, Behandlung der VR China im COCOM, Politisches Archiv des Auswärtigen Amts. For a contemporary report, see Philip Geyelin, "Arms Sales: The 'China

Differential,'" *Washington Post*, May 23, 1980. Also see Jing-dong Yuan, "The Politics of the Strategic Triangle: The U.S., COCOM, and Export Controls on China, 1979–1989," *Journal of Northeast Asian Studies* 14, no. 1 (1995).
72. Memorandum, "China: Military Modernization Efforts," 28 November 1979, NLC-21-15-11-9-1, Carter Library CREST.
73. Telegram, Paris to Bonn, "Behandlung der VR China im COCOM," October 30, 1980, File 141445, Folder 421–410. 55, Behandlung der VR China in COCOM, Politisches Archiv des Auswärtigen Amts.
74. Telegram, Paris to Bonn, "Behandlung der VR China," December 4, 1980, File 141445, Folder 421–410. 55, Behandlung der VR China im COCOM, Politisches Archiv des Auswärtigen Amts.
75. Flora Lewis, "Hua Guofeng in West Europe Stressed a New Pragmatism," *New York Times*, November 11, 1979.
76. Angela Romano, "Waiting for de Gaulle: France's Ten-Year Warm-Up to Recognizing the People's Republic of China," *Modern Asian Studies* 51, no. 1 (2016).
77. Cable, Paris to SECSTATE DC, October 14, 1979, NLC-21-15-11-24-4, Carter Library CREST. Warren Zimmermann later served as the US ambassador to Yugoslavia.
78. Cheol-sung Lee, "International Migration, Deindustrialization and Union Decline in 16 Affluent OECD Countries, 1962–1997," *Social Forces* 84, no. 1 (2005).
79. Christopher Kollmeyer and Florian Pichler, "Is Deindustrialization Causing High Unemployment in Affluent Countries? Evidence from 16 OECD Countries, 1970–2003," *Social Forces* 91, no. 3 (2013).
80. Memorandum, "Communique au Cabinet du Ministre du Commerce Exterieur et au Cabinet du ministre de L'industrie," August 17, 1979, Folder 10-11-5, AD Paris.
81. Li Xiannian 李先念, 建国以来李先念文稿 [Li Xiannian post-1949 papers] (中央文献出版社, 2011), 148.
82. Memorandum, "Nuclear Safeguards—Pakistan, South Africa, China," Vance to Brzezinski, July 14, 1977, National Security Archive, https://nsarchive2.gwu.edu/NSAEBB/NSAEBB114/chipak-4.pdf.
83. This message was passed through multiple channels, including the French embassy in Washington, D.C. Cable, AmbaFrance Washington to Diplomatie Paris, "Exportations de Centrales Nucléaires vers La Chine," July 4, 1978, Folder 10.11.5, Les centres des archives diplomatiques, La Courneuve.
84. Memorandum, "Mission en Chine (9 au 24 Novembre 1975)."
85. Memorandum, "Mission en Chine (9 au 24 Novembre 1975), Secrétariat a l'Énergie Atomique," December 11, 1975, Folder 10-11-9, Les centres des archives diplomatiques, La Courneuve.
86. Memorandum, "Pour M. Le Secrétaire Général, service des affaires scientifiques," December 16, 1975, Les centres des archives diplomatiques, La Courneuve.
87. Cable, Ambassadeur de France a Pekin to Paris, "Mission de géologues français de l'Uranium en Chine," November 18, 1976, Asie-Oceanie, Folder 10-11-5, Les centres des archives diplomatiques, La Courneuve.

88. Memorandum, "Audience de L'Ambassadeur de Chine: Coopération nucléaire franco-Chinoise," October 9, 1978, Asie-Oceanie, Folder 10-11-5, Les centres des archives diplomatiques, La Courneuve.
89. Note, December 18, 1978, Folder French-China, RG 59, UD-07D 106, Gerard Smith Files, National Archives.
90. Memorandum, "KKW-Export nach China." Der Bundesminister für Bildung und Wissenschaft, B196/56091, Bundesarchiv Koblenz.
91. Letter, VLR Rudolph to Bundesminister, September 19, 1978, File 141445, Folder 421–410, 55, Behandlung der VR China im COCOM, Politisches Archiv des Auswärtigen Amts.
92. Record of Discussion, "Uniformity of Application of the Controls Governing Exports of Strategic Commodities to Proscribed Destinations," May 31, 1977, File 141445, Folder COCOM, Ausfuhr von 3EDV-Systemen SIMENS 7,760-k Nach Der VR China, 1977, 1978/79, Politisches Archiv des Auswärtigen Amts.
93. Document 188, in *Akten Zur Auswärtigen Politik Der Bundesrepublik Deutschland*, vol. 1978 (De Gruyter Oldenbourg, 2009), 947.
94. Memorandum, "Britische Lieferung von Rüstungsgütern nach der VR China under Umgehung von COCOM," May 4, 1979, File 141445, Folder 421–410, COCOM: British Rüstungsgütern nach China, Politisches Archiv des Auswärtigen Amts.
95. Document 241, in *Akten Zur Auswärtigen Politik Der Bundesrepublik Deutschland*, vol. 1978 (De Gruyter Oldenbourg, 2009), 1227–28.
96. Memorandum, "Behandlung der VR China im COCOM," October 3, 1978, File 141445, Folder 421–410, Behandlung der VR China im COCOM, Politisches Archiv des Auswärtigen Amts.
97. Letter, Dr. Sutholt and Dr. Frewer to Herrn Staatssekretaer, August 16, 1978, Record B196/56091, Bundesarchiv Koblenz.
98. Memorandum, "Bezug von Kernkraftwerken durch die Volksrepublik China," Der Hessische Minister für Wirtschaft und Technique, July 25, 1978, Bundesarchiv Koblenz.
99. Memorandum, "Gespräch von Herrn M mit dem KWU-Vorstand am 18.9.1977," September 30, 1977, Bundesarchiv Koblenz.
100. Telegram, SECSTATE to WAHDC to AMEMBASSY Paris, "French Nuclear Reactor Sale to the Peoples Republic of China," December 6, 1978, RG 59, UD-07D 106, Gerard Smith Files, National Archives.
101. Telegram, SECSTATE to WAHDC to AMEMBASSY Paris, "French Nuclear Reactor Sale to the Peoples Republic of China."
102. Note, "Non-Proliferation Discussion with Congress," RG 59, UD-07D 106, Gerard Smith Files, National Archives.
103. Telegram, SECSTATE WASHDC to AMEMBASSY Paris, Peking, "Discussions with French on Framatome Sale to the PRC," December 25, 1978, RG 59, UD-07D 106, Gerard Smith Files, National Archives.
104. Telegram, Peiking to Paris, "Centrales Nucléaires," August 17, 1979, Asie-Oceanie, Folder 10-11-5, Les centres des archives diplomatiques, La Courneuve.
105. Li Xiannian, Li Xiannian post-1949 papers, 184.

106. Vermerk, "Unterrichtung des Bundeskabinetts uber unsere Haltung zum Amerikanischen Vorschlag auf Sonderbehandlung der VR China im COCOM," September 5, 1980, File 141445, Folder 421–410., Behandlung der VR China im COCOM, Politisches Archiv des Auswärtigen Amts.
107. Telegram, Peiking to Paris, "Projet de Centrale Électrique Nucléaire de Canton," June 5, 1980, Asie-Oceanie, Folder 10-11-5, Les centres des archives diplomatiques, La Courneuve.
108. S. Charbonneau, "Framatome Contribution to Chinese NPP Development and Standardization, Conference Record," International Nuclear Information System, 1996, https://inis.iaea.org/collection/NCLCollectionStore/_Public/29/035/29035049.pdf?r=1&r=1.
109. "China Launches French-Designed Next-Gen Nuclear Reactor," Nikkei Asia, December 14, 2018, https://asia.nikkei.com/Economy/China-launches-French-designed-next-gen-nuclear-reactor.
110. Memorandum, "Über aktuelle Problem in den Beziehungen UdSSR-GB," London to Berlin, July 6, 1978, File: M37 7564–90, Folder: Informationen über die sowjetische Außenpolitik 1980–1990, Politisches Archiv des Auswärtigen Amts.
111. Memorandum, "Политическая ситуации в Азии и проблемы коллективной безопасности" [The political situation in Asia and the problems of collective security], Sladkovskiĭ to International Department of the Communist Party of the Soviet Union, February 7, 1978, Fond 1970, Opis 2, Delo 10, Arkhiv Rossiiskoi Akademii nauk (hereafter cited as ARAN).
112. "Материалы к вступительному слову при открытии конференции—по проблемам маоизма" [Materials for the opening speech for the October conference—on the problems of Maoism], March 21, 1978, Fond 1970, Opis 2, Delo 10, ARAN.
113. "Внутренняя политика Китая и американо-китайские отношения" [Internal politics of China and US-China relations], July 7, 1978, Fond 2021, Opis 1, Delo 88, ARAN.
114. Attachment, "Defense Sale to China," November 20, 1978, DEFE11/977, UK National Archives.
115. Nickles, *China*, 965.
116. Transcript. "Chinese Foreign Minister Call on the Prime Minister: 11 October 1978," Foreign and Commonwealth Office, October 12, 1978, DEFE11/977, UK National Archives.
117. Telegram, Peking to Paris, "Entretien Avec M. Woodcock—Exportation de Centrales Nucleaires vers la Chine," July 26, 1978, Asie-Oceanie, Folder 10-11-5, Les centres des archives diplomatiques, La Courneuve.
118. Telegram, Paris to Peiking, "Ventes de Centrales Nucléaires A la Chine," October 23, 1978. Asie-Oceanie, Folder 10-11-5, Les centres des archives diplomatiques, La Courneuve.
119. Cable, Paris to Bonn, "Frankreich-VR China," October 26, 1978, Record B196/56091, Bundesarchiv Koblenz.
120. Cable, "USLO Peking to SECSTATE WASHDC," June 8, 1977, NLC-21-15-10-17, Carter Library CREST.
121. Melissa Jane Taylor, ed., *Soviet Union*, vol. 6 of *Foreign Relations of the United States, 1977–1980* (GPO, 2013), 469.
122. Taylor, *Soviet Union*, 503.

266   3. WESTERN EUROPEAN MILITARY AND DUAL-USE TECHNOLOGY

123. NSA Staff Material—Far East, Box 70, Folder: Brown Trip 1/80, Sullivan Files, JCPL.
124. NSA Staff Material—Far East, Box 70, Folder: Gen Biao Visit, June 10, 1980, Sullivan Files, JCPL.
125. Henry J. Kenny, *World Military Expenditures and Arms Transfers, 1986* (US Arms Control and Disarmament Agency, 1986).
126. Zuoyue Wang, "The Cold War and the Reshaping of Transnational Science in China," in *Science and Technology in the Global Cold War*, ed. Naomi Oreskes and John Krige (MIT Press, 2016); Susan Lawrence, " New Cracks in the Alliance: The US Is Desperate to Convince the EU That It Should Keep an Arms Embargo Imposed on China After Tiananmen Square 15 Years Ago; Europe Says That Times—and China—Have Changed," *Far Eastern Economic Review* 167, no. 32 (2004).

4. CHIANG CHING-KUO AND TAIWAN'S SEARCH FOR SECURITY

1. For the first Taiwan Strait Crisis, see Bruce A. Elleman, "The First Taiwan Strait Crisis, 1954–55," in *Taiwan Straits Standoff: 70 Years of PRC-Taiwan Cross-Strait Tensions* (Anthem, 2022), 43–46; and Ruping Xiao and Hsiao-ting Lin, "Inside the Asian Cold War Intrigues: Revisiting the Taiwan Strait Crises," *Modern Asian Studies* 52, no. 6 (2018).
2. Articles V and VI, Mutual Defense Treaty Between the United States and the Republic of China; December 2, 1954, https://avalon.law.yale.edu/20th_century/chin001.asp.
3. Lin Hsiao-ting 林孝庭, 台海 冷戰 蔣介石: 解密檔案中消失的台灣史 1948–1988 [Taiwan Strait, Cold War, Chiang Kai-shek: Taiwan's lost history in declassified archival materials 1948–1988] (Jinglian Chuban, 2015), 137. On the PRC's perspective and particularly Mao's thinking during both the First and the Second Taiwan Strait Crises, see Michael M. Sheng, "Mao and China's Relations with the Superpowers in the 1950s," *Modern China* 34, no. 4 (2008).
4. Lin Hsiao-ting, Taiwan Strait, Cold War, 140.
5. M. H. Halperin, *The 1958 Taiwan Strait Crisis* (RAND, 1966), 531. On the PRC's perspective, see Jian Chen, "Beijing and the Taiwan Strait Crisis of 1958," in *Mao's China and the Cold War* (University of North Carolina Press, 2012).
6. Chen Yishen 陳儀深, 戰後台灣對外關係史論集 [Postwar Taiwanese foreign relations essay collection] (國立政治大學, 2022), 55–57.
7. Lin Hsiao-ting, Taiwan Strait, Cold War, 142. For the KMT's overall intervention in South Asia, see Robert H. Taylor, *Foreign and Domestic Consequences of the KMT Intervention in Burma* (Department of Asian Studies, Cornell University, 1973).
8. Lin Hsiao-ting, Taiwan Strait, Cold War, 143.
9. Zhang Guocheng 張國城, "反攻大陸之可行性：從「國光計畫」探析1960年代國軍戰力" [The feasibility of counterattacking the mainland: An analysis of the National Army's combat power in the 1960s from the Guo-Guang plan], 國史館館刊 [Bulletin of Academia Historica], no. 76 (2023): 165, 167–201.
10. "Estimate of Communist China's Future Advanced Weapons Capabilities," August 27, 1963, CIA, CIA CREST, https://www.cia.gov/readingroom/document/cia-rdp66b00403r000 200060004-8.

4. CHIANG CHING-KUO AND TAIWAN'S SEARCH FOR SECURITY   267

11. Chiang Ching-kuo, Speech, "蔣經國對武漢部隊大隊長以上幹部講堅定信心迎接戰鬥演講稿," [Chiang Ching-kuo's Speech to the Officers Above Battalion Commander Level in the Wuhan Army, Encouraging Firm Confidence in Facing the Battle], 蔣經國先生全集 VI [Jiang Ching-kuo collections VI] (行政院新聞局, 1991), 675–84.
12. Jay Taylor, *The Generalissimo's Son: Chiang Ching-kuo and the Revolutions in China and Taiwan* (Harvard University Press, 2000), 518–19.
13. Telegram, American Embassy Taipei to Department of State, October 24, 1964, National Security Archive, https://nsarchive2.gwu.edu/NSAEBB/NSAEBB38/document20.pdf.
14. Koshiro Koko Gojiro Kotani 小谷豪治郎, and Chen Pengren 陳鵬仁, 經國先生傳 [Biography of Chiang Ching-kuo] (中央日報出版社, 1990), 255.
15. Airgram, American Embassy Tel Aviv to Department of State, March 22, 1966, National Security Archive, https://nsarchive2.gwu.edu/NSAEBB/NSAEBB20/docs/doc20.pdf.
16. Telegram, American Embassy Bonn to Department of State, March 25, 1966, National Security Archive, https://nsarchive2.gwu.edu/NSAEBB/NSAEBB20/docs/doc27.pdf.
17. Airgram, American Embassy Taipei to Department of State, April 8, 1966, National Security Archive, https://nsarchive2.gwu.edu/NSAEBB/NSAEBB20/docs/doc22.pdf.
18. Airgram, American Embassy Taipei to Department of State, April 8, 1966, National Security Archive, https://nsarchive2.gwu.edu/NSAEBB/NSAEBB20/docs/doc18.pdf.
19. David Albright and Corey Gay, "Taiwan: Nuclear Nightmare Averted," *Bulletin of the Atomic Scientists* 54, no. 1 (1998).
20. James Cameron and Or Rabinowitz, "Eight Lost Years? Nixon, Ford, Kissinger and the Non-Proliferation Regime, 1969–1977," *Journal of Strategic Studies* 40, no. 6 (2016).
21. Don Oberdorfer, "Taiwan to Curb A-Role, Agrees to Halt Nuclear Fuel Reprocessing," *Washington Post*, September 23, 1976. Also see Memorandum, "Visit of US Ambassador to Taiwan," October 22, 1976, CIA CREST, https://www.cia.gov/library/readingroom/docs/CIARDP83B00100R001001300129.pdf.
22. Testimony, "Honorable Gerard Smith, President's Special Representative for Non-Proliferation Matters Before the Subcommittee on Energy Research and Production," House Committee on Science and Technology, June 4, 1980, Box 33, Folder: 6/4/80, Gerard Smith Papers, Dwight D. Eisenhower Presidential Library, Abilene, KS.
23. Memorandum, "For Tel Sent Action SECSTATE DTD," Secretary of State to Brzezinski, March 11, 1977, National Security Archive, https://nsarchive2.gwu.edu/nukevault/ebb221/T-11a.pdf.
24. Cable, AMEMBASSY TOKYO to SECSTATE WASHDC, "ROC/IAEA Safeguards," March 21, 1977, National Security Archive, https://nsarchive2.gwu.edu/nukevault/ebb221/T-12.pdf.
25. Telegram, SECSTATE WASHDC to AMEMBASSY TAIPEI, "Nuclear Representation to the ROC," March 26, 1977, National Security Archive, https://nsarchive2.gwu.edu/nukevault/ebb221/T-13a.pdf.
26. David Albright and Andrea Stricker, *Taiwan's Former Nuclear Weapons Program* (Institute for Science and International Security, 2018), 84.
27. March 31, 1977, *Chiang Ching-kuo Diary*.
28. April 1, 1977, *Chiang Ching-kuo Diary*.

29. Memorandum, "Weekly National Security Report #11," Brzezinski to President Carter, April 29, 1977, National Security Archive, https://nsarchive2.gwu.edu/nukevault/ebb221/T-14.pdf.
30. 中華民國駐美大使沈劍虹電 [ROC Ambassador to US James C. H. Shen incoming telegram], File: 006-010804-00013-002, President Yen Chia-kan Files (1975/04至1978/05), Academia Historica, Taipei (hereafter cited as AH Taipei).
31. For the CIA's involvement in stopping Taiwan's nuclear weapons program, see Albright and Stricker, *Taiwan's Former Nuclear Weapons Program*, 120–25.
32. Tang Fei, Wang Changhe, and Ge Huimin, "捍衛臺海的F-104—用生命築長城 [F-104s defending the Taiwan Strait— building a Great Wall with their lives]," 空軍學術雙月刊 [Air Force Bimonthly Journal], no. 680 (February 2021): 127–40.
33. George C. Wilson, "Nationalist China to Be Offered New F5 Fighter," *Washington Post*, September 6, 1978.
34. "Conventional Arms Transfer Policy," PD 13, May 13, 1977, U.S. Department of State. https://history.state.gov/historicaldocuments/frus1977-80v26/d271.
35. Memorandum, From Mike Armacost, Mike Oksenberg, Les Dened, to Zbigniew Brzezinski, "Meeting on Korea and Taiwan," April 18, 1978, Box 7, Folder: 4/11–18/78, NSA 25 Staff Material, Armacost File, JCPL.
36. "Alfred Frauenknecht; Convicted of Selling Jet Secrets to Israel," *Los Angeles Times*, January 19, 1991, https://www.latimes.com/archives/la-xpm-1991-01-19-mn-255-story.html.
37. Harrison Kass, "IAI Kfir: Israel's Classic Fighter Jet No Nation Wanted to Ever Fight," *The National Interest*, August 7, 2024.
38. "F-21 Kfir Fighter Jet," *Airforce Technology*, July 13, 2020, https://www.airforce-technology.com/projects/f-21-kfir-jet/.
39. The exact date of the letter and its contents were classified, but the reply letter from an Israeli general suggested it was between 1951 and 1957. The letter was also categorized as "Military and Nuclear Energy." "蒋金国总统文物, '军事访问以色列空军报告等'" [Chiang Ching-kuo presidential files, "Military—Visit to Israeli Air Force and others"], Record 005000000841A, AH Taipei.
40. Guo Peiqing 郭培清, 台灣與以色列軍事貿易關係探析 [Study of Taiwan-Israel military trade relations] (Ershiyi Shijie, 2007), 58.
41. Airgram, American Embassy Tel Aviv to Department of State, "More on Nationalist Chinese Atomic Experts' Visit to Israel," March 24, 1966, National Security Archive, https://nsarchive2.gwu.edu/NSAEBB/NSAEBB20/docs/doc21.pdf.
42. May 21, 1977, *Chiang Ching-kuo Diary*.
43. May 29 and May 30, 1977, *Chiang Ching-kuo Diary*.
44. Thomas A. Marks, *Counterrevolution in China: Wang Sheng and the Kuomintang* (Taylor and Francis, 2016), 243.
45. Hsiao-ting Lin 林孝庭. 蔣經國的台灣時代, 中華民國與冷戰下的台灣 [The Chiang Ching-kuo era: The Republic of China on Taiwan in the Cold War] (Yuan zu wen hua, 2021), 73–74.
46. Gideon Gil, "Taiwanese Program Terminated at MIT," *Harvard Crimson*, July 16, 1976.
47. November 21, 1978, *Chiang Ching-kuo Diary*.

4. CHIANG CHING-KUO AND TAIWAN'S SEARCH FOR SECURITY 269

48. Dinshaw Mistry, *Containing Missile Proliferation Strategic Technology, Security Regimes, and International Cooperation in Arms Control* (University of Washington Press, 2003), 97.
49. Dennis M. Gormley, "Missile Contagion," *Survival* 50, no. 4 (2008).
50. A. W. Schwimmer 史溫摩, 往來函件, 蔣經國總統文物, [A. W. Schwimmer communication files], Record 005000001712A, President Chiang Ching-kuo Files, AH Taipei.
51. "The Impact of Cancelling the Lavi on Israel's Aircraft Industry," Directorate of Intelligence, October 13, 1987, CIA CREST, https://www.cia.gov/readingroom/docs/CIA-RDP90T00114R000700610001-4.pdf.
52. "英文中國郵報關於以色列超音速幻想式戰鬥轟炸機已於日前試飛成功擬於一九七二年開始量產等報導" [English language *China Post* on the testing and production of Israeli hypersonic fighter-bomber and others], Record 005-010502-00693-002, President Chiang Ching-kuo Files, AH Taipei.
53. 軍事—國防軍務散件資料 [Military and defense miscellaneous files], June 14, 1978, Record 005-010202-00168-001, Chiang Ching-kuo President Files, AH Taipei.
54. 軍事—國防軍務散件資料 [Military and defense miscellaneous files], June 14, 1978.
55. "Minutes of a Policy Review Committee Meeting," February 4, 1977, quoted in David P. Nickles, ed., *China*, vol. 13 of *Foreign Relations of the United States, 1977–1980* (GPO, 2013), 9.
56. Nickles, *China*, 48.
57. Cable, SECSTATE WASHDC to USDEL SECRETARY, "US-Israeli Consultative Group Meeting," August 2, 1977, National Archives, https://aad.archives.gov/aad/createpdf?rid=200409&dt=2532&dl=1629.
58. Cable, SECSTATE WASHDC to AMEMBASSY TEL AVIV, "Israeli Request for Permission to Sell KFIR to Taiwan," February 25, 1978, National Archives, https://aad.archives.gov/aad/createpdf?rid=48032&dt=2694&dl=2009.
59. Cable, SECSTATE WASHDC to AMEMBASSY TEL AVIV, "Weizman Visit: Hardware and Peace Strategy," March 14, 1978, National Archives, https://aad.archives.gov/aad/createpdf?rid=76238&dt=2694&dl=2009.
60. Nickles, *China*, 347.
61. "Taiwan Rejects Israeli Plane Offer," *New York Times*, July 7, 1978.
62. Cable, AMEMBASSY TEL AVIV to SECSTATE WASHDC, "Israel Aircraft Industries (IAI)," August 2, 1978, National Archives, https://aad.archives.gov/aad/createpdf?rid=216409&dt=2694&dl=2009.
63. Nickles, *China*, 578.
64. Cable, SECSTATE WASHDC to AMEMBASSY TAIPEI, "Demarche to President Chiang re ROC Arms Requests," November 2, 1978, National Archives, https://aad.archives.gov/aad/createpdf?rid=299546&dt=2694&dl=2009.
65. Cable, STATE to CINCPAC, "Demarche to President Chiang re ROC Arms Request," November 7, 1978, National Archives, https://aad.archives.gov/aad/createpdf?rid=276745&dt=2694&dl=2009.
66. Associated Press, "Israel Gets US Consent to Offer Jet Fighters to Taiwan," *Los Angeles Times*, April 17, 1992.

270   4. CHIANG CHING-KUO AND TAIWAN'S SEARCH FOR SECURITY

67. James Mann, "U.S. Says Israel Gave Combat Jet Plans to China," *Los Angeles Times*, December 28, 1994, https://www.latimes.com/archives/la-xpm-1994-12-28-mn-13774-story.html.
68. John Gee, "Has Israel's U.S.-Funded Lavi Jet Been Reborn as China's J-10 Warplane?," *Washington Report on Middle East Affairs* 26, no. 3 (2007).
69. "Hail to the Thief," *The Economist*, November 12, 2016, https://www.economist.com/asia/2016/11/12/hail-to-the-thief.
70. Stephen J. Morris, "The Soviet Union and the Philippine Communist Movement," *Communist and Post-Communist Studies* 27, no. 1 (1994). Also see "The Communist Party of the Philippines, Organizing for Revolution," December 30, 1981, CIA CREST, https://www.cia.gov/readingroom/docs/CIA-RDP83B00227R000100020004-3.pdf
71. "Marcos' Decline Is U.S. Dilemma," November 3, 1985, CIA CREST, https://www.cia.gov/library/readingroom/document/cia-rdp90-00965r000504130046-2.
72. "Philippines Visit Report," December 18, 1979, Box 13, Folder: Director's Visit to Philippines Special Files, Wang Shen Papers, Hoover Institute, Stanford University (hereafter cited as Wang Shen Papers).
73. Hand-Drafted Report, "The Current Crisis in the Philippines," December 17, 1979, Box 13, Folder: Director's Visit to Philippines Special Files, Wang Shen Papers.
74. "Visit Report," August 30, 1980, Folder: South Africa Visit Special Files, Wang Shen Papers.
75. Marks, *Counterrevolution in China*, 289.

5. FROM CLASSMATES TO ENEMIES: DENG XIAOPING AND CHIANG CHING-KUO

1. Chiang Ching-kuo, "孫逸仙大學" [Sun Yat-sen University], in 我在蘇聯的生活 [My days in the Soviet Union], Academia Historica, accessed September 17, 2025. On Deng's time at the university, see Alexander V. Pantsov and Steven I. Levine, *Deng Xiaoping: A Revolutionary Life* (Oxford University Press, 2015), 44–46.
2. Jie Yu 余杰, 偽裝的改革者：破解鄧小平和蔣經國神話 [Reformers in disguise: Deciphering the myths of Deng Xiaoping and Chiang Ching-kuo] (Ba qi wen hua chu ban, 2022), 43–45.
3. Chiang Ching-kuo, My days in the Soviet Union, appendix.
4. Jie Yu, Reformers in disguise, 58.
5. Jie Yu, Reformers in disguise, 59.
6. Jay Taylor, *The Generalissimo's Son: Chiang Ching-kuo and the Revolutions in China and Taiwan* (Harvard University Press, 2000), 163–73. For more details on the commissar system in the ROC's army, see Monte R. Bullard, *The Soldier and the Citizen: The Role of the Military in Taiwan's Development* (Sharpe, 1997), 44, 69.
7. Hsiao-ting Lin, *Taiwan, the United States, and the Hidden History of the Cold War in Asia: Divided Allies* (Routledge, 2022), 53.
8. "History and Politics of Taiwan," Class note, George Washington University, Fall 2015.
9. For the most up-to-date coverage of the assassination, see *Newstalk* (Taipei), December 11, 2018. Also see the revelation of Taiwan's former intelligence chief: Jianguo Wu

5. FROM CLASSMATES TO ENEMIES 271

吳建國, 破局: 揭祕！蔣經國晚年權力佈局改變的內幕 [Breakthrough: Revealed! The inside story of Chiang Ching-kuo's change in power structure in his later years] (Shibao wenhua, 2017).

10. Deng Xiaoping 邓小平, *Deng Xiaoping Wenxuan II* 邓小平文选 II [Deng Xiaoping Wenxuan OO] (Renmin Chubanshe, 1993), 154.
11. David P. Nickles, ed., *China*, vol. 13 of *Foreign Relations of the United States, 1977–1980* (GPO, 2013), 706–7.
12. Czeslaw Tubilewicz, "Taiwan and the Soviet Union During the Cold War: Enemies or Ambiguous Friends?," *Cold War History* 5, no. 1 (2005).
13. Lin, *Taiwan, the United States*, 187.
14. Lin, *Taiwan, the United States*, 194–95.
15. "Staff Note: China Affairs," August 4, 1975, CIA, CIA CREST, https://www.cia.gov/readingroom/document/cia-rdp86t00608r000300080018-3.
16. Lin, *Taiwan, the United States*, 53–54; for English language readers, a less detailed account of Taiwan-Soviet relations can be found on page 195.
17. Hsiao-ting Lin, *Taiwan, the United States*, 54.
18. Chiang Ching-kuo 蔣經國, 蔣經國先生全集 II [Chiang Ching-kuo collections, vol. 2] (行政院新聞局, 1991), 642.
19. September 1, 1977, *Chiang Ching-kuo Diary*.
20. January 8, 1978, *Chiang Ching-kuo Diary*.
21. Xu Keli 徐克礼, Jia Yaowu 贾耀斌, 国共两党关系90年图鉴 [CCP-KMT relations in ninety years] (Jiuzhou Chubanshe, 2011), 493.
22. "遵照蔣經國指示根據孫運璿所發表之對中共最近各種統戰活動的嚴正聲明重擬針對中共和平攻勢我們在海外的說法與做法綱要" [Under Chiang Ching-kuo's instructions, Sun Yunhuang publishes address and instructions on the CCP's united front efforts and peace offensive], Record: 005000001013A, Chiang Ching-kuo Files, AH Taipei.
23. February monthly entry, 1979, *Chiang Ching-kuo Diary*.
24. February 1, 1979, *Chiang Ching-kuo Diary*.
25. "民國六十八年蔣經國約見外賓談話紀錄" [Sixty-Eighth Republic year, Chiang Ching-kuo meeting with foreign dignitaries], Record: 005-010303-00001-011, Chiang Ching-kuo Files, AH Taipei.
26. "民国68年3月12日" [Madame Chiang letter on Republic Era 68, March 12], 蔣夫人來電 [Chiang Ching-kuo presidential files], Record: 005-010502-00004-089, Chiang Ching-kuo Files, AH Taipei.
27. Barry M. Goldwater, *The Conscience of a Conservative*, ed. CC Goldwater, reprint edition (Princeton University Press, 2007); William F. Buckley, *Flying High: Remembering Barry Goldwater* (Perseus, 2010).
28. Robert Alan Goldberg, *Barry Goldwater* (Yale University Press, 1995), 65.
29. Fendall W. Yerx, "Goldwater Says Generals Have a Nuclear Authority," *New York Times*, September 23, 1964.
30. Lloyd Grove, "Barry Goldwater's Left Turn," *Washington Post*, July 28, 1994, quoted in Goldberg, *Barry Goldwater*, 191.

31. Speech, "Red China and the U.N.," Box 185, Series: Legislative III, Folder: Legislative Foreign Relations, Red China, 1969, Goldwater Papers, Arizona State University, Tempe (hereafter cited as ASU).
32. Goldberg, *Barry Goldwater*, 296–97.
33. News Clip, *Taipei Central Press*, Box 421, Folder: Jan–July 1977, Goldwater Papers, ASU.
34. Letter, Barry Goldwater to Zbigniew Brzezinski, May 3, 1978, Box 220, Series: Legislative III, Folder: Goldwater vs. Carter Lawsuit, Goldwater Papers, ASU.
35. Letter, Zbigniew Brzezinski to Barry Goldwater, May 4, 1978, Box 220, Series: Legislative III, Folder: Goldwater vs. Carter Lawsuit, Goldwater Papers, ASU.
36. Letter, Reuben M. Burnham to Barry Goldwater, December 15, 1978, Box 220, Folder: Issue Mail Taiwan Treaty, Goldwater Papers, ASU.
37. Letter, James F. Byrne, to Barry Goldwater, December 17, 1978, Box 220, Folder: Issue Mail Taiwan Treaty, Goldwater Papers, ASU.
38. Letter, Gary and Joyce Hawkings to Barry Goldwater, December 16, 1978, Box 220, Folder: Issue Mail Taiwan Treaty, Goldwater Papers, ASU.
39. Letter, Students at Fu-Jen University, Taipei, to Barry Goldwater, undated, likely from early 1979 based on other letters in the same collection: 1979, Box 423, Folder: Constituent Service, 95th Congress, Goldwater Papers, ASU.
40. Card, J. Chen to Barry Goldwater, undated, Box 423, Folder: Constituent Service, 95th Congress, Goldwater Papers, ASU.
41. Card, W. He Lin to Barry Goldwater, December 26, 1978, Box 423, Folder: Constituent Service, 95th Congress, Goldwater Papers, ASU.
42. Goldwater v. Carter, 444 U.S. 996 (1979), https://supreme.justia.com/cases/federal/us/444/996/.
43. "美國前農業部長幕僚陳文柯函總統蔣金國為美國與中共建交國家面臨歷史緊要關頭之際為黨國效力，隨函附上美國國會政界領袖資料以供參考" [Former U.S. Department of Agriculture adviser Chen Wen-ke's letter to Chiang Ching-kuo, President, ready to serve the party-state at the critical moment of U.S.-Communist China normalization of diplomatic relations, with attached materials on U.S. congressional and political elites], 蔣經國總統文物 [Chiang Ching-kuo files], Record: 005-010502-00035-012, Academic Sinica, Taipei. Dr. Chen's name appeared again and again in Taiwanese sources associated with US intelligence reports, making one wonder which government he really worked for.
44. David F. Schmitz and Natalie Fousekis, "Frank Church, the Senate, and the Emergence of Dissent on the Vietnam War," *Pacific Historical Review* 63, no. 4 (1994).
45. "Alleged Assassination Plots Involving Foreign Leaders: An Interim Report of the Select Committee to Study Governmental Operations with Respect to Intelligence Activities," 1975, CIA CREST, https://www.cia.gov/library/readingroom/document/cia-rdp83-01042r000200090002-0.
46. Letter, Frank Church to Howard Luger, January 16, 1979, Box 9, Folder 3, Frank Church Papers, Boise State University.
47. "Salter-Sponsored Nut Calls," 1971, Box 21, Folder 3, Frank Church Papers, Boise State University.

48. Letter, Thomas C. Reina to Frank Church, February 1, 1979, Box 9, Folder 3, Frank Church Papers, Boise State University.
49. Letter, Helan Tsai to Frank Church, December 16, 1978, Box 24, Folder 7, Frank Church Papers, Boise State University.
50. Letter, M. I. Wheeler to Frank Church, February 2, 1979, Box 24, Folder 9, Frank Church Papers, Boise State University.
51. He Zhilin 何智霖 [ed.], 蔣经国与台湾: 相关人物访谈录 I [Chiang Ching-kuo and Taiwan: An oral history of related persons, vol. 1] (Academia Historica, 2010), 252.
52. Martin B. Gold, *A Legislative History of the Taiwan Relations Act* (Lexington Books, 2017), 237–42.
53. Richard C. Bush, *At Cross Purposes: U.S.-Taiwan Relations Since 1942* (East Gate Book, 2004), 182–85.
54. "Hearing Before the Committee on Foreign Relations," US Senate, Ninety-Sixth Congress, First Session, February 5, 1979, Box 220, Folder: Congress 1979, Barry Goldwater Papers, ASU, 80.
55. "Hearing Before the Committee on Foreign Relations," February 5, 1979, 89.
56. Gold, *A Legislative History of the Taiwan Relations Act*, 64.
57. "Hearing Before the Committee on Foreign Relations," February 5, 1979, 40. In the records, Brown either refused to answer questions or deflected them to Christopher, appearing to be completely disinterested in the testimony.
58. David Tawei Lee, *The Making of the Taiwan Relations Act: Twenty Years in Retrospect* (Oxford University Press, 2000).
59. Bush, *At Cross Purposes*, 155.
60. Cable, STATE to BEIJING, "Reply to Chinese Note of April 28," June 28, 1979, National Archives, https://aad.archives.gov/aad/createpdf?rid=169772&dt=2776&dl=2169.
61. *Time*, 15/1 (1979); Fred Halliday, "The Arc of Crisis and the New Cold War," *MERIP Reports*, no. 100/101 (1981).
62. Cable, BEIJING to STATE, "Deng Xiaoping Meeting with Codel/Church/Javits," April 21, 1979, National Archives, https://aad.archives.gov/aad/createpdf?rid=13829&dt=2776&dl=2169.
63. Nickles *China*, 941–44.
64. Memorandum, "Sino-US Relations: An Appraisal," Michel Oksenberg to Zbigniew Brzezinski, August 1, 1979, NSA Country File: China [PRC] 8–9/79, Box 9, JCPL.
65. 邓小平讲话实录: 会谈卷 [Deng Xiaoping conversation records: Meetings] (Hongqi Chubanshe, 2018), 161.
66. Gong Li 宫力, 邓小平与中美外交风云 [Deng Xiaoping and US-China Diplomatic Relations] (红旗出版社, 2015), 57–60.
67. "蔣經國接見美國華盛頓郵報總經理梅耶夫婦" [Chiang Ching-kuo meeting with Washington Post CEO Mr. and Mrs. Meyer], Chiang Ching-kuo Files, Record: 005-010303-00004-022, AH Taipei.
68. Xu Chengji 涂成吉, 克萊恩與台灣: 反共理想與理性之衝突和妥協 [Xu Chenji, Ke Laien, and Taiwan: The conflict and compromise between anti-communist inspiration and rationality] (Xiu wei zi xun ke ji gu fen you xian gong si, 2007), 309.

69. 蔣經國電宋美齡等 [Chiang Ching-kuo telegram to Song Meiling and others], Record: 005-010502-00007-046, Chiang Ching-kuo Files, AH Taipei.
70. "The August 17, 1982 U.S.-China Communiqué on Arms Sales to Taiwan," Office of the Historian, US Department of State, accessed May 21, 2024, https://history.state.gov/milestones/1981-1988/china-communique.
71. Daryl G. Kimball, ed., "US Conventional Arms Sales to Taiwan 1980–2010," Arms Control Association, updated October 2012, https://www.armscontrol.org/factsheets/taiwanarms.
72. "Declassified Cables: Taiwan Arms Sales & Six Assurances (1982)," July 10, 1982, American Institute in Taiwan, https://www.ait.org.tw/declassified-cables-taiwan-arms-sales-six-assurances-1982/.
73. Jie Yu, Reformers in disguise, 59, also see, James C. Hsiung, "Taiwan in 1984: Festivity, New Hope, and Caution," *Asian Survey* 25, no. 1 (1985). For an overview of the US Congress's relations with Taiwan, see Gang Lin et al., Wenxing Zhou, and Weixu Wu, "What Shapes Taiwan-Related Legislation in U.S. Congress?," *Journal of Contemporary China* 31, no. 136 (2021).
74. "Liao Zhongkai," History of Ministry of Finance, R.O.C. Online, accessed September 17, 2024, https://museum.mof.gov.tw/singlehtml/e5e41f7426964fee825cd37a87a6ca75?cntId=6688db3f31c6460e999eeb38d5d61f44.
75. Letter, Liao Cheng-chin to Chiang on reunification, July 24, 1982. Sub-Series A: Alpha Files, Box 4, Folder 10: Madame Chiang Kai-shek, 1967–1986, Goldwater Papers. ASU. Subsequent references in the next few pages are to this source.
76. Guo Moruo (1892–1978), Mao's favorite poet, was the longtime chairman of the China Federation of Literary and Art Circles. Encyclopedia Britannica, https://www.britannica.com/biography/Guo-Moruo.
77. "Madam Chiang Kai-shek's Reply to Open Letter from Liao Cheng-chin," August 18, 1982 (translated by Tao-Tai Hsia, Library of Congress), Sub-Series A: Alpha Files, Box 4, Folder 10: Madame Chiang Kai-shek, 1967–1986, Goldwater Papers. ASU.
78. Adjusted to current prices using IMF data, https://www.imf.org/external/datamapper/NGDPD@WEO/TWN?zoom=TWN&highlight=TWN.
79. J. Bruce Jacobs, "One China, Diplomatic Isolation and a Separate Taiwan," in *China's Rise, Taiwan's Dilemmas and International Peace*, ed. Edward Friedman (Routledge, 2006), 98.
80. Deng Xiaoping conversation records: Meetings, 53.
81. Shelley Rigger, *Taiwan's Rising Rationalism: Generations, Politics, and "Taiwanese Nationalism."* East-West Center, 2006.

6. THE GLOBAL RESPONSE TO CARTER'S CHINA POLICY: UNHEEDED WARNINGS FROM MOSCOW TO WASHINGTON

1. Vitaly Kozyrev, "Soviet Policy Toward the United States and China, 1969–1979," in *Normalization of U.S.-China Relations: An International History*, ed. William C. Kirby et al. (Harvard University Asia Center, 2007), 261–62.

6. THE GLOBAL RESPONSE TO CARTER'S CHINA POLICY 275

2. Olyegu B. Borisov and Boris T. Koloskov, *Советско-китайские отношения. 1945–1970* [Soviet-Chinese relations, 1945–1970] (Mysl', 1971), 527–28.
3. On the PRC's early break with the USSR, see Lorenz M. Lüthi, *The Sino-Soviet Split: Cold War in the Communist World* (Princeton University Press, 2008), 4–6; on Albania, see pages 169–74. On the proposed Soviet radio station, see Yang Kuisong 杨奎松 [et al.], 中苏关系史纲 [Survey of Sino-Soviet relations] (Shehui Kexue Chuban She, 2016), 228–31. On the PRC and the Warsaw Pact, see Lorenz M. Lüthi, "The People's Republic of China and the Warsaw Pact Organization, 1955–63," *Cold War History* 7, no. 4 (2007).
4. China and the Soviet Union were also divided by their approaches to decolonization. China preferred military struggles, and the Soviet Union preferred a more pragmatic and peaceful path within the framework of détente. Jeremy Friedman, *Shadow Cold War: The Sino-Soviet Competition for the Third World* (University of North Carolina Press, 2015), 66–70. On Liu Shaoqi and the pro-Soviet faction of the CCP, see Lüthi, *The Sino-Soviet Split*, 305–97. On the border conflicts, see Thomas W. Robinson, "The Sino-Soviet Border Conflicts of 1969: New Evidence Three Decades Later," in *Chinese Warfighting: The PLA Experience Since 1949*, ed. Mark A. Ryan et al. (Sharpe, 2003), 196–97.
5. Andrei A. Kokoshin, *Soviet Strategic Thoughts, 1917–91* (MIT Press, 1998), 127.
6. On Mao's various health conditions, see Zhisui Li, *The Private Life of Chairman Mao: The Memoirs of Mao's Personal Physician* (Chatto & Windus, 1994). 581, 583, 597.
7. May 21, 1976, *Anatoly S. Chernyaev Diary*, National Security Archive. https://nsarchive.gwu.edu/briefing-book/russia-programs/2016-05-25/anatoly-s-chernyaev-diary-1976.
8. Kuisong et al., Survey of Sino-Soviet relations, 518–20.
9. UN General Assembly, Thirty-Fifth Session, Eighth Plenary Meeting, September 28, 1976, United Nations Records. https://documents-dds-ny.un.org/doc/UNDOC/GEN/NL7/703/11/PDF/NL770311.pdf.
10. "Отчет: О Работе Общества Советско-Китайской Дружбы в 1977 Году" [Report: On the work of Soviet-Chinese Friendship Society in 1977], July 31, 1977, Fond 9570, Opis 20, Dela 1741, Gosudarstvennyy Arkhiv Rossiyskoy Federatsii (State Archive of the Russian Federation) (hereafter cited as GARF).
11. "Программа: Вечер Встречи Первых Советских военных Советников участвовавших в Оказании Помощи в создании базы Китайской револоузии на юге станы 1925–1927 ГГ" [Program: Evening of the meeting of the first Soviet military advisers who participated in assistance in the creation of the Chinese Revolution base in the south of the country 1925–1927], Fond 9570, Opis 20, Dela 1741, July 31, 1977, GARF.
12. "50-Летние Наньчангского Восстания и Создания Народной-Освобождения Армии Китай" [Fiftieth anniversary of the Nanchang Uprising and the establishment of the People's Liberation Army of China], July 27, 1977, Fond 9570, Opis 20, Dela 1741, GARF.
13. "К 75-Летнию Ван Мина" [On Wang Ming's seventy-fifth anniversary], Fond 9576-P, Opis 20, Dela 2509, GARF.
14. Gong Li 宫力, [ed.], 邓小平在重要历史关头 [Deng Xiaoping at key historical moments] (Jiu zhou chu ban she, 2012), 57–60. Only recently have Chinese academics started to evaluate Wang more realistically, especially his criticism of Mao's political

campaigns. Guo Dehong 郭德宏, 王明年谱 [Wang Ming yearbook] (Shehui Wenxian Chubanshe, 2014).

15. "Отчет: О Деятельности ОСКД в 1979 Году" [Report: On Association 1979 activities], x, Fond 9576-P, Opis 20, Dela 2509, GARF.

16. The only other study on the Soviet-Chinese Friendship Association also suggests its effort was fruitless in the 1970s. Alsu Tagirova, "Soviet Public Diplomacy in China: 'Small Steps' Towards Bilateral Rapprochement (1978–1985)," *Cold War History* 17, no. 4 (2017).

17. Hua Guofeng 华国锋, 十一大上的政治报告 [Report on the Eleventh People's Congress of the Communist Party of China], Gov.cn, August 12, 1977.

18. "Отчет" [Report], September 27, 1977, Fond 1970, Opis 2, Dela 10, Archive of the Russian Academy of Sciences, Moscow (hereafter cited as ARAN).

19. Suslov believed that the Soviet Union's path of development—its centralized planned economy, in particular—represented the most ideal and "scientific" path toward communism. His work was frequently cited as a theoretical base by Soviet scholars during the Sino-Soviet split. Serge Petroff, *The Red Eminence: A Biography of Mikhail A. Suslov* (Kingston Press, 1988); Paul Milton Carter Jr., "Suslov and Soviet Scientific Communism" (PhD diss., Indiana University, 1997). For Suslov's most cited works in late 1970s, see his two-volume collection of writings and speeches: Mikhail A. Suslov, *На Путях Строительства Коммунизма* [On the path to the construction of communism] (Politizdat, 1977).

20. "Новое Свидетельство Продолжения и Усугубления Кризиса Идеологии Маоизма в КНР" [New evidence of continuation and exacerbation of the crisis of the ideology of Maoism in China], August 30, 1978, Fond 1970, Opis 2, Dela 11, ARAH.

21. "Идеологические вопросы" [Ideological problems], October 3, 1979, Fond 1970, Opis 20, Delo 19, ARAH.

22. Gulnin V. Astaf'ev, "Великодержавный шовинизм и «левый» авантюризм во внешней политике группы Мао Цзэдуна" [Great power chauvinism and "left" adventurism in the foreign policy of the Mao Zedong group], in *Антимарксистская сущность взглядов и политики Мао Цзэдуна* [The anti-Marxist essence of the views and policies of Mao Zedong], [ed.] Mikhail I. Sladkovskiĭ (Akademiia nauk, 1965).

23. Sergey Radchenko, *To Run the World: The Kremlin's Cold War Bid for Global Power* (Cambridge University Press, 2024), 483.

24. Radchenko, *To Run the World*, 483.

25. "Родезийская проблема и политика Китая" [The Rhodesian problem and Chinese policy], March 18, 1980, Fond 1970, Opis 2, Delo 25, ARAN.

26. "К Вопросу о Создании в КНР 'Зон Свободных Городов'" [On the question of establishing in China "free city zones"], January 28, 1980, Fond 1970, Opis 2, Delo 25, ARAH.

27. "Об изучении Китая в капиталистических странах" [On the study of China in the capitalist countries], V. A. Krivzov to Secretariat of the Central Committee of the Communist Party of the Soviet Union, November 23, 1979, Fond 1970, Opis, 2, Delo 20, ARAN.

28. Record of Conversation Between Soviet Foreign Minister Gromyko and President Carter, September 23, 1977, Woodrow Wilson Center, https://digitalarchive.wilsoncenter.org/document/111256.

6. THE GLOBAL RESPONSE TO CARTER'S CHINA POLICY   277

29. David Paull Nickles, ed., *China*, vol. 13 of *Foreign Relations of the United States, 1977–1980* (GPO, 2013), 69.
30. Nickles, *China*, 96 and nn13–15.
31. Armacost Evening and Weekly Reports Files, January 3, 1978, Box 1, 1–2/78, JCPL.
32. Armacost Evening and Weekly Reports Files, January 4, 1978, Box 1, 1–2/78, JCPL.
33. Memo, Michel Oksenberg and Michael Armacost to Zbigniew Brzezinski, March 24, 1978, Box 6, Armacost Chron File, 3/22–31/78, JCPL.
34. Nickles, *China*, 440–41.
35. "Материалы к вступительному слову при открытии конференции по проблемам маоизма" [Conference opening material on the problems of Maoism], May 23, 1978, Fond 1970, Opis, 2, Delo 10, ARAN.
36. Speech by L. I. Brezhnev to CPSU CC Politburo, June 8, 1978, Woodrow Wilson Center, https://digitalarchive.wilsoncenter.org/document/111257.
37. "Стенограмма: внутренняя политика Китая и американо-китайские отношения" [Transcript: Domestic politics of China and US-China relations], Fond 2021, Opis 1, Delo 88, ARAN.
38. "Владимир Петрович Лукин [Vladimir Petrovich Lukin]," РСМД [Russian International Affairs Council], accessed September 18, 2024, https://russiancouncil.ru/vladimir-lukin/.
39. "Стенограмма: внутренняя политика Китая и американо-китайские отношения" [Transcript: Domestic politics of China and US-China relations]. For Lukin's professional relationship with Arbatov, see Georgiĭ Arbatov, "Владимир Петрович Лукин, политик с чистыми руками" [Vladimir Petrovich, politician with clean hands], in *К 80-летию В.П. Лукина* [On the eightieth anniversary of V. P. Lukin], ed. Andrey Dikarev and Alexander Lukin (Ves' Mir, 2018), 75.
40. "Transcript, Meeting of East German Leader Erich Honecker and Soviet Leader Leonid Brezhnev, Crimea (excerpt)," July 25, 1978, DY30 JIV 2/201/1495, Bundesrachiv Berlin, obtained and translated by Christian Ostermann, Woodrow Wilson Center, https://digitalarchive.wilsoncenter.org/document/117047.
41. Cable, Zbigniew Brzezinski to Cyrus Vance, October 14, 1978, Box 6, Folder: Backchannel Messages: Africa 4/77–11/78, NSA Office File, JCPL.
42. Taylor, Howard, *Soviet Union*, 495.
43. "Global Competition and the Deterioration of U.S.-Soviet Relations, 1977–1980," The Carter-Brezhnev Project, November 12, 2012, National Security Archive, 132. https://nsarchive2.gwu.edu/carterbrezhnev/docs_global_competition/part7.PDF.
44. Melissa Jane Taylor, ed., *Soviet Union*, vol. 6 of *Foreign Relations of the United States, 1977–1980* (GPO, 2013), 504–5.
45. Xiaoming Zhang, *Deng Xiaoping's Long War: The Military Conflict Between China and Vietnam 1979–1991* (University of North Carolina Press, 2018), 1–2; for the "counterattack" terminology, see page 60.
46. "К вопросу о вооруженной агрессии Китая против социалистической республики Вьетнам" [On the question of China's armed aggression against the Socialist Republic of Vietnam], February 21, 1979, Fond 1970, Opis 2, Delo 18, ARAN.

47. "Критический анализ буржуазных и ревизионистских точек зрения относительно китайской модели социализма, неприменимости в условиях Китая принципов марксистско-ленинистского научного социализма" [A critical analysis of the bourgeois and revisionist points of view regarding the Chinese model of socialism and the nonapplicability of the principle of Marxist-Leninist scientific socialism in China], September 10, 1979, Fond 1970, Opis 20, Delo 19, ARAN.

48. "К оценке современного Китая" [On China], Fond 1976, Opis 2, Delo 20, ARAN.

49. The Soviet Union was represented by Vice Minister Leonid Fedorovich Ilyichev and China by Vice Minister Wang Youping. Sergeĭ L. Tikhvinskiĭ, *Китай в моей жизни* [China in my life] (Akademīi͡a nauk, 1992), 192.

50. Fan Zhenshui 范振水, "王幼平同志回忆1979年中苏国家关系谈判" [Comrade Wang Youpin's recollection on 1979 Sino-Soviet negotiations]," in 新中国外交风云:中国外交官回忆录 IV [Diplomatic history of new China: Memoirs of a Chinese diplomat 4] (Waijiaobu Waijiaoshi Bianji Chubanshe 外交部外交史编辑室编出版社, 1996), 144–57.

51. Sun Qiming 孙其明, Zhong su guanxi shimo 中苏关系始末 [Sino-Soviet relations from the beginning till the end] (Shanghai Renmin Chubanshe, 2002), 644.

52. Taylor, *Soviet Union*, 571, 572.

53. "Transcript of Conversation Between Foreign Minister Gromyko and President Carter," September 23, 1977, National Security Archive, https://nsarchive2.gwu.edu/carterbrezhnev/salt_ii_ebb.html.

54. Taylor, *Soviet Union*, 608–12.

55. "Minutes of Conversation, Todor Zhivkov and Leonid Brezhnev," January 13, 1979, Woodrow Wilson Center, https://digitalarchive.wilsoncenter.org/document/113584.

56. Memorandum, "Meeting Between Dr. Gerald P. Dinnen, Principal Deputy Under Secretary of Defense for Research and Engineering, and Liu Huaqing, Assistant to Chief of General Staff," Box 69, Folder: 1/80, NSA Staff Files, Far East, JCPL.

57. George C. Wilson, "Brown Going to China; Afghanistan on Agenda," *Washington Post*, January 3, 1980.

58. "Memorandum of Conversation with Vice Premier Deng Xiaoping," 10 am, January 8,1980, Great Hall of the People, Box 69, Folder: Brown (Harold) Trip Memcons, 1/80, NSA Staff Files, Far East, JCPL.

59. Transcript, Department of Defense, January 16, 1980, NLC-21-15-11-28-0, Carter Library CREST.

60. Harry Harding, *A Fragile Relationship: The United States and China Since 1972* (Brookings Institution, 1992), 91–92.

61. James R. Lilley with Jeffrey Lilley, *China Hands: Nine Decades of Adventure, Espionage, and Diplomacy in Asia* (PublicAffairs, 2004), 214–15

62. Robert Michael Gates, *From the Shadows: The Ultimate Insider's Story of Five Presidents and How They Won the Cold War* (Pocket, 2008), 122–23.

63. Speech by Assistant Secretary David R. Stillwell, "US-China Bilateral Relations: The Lessons of History," December 23, 2019, US Embassy China, https://china.usembassy-china.org.cn/u-s-china-bilateral-relations-the-lessons-of-history/.

6. THE GLOBAL RESPONSE TO CARTER'S CHINA POLICY 279

64. Dennis Heves, "Mohammad Zia Ul-Haq: Unbending Commander for Era of Atom and Islam," *New York Times*, August 18, 1988.
65. Only a few books shed light on this strange episode; see, for example, Steve Coll, *Ghost Wars: The Secret History of the CIA, Afghanistan, and Bin Laden, from the Soviet Invasion to September 10, 2001* (Penguin, 2005).
66. "Name CIA Men in Afghanistan," February 22, 1980, General CIA Record, CIA CREST, RDP90-00845R000100120026-6. https://www.cia.gov/readingroom/document/cia-rdp90-00845r000100120026-6, Accessed September 21, 2025.
67. *Cold War, Soldiers of God*, episode 20, CNN, 1998.
68. Working Notes, May 1, May 2, May 4, July 26, 1979, Box 55, Folder: August–Sept 1979, Gerard Smith Papers, Dwight D. Eisenhower Presidential Library, Abilene, KS.
69. Working Notes, "Pakistan," April 21, 1980. Gerald R. Smith Papers, Folder: Notes April 1980, Box 55, Dwight D. Eisenhower Presidential Library, Abilene, KS.
70. Memorandum, DIA Defense Intelligence Notice, NLC-21-15-12-4-5, Carter Library CREST.
71. Memorandum for Brzezinski, from Marshall Brement, "Embassy Moscow's 'Policy Recommendations' Regarding the Soviet Invasion of Afghanistan, February 7, 1980, Folder: Meetings—Vance/Brown/Brzezinski, 1/80-2/80, Box 34, Brzezinski Collection, JCPL.
72. Memorandum, "Embassy Moscow's Analysis of US-Soviet Relations," from Brzezinski, to The Secretary of State/The Secretary of Defense, February 8, 1980, Box 20, Alpha Channel (1/80-3/80), Brzezinski Collection, JCPL.
73. Nickles, *China*, 1114.
74. "Новая фаза в блокировании Китая и США—к визиту министра обороны США в Пекин" [A new phase in the US-China bloc—on the visit of the U.S. defense secretary in Beijing], January 14, 1980, Fond 1970, Opis 2, Delo 25, ARAN.
75. "Китай после смерти Мао Цзэдуна" [China after Mao Zedong], Fond 1970, Opis 2, Delo 26, ARAN.
76. Vladimir P. Lukin, "Вашингтон–Пекин: квазисоюзники?" [Washington–Beijing: quasi-Alliance?], *США—экономика, политика, идеология* [USA: Economics, politics, ideology], no. 12 (1979).
77. Vladimir P. Lukin, "О Современном этапе американо-китайских отношений [On the current stage of US-China relations]," in Dikareva and Lukin, *К 80-летию В.П. Лукина*, 385–89.
78. Vladimir P. Lukin, "Китайская карта в предвыборном покере [Chinese card in the election poker]" in Dikareva, Lukin, *К 80-летию В.П. Лукина*, 391–98.
79. Qian Jiang 钱江, 邓小平与中美建交风云 (中共党史出版社, 2005); Gong Li 宫力, *Deng Xiaoping Yu Zhong Mei Waijiao Feng Yun* 邓小平与中美外交风云 (红旗出版社, 2015).
80. Ni Shixiong 倪世雄, "邓小平与中美关系" [Deng Xiaoping and US-China relations], 毛泽东邓小平理论研究, no. 5 (2009).
81. "中美关系的症结何在?" [Where is the main blockage of US-China relations?], 国际问题研究, no. 2 (1981).
82. Zheng Zhongbing 鄭仲兵 [et al.], [eds.], 胡耀邦年譜資料長編 [Hu Yaobang yearbook extended edition], vol. 1 (時代國際, 2005), entry for March 9, 1981, 539–40.

280 6. THE GLOBAL RESPONSE TO CARTER'S CHINA POLICY

83. Zheng Zhongbing, Hu Yaobang yearbook extended edition, entry for entry fo mid-March 1981, 540
84. Zhao Ziyang 赵紫阳, 赵紫阳文集: 1980–1989 [Zhao Ziyang papers: 1980–1989] (香港中文大学出版社 Hongkong Chinese University Press, 2016), 460.
85. Zhao Ziyang, Zhao Ziyang papers: 1980–1989, 558–59.
86. "Action Memorandum," from Reginald Bartholomew, to Mr. Nimetz," August 29, 1980, NLC-21-15-12-19-9, Department of States, Carter Library CREST.
87. Memorandum, "Munitions Cases for the People's Republic of China," from Reginald Bartholomew, to Mr. Nimetz, November 17, 1980, Department of States, NLC-21-15-12-22-6, Carter Library CREST.
88. Memorandum, "Munitions Cases for the People's Republic of China," from Reginald Bartholomew, Richard Holbrooke, to Mr. Nimetz, October 30, 1980, NLC-21-15-12-22-5, Carter Library CREST.
89. Cable, "Chinese Attitudes Toward U.S. Arms Sales," Beijing to SECSTATE WASNDC, April 11, 1980, NLC-21-15-12-13-5, Carter Library CREST.
90. DIA Defense Intelligence Notice, June 13, 1980, NLC-21-16-3-6-2, Carter Library CREST.
91. Memorandum, Warren Christopher to President Carter, May 16, 1980, NLC-2-16-3-12-5, Carter Library CREST.

CONCLUSION: MULTILATERAL COMPETITION BEYOND THE COLD WAR

1. "China Village Elections Project," Carter Center, October 2002, https://www.cartercenter.org/documents/nondatabase/chinavillagefactsheet.pdf.
2. "Village Democracy Shrugs in Rural China," East Asia Forum, July 22, 2014, https://eastasiaforum.org/2014/07/22/village-democracy-shrugs-in-rural-china/.
3. Jimmy Carter, "Report by Former U.S. President Jimmy Carter on Trip to Beijing, Qingdao, Xian, and Shanghai, China, Sept. 1–10, 2014," Carter Center, September 11, 2014, https://www.cartercenter.org/news/trip_reports/china-2014.html. For the treatment of the Carters by the Chinese, see Orville Schell, "China Strikes Back!," *New York Review of Books*, October 23, 2014.
4. Carter, "Report by Former U.S. President Jimmy Carter on Trip to Beijing."
5. Michael Pillsbury, *The Hundred-Year Marathon: China's Secret Strategy to Replace America as the Global Superpower* (St. Martin's Griffin, 2016).
6. Kurt M. Campbell and Ely Ratner, "The China Reckoning: How Beijing Defied American Expectations," *Foreign Affairs* 97, no. 2 (2018), https://www.foreignaffairs.com/articles/china/2018-02-13/china-reckoning. Also see Aaron L. Friedberg, *Getting China Wrong* (Polity, 2022).
7. Matt Pottinger and Mike Gallagher, "No Substitute for Victory: America's Competition with China Must Be Won, Not Managed," *Foreign Affairs* 103, no. 3 (2024); Rush Doshi et al., "What Does America Want from China? Debating Washington's Strategy—and the Endgame of Competition," *Foreign Affairs* 103, no. 4 (2024).

8. Hsiao Heng-chung 蕭衡鍾, "台灣在當代美國對外戰略部署中的定位：夥伴或棋子" [Taiwan's role in US foreign policy strategy], 台灣國際研究季刊 3, no. 17 (2021).
9. "Taiwan Initiates Its New One-Year Military Conscription Program," Global Taiwan Institute, February 6, 2024, https://globaltaiwan.org/2024/02/taiwan-initiates-its-new-one-year-military-conscription-program/.
10. "《台湾关系法》45周年 萧美琴：台湾将持续强化国防 台学者：美国应转向'战略清晰'" [The forty-fifth anniversary of the Taiwan Relations Act; Hsiao Mei-ching: Taiwan will continue to strengthen its national defense; Taiwanese scholars: The United States should turn to "strategic clarity"], Voice of America, April 14, 2024, https://www.voachinese.com/a/taiwan-relations-act-hsiao-20240413/7569245.html.
11. Michał Lubina, *Russia and China: A Political Marriage of Convenience—Stable and Successful* (Barbara Budrich, 2017), 112–20.
12. Tadeusz Dmochowski, "The Settlement of the Russian-Chinese Border Dispute," *Polish Political Science Yearbook* 44, no. 1 (2015), https://doi.org/10.15804/ppsy2015006. On Chinese nationalism's potential threat to China-Russia relations.
13. Jamshed Khan and Razia Sultana, "Sino-Russia Strategic Partnership: The Case Study of Shanghai Cooperation Organization (SCO)," *FWU Journal of Social Sciences* 15, no. 2 (2021), https://doi.org/10.51709/19951272/summer-2/1.
14. Bobo Lo, *Axis of Convenience: Moscow, Beijing, and the New Geopolitics* (Chatham House and Brookings Institution Press, 2008), 53–64.
15. On the most recent Chinese-Russian dispute over the Far East, see "PRC-Backed Projects Raise Suspicion in Russia's Far East," Indo-Pacific Defense Forum, November 21, 2020, https://ipdefenseforum.com/2020/11/prc-backed-projects-raise-suspicion-in-russias-far-east/. On Russian elites' view of Chinese nationalism and the potential threat to the Russian Far East, see Lo, *Axis of Convenience*, 71.
16. Zhang Lihua, "Explaining China's Position on the Crimea Referendum," Carnegie Endowment for International Peace, April 1, 2015, https://carnegieendowment.org/research/2015/04/explaining-chinas-position-on-the-crimea-referendum?lang=en&center=global.
17. "Russia, China to Discuss 'U.S. Meddling' in Moscow and Hong Kong Protests," *Moscow Times*, May 28, 2024, https://www.themoscowtimes.com/2019/08/13/russia-china-to-discuss-us-meddling-in-moscow-and-hong-kong-protests-a66828#google_vignette.
18. Michael Beckley, "Enemies of My Enemy: How Fear of China Is Forging a New World Order," *Foreign Affairs* 101, no. 2 (2022).
19. "Special Report: How U.S.-Made Chips Are Flowing Into Russia," Nikkei Asia, April 11, 2023, https://asia.nikkei.com/Business/Tech/Semiconductors/Special-report-How-U.S.-made-chips-are-flowing-into-Russia.
20. Olena Bilousova et al., "Challenges of Export Controls Enforcement: How Russia Continues to Import Components for Its Military Production," Kyiv School of Economics, January 2024, https://kse.ua/about-the-school/news/challenges-of-export-controls-enforcement-how-russia-continues-to-import-components-for-its-military-production/.
21. Reuters, "Ukraine Says It Is Finding More Chinese Components in Russian Weapons," April 16, 2023, https://www.reuters.com/world/europe/ukraine-says-it-is-finding-more-chinese-components-russian-weapons-2023-04-14/.

22. Lyle Goldstein and Nathan Waechter, "2 Years on, Ukraine's Sinking of the *Moskva* Intrigues China's Naval Strategists," *The Diplomat*, April 15, 2024, https://thediplomat.com/2024/04/2-years-on-ukraines-sinking-of-the-moskva-intrigues-chinas-naval-strategists/.
23. C. Todd Lopez, "Supplemental Bill Becomes Law, Provides Billions in Aid for Ukraine, Israel, Taiwan," U.S. Department of Defense, April 24, 2024, https://www.defense.gov/News/News-Stories/Article/Article/3754718/supplemental-bill-becomes-law-provides-billions-in-aid-for-ukraine-israel-taiwan/.
24. Michael McFaul and Evan S. Medeiros, "China and Russia Will Not Be Split," *Foreign Affairs*, April 4, 2025, https://www.foreignaffairs.com/china/china-and-russia-will-not-be-split.
25. Reuters, "Russia Says U.S. Withdrawal from INF Treaty 'Created Vacuum,'" December 8, 2022, https://www.reuters.com/world/europe/russia-says-us-withdrawal-inf-treaty-created-vacuum-2022-12-08/.
26. "Russia Formally Withdraws from INF Nuclear Treaty," Deutsche Welle, March 4, 2019, https://www.dw.com/en/russia-formally-withdraws-from-inf-nuclear-treaty/a-47766621.
27. Kingston Reif, "Trump to Withdraw U.S. from INF Treaty," Arms Control Association, November 2018, https://www.armscontrol.org/act/2018-11/news/trump-withdraw-us-inf-treaty.
28. US Department of Defense, *Military and Security Developments Involving the People's Republic of China*, December 2024, https://media.defense.gov/2024/Dec/18/2003615520/-1/-1/0/MILITARY-AND-SECURITY-DEVELOPMENTS-INVOLVING-THE-PEOPLES-REPUBLIC-OF-CHINA-2024.PDF, 166.
29. Thomas G. Mahnken, "China's Anti-Access Strategy in Historical and Theoretical Perspective," *Journal of Strategic Studies* 34, no. 3 (2011).
30. The quotation is from Heritage Foundation expert Michaela Dodge, "The End of an Era? The INF Treaty, New Start, and the Future of Strategic Stability," Brookings, March 27, 2019, https://www.brookings.edu/events/the-end-of-an-era-the-inf-treaty-new-start-and-the-future-of-strategic-stability/. Also see Richard H. Speier, *Hypersonic Missile Nonproliferation: Hindering the Spread of a New Class of Weapons* (RAND, 2017).
31. See the work of two PLA analysts: Mei Yuyuan 梅育源, Sun Qianjie 孙迁杰, "从《中导条约》的失效看未来国际军控走向" [Analysis on the trends of international arms control after the expiration of the Intermediate-Range Nuclear Forces Treaty], 国防科技 [National defense technology] 41, no. 4 (2020). Also see an article written by two scholars from the PLA Academy of Military Sciences: Yang Weili 杨卫丽, Zhang Wenming 张文明, "美正式退出《中导条约》的主要动因及影响分析" [Analysis of the main reasons and impacts of US formal withdrawal from the INF Treaty], 战术导弹技术 [Tactical missile technology] 5 (2019).
32. Tai Ming Cheung, "Sukhois, Sams, Subs: China Steps Up Arms Purchases from Russia," *Far Eastern Economic Review* 156, no. 14 (1993).
33. Arms Control Association, "China Buying Russian Combat Jets," accessed September 23, 2025, https://www.armscontrol.org/act/2003-03/china-buying-russian-combat-jets; The Diplomat, "Russia Completes Delivery of 24 Su-35 Fighter Jets to China," accessed September 23, 2025, https://thediplomat.com/2019/04/russia-completes-delivery-of-24-su-35-fighter-jets-to-china/.

34. Patrick Devenny, "PLAN Procurement of Sovremenny-Class Destroyers: Developments and Repercussions," Royal United Services Institute, May 23, 2005, https://rusi.org/publication/plan-procurement-sovremenny-class-destroyers-developments-and-repercussions.
35. For fighter purchases, see "Russia Completes Delivery of Su-35 Fighter Jets to China for $2.5bln," *Moscow Times*, September 2, 2023, https://www.themoscowtimes.com/2019/04/17/russia-completes-delivery-of-su-35-fighter-jets-to-china-for-25bln-a65271.
36. Wei-Chin Lee, "US Arms Transfer Policy to Taiwan: From Carter to Clinton," *Journal of Contemporary China* 9, no. 23 (2000).
37. Oliver Bräuner, "How Europe Shies from Taiwan," *The Diplomat*, March 20, 2012, https://thediplomat.com/2012/03/how-europe-shies-from-taiwan/.
38. James R. Holmes, "The Long, Strange Trip of China's First Aircraft Carrier," *Foreign Policy*, February 3, 2015, https://foreignpolicy.com/2015/02/03/the-long-strange-trip-of-chinas-first-aircraft-carrier-liaoning/.
39. "Exclusive: PLA Brass 'Defied Beijing' Over Plan to Buy China's First Aircraft Carrier Liaoning," *South China Morning Post*, May 1, 2015, https://www.scmp.com/news/china/diplomacy-defence/article/1779721/pla-brass-defied-beijing-over-plan-buy-aircraft-carrier.
40. Hugo Meijer, *Trading with the Enemy: The Making of US Export Control Policy Toward the People's Republic of China* (Oxford University Press, 2018), 237.
41. Oliver Bräuner, "Beyond the Arms Embargo: EU Transfers of Defense and Dual-Use Technologies to China," *Journal of East Asian Studies* 13, no. 3 (2013).
42. Nicola Casarini, *Remaking Global Order: The Evolution of Europe-China Relations and Its Implications for East Asia and the United States* (Oxford University Press, 2011), 94.
43. "Fact Sheet: President Xi Jinping's State Visit to the United States," Office of the Press Secretary, White House, September 25, 2015, https://obamawhitehouse.archives.gov/the-press-office/2015/09/25/fact-sheet-president-xi-jinpings-state-visit-united-states.
44. Cory Bennett and Bryan Bender, "How China Acquires 'the Crown Jewels' of U.S. Technology," *Politico*, May 22, 2018, https://www.politico.com/story/2018/05/22/china-us-tech-companies-cfius-572413; Ryan Hass and Abraham Denmark, "More Pain than Gain: How the US-China Trade War Hurt America," Brookings, August 7, 2020, https://www.brookings.edu/articles/more-pain-than-gain-how-the-us-china-trade-war-hurt-america.
45. "Nobelpreis Für Quantenphysiker Anton Zeilinger," *Rudolphina*, December 10, 2022, https://rudolphina.univie.ac.at/nobelpreis-fuer-quantenphysiker-anton-zeilinger.
46. Gregor Weihs et al., "Violation of Bell's Inequality Under Strict Einstein Locality Conditions," *Physical Review Letters* 81, no. 23 (1998).
47. The original idea for such a satellite was detailed in M. Aspelmeyer et al., "Long-Distance Quantum Communication with Entangled Photons Using Satellites," *IEEE Journal of Selected Topics in Quantum Electronics* 9, no. 6 (2003).
48. Martin Giles, "The Man Turning China Into a Quantum Superpower," *MIT Technology Review*, December 19, 2018, https://www.technologyreview.com/2018/12/19/1571/the-man-turning-china-into-a-quantum-superpower/.
49. "China Launches Quantum-Enabled Satellite Micius," BBC News, August 16, 2016, https://www.bbc.com/news/world-asia-china-37091833.

50. Elsa B. Kania and John K. Costello, "Quantum Technologies, U.S.-China Strategic Competition, and Future Dynamics of Cyber Stability," in *2017 International Conference on Cyber Conflict (CyCon U.S.)* (IEEE, 2017).
51. Tom Stefanick, "The State of U.S.-China Quantum Data Security Competition," Brookings, September 21, 2020, https://www.brookings.edu/articles/the-state-of-u-s-china-quantum-data-security-competition/.
52. Doug Quinn et al., "Quantum Computing: A New Competitive Factor with China," *Joint Force Quarterly* 110, no. 3 (2023).
53. Sandra Petersmann and Esther Felden, "China's Quantum Leap—Made in Germany," Deutsche Welle, August 27, 2023, https://www.dw.com/en/chinas-quantum-leap-made-in-germany/a-65890662.
54. Chun Han Wong, "China's Xi Jinping Takes Third Term as President with Eye on U.S.," *Wall Street Journal*, March 9, 2023, https://www.wsj.com/articles/chinas-xi-takes-third-term-as-president-with-eye-on-u-s-eaebef4c.
55. Shelley Rigger, *From Opposition to Power: Taiwan's Democratic Progressive Party* (Lynne Rienner, 2001), 25–27. For Chiang's own decision to liberalize Taiwan, see Jay Taylor, *The Generalissimo's Son: Chiang Ching-kuo and the Revolutions in China and Taiwan* (Harvard University Press, 2000), 25–28.
56. Jieh-min Wu, "Taiwan's Sunflower Occupy Movement as a Transformative Resistance to the 'China Factor,'" in *Take Back Our Future: An Eventful Sociology of the Hong Kong Umbrella Movement*, ed. Ching Kwan Lee and Sing Ming (Cornell University Press, 2019). Also see Ian Rowen, "Inside Taiwan's Sunflower Movement: Twenty-Four Days in a Student-Occupied Parliament, and the Future of the Region," *Journal of Asian Studies* 74, no. 1 (2015), https://doi.org/10.1017/S0021911814002174.
57. Ming-sho Ho, "The Activist Legacy of Taiwan's Sunflower Movement," Carnegie Endowment for International Peace, August 2, 2018, https://carnegieendowment.org/2018/08/02/activist-legacy-of-taiwan-s-sunflower-movement-pub-76766.
58. Chris Miller, "The Taiwan Dilemma," in *Chip War: The Fight for the World's Most Critical Technology* (Simon & Schuster, 2022), 334–35.
59. AP News, "Taiwan Says Chipmaker's Move to Invest $100 Billion in the US Wasn't Because of US Pressure," March 6, 2025, https://apnews.com/article/taiwan-us-tsmc-chips-investment-71d3aeb2bc403a92ce8eccdd8c51c0c8.
60. Reuters, "Sanctions China Has Imposed on Taiwan Over Pelosi Visit," August 3, 2002, https://www.reuters.com/world/asia-pacific/economic-sanctions-china-has-imposed-taiwan-over-pelosi-visit-2022-08-03/.
61. Simone McCarthy and Joyce Jiang, "Food Safety Scandal Rocks China As Report Claims Cooking Oil Carried in Same Trucks as Fuel," CNN, July 10, 2024, https://www.cnn.com/2024/07/10/food/china-oil-food-safety-scandal-sinograin-intl-hnk/index.html.
62. "接替刘鹤副总理何立峰任中央财办主任" [Vice Premier He Lifeng replaces Liu He as director of Central Finance Office], Deutsche Welle, October 30, 2023, https://p.dw.com/p/4YC0d?maca=zh-EMail-sharing.

63. Alexander Dukalskis, "Promoting and Controlling the China Dream: China's External Propaganda and Repression," in *Making the World Safe for Dictatorship* (Oxford University Press, 2021).
64. Professor David Shambaugh told me this in 2014; allegedly the Obamas found out only much later after Michele had returned to the United States.
65. Madeline Coggins, "San Francisco Gym Owner Describes 'Unrecognizable' City After Returning to Den of Homelessness, Drugs," Fox Business, December 13, 2023, https://www.foxbusiness.com/economy/san-francisco-gym-owner-describes-unrecognizable-city-returning-den-of-homelessness-drugs.

BIBLIOGRAPHY

BOOKS AND ARTICLES

Adamsky, Viktor, and Yuri Smirnov. "Moscow's Biggest Bomb: The 50-Megaton Test of October 1961." *Cold War International History Project Bulletin* 4 (1994): 19–21.

Albers, Martin. *Britain, France, West Germany and the People's Republic of China, 1969–1982: The European Dimension of China's Great Transition*. Palgrave Macmillan, 2016.

Albers, Martin. "Business with Beijing, Détente with Moscow: West Germany's China Policy in a Global Context, 1969–1982." *Cold War History* 14, no. 2 (2013): 237–57.

Albers, Martin, and Zhong Zhong Chen. "Socialism, Capitalism, and Sino-European Relations in the Deng Xiaoping Era, 1978–1992." *Cold War History* 17, no. 2 (2017): 115–19.

Albright, David, and Corey Gay. "Taiwan: Nuclear Nightmare Averted." *Bulletin of the Atomic Scientists* 54, no. 1 (1998): 54–60.

Albright, David, and Andrea Stricker. *Taiwan's Former Nuclear Weapons Program*. Institute for Science and International Security, 2018.

Aspelmeyer, M., T. Jennewein, M. Pfennigbauer, W. R. Leeb, and A. Zeilinger. "Long-Distance Quantum Communication with Entangled Photons Using Satellites." *IEEE Journal of Selected Topics in Quantum Electronics* 9, no. 6 (2003): 1541–51.

Associated Press. "Israel Gets US Consent to Offer Jet Fighters to Taiwan." *Los Angeles Times*, April 17, 1992.

Associated Press. "Russian Journalist Victor Louis Dies." *Washington Post*, March 21, 1992.

Auten, Brian J. *Carter's Conversion: The Hardening of American Defense Policy*. University of Missouri Press, 2008.

Baldwin, David A. *Economic Statecraft*. Princeton University Press, 2020.

Baylis, John, and Kristan Stoddart. *The British Nuclear Experience: The Role of Beliefs, Culture, and Identity*. Oxford University Press, 2015.

Beckley, Michael. "Enemies of My Enemy: How Fear of China Is Forging a New World Order." *Foreign Affairs* 101, no. 2 (2022): 68–85.

Bennett, M. Todd, ed. *National Security Policy, 1973–1976*. Vol. 35 of *Foreign Relations of the United States, 1969–1976*. GPO, 2014.

Bösch, Frank. *Zeitenwende 1979: Als Die Welt von Heute Begann*. Beck, 2019.

Brands, H. W. "Vietnam and the Origins of Détente." In *The Search for Peace in Vietnam, 1964–1968*, ed. Lloyd C. Gardner and Ted Gittinger. Texas A&M University Press, 2004.

Bräuner, Oliver. "Beyond the Arms Embargo: EU Transfers of Defense and Dual-Use Technologies to China." *Journal of East Asian Studies* 13, no. 3 (2013): 457–82.

Bräutigam, Deborah A. *The Dragon's Gift: The Real Story of China in Africa*. Oxford University Press, 2009.

Bräutigam, Deborah, and Tang Xiaoyang. "Economic Statecraft in China's New Overseas Special Economic Zones: Soft Power, Business or Resource Security?" *International Affairs* 88, no. 4 (2012): 799–816.

Brazinsky, Gregg. *Winning the Third World: Sino-American Rivalry During the Cold War*. University of North Carolina Press, 2017.

Brown, Kerry, and Kalley Wu Tzu-Hui. *The Trouble with Taiwan: History, the United States and a Rising China*. Bloomsbury Academic, 2022.

Brzezinski, Zbigniew K. *Between Two Ages: America's Role in the Technetronic Era*. Viking, 1970.

Brzezinski, Zbigniew K. *The Permanent Purge: Politics in Soviet Totalitarianism*. Harvard University Press, 1956.

Brzezinski, Zbigniew K. *Power and Principle: Memoirs of the National Security Adviser 1977–1981*. Farrar, Straus & Giroux, 1985.

Brzezinski, Zbigniew K. *The Soviet Bloc: Unity and Conflict*, rev. ed. Harvard University Press, 1967.

Buckley, William F. *Flying High: Remembering Barry Goldwater*. Perseus, 2010.

Bullard, Monte R. *The Soldier and the Citizen: The Role of the Military in Taiwan's Development*. Sharpe, 1997.

Burr, William, and Hector L. Montford, eds. "The Making of the Limited Test Ban Treaty, 1958–1963." August 8, 2003, National Security Archive, https://nsarchive2.gwu.edu/NSAEBB/NSAEBB94/#29.

Burr, William, and Jeffrey T. Richelson. "Whether to 'Strangle the Baby in the Cradle': The United States and the Chinese Nuclear Program, 1960–64." *International Security* 25, no. 3 (2001): 54–99.

Burton, Myra F., ed., *Middle East Region; Arabian Peninsula*, vol. 18 of *Foreign Relations of the United States, 1977–1980*. GPO, 2015.

Bush, Richard C. *At Cross Purposes: U.S.-Taiwan Relations Since 1942*. Routledge, 2004.

Bush, Richard C. *Uncharted Strait: The Future of China-Taiwan Relations*. Brookings Institution Press, 2013.

Bush, Richard C. *Untying the Knot: Making Peace in the Taiwan Strait*. Brookings Institution Press, 2006.

Cahn, Anne Hessing. "Team B Panel Report on Soviet Strategic Objectives." In *Killing Detente: The Right Attacks the CIA*. Pennsylvania State University Press, 1998.

Cahn, Anne Hessing. "Team B: The Trillion Dollar Experiment." *Bulletin of the Atomic Scientists* 49, no. 3 (1993): 22–31.
Cain, Frank. "America's Trade Embargo Against China and the East in the Cold War Years." *Journal of Transatlantic Studies* 18, no. 1 (2020): 19–35.
Cain, Frank. *Economic Statecraft During the Cold War: European Responses to the US Trade Embargo.* Routledge, 2007.
Cain, Frank. "The US-Led Trade Embargo on China: The Origins of CHINCOM, 1947-52." *Journal of Strategic Studies* 18, no. 4 (1995): 33–54.
Cameron, James. "Moscow 1972." In *Transcending the Cold War: Summits, Statecraft, and the Dissolution of Bipolarity in Europe, 1970–1990*, ed. Kristina Spohr and David Reynolds. Oxford University Press, 2016.
Cameron, James, and Or Rabinowitz. "Eight Lost Years? Nixon, Ford, Kissinger and the Non-Proliferation Regime, 1969–1977." *Journal of Strategic Studies* 40, no. 6 (2016): 839–66.
Carter, Jimmy. *Keeping Faith: Memoirs of a President.* University of Arkansas Press, 1995.
Carter, Jimmy. *The Presidential Campaign 1976.* Vol. 1. GPO, 1979.
Carter, Paul Milton, Jr. "Suslov and Soviet Scientific Communism." PhD diss., Indiana University, 1997.
Casarini, Nicola. *Remaking Global Order: The Evolution of Europe-China Relations and Its Implications for East Asia and the United States.* Oxford University Press, 2011.
Chang, Hui-ching, and Richard Holt. *Language, Politics and Identity in Taiwan: Naming China.* Routledge, 2017.
Chen, Jian. "Beijing and the Taiwan Strait Crisis of 1958." In *Mao's China and the Cold War.* University of North Carolina Press, 2012.
Cheung, Tai Ming. "Sukhois, Sams, Subs: China Steps Up Arms Purchases from Russia." *Far Eastern Economic Review* 156, no. 14 (1993): 23.
Chiang, Min-hua. "Contemporary China-Japan Relations: The Politically Driven Economic Linkage." *East Asia* 36, no. 4 (2019): 271–90.
CNN. *Cold War, Soldiers of God.* Episode 20. 1998.
Coll, Steve. *Ghost Wars: The Secret History of the CIA, Afghanistan, and Bin Laden, from the Soviet Invasion to September 10, 2001.* Penguin, 2005.
Crane, David. "The Harrier Jump-Jet and Sino-British Relations." *Asian Affairs: An American Review* 8, no. 4 (1981): 227–50.
Current Negotiations on the Comprehensive Test Ban Treaty: Hearings Before the Intelligence and Military Application of Nuclear Energy Subcommittee of the Committee on Armed Services, House of Representatives, 95th Congress, 2nd Session (March 15 and 16, 1978). GPO, 1978.
Dillon, Michael. *China in the Age of Xi Jinping.* Routledge, 2021.
Dmochowski, Tadeusz. "The Settlement of the Russian–Chinese Border Dispute." *Polish Political Science Yearbook* 44, no. 1 (2015): 56–74.
Dobrynin, Anatoly. *In Confidence: Moscow's Ambassador to America's Six Cold War Presidents.* Random House, 1995.
Doshi, Rush, Jessica Chen Weiss, James B. Steinberg, Paul Heer, Matt Pottinger, and Mike Gallagher. "What Does America Want from China? Debating Washington's Strategy—and the Endgame of Competition." *Foreign Affairs* 103, no. 4 (2024): 174–87.

Dukalskis, Alexander. "Promoting and Controlling the China Dream: China's External Propaganda and Repression." In *Making the World Safe for Dictatorship*. Oxford University Press, 2021.

Dunmire, Patricia L. "'Alerting America': The Committee on the Present Danger and the Re-Securitization of the Soviet Union." In *The Great Nation of Futurity: The Discourse and Temporality of American National Identity*. Oxford University Press, 2023.

Elleman, Bruce A. "The First Taiwan Strait Crisis, 1954–55." In *Taiwan Straits Standoff: 70 Years of PRC-Taiwan Cross-Strait Tensions*. Anthem, 2022.

Evron, Yoram. "The Enduring US-Led Arms Embargo on China: An Objectives-Implementation Analysis." *Journal of Contemporary China* 28, no. 120 (2019): 995–1010.

Fairbank, John King. *The United States and China*. 4th ed. Harvard University Press, 1983.

Fardella, Enrico. "A Significant Periphery of the Cold War: Italy-China Bilateral Relations, 1949–1989." *Cold War History* 17, no. 2 (2016): 181–97.

Fardella, Enrico. "The Sino-American Normalization: A Reassessment." *Diplomatic History* 33, no. 4 (2009): 545–78.

Foot, Rosemary. *The Practice of Power: US Relations with China Since 1949*. Oxford University Press, 1995.

Ford, Matthew, and Alex Gould. "Military Identities, Conventional Capability and the Politics of NATO Standardisation at the Beginning of the Second Cold War, 1970–1980." *International History Review* 41, no. 4 (2018): 775–92.

Friedberg, Aaron L. *Getting China Wrong*. Polity, 2022.

Friedman, Jeremy. *Shadow Cold War: The Sino-Soviet Competition for the Third World*. University of North Carolina Press, 2015.

Frieman, Wendy. *China, International Arms Control and Non-Proliferation*. Routledge, 2004.

Futter, Andrew. *The Politics of Nuclear Weapons*. Sage, 2015.

Gaddis, John Lewis. *George F. Kennan: An American life*. Penguin, 2012.

Gallagher, Nance W. *Arms Control: New Approaches to Theory and Policy*. Routledge, 1998.

Garner, William V. "SALT II: China's Advice and Dissent." *Asian Survey* 19, no. 12 (1979): 1224–40.

Garthoff, Raymond L. *Detente and Confrontation: American-Soviet Relations from Nixon to Reagan*. Brookings Institution, 1994.

Garthoff, Raymond L. *A Journey Through the Cold War: A Memoir of Containment and Coexistence*. Brookings Institution, 2002.

Garthoff, Raymond L. "Soviet Perspective." In *Cruise Missiles: Technology, Strategy, Politics*, ed. Richard K. Betts. Brookings Institution, 1981.

Garver, John W. *China's Quest: The History of the Foreign Relations of the People's Republic of China*. Oxford University Press, 2018.

Gates, Robert Michael. *From the Shadows: The Ultimate Insider's Story of Five Presidents and How They Won the Cold War*. Pocket, 2008.

Gee, John. "Has Israel's U.S.-Funded Lavi Jet Been Reborn as China's J-10 Warplane?" *Washington Report on Middle East Affairs* 3, no. 26 (2007): 42.

Gewirtz, Julian. *Never Turn Back: China and the Forbidden History of the 1980s*. Harvard University Press, 2022.

Gewirtz, Julian. *Unlikely Partners: Chinese Reformers, Western Economists, and the Making of Global China*. Harvard University Press, 2017.

Geyelin, Philip. "Arms Sales: The 'China Differential.'" *Washington Post*, May 23, 1980.
Gil, Gideon. "Taiwanese Program Terminated at MIT." *Harvard Crimson*, July 16, 1976.
Gill, Bates, and Taeho Kim. *China's Arms Acquisitions from Abroad Are a Quest for "Superb and Secret Weapons."* Oxford University Press, 1995.
Glad, Betty. *An Outsider in the White House: Jimmy Carter, His Advisors, and the Making of American Foreign Policy*. Cornell University Press, 2009.
Gleijeses, Piero. *Conflicting Missions: Havana, Washington, and Africa, 1959–1976*. University of North Carolina Press, 2011.
Goh, Evelyn. "Nixon, Kissinger, and the 'Soviet Card' in the U.S. Opening to China, 1971–1974." *Diplomatic History* 29, no. 3 (2005): 475–502.
Gold, Martin B. *A Legislative History of the Taiwan Relations Act: Bridging the Strait*. Lexington Books, 2017.
Goldwater, Barry M. *The Conscience of a Conservative*, ed. CC Goldwater. Princeton University Press, 2007.
Gormley, Dennis M. "Missile Contagion." *Survival* 50, no. 4 (2008): 137–54.
Gormley, Dennis M., Andrew S. Erickson, and Jingdong Yuan. "A Potent Vector: Assessing Chinese Cruise Missile Developments." *Joint Force Quarterly*, no. 4 (2014): 99–105.
Greenway, H. D. S., and Yuval Elizur. "US Ban on Fighter Sales Put to Israeli Voters." *Washington Post*, March 9, 1977.
Gries, Peter Hays, Qingmin Zhang, H. Michael Crowson, and Huajian Cai. "Patriotism, Nationalism and China's US Policy: Structures and Consequences of Chinese National Identity." *China Quarterly* 205 (2011): 1–17.
Halliday, Fred. "The Arc of Crisis and the New Cold War." *MERIP Reports*, no. 100/101 (1981): 14–25.
Halperin, M. H. *The 1958 Taiwan Strait Crisis*. RAND, 1966.
Hanska, Jan. "Rethinking the Unthinkable—Revisiting Theories of Nuclear Deterrence and Escalation." *Journal of Military Studies* 9, no. 1 (2018): 49–60.
Harding, Harry. *A Fragile Relationship: The United States and China Since 1972*. Brookings Institution, 1992.
Heckrotte, Warren. "A Soviet View of Verification." *Bulletin of the Atomic Scientists* 42, no. 8 (1986): 12–15.
Hennessy, Peter. *Cabinets and the Bomb*. Oxford University Press, 2007.
Hershberg, James, Sergey Radchenko, Péter Vámos, and David Wolff. *The INTERKIT Story: A Window Into the Final Decades of the Sino-Soviet Relationship*. Woodrow Wilson Center, 2011.
Heves, Dannis. "Mohammad Zia Ul-Haq: Unbending Commander for Era of Atom and Islam." *New York Times*, August 18, 1988.
Holdridge, John H. *Crossing the Divide: An Insider's Account of Normalization of US-China Relations*. Rowman and Littlefield, 1997.
Hong, Luong Thi. "Economic Cold War: Chinese Economic Aid to Vietnam, 1954–1975." *South East Asia Research* 30, no. 3 (2022): 325–40.
Horsburgh, Nicola. *China and Global Nuclear Order: From Estrangement to Active Engagement*. Oxford University Press, 2015.

Hovi, Jon, Robert Huseby, and Detlef F. Sprinz. "When Do (Imposed) Economic Sanctions Work?" *World Politics* 57, no. 4 (2005): 479–99.
Howard, Michael. *The Causes of War: And Other Essays*. Unwin, 1985.
Hsiung, James C. "Taiwan in 1984: Festivity, New Hope, and Caution." *Asian Survey* 25, no. 1 (1985): 90–96.
Hufbauer, Gary Clyde, Jeffrey J. Schott, and Kimberly Ann Elliott. *Economic Sanctions Reconsidered*. 3rd ed. Peter G. Peterson Institute for International Economics, 2007.
Huisken, Ron. *Rising China: Power and Reassurance*. Australian National University, 2009.
Ingold, Beth. "The Committee on the Present Danger: A Study of Elite and Public Influence, 1976–1980." PhD diss., University of Pittsburgh, 1989.
Jackson, Ian. "Compromise: America, COCOM and the Extension of the East-West Trade Embargo, 1950." In *The Economic Cold War*. Springer, 2001.
Jackson, Steven F. "China's Third World Foreign Policy: The Case of Angola and Mozambique, 1961–93." *China Quarterly* 142 (1995): 388–422.
Jacob, Stokes. *China's Missile Program and U.S. Withdrawal from the Intermediate-Range Nuclear Forces (INF) Treaty*. U.S.-China Economic and Security Review Commission, 2019.
Jacobs, J. Bruce. "One China, Diplomatic Isolation and a Separate Taiwan." In *China's Rise, Taiwan's Dilemmas and International Peace*, ed. Edward Friedman. Routledge, 2006.
Jenkins, Rhys. *How China Is Reshaping the Global Economy: Development Impacts in Africa and Latin America*. Oxford University Press, 2018.
Jervis, Robert. "Mutual Assured Destruction." *Foreign Policy*, no. 133 (2002): 40–42.
Jian, Chen. "China, the Vietnam War, and the Sino-American Rapprochement, 1968–1973." In *The Third Indochina War: Conflict Between China, Vietnam and Cambodia, 1972–79*, ed. Odd Arne Westad and Sophie Quinn-Judge. Routledge, 2006.
Jin, Berber. "Following Stanford Physics Professor's Passing, Rumors of Ties to Chinese Government Emerge." *Stanford Daily*, December 30, 2018.
Kania, Elsa B., and John K. Costello. "Quantum Technologies, U.S.-China Strategic Competition, and Future Dynamics of Cyber Stability." In *2017 International Conference on Cyber Conflict (CyCon U.S.)*. IEEE, 2017.
Kaplan, Edward. *To Kill Nations: American Strategy in the Air-Atomic Age and the Rise of Mutually Assured Destruction*. Cornell University Press, 2020.
Kass, Harrison. "IAI Kfir: Israel's Classic Fighter Jet No Nation Wanted to Ever Fight." *National Interests*, August 7, 2024.
Kaufman, Michael T. "Ogaden Conflict Termed Threat to Africa's Stability." *New York Times*, October 9, 1977.
Kaufman, Robert Gordon. *Henry M. Jackson: A Life in Politics*. University of Washington Press, 2000.
Keefer, Edward C., ed. *China*. Vol. 17 of *Foreign Relations of the United States, 1969–1976*. GPO, 2006.
Keefer, Edward C. *Harold Brown: Offsetting the Soviet Military Challenge 1977–1981*. Historical Office, Office of the Secretary of Defense, 2017.
Keefer, Edward C., David W. Mabon, and Harriet Dashiell Schwar, eds. *Northeast Asia*. Vol. 22 of *Foreign Relations of the United States 1961–1963*. GPO, 1996.

Kennedy, Paul M. *The Rise and Fall of the Great Powers: Economic Change and Military Conflict from 1500 to 2000.* Random House, 1988.
Kenny, Henry J. *World Military Expenditures and Arms Transfers, 1986.* US Arms Control and Disarmament Agency, 1986.
Kent, Ann. *Beyond Compliance: China, International Organizations, and Global Security.* Stanford University Press, 2010.
Khan, Jamshed, and Razia Sultana. "Sino-Russia Strategic Partnership: The Case Study of Shanghai Cooperation Organization (SCO)." *FWU Journal of Social Sciences* 15, no. 2 (2021): 1–19.
Kirby, William C. "Traditions of Centrality, Authority, and Management in Modern China's Foreign Relations." In *Chinese Foreign Policy: Theory and Practice*, ed. Thomas W. Robinson and David Shambaugh. Clarendon, 2006.
Kirby, William C., Robert S. Ross, and Li Gong, eds. *Normalization of U.S.-China Relations: An International History.* Harvard University Asia Center, 2007.
Kissinger, Henry. *White House Years.* Little, Brown, 1979.
Klein, Donald W. "The Political Economy of Taiwan's International Commercial Links." In *Taiwan: Beyond the Economic Miracle*, ed. Denis Fred Simon and Michael Y. M. Kau. Routledge, 1992.
Kokoshin, Andrei A. *Soviet Strategic Thoughts, 1917–91.* MIT Press, 1998.
Kollmeyer, Christopher, and Florian Pichler. "Is Deindustrialization Causing High Unemployment in Affluent Countries? Evidence from 16 OECD Countries, 1970–2003." *Social Forces* 91, no. 3 (2013): 785–812.
Kozyrev, Vitaly. "Soviet Policy Toward the United States and China, 1969–1979." In *Normalization of U.S.-China Relations: An International History*, ed. William C. Kirby, Robert S. Ross, and Gong Li. Harvard University Press, 2007.
Kung, Chien-wen. *Diasporic Cold Warriors: Nationalist China, Anticommunism, and the Philippine Chinese, 1930s–1970s.* Cornell University Press, 2022.
Lackner, Helen. "The People's Democratic Republic of Yemen: Unique Socialist Experiment in the Arab World at a Time of World Revolutionary Fervour." *Interventions* 19, no. 5 (2017): 677–91.
Ladley, Eric. *Nixon's China Trip.* Writers Club Press, 2002.
Lee, Cheol-sung. "International Migration, Deindustrialization and Union Decline in 16 Affluent OECD Countries, 1962–1997." *Social Forces* 84, no. 1 (2005): 71–88.
Lee, David Tawei. *The Making of the Taiwan Relations Act: Twenty Years in Retrospect.* Oxford University Press, 2000.
Lee, Wei-chin. "US Arms Transfer Policy to Taiwan: From Carter to Clinton." *Journal of Contemporary China* 9, no. 23 (2000): 53–75.
Lewis, Flora. "Hua Guofeng in West Europe Stressed a New Pragmatism." *New York Times*, November 11, 1979.
Li, Zhisui. *The Private Life of Chairman Mao: The Memoirs of Mao's Personal Physician.* Chatto & Windus, 1994.
Libbey, James. "COCOM, Comecon, and the Economic Cold War." *Russian History* 37, no. 2 (2010): 133–52.
Lieberthal, Kenneth G., and Michel Oksenberg. *Policy Making in China: Leaders, Structures, and Processes.* Princeton University Press, 1988.

Lilley, James. *China Hands: Nine Decades of Adventure, Espionage, and Diplomacy in Asia*. With Jeffrey Lilley. PublicAffairs, 2005.
Lin, Gang, Wenxing Zhou, and Weixu Wu. "What Shapes Taiwan-Related Legislation in U.S. Congress?" *Journal of Contemporary China* 31, no. 136 (2021): 609–25.
Lin, Herbert. *Cyber Threats and Nuclear Weapons*. Stanford University Press, 2021.
Lin, Hsiao-ting. *Accidental State: Chiang Kai-shek, the United States, and the Making of Taiwan*. Harvard University Press, 2016.
Lin, Hsiao-ting. *Taiwan, the United States, and the Hidden History of the Cold War in Asia: Divided Allies*. Routledge, 2022.
Litwak, Robert S. *Détente and the Nixon Doctrine: American Foreign Policy and the Pursuit of Stability, 1969–1976*. Cambridge University Press, 2008.
Liu, Qianer, and Andy Lin. "China Imports Record Amount of Chipmaking Equipment." *Financial Times*, August 25, 2023.
Liu, Yanqiong, and Jifeng Liu. "Analysis of Soviet Technology Transfer in the Development of China's Nuclear Weapons." *Comparative Technology Transfer and Society* 7, no. 1 (2009): 66–110.
Lo, Bobo. *Axis of Convenience: Moscow, Beijing, and the New Geopolitics*. Chatham House and Brookings Institution Press, 2008.
Logevall, Fredrik, and Andrew Preston, eds. *Nixon in the World: American Foreign Relations, 1969–1977*. Oxford University Press, 2009.
Long, William J. "Economic Incentives and International Cooperation: Technology Transfer to the People's Republic of China, 1978–86." *Journal of Peace Research* 28, no. 2 (1991): 175–89.
Lorell, Mark A., and Hugh P. Levaux. *The Cutting Edge: A Half Century of U.S. Fighter Aircraft R&D*. RAND, 1998.
Lorenzo, David. "Why Do Many Taiwanese Resist Unification with the People's Republic of China? An Overview of Explanations." *Journal of Indo-Pacific Affairs*, May 8, 2024, 35–49.
Lubina, Michał. *Russia and China: A Political Marriage of Convenience—Stable and Successful*. Barbara Budrich, 2017.
Lukin, Aleksandr. *The Bear Watches the Dragon: Russia's Perceptions of China and the Evolution of Russian-Chinese Relations Since the Eighteenth Century*. Sharpe, 2015.
Lüthi, Lorenz M. *Cold Wars: Asia, the Middle East, Europe*. Cambridge University Press, 2020.
Lüthi, Lorenz M. "The People's Republic of China and the Warsaw Pact Organization, 1955–63." *Cold War History* 7, no. 4 (2007): 479–94.
Lüthi, Lorenz M. "Rearranging International Relations? How Mao's China and de Gaulle's France Recognized Each Other in 1963–1964." *Journal of Cold War Studies* 16, no. 1 (2014): 111–45.
Lüthi, Lorenz M. *The Sino-Soviet Split: Cold War in the Communist World*. Princeton University Press, 2008.
MacMillan, Margaret. *Nixon in China: The Week That Changed the World*. Penguin Canada, 2008.
Made in China 2025 China: Manufacturing in the 21st Century—Opportunities for UK-China Partnership. China-British Business Council, 2018.
Made in China 2025. State Council Information Office of the People's Republic of China, 2016.
Mahnken, Thomas G. "China's Anti-Access Strategy in Historical and Theoretical Perspective." *Journal of Strategic Studies* 34, no. 3 (2011): 299–323.

Mann, James. *About Face: A History of America's Curious Relationship with China from Nixon to Clinton*. Vintage, 2000.
Mann, James. "U.S. Says Israel Gave Combat Jet Plans to China." *Los Angeles Times*, December 28, 1994. https://www.latimes.com/archives/la-xpm-1994-12-28-mn-13774-story.html.
Mao, Lin. "More Than a Tacit Alliance: Trade, Soft Power, and U.S.-Chinese Rapprochement Reconsidered." *Journal of American-East Asian Relations* 24, no. 1 (2017): 41–77.
Mao, Lin. "Traders as Diplomats: Trade and Sino-American Rapprochement, 1971–78." *International Journal of Social Science Studies* 5, no. 10 (2017): 52–66.
Mark, Chi-kwan. *The Everyday Cold War: Britain and China, 1950–1972*. Bloomsbury Academic, 2017.
Marks, Thomas A. *Counterrevolution in China: Wang Sheng and the Kuomintang*. Taylor and Francis, 2016.
Martin, Garret. "Playing the China Card? Revisiting France's Recognition of Communist China, 1963–1964." *Journal of Cold War Studies* 10, no. 1 (2008): 52–80.
Martin, Lisa L. *Coercive Cooperation: Explaining Multilateral Economic Sanctions*. Princeton University Press, 1994.
Mastanduno, Michael. *Economic Containment: COCOM and the Politics of East-West Trade*. Cornell University Press, 1993.
Mastanduno, Michael. "System Maker and Privilege Taker: US Power and the International Political Economy." In *International Relations Theory and the Consequences of Unipolarity*, ed. G. John Ikenberry, Michael Mastanduno, and William C. Wohlforth. Cambridge University Press, 2011.
McFarland, Kelly M., ed. *Middle East Region; Arabian Peninsula*. Vol. 18 of *Foreign Relations of the United States, 1977–1980*. GPO, 2015.
McFaul, Michael, and Evan S. Medeiros. "China and Russia Will Not Be Split." *Foreign Affairs*, April 4, 2025. https://www.foreignaffairs.com/china/china-and-russia-will-not-be-split.
Mearsheimer, J. J. "The Gathering Storm: China's Challenge to US Power in Asia." *Chinese Journal of International Politics* 3, no. 4 (2010): 381–96.
Medeiros, Evan S. *Reluctant Restraint: The Evolution of China's Nonproliferation Policies and Practices, 1980–2004*. NUS Press, 2009.
Meijer, Hugo. "Balancing Conflicting Security Interests: U.S. Defense Exports to China in the Last Decade of the Cold War." *Journal of Cold War Studies* 17, no. 1 (2015): 4–40.
Meijer, Hugo. *Trading with the Enemy: The Making of US Export Control Policy Toward the People's Republic of China*. Oxford University Press, 2018.
Miller, Chris. "The Taiwan Dilemma." In *Chip War: The Fight for the World's Most Critical Technology*. Simon & Schuster, 2022.
Miller, Judith. "US Said to Decide Against New Talks to Ban All A-Tests." *New York Times*, July 20, 1982.
Millwood, Pete. *Improbable Diplomats: How Ping-Pong Players, Musicians, and Scientists Remade US-China Relations*. Cambridge University Press, 2023.
Mistry, Dinshaw. *Containing Missile Proliferation, Strategic Technology, Security Regimes, and International Cooperation in Arms Control*. University of Washington Press, 2003.
Mitcham, Chad. *China's Economic Relations with the West and Japan, 1949–1979: Grain, Trade, and Diplomacy*. Taylor and Francis, 2005.

Mitchell, Nancy. "The Cold War and Jimmy Carter." In *The Cambridge History of the Cold War*, ed. Melvyn P. Leffler and Odd Arne Westad. Cambridge University Press, 2010.

Mitchell, Nancy. *Jimmy Carter in Africa: Race and the Cold War*. Woodrow Wilson Center Press, 2016.

Müller, Julian M., and Kai-Ingo Voigt. "Sustainable Industrial Value Creation in SMEs: A Comparison Between Industry 4.0 and Made in China 2025." *International Journal of Precision Engineering and Manufacturing—Green Technology* 5, no. 5 (2018): 659–70.

New York Times. "Taiwan Rejects Israeli Plane Offer." July 7, 1978.

Nickles, David Paull, ed. *China*. Vol. 13 of *Foreign Relations of the United States, 1977–1980*. GPO, 2013.

Noring, Nina J., ed. *Near East*. Vol. 18 of *Foreign Relations of the United States, 1961–1963*. GPO, 1995.

Nuclear Energy Cooperation with China: Hearing Before the Special Subcommittee on US-Pacific Rim Trade of the Committee on Energy and Commerce, House of Representatives, 99th Congress, 1st Session. GPO, 1986.

Nuclear Posture Review 2018. Office of the Secretary of Defense, 2018.

Oberdorfer, Don. "Taiwan to Curb A-Role, Agrees to Halt Nuclear Fuel Reprocessing." *Washington Post*, September 23, 1976.

Oksenberg, Michel. "A Decade of Sino-American Relations." *Foreign Affairs* 61, no. 1 (1982): 175.

Oliver, Kendrick. *Kennedy, Macmillan and the Nuclear Test-Ban Debate, 1961–63*. Macmillan, 1998.

Organski, Abramo F. *World Politics*. Knopf, 1968.

Ouimet, Matthew J. *The Rise and Fall of the Brezhnev Doctrine in Soviet Foreign Policy*. University of North Carolina Press, 2003.

Owen, David. *Nuclear Papers*. Liverpool University Press, 2009.

Paine, Sarah C. M. *The Sino-Japanese War of 1894–1895: Perceptions, Power, and Primacy*. Cambridge University Press, 2009.

Pantsov, Alexander V., and Steven I. Levine. *Deng Xiaoping: A Revolutionary Life*. Oxford University Press, 2015.

Pape, Robert A. "Why Economic Sanctions Do Not Work." *International Security* 22, no. 2 (1997): 90–136.

Pape, Robert A. "Why Economic Sanctions Still Do Not Work." *International Security* 23, no. 1 (1998): 66–77.

Patman, Robert G. *The Soviet Union in the Horn of Africa: The Diplomacy of Intervention and Disengagement*. Cambridge University Press, 2009.

Peters, Michael A. "The Emerging Multipolar World Order: A Preliminary Analysis." *Educational Philosophy and Theory* 55, no. 14 (2023): 1653–63.

Petroff, Serge. *The Red Eminence: A Biography of Mikhail A. Suslov*. Kingston Press, 1988.

Phillips, Steven E., ed. *China, 1969–1972*. Vol. 17 of *Foreign Relations of the United States, 1969–1976*. GPO, 2006.

Piao, Long, and Hsin-che Wu. "The Effect of the Chinese Government's Political Propaganda and Individual Characteristics on Anti-US Sentiment." *Asian Survey* 63, no. 3 (2023): 381–406.

Pillsbury, Michael. *The Hundred-Year Marathon: China's Secret Strategy to Replace America as the Global Superpower*. St. Martin's Griffin, 2016.

Politi, John J. "Concerning a Comprehensive Nuclear Test Ban." *US Army War College Quarterly: Parameters* 8, no. 1 (1978): 73–85.

Pollack, Kenneth M. *Armies of Sand: The Past, Present, and Future of Arab Military Effectiveness*. Oxford University Press, 2020.

Polmar, Norman, and Robert S. Norris. *The US Nuclear Arsenal: A History of Weapons and Delivery Systems Since 1945*. Naval Institute Press, 2009.

Powell, Robert. "Nuclear Brinkmanship, Limited War, and Military Power." *International Organization* 69, no. 3 (2015): 589–626.

Press, Frank. "Science and Technology in the White House, 1977 to 1980: Part 2." *Science* 211, no. 4479 (1981): 249–56.

Pugach, Noel H. "Anglo-American Aircraft Competition and the China Arms Embargo, 1919–1921." *Diplomatic History* 2, no. 4 (1978): 351–72.

Qingmin, Zhang. "The Bureaucratic Politics of US Arms Sales to Taiwan." *Chinese Journal of International Politics* 1, no. 2 (2006): 231–65.

Quinn, Doug, Patrick Wolverton, and Scott Storm. "Quantum Computing: A New Competitive Factor with China." *Joint Force Quarterly* 110, no. 3 (2023): 35–45.

Rabinowitz, Or, and Nicholas L. Miller. "Keeping the Bombs in the Basement: U.S. Nonproliferation Policy Toward Israel, South Africa, and Pakistan." *International Security* 40, no. 1 (2015): 47–86.

Radchenko, Sergey. *To Run the World: The Kremlin's Cold War Bid for Global Power*. Cambridge University Press, 2024.

Radchenko, Sergey. *Two Suns in the Heavens: The Sino-Soviet Struggle for Supremacy, 1962–1967*. Stanford University Press, 2009.

Reid, Richard J. *Frontiers of Violence in North-East Africa: Genealogies of Conflict Since C. 1800*. Oxford University Press, 2011.

Rhinelander, John B. "The Comprehensive Test Ban Treaty as a Prelude to SALT II." *Arms Control Today* 8, no. 4 (1978): 1–3.

Rigger, Shelley. *From Opposition to Power: Taiwan's Democratic Progressive Party*. Lynne Rienner, 2001.

Rigger, Shelley. *Taiwan's Rising Rationalism: Generations, Politics, and "Taiwanese Nationalism."* East-West Center, 2006.

Robinson, Thomas W. "The Sino-Soviet Border Conflicts of 1969: New Evidence Three Decades Later." In *Chinese Warfighting: The PLA Experience Since 1949*, ed. Mark A. Ryan, David Michael Finkelstein, and Michael A. McDevitt. Sharpe, 2003.

Romano, Angela. "Waiting for de Gaulle: France's Ten-Year Warm-Up to Recognizing the People's Republic of China." *Modern Asian Studies* 51, no. 1 (2016): 44–77.

Romano, Angela, and Valeria Zanier. "Circumventing the Cold War: The Parallel Diplomacy of Economic and Cultural Exchanges Between Western Europe and Socialist China in the 1950s and 1960s: An Introduction." *Modern Asian Studies* 51, no. 1 (2016): 1–16.

Ross, Robert S., ed. *China, the United States, and the Soviet Union: Tripolarity and Policy Making in the Cold War*. Sharpe, 1993.

Ross, Robert S. *Negotiating Cooperation: The U.S. and China, 1969–89*. Stanford University Press, 1997.

Rowen, Ian. "Inside Taiwan's Sunflower Movement: Twenty-Four Days in a Student-Occupied Parliament, and the Future of the Region." *Journal of Asian Studies* 74, no. 1 (2015): 5–21. https://doi.org/10.1017/s0021911814002174.

Rozman, Gilbert. "Moscow's China-Watchers in the Post-Mao Era: The Response to a Changing China." *China Quarterly* 94 (1983): 215–41.

Sanders, Jerry W. *Peddlers of Crisis: The Committee on the Present Danger and the Politics of Containment*. South End Press, 1983.

Schaeffer, Bernd. "Ostpolitik, 'Fernostpolitik,' and Sino-Soviet Rivalry: China and the Two Germanys." In *Ostpolitik, 1969–1974: European and Global Responses*, ed. Carole Fink and Bernd Schaefer. Cambridge University Press, 2008.

Schell, Orville. "China Strikes Back!" *New York Review of Books*, October 23, 2014.

Schwar, Harriet Dashiell, ed. *China*. Vol. 30 of *Foreign Relations of the United States, 1964–1968*. GPO, 1998.

Shambaugh, David L. *China's Communist Party: Atrophy and Adaptation*. Woodrow Wilson Center Press and University of California Press, 2008.

Shambaugh, David L. *Modernizing China's Military: Progress, Problems, and Prospects*. University of California Press, 2004.

Shambaugh, David L. "Patterns of Interaction in Sino-American Relations." In *Chinese Foreign Policy: Theory and Practice*, ed. Thomas W. Robinson and David L. Shambaugh. Clarendon, 1995.

Shen, Zhihua, and Danhui Li. *After Leaning to One Side: China and Its Allies in the Cold War*. Woodrow Wilson Center Press, 2011.

Sheng, Michael M. "Mao and China's Relations with the Superpowers in the 1950s." *Modern China* 34, no. 4 (2008): 477–507.

Solomon, Richard H. *Chinese Political Negotiating Behavior, 1967–1984*. RAND, 1995.

Speier, Richard H. *Hypersonic Missile Nonproliferation: Hindering the Spread of a New Class of Weapons*. RAND, 2017.

Sutter, Robert G. "China Policy During the Nixon and Ford Administrations." In *The China Quandary: Domestic Determinants of U.S. China Policy, 1972–1982*. Routledge, 2019.

Sutter, Robert G. *US-China Relations: Perilous Past, Uncertain Present*. Rowman & Littlefield, 2022.

Tagirova, Alsu. "From Crisis Management to Realignment of Forces: The Diplomatic 'Geometry' of the 1969–1978 Sino-Soviet Border Talks." *Journal of Cold War Studies* 24, no. 1 (2022): 116–54.

Talbott, Strobe. *Endgame: The Inside Story of SALT II*. Harper & Row, 1980.

Tan, Qingshan. "U.S.-China Nuclear Cooperation Agreement: China's Nonproliferation Policy." *Asian Survey* 29, no. 9 (1989): 870–82.

Tareke, Gebru. "The Ethiopia-Somalia War of 1977 Revisited." *International Journal of African Historical Studies* 33, no. 3 (2000): 635.

Taylor, Jay. *The Generalissimo's Son: Chiang Ching-kuo and the Revolutions in China and Taiwan*. Harvard University Press, 2000.

Taylor, Melissa Jane, ed. *Soviet Union*. Vol. 6 of *Foreign Relations of the United States, 1977–1980*. GPO, 2013.

Taylor, Robert H. *Foreign and Domestic Consequences of the KMT Intervention in Burma.* Department of Asian Studies, Cornell University, 1973.

Tertrais, Bruno. "France and Nuclear Non-Proliferation: From Benign Neglect to Active Promotion." In *Nuclear Proliferation and International Order: Challenges to the Non-Proliferation Treaty,* ed. Olav Njølstad. Routledge, 2011.

Thompson, Nicholas. *The Hawk and the Dove: Paul Nitze, George Kennan, and the History of the Cold War.* Picador, 2010.

Toggia, Pietro. "The Revolutionary Endgame of Political Power: The Genealogy of 'Red Terror' in Ethiopia." *African Identities* 10, no. 3 (2012): 265–80.

Tsipis, Kosta, Herbert York, Fred Kaplan, and Thomas J. Downey. "Thirty-Seven Years of Nuclear Weapons." *Bulletin of the Atomic Scientists* 38, no. 10 (1982): 46–58.

Tubilewicz, Czeslaw. "Taiwan and the Soviet Union During the Cold War: Enemies or Ambiguous Friends?" *Cold War History* 5, no. 1 (2005): 75–86.

Tucker, Nancy Bernkopf. *Strait Talk: United States–Taiwan Relations and the Crisis with China.* Harvard University Press, 2011.

Tudda, Chris, ed. *Arms Control and Nonproliferation.* Vol. 26 of *Foreign Relations of the United States, 1977–1980.* GPO, 2015.

Tudda, Chris. *A Cold War Turning Point: Nixon and China, 1969–1972.* Louisiana State University Press, 2012.

Tyler, Patrick. *A Great Wall: Six Presidents and China; An Investigative History.* PublicAffairs, 2000.

Ulsamer, Edgar. "Alarming Soviet Developments." *Air & Space Forces Magazine,* November 1, 1980.

Vaïsse, Justin, and Catherine Porter. *Zbigniew Brzezinski: America's Grand Strategist.* Harvard University Press, 2018.

Vance, Cyrus R. *Hard Choices: Critical Years in America's Foreign Policy.* Simon & Schuster, 1983.

Wang, Zuoyue. "The Cold War and the Reshaping of Transnational Science in China." In *Science and Technology in the Global Cold War,* ed. Naomi Oreskes and John Krige. MIT Press, 2015.

Weihs, Gregor, Thomas Jennewein, Christoph Simon, Harald Weinfurter, and Anton Zeilinger. "Violation of Bell's Inequality Under Strict Einstein Locality Conditions." *Physical Review Letters* 81, no. 23 (1998): 5039–43.

Westad, Odd Arne. "China and the End of the Cold War in Europe." *Cold War History* 17, no. 2 (2017): 111–13.

Westad, Odd Arne. *The Global Cold War: Third World Interventions and the Making of Our Times.* Cambridge University Press, 2005.

Westad, Odd Arne, and Sophie Quinn-Judge, eds. *The Third Indochina War: Conflict Between China, Vietnam, and Cambodia, 1972–79.* Routledge, 2006.

Wilson, George C. "Brown Going to China; Afghanistan on Agenda." *Washington Post,* January 3, 1980.

Wilson, George C. "Nationalist China to Be Offered New F5 Fighter." *Washington Post,* September 6, 1978.

Wishnick, Elizabeth. *Mending Fences: The Evolution of Moscow's China Policy from Brezhnev to Yeltsin.* University of Washington Press, 2014.

Woodroofe, Louise P., ed. *Horn of Africa*. Vol. 17, pt. 1 of *Foreign Relations of the United States, 1977–1980*. GPO, 2016.

Wu, Jieh-min. "Taiwan's Sunflower Occupy Movement as a Transformative Resistance to the 'China Factor.'" In *Take Back Our Future: An Eventful Sociology of the Hong Kong Umbrella Movement*, ed. Ching Kwan Lee and Sing Ming. Cornell University Press, 2019.

Xia, Yafeng. *Negotiating with the Enemy: U.S.-China Talks During the Cold War, 1949–1972*. Indiana University Press, 2006.

Xiao, Ruping, and Hsiao-ting Lin. "Inside the Asian Cold War Intrigues: Revisiting the Taiwan Strait Crises." *Modern Asian Studies* 52, no. 6 (2018): 2109–36.

Yeong, Kuang Ger. "Cross-Strait Relations and the Taiwan Relations Act." *American Journal of Chinese Studies* 22, special issue no. 2 (2015): 235–52.

Yuan, Jing-dong. "The Politics of the Strategic Triangle: The U.S., COCOM, and Export Controls on China, 1979–1989." *Journal of Northeast Asian Studies* 14, no. 1 (1995): 47–79.

Yuan, Jing-dong. "The U.S., COCOM, and the China Differentials: The Making of Western Export-Control Policies, 1949–1994." Diss., Queen's University, 1994.

Zanchetta, Barbara. "Re-Creating the Strategic Triangle: Normalization with China and SALT II." In *The Transformation of American International Power in the 1970s*. Cambridge University Press, 2014.

Zhan, Xin. "Prelude to the Transformation: China's Nuclear Arms Control Policy During the U.S.-China Rapprochement, 1969–1976." *Diplomatic History* 41, no. 2 (2017): 288–304.

Zhang, Xiaoming. *Deng Xiaoping's Long War: The Military Conflict Between China and Vietnam 1979–1991*. University of North Carolina Press, 2018.

Zhihua, Shen, and Neil E. Silver. *Mao, Stalin and the Korean War: Trilateral Communist Relations in the 1950s*. Routledge, 2013.

Zhong, Yang. "Explaining National Identity Shift in Taiwan." *Journal of Contemporary China* 25, no. 99 (2016): 336–52.

Zubok, Vladislav M. *A Failed Empire: The Soviet Union in the Cold War from Stalin to Gorbachev*. University of North Carolina Press, 2010.

Zubok, Vladislav M. "Look What Chaos in the Beautiful Socialist Camp: Deng Xiaoping and the Sino-Soviet Split, 1956–1963." *Cold War International History Project Bulletin* 10 (1998): 153–62.

INTERNET RESOURCES

Air Force Technology. "F-21 Kfir Fighter Jet." July 13, 2020. https://www.airforce-technology.com/projects/f-21-kfir-jet/.

American Institute in Taiwan. "Declassified Cables: Taiwan Arms Sales & Six Assurances (1982)." https://www.ait.org.tw/declassified-cables-taiwan-arms-sales-six-assurances-1982/.

Arms Control Association. "The Nuclear Testing Tally 1945–2017." Last reviewed January 2024. https://www.armscontrol.org/factsheets/nucleartesttally.

Arms Control Association. "U.S. Conventional Arms Sales to Taiwan 1980–2010." Last updated October 2012. https://www.armscontrol.org/factsheets/taiwanarms.

BBC News. "China Launches Quantum-Enabled Satellite Micius." August 16, 2016. https://www.bbc.com/news/world-asia-china-37091833.

Bennett, Cory, and Bryan Bender. "How China Acquires 'the Crown Jewels' of U.S. Technology." *Politico*, May 22, 2018. https://www.politico.com/story/2018/05/22/china-us-tech-companies-cfius-572413.

Bergkvist, Nils-Olov, and Ragnhild Ferm. "Nuclear Explosions 1945–1998." International Atomic Energy Agency. January 1, 1970. https://inis.iaea.org/search/search.aspx?orig_q=RN%3A31060372.

Bilousova, Olena, Oleksii Gribanovskiy, Benjamin Hilgenstock, Elina Ribakova, Nataliia Shapoval, and Vladyslav Vlasiuk. "Russia's Military Capacity and the Role of Imported Components." KSE Institute. June 19, 2023. https://kse.ua/wp-content/uploads/2023/06/Russian-import-of-critical-components.pdf.

Bilousova, Olena, Benjamin Hilgenstock, Elina Ribakova, Nataliia Shapoval, Anna Vlasyuk, and Vladyslav Vlasiuk. "Challenges of Export Controls Enforcement: How Russia Continues to Import Components for Its Military Production." Kyiv School of Economics. January 2024. https://kse.ua/about-the-school/news/challenges-of-export-controls-enforcement-how-russia-continues-to-import-components-for-its-military-production/.

Bräuner, Oliver. "How Europe Shies from Taiwan." *The Diplomat*, March 20, 2012. https://thediplomat.com/2012/03/how-europe-shies-from-taiwan/.

Braw, Elisabeth. "How China Is Buying Up the West's High-Tech Sector." *Foreign Policy*, December 3, 2020. https://foreignpolicy.com/2020/12/03/how-china-is-buying-up-the-wests-high-tech-sector/.

Buckley, Chris. "Liu Xiaobo, Chinese Dissident Who Won Nobel While Jailed, Dies at 61." *New York Times*, July 13, 2017. https://www.nytimes.com/2017/07/13/world/asia/liu-xiaobo-dead.html.

Burr, William. "The Limited Test Ban Treaty—50 Years Later: New Documents Throw Light on Accord Banning Atmospheric Nuclear Testing." The Nuclear Vault, August 2, 2013. https://nsarchive2.gwu.edu/nukevault/ebb433/.

Burr, William. "Nixon's Trip to China." December 11, 2011. https://nsarchive2.gwu.edu/NSAEBB/NSAEBB106/.

Burr, William, and Svetlana Savranskaya, eds. "Previously Classified Interviews with Former Soviet Officials Reveal U.S. Strategic Intelligence Failure Over Decades." September 11, 2009. National Security Archive. https://nsarchive2.gwu.edu/nukevault/ebb285/.

Caixin Global. "China's CITIC Group Corp Executive Probed for Suspected Corruption." June 10, 2024. https://www.caixinglobal.com/2024-06-10/chinas-citic-group-corp-executive-probed-for-suspected-corruption-102204792.html.

Campbell, Kurt M., and Ely Ratner. "The China Reckoning: How Beijing Defied American Expectations." *Foreign Affairs* 97, no. 2 (2018). https://www.foreignaffairs.com/articles/china/2018-02-13/china-reckoning.

Carter, Jimmy. "Report by Former U.S. President Jimmy Carter on Trip to Beijing, Qingdao, Xian, and Shanghai, China, Sept. 1–10, 2014." Carter Center. September 11, 2014. https://www.cartercenter.org/news/trip_reports/china-2014.html.

Carter, Jimmy. "Trip Report by Former U.S. President Jimmy Carter to China, Sept. 4–10, 2010." Carter Center. https://www.cartercenter.org/news/trip_reports/china-090410.html.

CBS News. "Read Trump's Statements on Jimmy Carter's Death." December 30, 2024. https://www.cbsnews.com/news/jimmy-carter-death-donald-trump-statement/.

Charbonneau, S. "Framatome Contribution to Chinese NPP Development and Standardization." International Nuclear Information System, 1996. https://inis.iaea.org/collection/NCLCollectionStore/_Public/29/035/29035049.pdf?r=1.

"China Village Elections Project." Carter Center. October 2002. https://www.cartercenter.org/documents/nondatabase/chinavillagefactsheet.pdf.

Coggins, Madeline. "San Francisco Gym Owner Describes 'Unrecognizable' City After Returning to Den of Homelessness, Drugs." Fox Business. December 13, 2023. https://www.foxbusiness.com/economy/san-francisco-gym-owner-describes-unrecognizable-city-returning-den-of-homelessness-drugs.

Council on Foreign Relations. *U.S.-Taiwan Relations in a New Era: Responding to a More Assertive China*, June 2023. https://www.cfr.org/task-force-report/us-taiwan-relations-in-a-new-era.

Hass, Ryan and Abraham Denmark. "More Pain than Gain: How the US-China Trade War Hurt America." Brookings. March 9, 2022. https://www.brookings.edu/articles/more-pain-than-gain-how-the-us-china-trade-war-hurt-america/.

Deutsche Welle. "Russia Formally Withdraws from INF Nuclear Treaty." March 4, 2019. https://www.dw.com/en/russia-formally-withdraws-from-inf-nuclear-treaty/a-47766621.

Devenny, Patrick. "PLAN Procurement of Sovremenny-Class Destroyers: Developments and Repercussions." Royal United Services Institute. May 23, 2005. https://rusi.org/publication/plan-procurement-sovremenny-class-destroyers-developments-and-repercussions.

Dodge, Michaela. "The End of an Era? The INF Treaty, New Start, and the Future of Strategic Stability." Brookings. March 27, 2019. https://www.brookings.edu/events/the-end-of-an-era-the-inf-treaty-new-start-and-the-future-of-strategic-stability/.

Duster, Chandelis. "Top Military Leader Says China's Hypersonic Missile Test 'Went Around the World.'" CNN. November 18, 2021. https://edition.cnn.com/2021/11/17/politics/john-hyten-china-hypersonic-weapons-test/index.html.

East Asia Forum. "Village Democracy Shrugs in Rural China." December 7, 2023. https://eastasiaforum.org/2014/07/22/village-democracy-shrugs-in-rural-china/.

The Economist. "The End of Apple's Affair with China." October 24, 2022. https://www.economist.com/business/2022/10/24/the-end-of-apples-affair-with-china.

Fadel, Leila. "A Review of Carter's Foreign Policy and Views on Global Affairs Post Presidency." NPR. December 30, 2024. https://www.npr.org/2024/12/30/nx-s1-5241005/a-review-of-carters-foreign-policy-and-views-on-global-affairs-post-presidency.

"A Former PLA Soldier Hired by Russians Gives a Reality Check on Russia-Ukraine War." YouTube. May 24, 2024. https://www.youtube.com/watch?v=K_jdfaI5dyQ.

Fritz, Audrey. "China's Evolving Conception of Civil-Military Collaboration." Center for Strategic and International Studies. August 2, 2019. https://www.csis.org/blogs/trustee-china-hand/chinas-evolving-conception-civil-military-collaboration.

Garanich, Gleb, and Sergiy Karazy. "Kyiv Says It Shoots Down Volley of Russian Hypersonic Missiles." Reuters. May 17, 2023. https://www.reuters.com/world/europe/air-defence-systems-repelling-attacks-ukraine-early-tuesday-officials-2023-05-16/.

Giles, Martin. "The Man Turning China Into a Quantum Superpower." *MIT Technology Review*, December 19, 2018. https://www.technologyreview.com/2018/12/19/1571/the-man-turning-china-into-a-quantum-superpower/.

Global Taiwan Institute. "Taiwan Initiates Its New One-Year Military Conscription Program." February 6, 2024. https://globaltaiwan.org/2024/02/taiwan-initiates-its-new-one-year-military-conscription-program/.

Goldstein, Lyle, and Nathan Waechter. "2 Years on, Ukraine's Sinking of the *Moskva* Intrigues China's Naval Strategists." *The Diplomat*, April 15, 2024. https://thediplomat.com/2024/04/2-years-on-ukraines-sinking-of-the-moskva-intrigues-chinas-naval-strategists/.

Goldwater v. Carter, 444 U.S. 996 (1979). https://supreme.justia.com/cases/federal/us/444/996/.

Gordon, Susan, Michael Mullen, and David Sacks, eds. "U.S.-Taiwan Relations in a New Era." Council on Foreign Relations. 2023. https://www.cfr.org/task-force-report/us-taiwan-relations-in-a-new-era.

Gorman, Lindsay. "Testimony: The United States, Europe, and China: Convergence and Divergence on Technology, Standards/Data, and Trade." German Marshall Fund. June 15, 2023. https://www.gmfus.org/news/testimony-united-states-europe-and-china-convergence-and-divergence-technology-standardsdata.

Hearing Before the Congressional-Executive Commission on China. The Broken Promises of China's WTO Accession: Reprioritizing Human Rights. March 1, 2017. https://www.congress.gov/event/115th-congress/house-event/LC47864/text?s=1&r=4.

Hille, Kathrin. "China's Chip Breakthrough Poses Strategic Dilemma." *Financial Times*, August 15, 2022. https://www.ft.com/content/foddae61-a8a3-456d-8768-971c71ccb6dd.

Ho, Ming-sho. "The Activist Legacy of Taiwan's Sunflower Movement." Carnegie Endowment for International Peace. August 2, 2018. https://carnegieendowment.org/2018/08/02/activist-legacy-of-taiwan-s-sunflower-movement-pub-76966.

Holmes, James R. "The Long, Strange Trip of China's First Aircraft Carrier." *Foreign Policy*, February 3, 2015. https://foreignpolicy.com/2015/02/03/the-long-strange-trip-of-chinas-first-aircraft-carrier-liaoning/.

Hoppens, Robert. "Deng Xiaoping Visits Tokyo, October 1978 and February 1979." Wilson Center. May 18, 2020. https://www.wilsoncenter.org/blog-post/deng-xiaoping-visits-tokyo-october-1978-and-february-1979.

Indo-Pacific Defense Forum. "PRC-Backed Projects Raise Suspicion in Russia's Far East." November 21, 2020. https://ipdefenseforum.com/2020/11/prc-backed-projects-raise-suspicion-in-russias-far-east/.

Jenkins, Maureen. "Boeing's Ties to China Turn 30." Boeing Frontiers Online. December 2002. https://www.boeing.com/news/frontiers/archive/2002/december/mainfeature.html.

Kimball, Daryl G., ed. "US Conventional Arms Sales to Taiwan 1980–2010." Arms Control Association. Updated October 2012. https://www.armscontrol.org/factsheets/taiwanarms.

Korteweg, Rem, Vera Kranenburg, and Frans-Paul van der Putten. "Sino-European Joint Ventures and the Risk of Technology Transfers." Clingendael. August 29, 2022. https://www.clingendael.org/publication/sino-european-joint-ventures-and-risk-technology-transfers.

Lee, Yen Nee. "2 Charts Show How Much the World Depends on Taiwan for Semiconductors." CNBC. March 16, 2021. https://www.cnbc.com/2021/03/16/2-charts-show-how-much-the-world-depends-on-taiwan-for-semiconductors.html.

Lee, Yoojung. "TSMC Founder Says U.S. Welcomes Chipmaker's Arizona Plant Plan." Bloomberg. November 20, 2022. https://www.bloomberg.com/news/articles/2022-11-20/tsmc-founder-says-u-s-welcomes-chipmaker-s-arizona-plant-plan.

Lewis, Jeffrey. "Point and Nuke." *Foreign Policy*, September 12, 2018. https://foreignpolicy.com/2018/09/12/point-and-nuke-davy-crockett-military-history-nuclear-weapons/.

Liboreiro, Jorge, and Efi Koutsokosta. "EU Agrees New Sanctions Against Russia, Targeting Chinese Companies." Euronews. June 21, 2023. https://www.euronews.com/my-europe/2023/06/21/eu-agrees-new-sanctions-against-russia-targeting-companies-suspected-of-circumvention.

Lihua, Zhang. "Explaining China's Position on the Crimea Referendum." Carnegie Endowment for International Peace. April 1, 2015. https://carnegieendowment.org/research/2015/04/explaining-chinas-position-on-the-crimea-referendum?lang=en&center=global.

Lopez, C. Todd. "Supplemental Bill Becomes Law, Provides Billions in Aid for Ukraine, Israel, Taiwan." US Department of Defense. April 24, 2024. https://www.defense.gov/News/News-Stories/Article/Article/3754718/supplemental-bill-becomes-law-provides-billions-in-aid-for-ukraine-israel-taiwan/.

Los Angeles Times. "Alfred Frauenknecht; Convicted of Selling Jet Secrets to Israel." January 19, 1991. https://www.latimes.com/archives/la-xpm-1991-01-19-mn-255-story.html.

Martina, Michael. "China's Tech Transfer Problem Is Growing, EU Business Group Says." Reuters. May 20, 2019. https://www.reuters.com/article/us-china-eu-idUSKCN1SQ0I7.

McCarthy, Simone, and Joyce Jiang. "Food Safety Scandal Rocks China as Report Claims Cooking Oil Carried in Same Trucks as Fuel." CNN. July 10, 2024. https://www.cnn.com/2024/07/10/food/china-oil-food-safety-scandal-sinograin-intl-hnk/index.html.

McKinney, Jared M. "TSMC's Fate Will Indeed Be at Stake If China Attacks Taiwan." Nikkei Asia. June 2, 2023. https://asia.nikkei.com/Opinion/TSMC-s-fate-will-indeed-be-at-stake-if-China-attacks-Taiwan.

Morris, David Z. "Hackers Stole Restricted F-35 Data from Australian Contractor. *Fortune*, October 14, 2017. https://fortune.com/2017/10/14/hacked-f-35-data/.

Moscow Times. "Russia, China to Discuss 'U.S. Meddling' in Moscow and Hong Kong Protests." May 28, 2024. https://www.themoscowtimes.com/2019/08/13/russia-china-to-discuss-us-meddling-in-moscow-and-hong-kong-protests-a66828#google_vignette.

Moscow Times. "Russia Completes Delivery of Su-35 Fighter Jets to China for $2.5bln." September 2, 2023. https://www.themoscowtimes.com/2019/04/17/russia-completes-delivery-of-su-35-fighter-jets-to-china-for-25bln-a65271.

Mozur, Paul. "In Hong Kong Protests, Faces Become Weapons." *New York Times*, July 26, 2019. https://www.nytimes.com/2019/07/26/technology/hong-kong-protests-facial-recognition-surveillance.html.

Mozur, Paul, and Don Clark. "China's Surveillance State Sucks Up Data: U.S. Tech Is Key to Sorting It." *New York Times*, November 23, 2020. https://www.nytimes.com/2020/11/22/technology/china-intel-nvidia-xinjiang.html.

Mozur, Paul, Jonah M. Kessel, and Melissa Chan. "Made in China, Exported to the World: The Surveillance State." *New York Times*, April 24, 2019. https://www.nytimes.com/2019/04/24/technology/ecuador-surveillance-cameras-police-government.html.

Nelson, Amy J., and Alexander H. Montgomery. "Ukraine and the Kinzhal: Don't Believe the Hypersonic Hype." Brookings. June 29, 2023. https://www.brookings.edu/articles/ukraine-and-the-kinzhal-dont-believe-the-hypersonic-hype/.

Nikkei Asia. "China Eyes 'Armed Unification' with Taiwan by 2027: Key Academic." January 30, 2022. https://asia.nikkei.com/Politics/International-relations/China-eyes-armed-unification-with-Taiwan-by-2027-key-academic.

Nikkei Asia. "China Launches French-Designed Next-Gen Nuclear Reactor." December 14, 2018. https://asia.nikkei.com/Economy/China-launches-French-designed-next-gen-nuclear-reactor.

Nikkei Asia. "Special Report: How U.S.-Made Chips Are Flowing Into Russia." April 11, 2023. https://asia.nikkei.com/Business/Tech/Semiconductors/Special-report-How-U.S.-made-chips-are-flowing-into-Russia.

The Nobel Prize. "Nobel Prize in Physiology or Medicine 2015." Accessed September 4, 2023. https://www.nobelprize.org/prizes/medicine/2015/tu/facts/.

Office of the Historian, US Department of State. "The August 17, 1982 U.S.-China Communiqué on Arms Sales to Taiwan." https://history.state.gov/milestones/1981-1988/china-communique.

Perlez, Jane. "President Xi Jinping of China Arrives in Seattle." *New York Times*, September 22, 2015. https://www.nytimes.com/interactive/projects/cp/reporters-notebook/xi-jinping-visit/president-xi-of-china-arrives-in-seattle.

Petersmann, Sandra, and Esther Felden. "China's Quantum Leap—Made in Germany." Deutsche Welle. June 23, 2023. https://www.dw.com/en/chinas-quantum-leap-made-in-germany/a-65890662.

Pike, John. "Atomic Artillery." Global Security. Accessed December 30, 2022. https://www.globalsecurity.org/military/world/russia/atomnaya-artilleriya.htm.

Reif, Kingston. "Trump to Withdraw U.S. From INF Treaty." Arms Control Association. November 2018. https://www.armscontrol.org/act/2018-11/news/trump-withdraw-us-inf-treaty.

Reinsch, William Alan, John Hoffner, and Jack Caporal. "Unpacking Expanding Export Controls and Military-Civil Fusion." Center for Strategic and International Studies. May 14, 2020. https://www.csis.org/analysis/unpacking-expanding-export-controls-and-military-civil-fusion.

Reuters. "Nvidia Sees Permanent Loss of Opportunities from China Export Curbs." June 28, 2023. https://www.reuters.com/technology/nvidia-sees-no-material-impact-reported-ai-chip-restrictions-china-cnbc-2023-06-28/.

Reuters. "Report Says China Internet Firms Censored Coronavirus Terms, Criticism Early in Outbreak." March 3, 2020. https://www.reuters.com/article/us-health-coronavirus-china-censorship-idUSKBN20Q1VS.

Reuters. "Russia Says U.S. Withdrawal from INF Treaty 'Created Vacuum.'" December 8, 2022. https://www.reuters.com/world/europe/russia-says-us-withdrawal-inf-treaty-created-vacuum-2022-12-08/.

Reuters. "Sanctions China Has Imposed on Taiwan Over the Pelosi Visit." August 3, 2002. https://www.reuters.com/world/asia-pacific/economic-sanctions-china-has-imposed-taiwan-over-pelosi-visit-2022-08-03/.

Reuters. "Ukraine Says It Is Finding More Chinese Components in Russian Weapons." April 16, 2023. https://www.reuters.com/world/europe/ukraine-says-it-is-finding-more-chinese-components-russian-weapons-2023-04-14/.

Rudolphina. "Nobelpreis Für Quantenphysiker Anton Zeilinger." December 10, 2022. https://rudolphina.univie.ac.at/nobelpreis-fuer-quantenphysiker-anton-zeilinger.

Sacks, David. "How Taiwan Is Assessing and Responding to Growing Threats from China." Council on Foreign Relations. November 14, 2022. https://www.cfr.org/blog/how-taiwan-assessing-and-responding-growing-threats-china.

Savranskaya, Svetlana, and David A. Welch, eds. "SALT II and the Growth of Mistrust." The Carter-Brezhnev Project. February 5, 1995. https://nsarchive2.gwu.edu/carterbrezhnev/salt_ii_intro.html.

Savranskaya, Svetlana, and David A. Welch, eds. "Transcript, Global Competition and the Deterioration of U.S.-Soviet Relations, 1977–1980." The Carter-Brezhnev Project. June 8, 1995. https://nsarchive2.gwu.edu/carterbrezhnev/.

Schlesinger, James. "James Schlesinger Oral History." Miller Center. Accessed August 9, 2023. https://millercenter.org/the-presidency/presidential-oral-histories/james-schlesinger-oral-history.

Sentner, Irie. "Trump Slams Carter's Panama Canal Deal As He's Set to Lie in State." *Politico*. January 7, 2025. https://www.politico.com/live-updates/2025/01/07/congress/trump-jimmy-carter-panama-canal-00196862.

Smith, Gordon. "Goldman Sachs Tapped Chinese State Money to Buy Western Companies." *Financial Times*, August 30, 2023. https://www.ft.com/content/a940f22f-a79d-4165-9ca2-f15ec218c3b5.

South China Morning Post. "Exclusive: PLA Brass 'Defied Beijing' Over Plan to Buy China's First Aircraft Carrier *Liaoning*." May 1, 2015. https://www.scmp.com/news/china/diplomacy-defence/article/1779791/pla-brass-defied-beijing-over-plan-buy-aircraft-carrier.

South China Morning Post. "Expired US-China Science Treaty Signals Deep Uncertainty Amid High Tensions." August 30, 2024. https://www.scmp.com/news/china/diplomacy/article/3276479/expiration-major-us-china-science-treaty-signals-deep-uncertainty-amid-high-tensions.

South China Morning Post. "The Inside Story of the *Liaoning*: How Xu Zengping Sealed a Deal for China's First Aircraft Carrier." January 19, 2015. https://www.scmp.com/news/china/article/1681755/how-xu-zengping-became-middleman-chinas-deal-buy-liaoning.

Stefanick, Tom. "The State of U.S.-China Quantum Data Security Competition." Brookings. September 21, 2020. https://www.brookings.edu/articles/the-state-of-u-s-china-quantum-data-security-competition/.

Tanner, Murray Scot. "Beijing's New National Intelligence Law: From Defense to Offense." Lawfare Institute. July 20, 2017. https://www.lawfaremedia.org/article/beijings-new-national-intelligence-law-defense-offense.

United Nations. "Chapter XXVI, Disarmament, 4. Comprehensive Nuclear-Test-Ban Treaty, September 10, 1996, Accessed September 11, 2025. https://treaties.un.org/pages/ViewDetails.aspx?src=TREATY&mtdsg_no=XXVI-4&chapter=26

US Department of Defense. *Military and Security Developments Involving the People's Republic of China*. December 2024. https://media.defense.gov/2024/Dec/18/2003615520/-1/-1/0/MILITARY-AND-SECURITY-DEVELOPMENTS-INVOLVING-THE-PEOPLES-REPUBLIC-OF-CHINA-2024.PDF.

US Department of State. Protocol Between the United States of America and China Extending the Agreement of January 31, 1979, as Amended and Extended. January 30 and 31, 2018. https://www.state.gov/wp-content/uploads/2019/02/18-131-China-Scientif-and-Tech-Extens.pdf.

US Department of State. "Treaty Between the United States of America and the Union of Soviet Socialist Republics on the Limitation of Strategic Offensive Arms (SALT II)." June 18, 1979. https://2009-2017.state.gov/t/isn/5195.htm.

US Department of State, "U.S.-China: Thirty Years of Science and Technology Cooperation." October 15, 2009. https://2009-2017.state.gov/e/oes/rls/fs/2009/130625.htm.

Warnke, Paul. "War and Peace in the Nuclear Age; Interview with Paul Warnke, 1986." November 19, 1986. https://openvault.wgbh.org/catalog/V_12C9C3E486D44769A6AF4B243D6D5E4E.

White House, Office of the Press Secretary. "Fact Sheet: President Xi Jinping's State Visit to the United States." September 25, 2015. https://obamawhitehouse.archives.gov/the-press-office/2015/09/25/fact-sheet-president-xi-jinpings-state-visit-united-states.

Wong, Chun Han. "China's Xi Jinping Takes Third Term as President with Eye on U.S." *Wall Street Journal*, March 9, 2023. https://www.wsj.com/articles/chinas-xi-takes-third-term-as-president-with-eye-on-u-s-eaebef4c.

World Bank. "GDP per Capita Growth (Annual %)—China." Accessed September 7, 2023. https://data.worldbank.org/indicator/NY.GDP.PCAP.KD.ZG?locations=CN.

Wright, Rebecca, Ivan Watson, Olha Konovalova, and Tom Booth. "Exclusive: Chinese-Made Drone, Retrofitted and Weaponized, Downed in Eastern Ukraine." CNN. March 16, 2023. https://edition.cnn.com/2023/03/16/europe/china-made-drone-downed-eastern-ukraine-hnk-intl/index.html.

Zhao, Kejin. "China's National Security Commission." Carnegie Endowment for International Peace. July 14, 2015. https://carnegieendowment.org/2015/07/14/china-s-national-security-commission-pub-60637.

CHINESE-LANGUAGE RESOURCES

Chen Jinhua 陈锦华. *Guo Shi Yi Shu* 国事忆述 [The Eventful Years: Memoirs of Chen Jinhua]. Zhong gong dang shi chu ban she, 2005.

Chen Yishen 陈仪深. 战后台湾对外关系史论集 [Post-war Taiwanese foreign relations essay collection]. 国立政治大学, 2022.

Fan Chao 樊超, Wang Ke 王珂. "间接消耗战略:20世纪80年代中国对苏联安全战略再考察" [Indirect attrition strategy: A re-examination of China's security strategy against the USSR in the 1980s of the 20th century]. 国际政治研究 [The Journal of International Studies] 1 (2020): 81–116.

Fang Yi 方毅. 方毅文集 [Fang Yi papers]. Renmin Chubanshe, 2008.
Gong Li 宫力, [ed.]. 邓小平在重要历史关头 [Deng Xiaoping at key historical moments]. Jiu zhou chu ban she, 2012.
Gong Li 宫力. 邓小平与中美外交风云 [Deng Xiaoping and the Establishment of Diplomatic Relations between China and the United States]. 红旗出版社, 2015.
Guo Dehong 郭德宏. 王明年谱 [Wang Ming yearbook]. Shehui Wenxian Chubanshe, 2014.
Guo Peiqing 郭培清. 台湾与以色列军事贸易关系探析 [Study of Taiwan-Israel military trade relations]. Ershiyi Shijie, 2007.
He Zhilin 何智霖. 蔣经国与台湾: 相关人物访谈录(一) [Chiang Ching-kuo and Taiwan: An oral history of related persons, vol. 1]. Academica Historica, 2010.
Hsiao Heng-chung 萧衡钟. "台湾在当代美国对外战略部署中的定位" [Taiwan's role in US foreign policy strategy]. 台灣國際研究季刊 [Taiwan International Studies Quarterly] 3, no. 17 (2021): 121–39.
Hsiao-ting Lin. 蔣經國的台灣時代, 中華民國與冷戰下的台灣 [The Chiang Ching-kuo era: The Republic of China on Taiwan in the Cold War]. Yuan zu wen hua, 2021.
Hsiao-ting Lin. 林孝庭, 台海 冷戰 蔣介石: 解密檔案中消失的台灣史 1948–1988 [Taiwan Strait, Cold War, Chiang Kai-shek: Taiwan's lost history in declassified archival materials 1948–1988]. Jinglian Chuban, 2015.
Hua Guofeng 华国锋. 十一大上的政治报告 [Report on the Eleventh People's Congress of the Communist Party of China]. Gov.cn. August 12, 1977.
Hua Xinmin 华新民. "文革中的钱学森" [Qian Xuesen during the Cultural Revolution]. *Ji Yi* 记忆 [Memories] 32, no. 3 (2010): 1–19.
Huang Qinglong 黄清龙. 蔣经国日记揭密 [Chiang Ching-kuo's diary revealed]. Shi bao wen hua, 2020.
Huang Wenjiang 黄文江. 国际关系, 商贸机会, 科技转移对1975年中英'斯贝202'发动机专利合同及其时代意义的解读 [Interpretation of the British Spey 202 engine technology transfer to China in 1975]. 外交评论 [Foreign Affairs Review] 1 (2010): 78–87.
Chiang Ching-kuo 蒋经国, 蒋经国先生全集 VI [Chiang Ching-kuo collections VI]. 行政院新闻局, 1991.
Koshiro Koko 小古浩志郎, Chen Pengren 陳鵬仁, 蔣經國先生傳 [Biography of Chiang Ching-kuo]. Zhongyang Ribao Chubanshe 中央日報出版社, 1990.
Li Danhui 李丹慧, "走向分裂：从暗中斗争到公开论战, 1960年代中苏关系研究之二" [Toward the split: From intrigues to polemics, 1960s Sino-Soviet relations, Study 2]. 史学集刊 [Collected papers of history studies], no. 6 (2006): 51–67.
Li Xiannian 李先念. 李先念文选 [Li Xiannian papers]. Zhonggong Zhongyang Dangshi He Wenxian Yanjiu Yuan, 1989.
Lin Xiaoguang 林晓光, Sun Hui 孙辉. "中日和约的签定与20世纪70年代的中日关系" [Sino-Japanese Friendship Treaty and the 1970s Sino-Japanese relations]. *Riben Yanjiu Jilin* 日本研究集林 [Japanese Studies Collections, Fudan University Center for Japanese Studies] 2 (2008): 1–17.
Lu Peng 逯鹏. 明郑集团火炮在中西火器交流史上的地位 [Mingzheng Group's historical role in East-West military technology exchange]. *Nanfang Wenwu*, no. 3 (2019): 230–35.

Lu Qiming 陆其明, Fan Minruo 范敏若. 张爱萍与两弹一星 [Zhang Aiping and the "two missiles," "one satellite"]. Jiefangjun Chuban She, 2011.

Ni Shixiong 倪世雄. "邓小平与中美关系 [Deng Xiaoping and US-China Relations]c." 毛泽东邓小平理论研究 [Research on Mao Zedong and Deng Xiaoping Theories], no. 5 (2009): 23-32.

Nie Rongzhen 聂荣臻. 聂荣臻军事文选 [Nie Rongzhen military papers]. Jiefangjun Chubanshe, 1992.

Niu Dayong 牛大勇. "中美解冻关系时对日本问题的考量与角力" [The consideration and trial of strength over the issue of Japan in the period of the thawing of relations between China and the United States]. 美国研究 [American studies] 5 (2014): 44-59.

Qian Jiang 钱江. 邓小平与中美建交风云 [Deng Xiaoping and the Establishment of Diplomatic Relations Between China and the United States]. 中共党史出版社, 2005.

Su Shaoren 苏少壬, "毛泽东、周恩来的最后时光 [The final days of Mao Zedong and Zhou Enlai]." 福建党史月刊 [Fujian Dangshi Yuekan, or Fujian Provincial Communist Party History Monthly Journal]5 (2015): 26-29.

Sun Qiming 孙其明. 中苏关系始末 [Sino-Soviet Relations from the beginning till the end]. Shanghai Renmin Chubanshe, 2002.

Tao Wenjian. 中美关系史: 1972-2000 [US-China relations: 1972-2000] (Shanghai Renmin Chubanshe, 2004).

Wang Jian 王建. 战后美日台关系史研究 1945-1995 [Study on postwar US-Japan-Taiwanese relations 1945-1995]. Jiuzhou Chubanshe, 2013.

Wang Wenhua 王文华. 钱学森实录 [Qian Xuesen chronology]. 四川文艺出版社, 2001.

Wu Xiuquan 伍修权. 往事沧桑 [The vicissitudes of the past]. Shanghai wen yi chu ban she, 1986.

Xi Qixin 奚启新. 钱学森传 [Qian Xuesen biography]. Renmin Chuban She, 2011.

Xiao Dongxiang 萧冬连. 历史的转轨: 从拨乱反正到改革开放 [The historical transition: from rectifying the chaos to reform and opening up], 1979-1981. 香港中文大学当代中国文化研究中心, 2009.

Xiong Chenxi 熊晨曦. "卡特政府对华科技交流与合作政策研究" [The Carter administration's policy of science and technology exchange and cooperation toward China]. Diss., East China Normal University, 2021.

Yan Xuetong 阎学通. 权力中心转移与国际体系转变 [Power center shift and international system transformation]. 当代亚太 [Journal of Contemporary Asia-Pacific Studies], no. 6 (2012): 4-21.

Yang Kuisong 杨奎松, Shen Zhihua 沈志华, Li Danhui 李丹慧, Niu Jun 牛军, [eds.] 中苏关系史纲 [Survey of Sino-Soviet relations]. Shehui Kexue Chuban She, 2016.

Yu Jie 余杰. 偽裝的改革者: 破解鄧小平和蔣經國神話 [Reformers in disguise: Deciphering the myths of Deng Xiaoping and Chiang Ching-kuo]. Ba qi wen hua chu ban, 2022.

Zhang Guocheng 張國城. "反攻大陸之可行性: 從「國光計畫」探析 1960 年代國軍戰力" [The feasibility of counterattacking the mainland: An analysis of the National Army's combat power in the 1960s from the Guoguang Plan]. 國史館館刊 [Bulletin of Academia Historica], no. 76 (2023): 165, 167-201.

Zhao Ziyang 赵紫阳. 赵紫阳文集: 1980–1989 [Zhao Ziyang papers: 1980–1989]. 香港中文大学出版社, 2016.

Zheng Zhongbing 郑仲兵, Sheng Ping 盛平, Wang Sitong 王思彤, [eds.] 胡耀邦年谱资料长编 [Hu Yaobang yearbook extended edition]. 时代国际, 2005.

Zhong Wen 钟文, Wen Fu 文夫. 邓小平外交风采实录 [Records of Deng Xiaoping's foreign policy]. Renmin Chubanshe, 2004.

Zhu Feng 朱锋. "权力转移理论: 霸权性现实主义? [Power transition theory: Hegemonic realism]" 国际政治研究 [The Journal of International Studies] 3 (2018): 24–42.

Liu Huaqing 刘华清, 刘华清回忆录 [The memoir of Lui Huaqing]. Jiefangjun Chubanshe, 2004.

Tang Fei, Wang Changhe, Ge Huimin 唐飛, 王長河, 葛惠敏, "捍衛臺海的F-104" [The F-104 that defended Taiwan Strait]. 空軍學術雙月刊 [Airforce Bimonthly Journal], no. 680 (2021): 127–40.

CHINESE-LANGUAGE INTERNET RESOURCES

"厉害了！'厉害了，我的国' 累计票房已超过4亿 [Amazing! "Amazing China" surpasses 400 million at the box office." CCTV News. March 30, 2018. http://news.cctv.com/2018/03/30/ARTIN4qiVxZioZH0Ss482FIM180330.shtml.

"《台湾关系法》45周年 萧美琴：台湾将持续强化国防 台学者：美国应转向"战略清晰. [On the 45th anniversary of the Taiwan Relations Act, Hsiao Bi-khim stated that Taiwan will continue to strengthen its national defense. Taiwanese scholars stated that the United States should shift to a "clear strategy."]" 美国之音. Voice of America Chinese. April 14, 2024. https://www.voachinese.com/a/taiwan-relations-act-hsiao-20240413/7569245.html.

"张军大使在安理会《全面禁止核试验条约》问题公开会上的发言" [Ambassador Zhang Jun's speech at the UN Security Council public meeting on the Comprehensive Nuclear Test Ban Treaty]. Permanent Mission of the PRC to the UN. September 27, 2021. http://un.china-mission.gov.cn/zgylhg/jjalh/alhzh/qita1/202109/t20210928_9579278.htm.

"中国政府关于全面禁止和彻底销毁核武器的声明" [Chinese government's statement on the complete prohibition and thorough destruction of nuclear weapons]. *People's Daily*, October 21, 1964. Republished by, Chinese Ministry of Foreign Affair, https://www.mfa.gov.cn/ziliao_674904/wjs_674919/2159_674923/200011/t20001107_7950053.shtml, accessed September 23, 2025.

"1979年邓小平访美，在休斯顿宇航中心进行模拟飞行" [Deng Xiaoping's 1979 visit to the US and simulated flight at Houston Space Center]. ifeng. February 23, 2021. https://news.ifeng.com/c/846L5rXodRO.

"'Jieshu Guoqu, Kaipi Weilai'—Zhongsu Guanxi Zhengchang Hua" " '结束过去，开辟未来'—中苏关系正常化" ["End the past, open the future"—on the normalization of Sino-Soviet relations]. Ministry of Foreign Affairs. 2000. https://www.mfa.gov.cn/chn//pds/ziliao/wjs/2159/t8960.htm.

"封城76天，这家武汉芯片公司产能屡创新高，他们是如何做到的？" [How did this Wuhan chip company achieve record production during a seventy-six-day lockdown?]. April 19, 2020. http://www.semiinsights.com/s/electronic_components/23/38987.shtml.

"1972年欢迎尼克松的神秘晚宴" [The mysterious banquet welcoming Nixon in 1972]. June 4, 2019. http://zhouenlai.people.cn/n1/2019/0604/c409117-31119591-2.html.

"1949年后中国大陆科学家景况一览" [Overview of the situation of scientists in mainland China after 1949]. Qiushi.org. January 2012. http://www.qiushi.org/index.php?m=content&c=index&a=show&catid=30&id=197.

Hua Guofeng 华国锋. "十一大上的政治报告" [Report on the Eleventh People's Congress]. Central People's Government of the People's Republic of China. August 18, 1977. http://www.gov.cn/test/2007-08/28/content_729705.htm.

"接替刘鹤副总理何立峰任中央财办主任" [Vice Premier He Lifeng succeeds Liu He as director of the Central Finance Office]. Deutsche Welle. October 30, 2023. https://p.dw.com/p/4YCod?maca=zh-EMail-sharing.

RUSSIAN-LANGUAGE RESOURCES

Arbatpv, Georgiĭ. "Владимир Петрович Лукин, политик с чистыми руками" [Vladimir Petrovich, politician with clean hands], in *К 80-летию В.П. Лукина* [On the eightieth anniversary of V. P. Lukin], ed. A. D. Dikarev and A. V. Lukina. Ves' Mir, 2018.

Astaf'ev, Gulnin V. "Великодержавный шовинизм и «левый» авантюризм во внешней политике группы Мао Цзэдуна" [Great power chauvinism and "left" adventurism in the foreign policy of the Mao Zedong group]. In *Антимарксистская сущность взглядов и политики Мао Цзэдуна* [The anti-Marxist essence of the views and policies of Mao Zedong], [ed.] Mikhail I. Sladkovskiĭ. Akademiia nauk, 1965.

Borisov, Olyegu B., and Boris T. Koloskov. *Советско-китайские отношения, 1945–1970* [Soviet-Chinese relations, 1945–1970]. Mysl', 1971.

Fenenko, Aleksei. "Ядерные испытания в системе стратегической стабильности" [Nuclear testing and system strategic balance]. *Mezhdunarodnaia Zhizn* [International Affairs] 2 (2009). https://interaffairs.ru/jauthor/material/161.

Gromyko, Andreĭ Andreevich. *Памятное: Новые горизонты* [Memoir: New horizons]. Vol. 2, 2015.

Lukin, Vladimir P. "Вашингтон–Пекин: квазисоюзники?" [Washington–Beijing: Quasi-allies?]. *США—экономика, политика, идеология* [USA: Economics, politics, ideology], no. 12 (1979): 50–55.

Pravda. "Задача ограничения стратегических вооружений: перспективы и проблемы" [The task of limiting strategic weapons]. February 11, 1978.

Suslov, Mikhail A. *На путях строительства коммунизма* [On the path to the construction of communism]. Politizdat, 1977.

Tikhvinskiĭ, Sergeĭ L. *Китай в моей жизни* [China in my life]. Akademiia nauk, 1992.

Timerbaev, Roland M. *Рассказы о былом: воспоминания о переговорах по нераспространению и разоружению и о многом другом* [Tales of the past: A memoir on the negotiation of nonproliferation and disarmament]. PIR-Center, 2007.

INDEX

Abramowitz, Morton, 151
Acheson, Dean, 29, 247n28
aerospace manufacturer, 58–59
Afghanistan: Brzezinski to border of Pakistan and, 208–10; Soviet infiltration in, 54; Soviet invasion of, 114, 130, 205, 219
agriculture policy, 108
air superiority, 47
Alber, Martin, 10
Albright, David, 141
Al Saud, Fahd bin Abdulaziz, 36
ammunitions, nuclear components in, 86
amyotrophic lateral sclerosis, 189
Anti-Ballistic Missile Treaty (1972), 86
anti-imperial struggles, 217
antisatellite weapons, 39
anti-Soviet alliance: Brzezinski as scholar of, 32–35; China partnership in, 7; Deng Xiaoping as Maoist in, 198; Deng Xiaoping as politician in, 49, 102–3; Deng Xiaoping building, 10–12, 49; Deng Xiaoping on multilateral, 35; US policy in, 199
anti-Soviet struggle, 3–4, 10, 27
antitank missiles, 122

An Yang, 80
appeasement trend, 248n33
Arab-Israeli war, 2
Arbatov, G. A., 199
Armacost, Michael, 48, 144–45, 197
Arms Control and Disarmament Agency, 83
Arms Control Association, 64
arms control negotiations, 31–32
Ashbrook, John M., 168
Assad, Hafez al-, 36
Atkinson, Richard C., 101
Atomic Energy Council, 139
atomic research, by Israel, 139
atomic weapons, 138
authoritarianism, democracy compared to, 236–41

Bakr, Aḥmad Ḥassan al-, 36
banquet menu, in China, 45
Baruch, Jordan A., 101
Baryshnikov, V. N., 195
battleships, decommissioned, 86–87
Beckley, Michael, 226
Benn, Tony, 111
Between Two Ages (Brzezinski), 33

INDEX

Biao, Geng, 130, 207, 218
Biden, Joe, 176, 207–8, 223, 228, 233
BL755 antiarmor bomb, 110
Blumenthal, W. Michael, 34
Bösch, Frank, 10
Brands, Henry William, 19
Brave Wind I cruise missile, 147
Brezhnev, Leonid: J. Carter getting letter from, 25; J. Carter getting warning from, 201; J. Carter meeting with, 204; J. Carter mistrust and suspicions of, 204–5; J. Carter relations deteriorating with, 47; China relations repair attempts by, 13; frustration shown by, 127–28; NATO's weapon purchases disturbing, 127–28; Nixon on yacht with, 22; SALT II signed by J. Carter and, 204; Vance meeting with, 32
Britain: China buying Harrier jets from, 104–9, 111–12; China's trade with, 95–96; no comment policy from, 106; submarine-launched warheads from, 77; US misunderstanding with, 85
British Aerospace, 109–10, 115
Brown, Harold, 28–29, 34, 39; in China with US shopping menu from, 114; on Chinese military, 7; Deng Xiaoping meeting with, 205–6
Brzezinski, Zbigniew, 4; as anti-Soviet scholar, 32–35; *Between Two Ages* by, 33; J. Carter receiving note from, 34; as China policy authority, 211–12; commission impacting Japan and, 34–35; Deng Xiaoping enjoying vodka with, 57; Dobrynin's casual lunch talks with, 200–201; mainland China trip by, 53–55; nuclear weapons underground testing from, 83; to Pakistan-Afghanistan border, 208–10; *The Permanent Purge* by, 33; *The Soviet Bloc* by, 33; on US arms sales to China, 103, 197; US-PRC normalization advice from, 48–49; US top-secret weapons from, 53–54

Burnham, Reuben M., 170
Bush, George H. W., 24, 153, 231
Bush, George W., 225
Bush, Richard C., 173
business-oriented countries, 121–22
Byrne, James F., 170

Cage, Nicolas, 232
Cain, Frank, 11
Callaghan, James, 85, 105, 107, 110–11
Campbell, Kurt, 223
Camp David Accords (1978), 2
Carrington, Peter, 85
Carter, James Earl, 170
Carter, Jimmy, 1, 56; Brezhnev sending letter to, 25; Brezhnev sending warning to, 201; Brezhnev's meeting with, 204; Brezhnev's mistrust and suspicions of, 204–5; Brezhnev's relations deteriorating with, 47; Brzezinski sending note to, 34; Chiang Ching-kuo receiving offer from, 152–53; Chiang Ching-kuo's caution toward, 23; Chiang Ching-kuo's distrust of, 143; China and anti-Soviet advisers of, 7; China giving cold shoulder to, 222–23; China normalizing relations with, 50–53; China's engagement by, 12–13; China's visitation by, 14; China with grassroots democracy and, 221–24; Chinese regimes dealt with by, 163; Ching-kuo shocked by secret China deal by, 60; Cold War policy of, 9; document signed by, 5; first year as president of, 23–26; Goldwater's crusade against, 172; legacy of, 2–6; as naïve policy-maker, 6; 1979 Iranian Revolution testing policy of, 3; as nuclear nonproliferation president, 140–43; nuclear test ban choices of, 75–76; nuclear weapons testing halt from, 62–63; PRC embraced by, 4, 170–71; PRC with normalized relations by, 153–54; SALT II signed by Brezhnev and, 204; Soviet appeasement policy of, 29, 31; Taiwan

crack down by, 141–43; Taiwan's security endangered by, 173–74; White House gathering with, 240
Carter, Rosalynn, 56, 221
Castro, Fidel, 37, 38
CCP. See Chinese Communist Party
Central Asia, 225
Chamanan, Kriangsak, 51
Chang Hsien-yi, 143
charm offensive, of Soviets, 191–93
chemical weapon ban, 204
Chengdu J-10 fighter, 153
Chen Shui-bian, 14
Chen Wen-ke, 172–73, 272n43
Chiang Ching-kuo, 10; any friend at any cost of, 155; career path of, 160–61; J. Carter distrusted by, 143; J. Carter making offer to, 152–53; Carter's secret China deal shocking, 60; caution toward Carter from, 23; with Chiang Fang-liang, 134; Chiang Kai-shek son as, 134; as Chinese nationalists, 14; Deng Xiaoping's dealings with, 5–6, 236; Deng Xiaoping's negotiations with, 178–81; father renounced by, 160; Goldwater's meeting with, 169; Huang Hua feeling contempt for, 42; international politics engagement by, 155; Israeli defense industry interest of, 146; Israeli jet deal dropped by, 151–52; Kennedy lobbied by, 138; Madame Chiang Kai-shek writing and, 168, 182–84; nuclear program not admitted by, 142; nuclear program overseen by, 139–40; patience and strategy required by, 167; as ROC president, 162–63; Schwimmer visiting, 148; Soviet Communist Party joined by, 161; US hated by, 165–66; Vance's China trip angering, 44
Chiang Fang-liang, 134
Chiang Kai-shek, 10, 23, 42; Chiang Chin-kuo son of, 134; Dulles negotiations with, 135–36; nuclear bomb wanted by, 139–40; US handling of crisis and, 136

Chiang Kai-shek, Madame (Soong Mei-ling), 168, 173, 180–86, 183
Chiang Nan. See Liu, Henri
China. See mainland China
"China After Mao" (report), 212
China International Trust Investment Corporation (CITIC), 113
Chinese Communist Party (CCP), 2; Deng Xiaoping's new vision for, 56; détente warnings from, 27; Eleventh Party Congress of, 194; Hu Yaobang as general secretary of, 215; order achieved through, 199; people killed by, 184; Taiwan and managed competition with, 223
Chinese Nationalist Party (KMT), 2, 162
Chinese nationalists, 14
Chinese Village Elections Project, 221
Chirac, Jacques, 116
Chou Shu-k'ai, 141
Christopher, Warren, 177
Church, Frank, 177–78, 207
Ciechanover, Josef, 150
CITIC. See China International Trust Investment Corporation
Cline, Ray S., 180
COCOM. See Coordinating Committee for Multilateral Export Controls system
code of conduct, 20
Cold War: alliances shifting during, 56–57; anti-Soviet struggle of, 3–4; Carter's policy during, 9; China and Taiwan in global, 6–9; Deng Xiaoping's strategy during, 93–94; détente strategy in, 21; dynamic shift in, 224–28; global strategic balance of, 55; international history of, 8–9; political and ideological struggle during, 159–60; technology acquisition during, 233; US and, 1–2
Committee on the Present Danger (CPD), 29–30
communism, 168, 276n19
Communist Party of the Soviet Union (CPSU), 188–89

Communist Party Youth League, 241
Comprehensive Test Ban Treaty (CTBT), 12; France's concerns negotiations on, 80–82; negotiations collapse of, 83–90; nuclear weapons negotiations in, 83–85; Reagan ending talks for, 87; as trilateral treaty, 61–62; vertical proliferation halting in, 63
computer industry, 78, 198
computer technology, 33
Congress, US, 175
Conscience of a Conservative, The (Goldwater), 169
Coordinating Committee for Multilateral Export Controls (COCOM) system, 12, 95–96, 98; members of, 115; US as founder of, 103
CPD. *See* Committee on the Present Danger
CPSU. *See* Communist Party of the Soviet Union
Cradock, Percy, 104
Crimea, Russia annexing, 226
cruise missiles, 25
CTBT. *See* Comprehensive Test Ban Treaty
Cuba: African conflict involvement of, 41; Ethiopia backed by, 46–47; Ethiopia with military personnel from, 37; Somalia's defense agreement with, 41
Cultural Revolution, 2; China's scientists during, 68–69; Great, 189; on mainland China, 164; military expansionism during, 74
Cutler, Rupert, 101

decolonization, 275n4
decommissioned battleships, 86–87
de Gaulle, Charles, 67, 96, 116–17
democracy, 221–24, 236–41
Democratic Progressive Party (DPP), 223–24, 237
Deng Jiaxian, 69
Deng Rong, 222
Deng Xiaoping, 1, 4; anti-Soviet alliance built by, 10–12, 49; as anti-Soviet Maoist, 198; as anti-Soviet politician, 49, 102–3; anti-Soviet struggle partnerships of, 27; Brown meeting with, 205–6; Brzezinski enjoying vodka with, 57; career path of, 160–61; CCP's new vision from, 56; Chiang Ching-kuo's dealings with, 5–6, 236; Chiang Ching-kuo's negotiations with, 178–81; as Chinese nationalists, 14; Cold War strategy of, 93–94; Deng Rong as daughter of, 222; détente assaults by, 59–62; dual-use technology sought by, 197; German relations smothered by, 98; Horn of Africa conflict used by, 40–41; ideological problems from, 194; Jackson's unofficial meeting with, 50–51; Limited Test Ban triggering, 82–83; multilateral anti-Soviet alliance from, 35; NASA visit by, 58–59; nonproliferation efforts of, 88–89, 258n94; nuclear weapons underground technology request by, 87; one-China, two-systems option offered by, 13, 185–87; poster of, *186*; red carpet rolled out for, 56–57; ROC abandonment for US-China relations by, 22–23; SALT II attitude by, 32; Senate Foreign Relations Committee meeting with, 177–78; Soviet hostility from, 28–29; Soviet leadership challenged by, 202; Soviet not trusted by, 58; Soviets as evil empire from, 128; Taiwan influencing meeting with, 42; three no-changes from, 179; US industrial tour by, 58–59; on US interest in Taiwan, 42–43, 51–52; US technology desired by, 55; US trip of, 55–60, 56, 102–3, 167; Vance meeting with, 150; White House gathering with, *240*
Derg. *See* Provisional Military Government of Socialist Ethiopia
détente: CCP warnings on, 27; Cold War strategy of, 21; decolonization and, 275n4; Deng Xiaoping's assaults on, 59–62; SALT Treaty cornerstone of, 20–21; with Soviet Union, 19–23; US false hopes in, 51–52

Deutsche Welle (DW) media, 235
Dinneen, Gerald P., 205
disarmament, 27; China's concerns about, 80–81; with Soviet Union, 76–77; of US-Soviet relations, 74
disruptive technology, 235
Dobrynin, Anatoly, 25, 57, 200–201
Dole, Robert, 172
Dolgov, Vyacheslav Ivanovich, 127
domestic oppression, 226
Donovan, Hedley, 179
Doshi, Rush, 223
DPP. *See* Democratic Progressive Party
dual-use technology, 197
Duguid, Andrew, 108
Dulles, John Foster, 135–36
DW. *See* Deutsche Welle media

early warning radar system, 206
economic development, in Taiwan, 231–32
Ecuador, 149–50
Einstein, Alfred, 234
Eleventh Chinese Communist Party Congress (1977), 27
Eleventh Party Congress, of CCP, 194
Enrile, Juan Ponce, 154
EPRP. *See* Ethiopian People's Revolutionary Party
Ethiopia, 41, 249n52; in Africa Soviet backing, 46–47; Cuban military personnel in, 37; Somalia's attack on, 37–38
Ethiopian People's Revolutionary Party (EPRP), 36
Ethiopian Red Terror, 37
Europe, 126–30
European Security Conference, 109
expansionism, by Soviet Union, 31

F-4/F-5 supersonic jets, 144, 151
F-104 Starfighters, 144
Faina Chiang Fang-Liang, 161
Fairbank, John, 9
Fang Yi, 58, 79, 102, 123

Far East Institute, 202, 212
Fergusson, Ewen, 108
fighter jets: F/A-18, 106; F-4, 144, 145, 149, 151, 152; F5, 151; F-5, 47, 145, 151, 152; F-14, 106; F-104 Starfighters, 144; Harrier jets, 104–9; JH-7 tactical bombers, 96; Kfir jets, 144–45, 148–53; MiG, 38, 106; Tu-22M Backfire bombers, 25, 39
FitzGerald, Stephen, 190
food diplomacy, 44, *45*
Foot, Michael, 107
Foot, Rosemary, 10
Ford, Gerald, 19
Ford, Henry, II, 58
foreign currency reserves, 112
foreign policy, 3–4, 215–16
Framatome nuclear reactors, 117, 121, 124–25
France: antitank missiles from, 122; China's nuclear cooperation with, 8–9; China's reactor negotiations with, 117–18, 124; China's uranium resources interest of, 119–21; CTBT negotiations concerns of, 80–82; Hua Guofeng and Chirac in, *116*; Intervener Agreement on Supply of Nuclear Reactors by, 79–80; Li Xiannian on reactors sales by, 125; military technology exported by, 232; nuclear industry of, 118–19; nuclear reactor sales by, 116–18; nuclear technologies transfer role of, 97; as nuclear weapon states, 128–29; as peace-loving nation, 81; PRC's diplomatic relations with, 96; US technology in reactors from, 124–25
François-Poncet, Jean, 120
Fredrickson, Donald S., 101
free-market economy, 238
French-Indochina War, 136
FRG. *See* Germany
Frosch, Robert A., 101
fuel-processing technologies, 118
Fukuda, Takeo, 42, 50

318   INDEX

Garthoff, Raymond, 11, 21, 40, 62
Garver, John W., 10
Gates, Robert, 21, 208, *209*
Gates, Thomas S., 26–27
Gathering in the Crops (poster), *72*
GDP per capita, 185
gege jipo strategy, 95
Gelb, Leslie, 87, 150
Genscher, Hans-Dietrich, 123
Geocaris, James A., 85
Germany, 97–98; China's opportunities for, 122–23; military technology exported by, 232. *See also* West Germany
Girard, Yves, 125
Giscard d'Estaing, Valéry, 78–79, 96, 120
global relations. ROC's troubled, 5
Global Television Network, 241
Goldwater, Barry: against Carter, J., 172; Chiang Ching-kuo meeting with, 169; *The Conscience of a Conservative* by, 169; schoolchildren writing to, *171*; as Taiwan's friend, 169–70; Taiwan students writing to, 171–72
Goldwater v. Carter lawsuit, 172
Gong Li, 5
Gorbachev, Mikhail, 185
Gorce, François de la, 80
Goronwy-Roberts, Lord, 109
Great Cultural Revolution, 189
Great Leap Forward, 108
Gromyko, Andrei, 32, 129, 190, 196, 203
Grumman jets, 106
Gu Mu, 117
Guo-Guang Jihua (Nation's Light Plan), 137–39
Guo Moruo, 274n76

Haile Selassie I (Emperor of Ethiopia), 217
Halford, Scott, 102
Hansell, Herbert, 175–76
Han Xu, 101
Harding, Harry, 10
Harvard, viii, xi, 33, 68, 69, 101, 239, 240

Harrier jets, 104–9
Hasss, Richard, 3
Hauff, Volker, 123
Haunschild, Hans Hilger, 123
Hawkings, Joyce, 171
health issues, of Mao Zedong, 189–90
heavy water reactor, 143
Helan Tsai, 174
He Lifeng, 240
He Long, 185
Henderson, Nicholas, 98
Hermes, Peter, 122
high-tech arms race, 230–36
history, of Cold War, 8–9
Honecker, Erich, 38, 200
Hong Kong, 95
Horn of Africa, 39–40, 43; Cuba's conflict involvement in, 41; North Africa and, 36; South Africa and, 140, 154–55; Soviet backing Ethiopia in, 46–47; Soviet focus in, 48; Special Coordination Committee meeting in, 47–48
Horsburgh, Nicola, 64
Hotung, Eric, 180
Hsiao Bi-Khim, 224
Hsiao-ting Lin, 6, 10, 164
Hsiung Feng I (Brave Wind I) cruise missile, 147
Hua Guofeng, 19, 27, 116–17; on fighting socialist-imperialism, 193; hundred-day thaw launched for, 190; on international politics, 99; Mondale comments from, 128; in Paris, *116*
Huang Hua, 53, 79, 128; Chiang Ching-kuo contempt from, 42; Gates warning from, 26–27; Nitze comments with, 31; TRA concerns of, 177
Huang Zhen, 76
Hua Xinming, 69
Huberman, Benjamin, 101
Hu Jintao, 223
hundred-day thaw, by Soviets, 190
Hunt, John, 96

Hu Xu-Guang, 146
Hu Yaobang, 88, 214–15
hydrogen bomb, 68
hypersonic antiship missiles, 231
hypersonic missile test, 90

IAEA. *See* International Atomic Energy Agency
IAI. *See* Israeli Aerospace Industries
ICBM. *See* intercontinental ballistic missile
imperialism, of US, 216–17
INER. *See* Institute for Nuclear Energy Research
INF. *See* Intermediate-Range Nuclear Forces Treaty
information systems, 235
Institute for Nuclear Energy Research (INER), 139, 142
intercontinental ballistic missile (ICBM), 30; China joining club with, 230; China's program of, 71–72, 88; China's project for, 12
intermediate-range ballistic missiles (IRBMs), 64
Intermediate-Range Nuclear Forces Treaty (INF): PRC's strategic rocket forces influenced by, 226; Putin ending participation in, 229; US withdrawal from, 228–30
International Atomic Energy Agency (IAEA), 139, 141
international politics, 99, 155
International Studies (journal), 214
Intervener Agreement on Supply of Nuclear Reactors, 79–80
interventionists policy, 188–90
Iranian Revolution (1979), 3
IRBMs. *See* intermediate-range ballistic missiles
Israel: atomic research by, 139; Chiang Ching-kuo dropping jet deal with, 151–52; Chiang Ching-kuo interest in defense industry of, 146; Kfir jets from, 144–45,

148–53; military independence of, 148; ROC's nuclear collaboration with, 146, 268n38; Taiwan's fighter jet deal with, 143–53; US being offended concern of, 149; US blocking Kfir sales by, 149–50
Israeli Aerospace Industries (IAI), 146

Jackson, Henry ("Scoop"), 31, 50–51
Japan: formula, 43; PRC as part of China from, 50; Trilateral Commission impacting, 34–35
Jasmine Revolution, 222
Javits, Jacob, 177–78
JH-7 tactical bombers, from China, 96
Jiang Qing, 51
Jiang Zemin, 223
Jing-dong Yuan, 11
Johnson, Lyndon, 67, 138

Keatley, Anne, 101
Kennan, George F., 29, 247n28
Kennedy, John F., 65, 136, 138
Kennedy, Ted, 175
Kfir jets, 144–45, 148–53
Khmer Rouge, 202
Khrushchev, Nikita, 65
King, Coretta Scott, 58
King, Martin Luther, Jr., 58
Kissinger, Henry, 9, 14, 23
Klemow, Marvin, 148–49
KMT. *See* Chinese Nationalist Party
Kohl, Helmut, 97
Kokoshin, Andrei A., 189
Ko Mo-jo, 184
Kraft, Christopher C., 58
Krivzov, Vladimir Alexeyevich, 196
Kuomintang. *See* Chinese Nationalist Party

Labour Party, 111
Lai Ching-te, 239
Lake, Antony, 87
land-based missiles, of Soviet Union, 250n67
Le Duan, 202

320   INDEX

Lee Teng-hui, 239
Liao Cheng-chih, 181–82
Liao Zhongkai, 181–82
Li Danhui, 11
Limited Test Ban Treaty (LTBT), 26, 65, 77–78, 82–83, 256n54
Li Qiang, 104, 261n31
Liu, Henri, 163
Liu Bocheng, 69
Liu He, 240
Liu Huaqing, 130, 205, 207
Liu Shaoqi, 189
Li Xiannian, 108–9, 117; on French reactors sales, 125; photo with, 30; Soviet alarm from activities of, 195; technology import policy and, 112–13
Li Yuefei (Li Yue Fei), 72
Lord of War (film), 232
Louis, Victor, 164, 165
LTBT. *See* Limited Test Ban Treaty
Lu Hsiu-lien, Annette, 239
Lukin, Vladimir Petrovich, 199, 213
Lüthi, Lorenz M., 7

mainland China: anti-Soviet alliance partnership of, 7; Brezhnev's attempts to repair relations with, 13; British Harrier jet sales to, 104–9, 111–12; British trade with, 95–96; Brown on military of, 7; Brzezinski as policy authority on, 211–12; Brzezinski landing in, 53–55; Brzezinski on US arms sales to, 103, 197; J. Carter and visitation of, 14; J. Carter anti-Soviet advisers partnering with, 7; J. Carter dealing with regimes in, 163; J. Carter engagement with, 12–13; J. Carter getting cold shoulder from, 222–23; J. Carter helping in grassroots democracy for, 221–24; J. Carter normalizing relations with, 50–53; Chiang Ching-kuo as nationalists of, 14; Ching-kuo angered by Vance's trip to, 44; Ching-kuo shocked by Carter's secret deal with, 60; COCOM system dismantled by, 115; congress dealing with two regimes in, 175; Cultural Revolution and scientists from, 68–69; Cultural Revolution on, 164; disarmament concerns of, 80–81; domestic oppression in, 226; early warning radar system delivered to, 206; European arms sales to, 126–30; France's nuclear cooperation with, 8–9; France's reactor negotiations with, 117–18, 124; fuel-processing technologies for, 118; future goals of, 202; GDP per capita of, 185; Germany's opportunities from, 122–23; in global cold war, 6–9; *Guo-Guang Jihua* strategic plans for, 137–39; hypersonic missile test by, 90; ICBM program of, 12, 71–72, 88, 230; Japan on PRC as part of, 50; JH-7 tactical bombers from, 96; KMT defeated on, 162; Made-in-America shopping menu for, 114; manufacturing processes sought by, 115; Maoist influence in, 189; under Maoist rule, 200; military hardware shopping by, 94; military power of, 223; Mutual Defense Treaty with, 134; NATO countries selling military technologies to, 129; Nine Articles of Polemics from, 67; North Vietnam supported by, 20; nuclear arms race of, 68; nuclear bilateral cooperation by, 79–80, 257n71; nuclear first strike vulnerability of, 64; nuclear technologies transfer to, 97; as nuclear weapon states, 128–29; "one China" vision for, 13; as peace-loving nation, 81; PRC in, 1–2; Qian Xuesen deported back to, 73; quantum technology development in, 235; Russia receiving war materials from, 227; SALT II linked to, 39–45; SEZ of, 195; Somalia getting weapons from, 47; Soviet border with troops from, 49; Soviet celebrations themed after, 191; Soviet nuclear threat reevaluation by, 69–70; Soviet cartoon of nuclear testing by, 89; Soviet military presence on border

with, 203; Soviet relations with, 185–86; Soviet split from, 189; Soviets targeted by US arms to, 126–27; Soviet tensions with, 165; strategic weapon development of, 74; Taiwan's reunification with, 181–82; technology acquisition changes by, 113–14; TRA dissatisfaction of, 178; two-systems and one, 13, 185–87; uranium resources of, 119–21; US accepting demands of, 54; US card played by, 200; US defense-related shopping menu for, 114; US future relationship with, 236; US intelligence sharing with, 208; US military cooperation with, 212, 224–25; US military sales to, 206–7; US providing investment and weapons to, 230–32; US-Soviet relations problem of, 196–201; US strategic cooperation with, 130; US technology acquisition by, 55, 233–34; US trade embargo on, 95, 97; US willing to work with, 28; Vance normalizing relations with, 41; Vance's official dinner in, 43–44, 45; Vance visit to, 166; Vietnam invaded by, 110–11, 195; Western countries arms sales to, 129–31, 131–32; Western countries catch up in technology by, 99–101; Western Europe's military exchanges with, 94; West Germany conditionalities concerns of, 123–24; West Germany not selling weapons to, 125. *See also* People's Republic of China; Republic of China; US-China relations
Manhattan Project, 84
manufacturing processes, China seeking, 115
Mao Tse-tung, 184, 200
Mao Zedong, 19, 66, 189–90
Marcos, Ferdinand, 153–54
Marshall, George, 95
Marxist-Leninist principles, 192, 194, 216–17
Ma Ying-jeou, 169, 238–39
McClure, James A., 143
McDonnell Douglas, 106, 144, 149, 151
Meijer, Hugo, 11

Mengistu Haile Mariam, 37
Meng Qingshu, 192
MI-4 Helicopters, 115
Middle East, 35–36
military: Brown on Chinese, 7; Central Asia bases for, 225; China and US cooperation of, 212, 224–25; China's hardware shopping for, 94; China's power of, 223; Cuba and Ethiopian personnel of, 37; expansionism, 74; France and Germany exporting technologies for, 232; Israeli independence of, 148; NATO countries selling technologies for, 129; Soviets on China's border with, 203; supremacy of, 30; Taiwan fears of inadequate, 133; US-China relations and technologies, 93–94; US sales to China, 206–7; Western Europe's exchanges with China of, 94
MIRVs. *See* multiple independently targetable reentry vehicles
Mitchell, Nancy, 6, 11, 43
Mondale, Walter, 34, 48, 128, 178
Morrison, Herbert, 95
Muldoon, Robert, 190
Mulley, Fred, 105
multilateral negotiations, 77
multilateral network, 7–8
multiple independently targetable reentry vehicles (MIRVs), 25
Mutual Defense Treaty, 134, 176
mutual security, 127
My Days in the Soviet Union (pamphlet), 161

Nanking Treaty (1842), 195
NASA, 58–59, 73
National Chung-Shan Institute of Science and Technology (NCSIST), 147
National Defense Science Committee (NDSC), 71
National Defense Strategy, 228
national seismic station (NSS), 85
National University of Defense Technology (NUDT), 236

Nation's Light Plan (*Guo-Guang Jihua*), 137–39
NATO countries: Brezhnev's weapon purchases by, 127–28; China receiving military technologies from, 129; nuclear weapon use by, 169
navy fleet, of PLA, 88
NCSIST. *See* National Chung-Shan Institute of Science and Technology
NDSC. *See* National Defense Science Committee
Nie Rongzhen, 69
9K32 Strela-2 shoulder-fired antiair missiles, 210–11
Nine Articles of Polemics, from China, 67
Nitze, Paul, 29, 39, 247n28; on appeasement trend, 248n33; Huang Hua comments with, 31; photo with, *30*; on Soviet nuclear strategy, 24
Nitze, Phyllis Pratt, 30
Nixon, Richard, 9, 19, 57; Brezhnev on yacht with, 22; SALT II treaty signing criticism of, 70–71; structure of peace from, 20; White House gathering with, *240*
no contact, no negotiation, no compromise policy (Three "No's" Policy), 182
non-nuclear weapons states, 86
nonproliferation efforts, 88–89, 258n94
Non-Proliferation Treaty (1968), 26
North Africa, 36
North Korea, 233
Northrop jets, 106, 151
North Vietnam, 20
NSS. *See* national seismic station
nuclear arms race, 20, 61–62; of China, 68; high-tech arms race and, 230–36; Sino-Soviet relations reevaluation in, 69–70; US and Soviet, 24–25; US-Soviet relations agreements in, 74–75
nuclear nonproliferation cooperation, 62
Nuclear Nonproliferation Treaty, 68
nuclear program: Chiang Ching-kuo never admitting to, 142; China's bilateral cooperation on, 79–80, 257n71; of France, 118–19; of Taiwan, 135–37, 139–40; US nuclear advantage of, 40; US nuclear policy in, 63
nuclear technology: ammunition with components using, 86; China getting transfer of, 97; heavy water reactor as, 143; reactor sales of, 116–18; Sino-French cooperation in, 8–9; uranium resources for, 119–21, 140; US policy on, 63
nuclear test ban treaty, 61, 75–76
nuclear weapons: Brzezinski on underground testing of, 83; J. Carter on nonproliferation of, 140–43; Chiang Kai-shek wanting their own, 139–40; China and France as states with, 128–29; China's vulnerability in first strike, 64; countries testing, 64–65, 87–88; CTBT negotiations on, 83–85; Deng Xiaoping's requesting technology for, 87; NATO countries using, 169; plutonium for, 117, 119, 139–41; portable nuclear devices as, 65; PRC exploding first, 138–39; proliferation of, 210; superpowers superiority in, 81; vertical proliferation of, 66–67; warhead technology of, 63–64
nuclear weapons testing: J. Carter calling for halt to, 62–63; non-nuclear weapons states and, 86; Soviet cartoon about China with, *89*; vertical proliferation of, 62–63
NUDT. *See* National University of Defense Technology
Nunn, Sam, 163

Obama, Barack, 233, 241
Obama, Michelle, 241
Ōhira, Masayoshi, 179
Oksenberg, Michel, 9, 102, 144–45, 179; on China buying US technology, 197; on Soviets in Africa, 48; on US-China normalization talks, 51
one-China, two-systems option, 13, 185–87
open door policy, 10

Operation Chestnut, 208
Organization of African Unity, 46
Ostrova, Rosa Vladimirova, 192
Oval Office, document signed in, 5
Owen, David, 105, 111

Pacific Ocean strategy, 213
Panama Canal, 2–3
Panama Canal Treaty, 170
Pan Jianwei, 234
Parkinson's disease, 189
Party State (Tang Guo), 15
Patman, Robert G., 38
PDRY. *See* People's Democratic Republic of Yemen
Pelosi, Nancy, 239
Peng De-Huai, 192
People's Democratic Republic of Yemen (PDRY), 36
People's Liberation Army (PLA), 51, 88, 201–2
People's Republic of China (PRC), 1–2; Brzezinski on relations normalization with, 48–49; J. Carter embracing, 4, 170–71; J. Carter normalizing relations with, 153–54; France's diplomatic relations with, 96; independent foreign policy steps for, 215–16; Japan on PRC as part of, 50; nuclear weapon exploded by, 138–39; Soviet Union refusing demands of, 202–3; strategic rocket forces of, 226; superpowers policies toward, 21–23; Taiwan demands by, 52; US arms sales to, 217–18; US diplomatic relations with, 61–62; US export deals with, 112; US normalization with, 48–49, 240; US relations with, 225; US technology exchanges with, 101–2
people-to-people diplomacy, 166
Peres, Shimon, 150
Perle, Richard, 248n37
Permanent Purge, The (Brzezinski), 33

Perry, William, 206
Pickering, Thomas, 124
Pillsbury, Michael, 222
PLA. *See* People's Liberation Army
plutonium, 117, 119, 139–41
policy-making, of Carter, J., 6
Politburo meeting, 112
politics: Chiang Ching-kuo in international, 155; Cold War's struggle over, 159–60; Deng Xiaoping against Soviet, 49, 102–3; international, 99, 155; warfare using, 138
Ponomarev, Boris N., 190
portable nuclear devices, 65
Pottinger, Matthew, 223
Pratt and Whitney, 115
PRC. *See* People's Republic of China
presidency, J. Carter first year, 23–26
presidential elections, ROC's democratic, 237–38
Press, Frank, 53, 101
propaganda poster, *100*
Provisional Military Government of Socialist Ethiopia (Derg), 36
PT-6 Turboshaft engine, 115
Putin, Vladimir, 225–27, 229

QC. *See* quantum computer technology
Qian Xuesen (Tsien Hsue-shen), 69, *73*, 73–74
quantum computer (QC) technology, 235
quantum entanglement, 234

radar equipment, 218
Radchenko, Sergei, 195
Rakhmanin, Oleg B., 191
Rao Yutai, 69
rapid reload system, 40
Ratner, Ely, 223
Reagan, Ronald, 2, 62, 180; CTBT talks ended by, 87; Taiwan abandonment criticized by, 213
Reina, Thomas C., 174

Republic of China (ROC): aging fighter jet fleet of, 144; Atomic Energy Council of, 139; Chiang Ching-kuo president of, 162–63; democratic presidential election of, 237–38; fighter jet options for, 145–46; Israel's nuclear collaboration with, 146, 268n38; strategic missile program of, 147–48; in Taiwan, 1–2; troubled global relations of, 5; US arms sales to, 180–81; US-China relations and abandonment of, 22–23; US-ROC-IAEA safeguards agreement with, 141
Republic of China Army (ROCA), 133
Rockefeller, David, 33–35
rocket scientists, at NASA, 73
Rolls-Royce's Spey engine sales, 97
Rong Yiren, 113
Rose, Clive, 84
Ross, Robert C., 5, 10
Russia: China provided war materials to, 227; Crimea annexed by, 226; SALT II treaty negotiations of, 26

Sachs, Hans-Georg, 98
Sadat, Anwar, 35
SALT. *See* Strategic Arms Limitation Talks Treaty
SALT II treaty, 22, 48, 178, 201; J. Carter and Brezhnev signing, *204*; CPD's primary target of, 29–30; Deng Xiaoping's attitude toward, 32; mainland China linked to, 39–45; Nixon criticism in signing, 70–71; SLBM restrictions sought for, 40; superpower agreement in, 63; US and Russian negotiations in, 26; US-Soviet approaches to, 26, 203–4
SAM. *See* surface-to-air missile
Sánchez, Arnaldo Ochoa, 46
San Francisco, 241
Schlesinger, James, 101
Schmidt, Helmut, 97, 122
schoolchildren, Goldwater letters from, *171*
Schwimmer, Adolph William, 148

Seignious, George, 130
Selassie, Haile, 36
self-defense, Taiwan's capabilities for, 177
Senate Foreign Relations Committee, 177–78
Sequoia (yacht), 22
SEZ. *See* Special Economic Zones
Shah Pahlavi (of Iran), 217
Shambaugh, David, 10, 94
Shanghai Communique, 14, 51, 54, 76, 214
Siemens, 121
Shcherbakov, Ilyá S., 193
Shelepin, Alexander Nikolayevich, 164
Shen Hongjian, 141
Shen Zhihua, 11, 190
Shi Huyao, 193
Siad Barre, Mohamed, 37–38, 41
Siddeley, Hawker, 107
Simon, Jean, 119
Sino-American Mutual Defense Treaty, 28
Sino-Soviet relations: border in, 49; China's nuclear threat reevaluation in, 69–70; deteriorating, 65
Sixteenth Presidential Review Memorandum, 75
Sladkovskiĭ, Mikhail, 126, 191–94, 198, 202
SLBM. *See* submarine-launched ballistic missiles
Smith, Gerald C., 34, 124, 210
Snowden, Edward, 235
socialist-imperialism, 193
Solomon, Richard, 10
Somalia: Cuban defense agreement with, 41; Ethiopia attacked by, 37–38; mainland China's weapons to, 47; Soviet Union collision course of, 38
Soong, James, 14
South Africa, 140, 154–55
South Yemen, 36
Soviet Bloc, The (Brzezinski), 33
Soviet-Chinese Friendship Association, 193
Soviet Communist Party, 161
Soviet Union: Afghanistan infiltrated by, 54; Afghanistan invaded by, 114, 130,

205, 219; antisatellite weapons from, 39; anti-US propaganda campaign by, 39–40; Brzezinski as scholar against, 32–35; J. Carter appeasement policy toward, 29, 31; charm offensive launched by, 191–93; China's Maoist influence fought off by, 189; China's nuclear testing depicted by, *89*; China's relations with, 49, 65, 69–70, 185–86; China's split from, 189; China's troops on border of, 49; China tensions with, 165; Chinese border military presence of, 203; Chinese-themed celebrations in, 191; communism path of, 276n19; Deng Xiaoping as challenger to leadership of, 202; Deng Xiaoping as politician against, 49, 102–3; Deng Xiaoping not trusting, 58; Deng Xiaoping's hostility toward, 28–29; Deng Xiaoping stating evil empire of, 128; détente with, 19–23; disarmament talks with, 76–77; Ethiopia backed by, 46–47; expansionism as global threat by, 31; Gates dissertation on sinology of, *209*; Horn of Africa focus of, 48; hundred-day thaw by, 190; interventionists policy of, 188–90; land-based missiles of, 250n67; Li Xiannian causing alarm in, 195; LTBT violations by, 77–78, 256n54; military supremacy and, 30; 9K32 Strela-2 shoulder-fired antiair missiles, 210–11; Nitze on nuclear strategy of, 24; PRC demands refused by, 202–3; rapid reload system developed by, 40; SALT II treaty negotiations of, 26, 203–4; SALT Treaty restraining, 21; SAM missiles from, 211; Siad Barre ultimatum from, 38; Somalia's collision course with, 38; Tsar Bomba of, 65; US arming China to encircle, 126–27; US-China relations with constraints on, 28–29; US nuclear advantage over, 40; US nuclear arms race with, 24–25; US on ambitions of, 250n64; US policies against, 199; world conquest assumptions

about, 248n37. *See also* Russia; US-Soviet relations
Special Coordination Committee, 47–48
Special Economic Zones (SEZ), 185, 195
Stilwell, David R., 208
Stone, Richard, 175–76
Strategic Arms Limitation Talks (SALT) Treaty, 20–21
strategic missile program, of ROC, 147–48
strategic rocket forces, of PRC, *226*
strategic triangle, 22
strategic weapon development, 74
Strauss, Franz-Josef, 97
Stricker, Andrea, 141
Striving to Modernize National Defense poster, *100*
structure of peace, 20
submarine-launched ballistic missiles (SLBM), 40
submarine-launched warheads, 77
Sun Yat-sen University, 160
Sun Yat-sen, 167
Sun Yun-suan, 167
superpowers: nuclear superiority of, 81; PRC and policies of, 21–23; SALT II's agreement of, 63
surface-to-air missile (SAM), 211
surveillance radar, 218
Suslov, Mikhail A., 276n19
Sutter, Robert, 162

Taiping rebellion, 184
Taishan Nuclear Power Plant, 126
Taiwan: J. Carter cracking down on, 141–43; J. Carter endangering security of, 173–74; CCP and managed competition with, 223; China's reunification with, 181–82; communism struggle of, 168; Deng Xiaoping on US interest in, 42–43, 51–52; Deng Xiaoping's meeting influenced by, 42; economic development in, 231–32; free-market economy of, 238; GDP per capita of, 185; in global cold

326　INDEX

Taiwan (*continued*)
　war, 6–9; global influence of, 154–55; Goldwater friend to, 169–70; Goldwater getting letters from students from, 171–72; inadequate military fears of, 133; Institute of Nuclear Energy Research of, 142; Israel's fighter jet deal with, 143–53; nuclear program of, 135–37, 139–40; PRC's demands about, 52; Reagan criticizing abandonment of, 213; ROC in, 1–2; self-defense capability of, 177; US abandonment of, *171*, 173, 213, 223–24; US arms trade with, 214; US tied to fate of, 237
Taiwan Relations Act (TRA), 11, 13, 159, 214; China's dissatisfaction with, 178; final version of, 176–77; Huang Hua's concerns about, 177; strategic ambiguity of, 223–24; US congress and, 173–77
Taiwan Strait Crisis, 135–37, 231
Tanaka, Kakuei, 50
Tang Guo (Or Dang Guo, Party State), 15
Taylor, Jay, 10
technology: China chasing Western countries in, 99–101; China's acquisition changes for, 113–14; China's acquisition of US, 55, 233–34; China's development of quantum, 235; Cold War acquisition of, 233; computer, 33; disruptive, 235; dual-use, 197; France exporting military, 232; fuel-processing, 118; Li Xiannian and import policy on, 112–13; NATO countries selling military, 129; nuclear warhead, 63–64; nuclear weapons underground, 87; PRC and US exchanges with, 101–2; quantum, 235; US-China relations and military, 93–94; US reactor, 124–25; for weapons, 210–11
Teillac, Jean, 118–19
Thatcher, Margaret, 85
three no-changes, from Deng Xiaoping, 179
Three-People's Principles, 167
Threshold Test Ban Treaty, 64

Tiananmen Square, 185, 208, 215
Tikhvinskii, Sergei, 191–92, 212
Timerbaev, Roland, 64, 78, 85, 256n54
Tolstikov, Vasily S., 190
Torrijos-Carter Treaties, 2
TRA. *See* Taiwan Relations Act
Treaty of Peace and Friendship Between Japan and China (1978), 50
Trilateral Commission (1973), 33–35
trilateral treaty, 61–62
Trump, Donald, 228, 230
Tsai Ing-wen, 223, 239
Tsar Bomba, of Soviet Union, 65
TSMC (chipmaker), 238
Tu-22M Backfire bombers, 39
Tucker, Nancy, 5, 10
Tupolev Tu-22M Backfire bombers, 25
Turner, Stansfield, 208

Ukraine, Putin's invasion of, 226–27
underground testing, of nuclear weapons, 83
Unger, Leonard S., 141, 152
unguided nuclear artillery shells, 66
United States (US): anti-Soviet policy of, 199; arms sales to China by, 103, 197; Britain's misunderstanding between, 85; Brzezinski on top-secret weapons of, 53–54; Central Asia military bases of, 225; Chiang Ching-kuo hating, 165–66; Chiang Kai-shek on handling of crisis by, 136; China playing card of, 200; China receiving investment and weapons from, 230–32; China's acquisition of technology from, 55, 233–34; China's defense-related shopping menu from, 114; China's future relationship with, 236; China's intelligence sharing with, 208; China's military cooperation with, 212, 224–25; China's points accepted by, 54; China's strategic cooperation with, 130; China's trade embargo from, 95, 97; China willing to work with, 28; as COCOM system founder, 103; Cold War

and, 1–2; communism struggle of, 168; computer industry of, 78; Deng Xiaoping on Taiwan interest of, 42–43, 51–52; Deng Xiaoping's desire for technology from, 55; Deng Xiaoping's industrial tour in, 58–59; Deng Xiaoping's trip to, 55–60, 56, 102–3, 167; détente false hopes of, 51–52; Ecuador's Kfir purchase blocked by, 149–50; France and reactor technology from, 124–25; imperialism of, 216–17; information systems protections by, 235; INF withdrawal of, 228–30; Israel concerns about offending, 149; Israel's Kfir sales blocked by, 149–50; military sale questions to, 206–7; Mutual Defense Treaty with, 134; National Defense Strategy of, 228; nonproliferation efforts led by, 88–89, 258n94; nuclear advantage of, 40; nuclear policy of, 63; plutonium from, 140–41; PRC arms sales from, 217–18; PRC normalization with, 48–49, 240; PRC relations with, 225; PRC's diplomatic relations with, 61–62; PRC's import deals with, 112; PRC's technology exchanges with, 101–2; ROC getting weapons from, 180–81; SALT II treaty negotiations of, 26, 203–4; self-contradictory policy of, 4; Sino-American Mutual Defense Treaty and, 28; Soviet ambitions of, 250n64; Soviet propaganda campaign against, 39–40; Soviet nuclear arms race with, 24–25; Soviets targeted by arms to China by, 126–27; strategic triangle with, 22; Taiwan abandoned by, *171*, 173, 213, 223–24; Taiwan's arms trade with, 214; Taiwan's fate tied to, 237; Taiwan Strait Crisis intervention of, 231; TRA and, 173–77; zero-sum competitions view of, 6–7
uranium resources, 119–21, 140
US. *See* United States
USA: Economics, Politics, Ideology (journal), 213

US-China Agreement on Cooperation in Science and Technology, 102
US-China Nuclear Cooperation Agreement, 258n94
US-China relations: Deng on abandoning ROC for, 22–23; diplomatic, 107–9; military technologies in, 93–94; multilateral network in, 7–8; nuclear nonproliferation cooperation of, 62; rapprochement in, 98–99; Soviet constraints goal in, 28–29. *See also* mainland China
US-ROC-IAEA safeguards agreement, 141
US-Soviet relations: China's problem in, 196–201; disarmament talks of, 74; maintaining good, 97; nuclear arms agreements of, 74–75; SALT II treaty approaches of, 26, 203–4. *See also* Soviet Union

Vance, Cyrus, 4, 25, 34, 76; Brezhnev meeting with, 32; China normalizing relations with, 41; China's official dinner with, 43–44, *45*; Ching-kuo angered by China trip of, 44; Deng Xiaoping meeting with, 150; mainland China visit by, 166
Varley, Eric, 104
Varyag (aircraft carrier), 232
vertical proliferation, 62–63, 66–67
Vienna, 65, 123, 203, 204, 234
Vietnam: Chinese forces invading, 110–11, 195; North, 20; PLA invading, 201–2; War, 19, 60
Vladivostok Accord (1974), 26

Walden, George G., 127
Wang Shen, 153–55
Wang Sheng, 162, 275n14
Wang Zhen, 88
warhead technology, of nuclear weapons, 63–64
Warnke, Paul, 31, 83, 248n37
Washington, George, 4

"Washington-Beijing" (article), 213
Watson, Thomas J., 211
weapons: antisatellite, 39; atomic, 138; ban on chemical, 204; BL755 antiarmor bomb as, 110; Brave Wind I cruise missile, 147; China receiving US, 230–32; China's war materials used for, 227; cruise missiles as, 25; development of strategic, 74; Hsiung Feng I (Brave Wind I) cruise missiles, 147; hydrogen bomb as, 68; hypersonic antiship missiles as, 231; ICBM, 12, 30, 71–72, 88, 230; IRBMs, 64; land-based missiles as, 250n67; NATO's purchase of, 127–28; 9K32 Strela-2 shoulder-fired antiair missiles, 210–11; ROC buying US, 180–81; SAM as, 211; SLBM as, 40; Somalia getting Chinese, 47; strategic weapon development for, 74; technologies for, 210–11; US sales to PRC of, 217–18; US top-secret, 53–54; Western countries sales of, 129–31; West German not selling China, 125. *See also* fighter jets
Wei, James, 165
Weizman, Ezer, 150
Wen Haxiong, 148–49
Westad, Odd Arne, 11
Western countries, 99–101, 129–31, *131–32*
Western Europe, 94, 232
West Germany, 98; antitank missiles from, 122; business-oriented countries and, 121–22; China concerned about conditionalities of, 123–24; China not getting weapons from, 125; nuclear reactor sales by, 116–18
Wheeler, M. I., 174

White House, *240*
Wickert, Erwin, 122
Wishnick, Elizabeth, 11
Woodcock, Leonard, 177
world peace, 90
Wu Ta-you, 140
Wu Xiuquan, 51

Xiao Donglian, 112
Xiao Guangyan, 69
Xie Peiyi, 123
Xi Jinping, 226, 239, 241

Yao Tongbin, 69
Ye Jianying, 194, 216
Ye Qisun, 68
Yom Kippur War, 21
York, Herbert, 62, 83, *84*
Yu Jie, 6, 161

Zakharova, Maria, 229
Zametin, B. N., 200
Zeilinger, Anton, 234–35
zero-sum competitions, 6–7
Zhang Aiping, 71, 99
Zhang Jun, 88
Zhao Jiuzhong, 69
Zhao Shoubo, 175
Zhao Ziyang, 214, 216–17
Zhivkov, Todor, 205
Zhou Enlai, 49–50, 69, 95, 113
Zhou Ren, 68
Zhuo Lin, 56
Zhu Xinming, 164
Zia-ul-Haq, Muhammad, 208
Zimmermann, Warren, 116–17

GPSR Authorized Representative: Easy Access System Europe, Mustamäe tee 50, 10621 Tallinn, Estonia, gpsr.requests@easproject.com

www.ingramcontent.com/pod-product-compliance
Lightning Source LLC
Chambersburg PA
CBHW022030290426
44109CB00014B/809